THE AMERICAN BUSINESS CORPORATION

New Perspectives on Profit and Purpose

The MIT Press
Cambridge, Massachusetts,
and London, England

THE AMERICAN BUSINESS CORPORATION

New Perspectives on Profit and Purpose

Edited by

Eli Goldston,
Herbert C. Morton,
and G. Neal Ryland

Part I copyright © 1969 by
The American Academy of Arts and Sciences
Part II copyright © 1972 by
The Massachusetts Institute of Technology

Printed and bound by
The Colonial Press Inc.
in the United States of America.

Library of Congress Cataloging in Publication Data

Goldston, Eli, 1920–   comp.
  The American business corporation.

  (The Daedalus library, v. 20)
  Part 1 was originally published as the winter 1969
issue of Daedalus; part 2 contains 8 new articles and
a new preface.
  1. Corporations—U. S.—Addresses, essays, lectures.
I. Morton, Herbert Charles, joint comp. II. Ryland,
G. Neal, joint comp. III. Title. IV. Series.
HD2791.G64   338.7′4′0973   77–175716
ISBN 0–262–07052–9
ISBN 0–262–57028–9 (pbk)

CONTENTS

1693599

Part II

ELI GOLDSTON, HERBERT C. MORTON,
AND G. NEAL RYLAND

Foreword

THIS VOLUME reprints in Part I the eleven articles and the Preface
that comprised the Winter 1969 issue of *Dædalus*. In addition, as
Part II the editors have added a Preface and eight articles which
expand or illustrate some of the themes that emerged from the
Dædalus papers.

Because the original articles were prepared by eight academi-
cians, two scholarly journalists, and one businessman with a legal
background, they seem to whisper in a library rather than to shout
in the market place. As Stephen Graubard, editor of *Dædalus*,
comments in the Preface to Part I, "The authors have scrupulously
avoided the vocabulary that has often been used to condemn or to
praise what business has done or failed to do."

Verbal restraint, however, did not result in homogenization of
thought. The conference technique by which *Dædalus* is produced
makes each author aware of the thrust of the other articles, but it
does not require him to modify his views. The authors are invited
to contribute to a collection, not to provide one piece of a jigsaw
puzzle.

In expanding the volume we have held to the same approach,
seeking new perspectives without trying to influence the views of
our contributors. But we did seek out authors from private business,
government, academic administration, journalism, and a consulting
firm to comment from their viewpoints on American business life.
The viewpoint of the ichthyologists on the life around a coral reef
would be, we thought, enriched by the comments of a few articulate
fish.

These added articles reflect the same independence of judgment
that distinguished the contributions to the *Dædalus* issue. But even
with these new papers we do not pretend to have covered fully the
performance and prospects of American business. Our authors do
not include a student, a labor leader, a civil rights militant, or many
other possible perspectives. What is offered here is a collection of
informed observations, not a definitive analysis.

Acknowledgments

THIS BOOK owes a great deal to a large company who have advised the editors from the beginning. In addition to the authors, an expression of thanks is due: Kenneth R. Andrews, Daniel Bell, Warren Bennis, L. Earle Birdzell, Jr., Wayne G. Broehl, Harvey Brooks, Thomas C. Cochran, Anthony Downs, Henry W. Ehrmann, Gaylord A. Freeman, Jr., Thomas M. Garrett, Alexander Gerschenkron, Randall T. Klemme, Seymour Martin Lipset, Robert M. Macdonald, Daniel Marx, Jr., Isamu Miyazaki, Bernard J. Muller-Thym, John C. Parkin, Theodore V. Purcell, David Riesman, John H. Rubel, Raymond Stevens, and E. O. Vetter.

The initiative for this study came from the Amos Tuck School of Business Administration. A special debt is owed the former Dean of the School, Karl Hill. The present Dean, John W. Hennessey, Jr., has given generously of his time from the beginning.

Finally, mention should be made of those who have given funds for this study to the Amos Tuck School, permitting the School to join the American Academy in this effort. The Alfred P. Sloan Foundation, the I.B.M. Corporation, and the Amos Tuck School Associates Program provided the financial aid that made two conferences, the issue of *Dædalus*, and this book possible.

Part I

STEPHEN R. GRAUBARD

Preface

WHEN THE first part of this volume appeared as an issue of *Dædalus*, the title of the issue was bland and innocuous, "Perspectives on Business." I suggested at the time that the reader not be misled about what was being attempted. I wrote:

The authors have scrupulously avoided the vocabulary that has often been used to condemn or to praise what business has done or failed to do. They have chosen to consider whether business—and most particularly the large corporation—may presently be passing through a moment of change with major social and political significance. If we are, in fact, on the eve of a fundamental rethinking of the enterprises and activities appropriate to business involvement, this may lead to a reformulation of what have for some time appeared to be acceptable divisions of public and private responsibility and control. The authors in this volume discuss whether business, as presently constituted, is in a position to assume new roles linked, in one way or another, to the deepening social crises of our time.

The book opens with two essays that place the present situation in a historical setting. William Letwin suggests that America has always been a society in which business and businessmen have stood at the top. He argues that there has never been a fundamental cleavage in America between the businessman's view of things and that of society at large. Even in the so-called "trust-busting" era, anti-business sentiment was always more limited than some have tried to suggest. Anti-business feelings made considerable advances during the Great Depression, but these antipathies were reduced somewhat by the successful mobilization of business enterprise in World War II.

Today, when business is not subject to persistent obloquy, there is new talk of the demise of the conventional businessman. Three revolutions—the Managerial, the Technological, and the Planning— are said to be creating conditions that make the survival of the businessman in his traditional role unlikely. The author considers

1

these "threats" to the businessman and concludes that the report of his imminent death is premature. The Managerial Revolution, he writes, is not having the effect that had been predicted for it. There had been some expectation that large corporations would no longer be run primarily for profit—that managers would use their positions for other ends, a tendency stockholders would be powerless to resist. As a result, it has been contended, the old risk-taking business values would atrophy. Mr. Letwin sees no evidence of this change. He also suggests that the idea of a Technological Revolution in which technical experts replace the businessman is based on a misconception of the businessman's role. His function is still to define the ends that the engineer or expert seeks to realize. That many American business executives today are educated as scientists and engineers may confuse the issue for some people. Mr. Letwin argues, however, that the business manager does not reach his decisions on the basis of his competence as an engineer or scientist and that his managerial role is not defined by that competence. The Planning Revolution, which was supposed to see businessmen replaced by "expert public servants," has simply not occurred. Central planning has not enjoyed the bright future that was once predicted for it. Today the business executive is required to take into account the side effects of his industrial effort, but Mr. Letwin is not persuaded that he can do so chiefly through planning. While not prepared to say that the businessman "will continue to enjoy the high esteem that American society has usually accorded him," he argues that the businessman's managerial role will certainly remain a central one.

Alfred D. Chandler, Jr., charts the changing character of business enterprise in the United States. His interest is not simply to document the transition from an economy dominated by the merchant to one in which the wholesaler, the manufacturer, and, finally, the manager emerged as dominant figures. Under each of these "dominations," the values of business were significantly different. The colonial merchant was an all-purpose man of business—a wholesaler and retailer, importer and exporter. His calling required him to be broadly familiar with many things. With the beginning of specialization, the wholesaler came to the fore. He handled the marketing of finished products, but also financed the long-term growth of the economy. Specialization, however, had its price; the new breed of manufacturers generally lacked the international outlook of the colonial merchants. They tended to see their needs in sectional rather than national terms. After the recession of 1873, the manufacturer began to replace the wholesaler as the one who had the most to say about the economy. The manufacturer was in a position to adapt the economy to population and technological changes. Using profits from his own firm to provide capital for new enterprise, he employed factory production techniques to create a vastly greater industrial output that would satisfy the growing consumer demand. These enterprises, increasingly complex, required an efficient managerial class. By the first decades of the twentieth century, it was understood that a new class had made its way up the corporate bureaucratic ladder. Rarely owning a significant portion of the company's stock, these businessmen were prepared to organize and rationalize large industrial enterprises.

The horizons of managers were often national and international rather than local. This did not mean, however, that they had an extensive acquaintance with Americans of other social groups. Nor did it mean that other types of business atrophied. Small business, for example, remained a basic and essential part of the economy. The Depression and World War II dramatically altered the relations between business and the federal government; in the 1930's and 1940's, the growth of trade unions had other important effects on the role of managers. But Mr. Chandler agrees with Mr. Letwin that the decision-making powers of managers were not substantially reduced. The question posed is whether managers, having succeeded in creating a powerful production economy, will respond equally well to the new non-economic challenges of today. It is not self-evident that the managers of large corporations are suited, either by training or experience, to the new social responsibilities that call so insistently for their help. Mr. Chandler leaves the question open. Business may prove adequate to the new challenge; if it does not, such matters will come to be handled by men who are not businessmen.

While both Messrs. Letwin and Chandler parenthetically consider the relations of business with government, Richard H. Holton makes them the principal focus of his article. Setting aside the myth that there was once a time when government did not concern itself with business, he shows how government engaged actively from the nation's beginning to encourage business and commerce. Only in the late-nineteenth century did government turn its attention increasingly to the regulation of certain kinds of business. Regulatory legislation in its present pattern is generally thought to date from the passage of the Interstate Commerce Commission Act in 1887 and the Sherman Antitrust Act of 1890. The impulse to such regulatory action came, in part at least, from the farmers and ranchers of the Midwest and Far West who were increasingly suspicious of the financial and railroad interests that they associated with eastern business domination.

The Depression led to a new spurt of regulatory legislation, but Mr. Holton argues that it would be a mistake to dwell only on this one kind of legislation. Government activity supportive of business has always been a conspicuous part of the federal legislative record. Maximizing the rate of growth of the economy and, with it, the achievement of high employment levels are principal governmental objectives today. At the same time, the government seeks to regulate various markets, including the major consumer markets for goods and services. A third governmental objective is to redirect significant amounts of resources to agreed-upon social goals, such as improved housing and education. Finally, there is the persistent governmental effort to correct "external diseconomies" of the kind represented most obviously by pollution.

Because segments of the business community have complained both about the rationale for these public policies and their implementation, Mr. Holton attempts to explain what is involved in these various efforts. He sees significant differences between the attitudes of big and small business in respect to government. Among big businessmen, relations with the federal government are generally close, and many executives in the large American corporations have served at one time or other with governmental agencies in Washington. This relationship is not true of those who are in small business, among whom serious misgivings are expressed about the programs of the federal government. Mr. Holton points out that big business tends, with noteworthy exceptions, to be involved not at the state and local levels, but at the federal level, while the medium-sized or small firm seeks to maximize its influence on the state and local levels. If such businesses are hostile to governmental intervention, there is little likelihood that they will be willing to assist in the development of new and imaginative programs in the social field. On the state and local levels, there is a constant concern with a "good business climate"—which is often a shorthand expression for keeping taxes down. In these circumstances, additional pressures are put on Washington. Social problems may exist most acutely in local communities, but support for their resolution is constantly

being sought in the nation's capital. Small business is still insufficiently involved in the efforts that are required, and the federal
government is not in the best position to involve them.

Robert T. Averitt, in his taxonomical study of American business,
makes even more explicit the tensions that presently exist within the
system. The contemporary theories of macroeconomics indicate that
there is an "optimal level of employment in an industrial economy.
When the economic system operates below that level, potentially
available goods and services are lost," poverty increases, but prices
decline only slightly. "Above the optimum level, inflation becomes
unmanageable." Thus, Mr. Averitt suggests, "the economic system
is a finely tuned mechanism that operates well only within a narrow employment range." Theories of microeconomics, on the other
hand, argue that a maximization of consumer choice ought to be
the objective of an efficiently operating economic system.

Mr. Averitt divides the United States economy into two distinct
though interconnected systems. The first, which he calls the "center
economy," consists of large enterprises that operate nationally and
internationally; these are generally capital-rich firms that tend to
expand when the economy is growing. The other part of the system,
which he calls the "periphery economy," is made up of comparatively small enterprises, most of which are local in their orientation.
These firms are more craft-oriented; they are "labor-intensive," generally less interested in research and development, and rarely affluent in capital resources. Many of the firms in the "periphery economy" serve as "satellites" to firms in the "center economy."

Mr. Averitt suggests that the American economy is increasingly
made up of firms that wish to free themselves of the hazards incurred by being bound to some specific product or a single isolated
industry. Even the prospect of a single national market is seen to be
increasingly dangerous. Certain industries and services—housing,
health, education, medicine—are still largely craft-oriented. How
can they be made part of the center economy? Why should they
be? Mr. Averitt's answer is simple: "In the present economy, the
American consumer is confronted with a choice between the heavily
advertised, mass- and process-produced goods of center firms and
the ill-advertised, craftsmen-produced services of, for example,
health and education. The result is a price disparity that strongly
favors the expenditure of income gains on goods, even when these
yield satisfactions below additional health and education. Our imbalance in production techniques threatens us with a society where

comforts accumulate while human potentialities decay." Numerous center firms are now entering the education and health industries. The new consumer demands for these services must be met at reduced real costs, and if they are, Mr. Averitt suggests, business will have found a new place for itself in American society.

Eli Goldston has no doubt that this is the "new frontier" for American business. He starts with the premise that private business ought to be enlisted in working toward the solution of many of our more critical social problems. He makes the flat prediction "that American business will increasingly supply many of the physical goods and services we have obtained, at least since the New Deal era, from public sources." The involvement of American business, if guided and controlled by public agencies, may represent the only permanent solution to the urban problems that have so clearly overtaxed the capacities of our public agencies.

Mr. Goldston points out that net profit per share remains a major concern for every conscientious business executive. He further contends that the sense of social responsibility of such men ought not to be treated lightly because of their interest in profit. The two, when combined, make possible the new activities in which business must be expected to take a part.

Looking at big business today, he argues that the degree of separation between owners and managers has been overstated. The stockholders' interest in profits is in no way diminished; there is always a threat of a "takeover" or a merger where an executive does not give sufficient attention to his company's earnings. Because of modern technology, however, large enterprises, Mr. Goldston suggests, can once again be personally directed—sometimes by a single man. Management today is very exposed. Its public performance is known and advertised. Many managers, profiting from their stock option rights as employees, are significant property owners in the companies for which they work, and this is an additional incentive to their success. Personal financial gain is involved no less than a public reputation for a good performance.

Mr. Goldston has no doubt that earnings measure performance, and that business executives are acutely concerned with the performance of their companies. He sees four major areas of growth potential for business sales and profits: in new or more products in existing markets; new markets abroad; new markets among the emerging poor; and new activities in areas once considered the province of government. Mr. Goldston suggests that business will be pushed in all these directions, thus guaranteeing a growing concern by business with the major social problems of our day—most critically those of the cities, where public control of such activities has been found to be patently inadequate. But government must devise a proper package of incentives to induce business to enter such fields. Mr. Goldston imagines that such packages will include many kinds of inducements—subsidies, guarantees, franchises, tax benefits, contracts. To indicate the kinds of business involvement that suggest prototypes for what is possible, he mentions the large-scale development of Puerto Rico, business involvement in low- and middle-income housing in Boston, and the large-scale efforts by business to train and employ "hard-core" unemployables. The possibilities for the future are many. In education, particularly, an important opportunity exists. Mr. Goldston has no doubt that business will wish to take advantage of these new options.

Both Messrs. Averitt and Goldston give some attention to the growing importance of foreign investment for American business. This subject is the focus of Raymond Vernon's contribution to the volume. Reminding his readers that "the investments of United States companies in foreign subsidiaries and affiliates rose from $12 billion to $55 billion" between 1946 and 1967, Mr. Vernon discusses some of the problems that have arisen as a result of this vast expansion of American involvement abroad. It is important to distinguish between investment in less-developed countries from that which is occurring in the more advanced nations. Until a few decades ago, the principal object of the former was the extraction of raw materials. The governments of less-developed countries encouraged American (and other foreign) investment because too few local entrepreneurs were prepared to take the financial risks involved, particularly if the product had to be sold abroad. In these circumstances, special permission was granted foreigners to exploit the resource. During the interwar years, this situation began to change in many of the less-developed countries. This shift coincided with the development of new political structures in many of these countries, but also with certain new economic facts. The countries were no longer so impoverished as to capital, technology, and available markets—the indispensable reasons for originally encouraging the foreigner to enter. The operations already installed were providing profits (on which the local area could draw for its new capital needs), and the installation of machinery made the local community more familiar with the technology of the enterprise. One problem remained—that of gaining and keeping markets. But this difficulty was not insurmountable. The bargaining capacities of the less-developed countries grew considerably, and though both they and the investors may have had an interest in continuing the relation, there was no longer the same urgency for it.

The situation is entirely different in respect to the establishment of manufacturing facilities in less-developed countries. Here, if anything, the foreign investor's position has improved. In this area there is considerable risk and uncertainty. The host countries have a great interest in exporting the goods that are produced on their soil, and their concern is to invite foreign subsidiaries that have an extensive knowledge of foreign markets. Such production is always overwhelmingly intended for foreign sale. In these circumstances, considerable effort is made to establish some kind of partnership between foreign and local interests. The host country, seeking the benefits of having a powerful international company operating within its economy, wishes at the same time to retain control over that economy. The United States was prepared for ambivalent reactions in countries like Mexico, Nigeria, and India; it was less prepared for such responses in countries like France, Germany, and Great Britain. In these advanced nations, local businessmen are alarmed over the intrusion of American-owned enterprise. The unfamiliarity of local businessmen with the behavior patterns of these new firms has led to difficulty. But the governments have been no less wary; there is a constant worry over whether the local governments will be able to apply their fiscal and monetary policies to their subsidiaries. No advanced country (and no less-developed one) can accept easily the prospect of seeing subsidiaries controlled from some center outside their own frontiers.

The issue of sovereignty is a real one. Although the enterprises involved are generally thought of as being U. S.-owned, their identity in national terms is likely to become more ambiguous. As both material and human resources are increasingly drawn from many nations, and as more solutions to problems are attempted without reference to national boundaries, there is the possibility that the new multinational enterprise will no longer be identified with any one nation. It is by no means certain that firms will quickly accept the implications of an uncertain and ambiguous identity. Also, the national sovereign may remain quite suspicious of these vast organisms suddenly planted in its midst. The problem, as Mr. Vernon sees it, is to reconcile the nation-state to the multinational enterprise. He indicates many possible devices for achieving this objective, including the creation of new kinds of supranational authority. This, however, is a long-range objective; in the immediate future, there is the pressing problem of reconciling existing governments with the foreign economic empires that are building in their midst.

Neil W. Chamberlain sets himself the task of considering how the large corporate organization affects the intellectual activity of those who serve it. Modern corporate life necessitates a high degree of specialization, and Mr. Chamberlain asks whether this considerable specialization does not contribute to a narrowing of the perspectives of the men who are obliged to work in such an environment. Moreover, because any large corporation has many subunits, which cannot interfere with the larger company objectives, there is an additional serious restraint on "the play of the imagination," even for those who hold fairly elevated posts. In these circumstances, it is easy to believe that the only safe escape is in a steady climb to the higher reaches of the organizational ladder—where more time is devoted to planning and future-oriented activity; where efficiency concepts and standard routines are inapplicable; where, in short, imagination and insight command a premium. Such an escape is possible only for a few. Others who seek an intellectual escape may conclude that the only hope is to build one's interests outside one's working life. Mr. Chamberlain argues that this is a distorted representation of the situation in the larger corporation. He believes that size is an asset, creating an organizational environment calculated to contribute to intellectual vigor. Bigness provides a larger absolute pool of earnings with which the firm can play. Only the large corporation is in a position to undertake projects that require large sums of capital, high risk, and long periods of gestation. If the specialized character of work in the large firm is a limiting factor, the creation of opportunities that would not exist at all is a liberating one.

Like Mr. Goldston, Mr. Chamberlain believes that the large firm will increasingly assume responsibility for tasks presently performed by the government. While there will be no abandonment of the profit incentive, it will figure less prominently. Only large firms are in a position to involve themselves in this way. Looking to the future, Mr. Chamberlain can imagine corporations self-consciously choosing to operate in two quite different sectors—one defined as profit-making, the other as non-profit. The survival of business in its present dominant position may depend on its readiness to shift to such a broader set of social objectives.

There are subtle differences of emphasis in the approaches of Messrs. Goldston and Chamberlain. Both, however, are given new meaning in the article by Michel Crozier, appropriately entitled "A New Rationale for American Business." Mr. Crozier suggests that America's business superiority "lies not in the resources of its firms, however immense those may be, but in the capacities of its many corporations to create and develop efficient organizations rapidly, to recruit and employ able people anywhere," and to use the competition that results "to maintain the necessary pressure" while enforcing a sufficient amount of cooperation so that each organization is able to use its talent effectively.

Mr. Crozier suggests that the present-day model of American corporate enterprise may soon change dramatically. New fields, new societal responsibilities, and new cultural environments will provide the basic challenges for American business in the next two or three decades. These will constitute the new frontiers for American business and will provide the incentives for its renewal. A generation ago, activities like teaching, caring for the sick, assisting the poor, and organizing scientific research were not considered suitable areas for business involvement. Had business thought to enter such areas, it would have encountered considerable resistance. Today, the situation is greatly changed; it is increasingly recognized that business has a unique contribution to make in all such endeavors. The business corporation is in a position to identify and locate the basic problems in each of these areas, to experiment with pilot projects, and to arrange for large-scale applications of new techniques. Management techniques may be introduced into areas where market mechanisms have never existed. Mr. Crozier's concern is not simply to demonstrate that these areas will be transformed as a result of the involvement of business; he contends that the corporation itself will be fundamentally altered as the result of this encounter. Modern and efficient planning, he says, consists in foreseeing the consequences of purposive social action and then in feeding this knowledge back to the decision-makers. Individual firms are already doing this; the challenge is to pass from the stage of planning by individual firms to one that can be properly called public planning.

Noting the increased involvement of American corporations in foreign enterprise, Mr. Crozier asks whether they will become truly international, disassociating their business methods from their cultural background. He suggests that an organization capable of building efficient international teams will have a greater capacity for problem-solving than a culturally bound one. In its work to develop a world community, Mr. Crozier predicts, American business will be led to reconsider some of its basic thinking about economic and social rationality. In this area, no problem is more urgent than that which relates to the growing demand for participation and, with it, the necessity for innovation. Mr. Crozier maintains that vast human resources are wasted because of our inability to "organize social systems that allow people to mature, express themselves, and participate." He argues that American firms may be efficient without providing for any of these things, but that such effort will not prove effective in certain of the newer fields, like scientific research, education, and health.

The last two decades, he observes, have seen the emergence of a new and more complex hero; he is not so much an organizer as an expert in rational arrangements. The rationale of American business, according to Mr. Crozier, is "rationality itself." Profit is still the measure, he writes, and an indispensable one, but it is no longer the end. Mr. Crozier predicts that this trend will become accentuated in the next two decades. By broadening business mores and perspectives, this shift will mean that "business will leave what to some extent has become its ghetto." As a result, Mr. Crozier expects the antagonism between business and certain elements in the American community to subside.

He predicts that men will face severe psychological pressures in seeking to adjust to an increasingly rational society. It would be well to anticipate certain of the tensions that will develop, and Mr. Crozier foresees the emergence of "new opposing hedonistic tendencies" rising up to challenge the dominant rationalistic value system.

R. Joseph Monsen, while also concerned with the future, is more preoccupied with the contemporary ideologies of American businessmen. He divides businessmen into three major categories and seeks to define the ideology and role of each. A distinction is made between the traditional businessman, the professional manager, and the small businessman. The first still believes in the operation of the market, holds fast to many of the ideas of the Puritan ethic, placing a high value on thrift and hard work, finds his organizational affiliation generally in the National Association of Manufacturers, and often feels that he is under attack. The professional manager belongs to a quite different ideological family. Often an individual who has worked his way up in the corporate bureaucracy, he comes to his business career with a university degree and shows an early concern with achieving the goals that the corporation sets for itself. Many professional managers show little if any hostility to Keynesian economics. As a group, they are interested in new management techniques, principally as a way of increasing corporate efficiency, and they are frequently prepared to involve their corporations in helping to solve the critical social problems of our day. The small businessman is more difficult to characterize. The class is broad, and its members are highly differentiated. On the whole, they resemble traditional businessmen more than they do the professional managers. They have a strong customer orientation; being generally short of capital, they are more immediately affected by adverse conditions affecting their consumers. Governmental regulatory practices are expensive nuisances for many of them, or at least are thought to be that. The risks they take are large, and the prospect of failure is never far from their thinking. They tend to be "protectionist" and to place a high value on law and order. They are often prone to look on universities with considerable suspicion.

If this is how business looks at the world, how do others regard business? Mr. Monsen considers the opinions of only two groups—the young and what may be called the intellectual critics. Among the young, there is growing evidence of either indifference or hostility. Although the data are conflicting, certain small groups among the young severely criticize business practices and values. Mr. Monsen considers the views of both the New Left and the Hippies. He also provides evidence—there is not so much available as we would wish to have—on what university students generally think about business. The attitudes of intellectuals are just as disparate. Considering the views of what may be called the Conservative, Liberal, and New Left positions, Mr. Monsen concludes that the Liberal view probably carries the greatest weight at the moment among American intellectuals. They are not, Mr. Monsen says, opposed to business becoming involved in resolving society's major dilemmas. There is, in Liberal circles, an increased faith in business as a responsible partner in helping to remedy our more serious social problems.

Leonard S. Silk is concerned with the nature of business power in contemporary America, but has more than a little interest in how business is viewed. On the matter of power, he suggests that "big business actually has less power today than it had in the 1890's and the 1900's, that big labor has more, but that neither 'dominates' the society." The great corporations exercise considerable influence, particularly in the market place, but there are checks even on this power. On the question of how effective business will show itself to be in dealing with the larger social problems, Mr. Silk is inclined to reserve judgment. A too-close alliance between large corporations and the government may well create difficult problems, and charges of monopoly and privilege might well be heard. While there continue to be major misgivings on the part of business executives about their relations with government, there is every reason to believe that such relations will, in fact, continue and expand. Mr. Silk gives considerable weight to the increased economic knowledge presently available; this, he says, almost guarantees that there will be no booms or busts like those of the 1920's. Still, the existence of sophisticated economic and fiscal theories does not guarantee that this knowledge will be used intelligently. Political opportunism and narrow self-interest may well combine to defeat the reasonable use of economic policy for preserving full employment.

Like Mr. Averitt, Mr. Silk considers the maintenance of full employment essential to the working of an industrial economy constituted as the American one presently is. Efforts by the government to sponsor central planning and coordination are not much favored by business. The small businessman, as Mr. Monsen suggested, remains highly suspicious of Keynesian economics. In the large, American companies still seek to control the environment in which they operate not so much through an alliance with the government, as through their control of markets. "Risk and uncertainty," Mr. Silk contends, "still remain the dominant characteristics of the business environment." There is still a widespread distrust in the business community of "intellectuals"; technicians are exempted from this suspicion, but businessmen do not think of technicians as intellectuals. Mr. Silk notes in much contemporary writing a tendency to believe that power is shifting from the business corporation and its leaders to other sectors, especially to universities and research centers. Mr. Silk is unable to accept these arguments in the form that they presently take. He suggests that the "research revolution" has increased rather than diminished the capability of the corporation to survive and to grow. It will remain in a central position in the American economy. This, however, constitutes no verdict on how it will fare in its attempts to cope with the nation's growing social problems.

Andrew Shonfield's forward-looking essay, entitled "Business in the Twenty-First Century," offers a reasonable conclusion to Part I. He suggests that the dialogue between business and public authority today might be summed up in the assertion by the first: "Anything you can do, I can do better." Mr. Shonfield is impressed with this self-confidence; the corporation, which lost so much of its prestige during the Depression, appears to be entirely rehabilitated. The explanation, he thinks, is to be found in the general disappointment with the performance of the postwar state as the manager of economic enterprise. While the state, during the past quarter century, has provided a favorable economic environment for the corporation to live in, it has received little credit for its accomplishment. Instead, the business corporation has emerged with all the credit for its capacity to be flexible and to respond quickly and efficiently to changing consumer demands. By comparison, Mr. Shonfield suggests, agencies of the state seem ponderous and insensitive. Also, and very importantly, the corporation has become an exceptionally powerful instrument of innovation. Where once it was regarded as a somewhat sinister body pursuing restrictive policies, it is now seen to be open and ready to experiment. There can be no question but that the corporation's attachment to techniques of scientific management has contributed greatly to its raised reputation. Also, its readiness to serve as an active partner of the state in carrying out major national economic policies has added to its luster.

Mr. Shonfield asks what the corporation's future relations will be with the consumers of its products, its shareholders, organized labor, and the government itself. All his predictions, he insists, are based on the assumption that there will be "no economic slump in this period and no large-scale war involving the present industrial world." With these provisos, he suggests that we will see a vast expansion in the size of large corporations. The use of computers and other technologies will operate to remove many of the traditional constraints on the size of organizations that can be run efficiently by a single management board. A less authoritarian structure, offering the possibility of considerable initiative at the periphery as well as strict control over essential matters at the center, is likely to make the task of expansion much easier.

Corporations are showing today a growing interest in having wider and longer lasting contractual relationships with their customers. This is an attempt by the corporation to secure a firmer commitment from its customers. This practice will continue and expand. It is predicated, however, on the guarantee of reliable and fast service. In the future, both will be even more highly valued than today. Corporations will be judged severely, but those that show a capacity to meet such standards will be greatly used. They will be seen increasingly as major social instruments, performing services not essentially different from those public agencies (like the police) that have the authority of the state behind them. The corporation may see that it is in its interest to foster a sense of consumer participation. As the society grows more complex, there will be a greater recognition that no one can fend for himself. There will be a new reliance on the producer of essential services. The bond between management and shareholders will be loosened even more. Management will be less disposed to make shareholders' views all-important; other constituencies will concern them more. The corporation will have a greater interest in retaining its efficient labor and will not welcome a continuing loss of key personnel. The corporation will assume responsibility for retraining men and women in new skills. The sheer size of the corporation will greatly facilitate the task of job-changing. These giant corporations will appear as "formidable rivals" to government itself, and there will be growing demands for the close surveillance of these giants. Given their authority and position in society, they will have to be open to public scrutiny.

Such interpretations, whether they relate to business in the past, present, or future, will not go unchallenged. One of the principal objectives of this book is to encourage discussion of the options that presently exist. Nothing would be more hazardous than the failure to think through the implications of the proposals presented in these pages. The authors would be the first to welcome readers' reactions. would be the first to welcome readers' reactions.

The issue owes a great deal to a large company who have advised the Editors from the beginning. In addition to the authors, an expression of thanks is due: Kenneth R. Andrews, Daniel Bell, Warren Bennis, L. Earle Birdzell, Jr., Wayne G. Broehl, Harvey Brooks, M. B. E. Clarkson, Thomas C. Cochran, Anthony Downs, Henry W. Ehrmann, Gaylord A. Freeman, Jr., Thomas M. Garrett, Alexander Gerschenkron, Randall T. Klemme, Seymour Martin Lipset, Robert M. Macdonald, Daniel Marx, Jr., Isamu Miyazaki, Bernard J. Muller-Thym, John C. Parkin, Theodore V. Purcell, David Riesman, John H. Rubel, Raymond Stevens, and E. O. Vetter.

The initiative for this study came from the Amos Tuck School of

Business Administration. A special debt is owed the former Dean of the School, Karl Hill. The present Dean, John W. Hennessey, Jr., has given generously of his time from the beginning.

Finally, mention should be made of those who have given funds for this study to the Amos Tuck School, permitting the School to join the American Academy in this effort. The Alfred P. Sloan Foundation, the I.B.M. Corporation, and the Amos Tuck School Associates Program provided the financial aid that made two conferences and this publication possible.

S. R. G.

WILLIAM LETWIN

The Past and Future of the American Businessman

"THIS NATION'S business is business" instantly identifies the nation as the United States. Other nations have pursued glory, empire, peace—transcendent or secular—and commonly that most perplexing and troublesome of goals, national independence. The United States alone has devoted itself, deliberately and almost consistently from the start, to the double ideals of liberty and plenty. Elsewhere businessmen would not have been at home, for in a nation lacking economic liberty—its economy completely controlled by government—there would be no business, and there could be no businessmen. And in a nation indifferent to plenty, there would be no great need of businessmen. But in the United States, a community whose ideals and actual circumstances were so favorable, businessmen flourished. They did not merely become rich in that obscure or even surreptitious manner of certain Oriental businessmen who hope fervently to evade the notice of public officials and the envy of their neighbors. On the contrary, most American businessmen have lived as publicly as most other Americans; they have openly taken part not only in business, but also in public affairs, in politics, and in government. Their activities have been endorsed and even admired by the public, so that at last it was possible for Calvin Coolidge to call the private concerns of businessmen the chief public concern of the nation.

Business has been the national work of the United States just as baseball is its national sport; and the top of American society is occupied largely by businessmen. Historically this status is unusual, perhaps unique, for elsewhere businessmen have been despised or, if condoned, relegated to an inferior level of the social order. In Europe, they suffered consecutively from the disapproval of medieval theologians, eighteenth-century aristocrats, and mod-

ern socialists. In America, they have sometimes been censured
by the few, but those episodes of criticism have ended by renewed
approval of the many.

All this should stir the curiosity of historians more than it has.
How did American businessmen get to the top? How have they
stayed there? And who are "they" anyway? After answering those
questions, I will pass over the present condition of businessmen in
America to consider the more compelling question of their future,
another subject about which history has something to tell.

I

Businessmen were already established in their high status when
the United States emerged as a nation in 1789. Even as early as
that, the United States could have been described as a nation of
businessmen ruled by businessmen. That description would have
violated certain of the more acceptable images of American life,
but it would have fitted the larger facts.

In the first place, the North American colonies were originally
conceived as commercial ventures. John Cabot, on whose discoveries English claims in the New World were founded, undoubtedly shared that irrational impulse to adventure without
which the endurance of explorers and perpetual frontiersmen
would be incomprehensible. But Cabot was equally keen on making the most of his trip as a business undertaking, and so he
stipulated for a monopoly of all commerce with places he discovered, in return for which grant he undertook to pay 20 per cent
of his earnings to Henry VII. Leaving aside the political implications of such forays into the New World, the King and his successors saw these grants as counterparts of the charters they regularly
gave to trading companies—the Merchant Adventurers, Muscovy
Company, Levant Company, Royal African Company, and, above
all, the East India Company. Trading companies, organized by
private men for private profit, also colonized the New World. The
Virginia Companies of London and of Plymouth, incorporated in
1606, capped the energetic effort of merchants to break into a new
field of foreign trade. Their successor, the Virginia Company of
1609, was governed for fourteen years by Sir Thomas Smith,
magnate, investor in New World projects since 1589, head of the
East India Company for twenty years, and director of many
similar enterprises. From the efforts of such men to find profitable

imports, gold and silver having evaded them, resulted colonization; it was an afterthought, devised to settle on the foreign site a labor force that would catch or grow products that were commercially interesting—fish, furs, and at last tobacco. The colony once established, control passed little by little from the home investors to the settlers abroad. The trading company was transformed into a political community, and its joint enterprise disintegrated into the private enterprises of the colonists. After this happened, Virginia was no less mercantile in spirit than when it was originally conceived, though the spirit now resided in tidewater plantation owners like William Byrd, as well as in men called "merchants."

Pecuniary objectives were not the only reasons for colonization, as the history of Massachusetts Bay makes clear. On the other hand, the image of a single-minded flight to religious freedom also overstates the case. The fathers of the Puritan colony were men like John Endecott, leader of the first expedition, chosen by his uncle-in-law, Mathew Cradock, a leading merchant of London and first governor of the company. For legal adviser, Cradock had John White, lawyer and merchant-adventurer. Among his senior colleagues were Sir Richard Saltonstall, Simon Whetcome, and John Venn—wealthy London merchants. The company's charter followed that of the Virginia Company, because this company, too, intended to do what trading companies did. But in Massachusetts colonization was intended from the start, and the colonists took over the whole venture more decisively. The voyage of the *Mayflower* transmuted a mercantile enterprise into a theocratic commonwealth. Nevertheless, within twenty years, Boston began to change from a temple in the wilderness into a noisy market place of the Empire, its ships and selling managed by men of the best families—Governor Winthrop's son Stephen, John Leverett, and David Yale, whose son founded a college. How business fitted into such men's lives is illustrated by the career of William Pynchon. Born into Essex gentry, he sold his lands and emigrated to New England for religious reasons. There he set up as a fur trader and used the earnings to buy large holdings in the west of the colony, where he founded Springfield and operated trading posts that converted local crops into imported manufactures. Was he a landowner or a merchant? He was both, and most certainly a businessman—a maker, buyer, and seller. His career was duplicated by many other dignitaries of New England, who built their fortunes, families, and standing, until Massachusetts came to be led by Apthorps and Hancocks, New Hampshire by Pepperells and Sherburns, and Rhode Island by Browns.

What then of the legend that the United States began as a nation of small farmers ruled or, rather, led by upright frontier lawyers? Can we dismiss such national monuments as the minuteman and backwoodsman, Patrick Henry and Daniel Webster? It is not necessary to deny the overwhelming incidence of the independent farmer, but it is necessary to recognize that his daily occupation as a farmer did not prevent him from being partly a businessman in spirit. His regular encounters with snow and mud and wild beasts, the empty forests and silence that surrounded him, his heavy work and coarse comforts—these did not make him an ascetic nor obliterate the desire for worldly advancement in a man who, had he quite lacked it, could have stayed more quietly in England. Our liability to misgauge him comes partly from the habit of analyzing society in the threefold pattern: upper class, middle class, and lower class. These categories would do less harm to our understanding if they were not supposed to be mutually exclusive. As it is, they falsely suggest that a small farmer, because he falls within the lower class, could not also have been a businessman, since businessmen are in the middle class. In fact, many American farmers in 1700 and 1800 shared the attitudes and problems of businessmen. They borrowed to finance their operations; they sold goods into risky, remote, impersonal markets; their earnings rose and fell as times were good or bad. Some speculated, like their town cousins, in western lands; and many wanted government to be helpful and non-interfering at the same time. The farmer's way of life was different from that of the town merchant, but the commercial spirit—which feels no doubts about the worthiness of buying, selling, and profit—infused them all. They were not peasants, bound to crops and methods dictated by ritual habits, sentimentally tied to their land. Instead, like tradesmen, they followed fashions and prices. Despite all the striking differences, the independent American farmer and the town-bound full-time merchant easily understood each other.

And what of the lawyers who governed? It is true enough that Congress has always been supremely the province of lawyers. Granted that the American lawyer of the eighteenth century was not a learned man, discerning abstract justice from a perch high above the turmoil, it might be said that neither was he exactly a businessman. But it may be answered that he was a businessman, even exactly a businessman. First of all, lawyers who flourish in a commercial society are commercial lawyers. A commercial lawyer and his client speak the same language—the one slightly better informed about legal technicalities, the other slightly more conscious that his, not the lawyer's, money is at stake. Second, the American lawyer was more nearly a businessman than his English counterpart, for the English solicitor, the lawyer as drawn by Dickens and Trollope, was a family retainer, a faithful servitor, whereas the American attorney met his client as a social equal, as one man of affairs to another—a difference illustrated by the solicitor's habit of "attending" his employer, while the American client commonly called, for his advice, at the lawyer's office. And, finally, the American lawyer was often a businessman in the strict sense. Many of the congressmen classified as "lawyers" are men who, though admitted to the bar, spent a large part of their lives in business, dealing in land, managing shops, investing in trading ventures to China, floating mortages—acting, in short, as everything and anything between small-time bankers and jumped-up peddlers.

The interweaving of the various occupations in colonial America is exhibited in such a place as Groton, Connecticut. Of some five hundred taxpayers in 1783, about two thirds were farmers; and among the farmers were the wealthier men in town—they owned, for instance, the town's sixteen mills. About one quarter of the men were laborers, some indentured servants. The rest, just under one tenth, followed other occupations. There was a lawyer, a physician who also kept a shop, seven other shopkeepers, fifteen tavernkeepers, and a parcel of artisans—carpenters, tailors, shoemakers, and a goldsmith. As artisans were self-employed and often kept shops, that tenth were clearly businessmen. And the farmers in a community like Groton, based as it was on commercial agriculture, were businessmen in all but name. Groton was not altogether like towns closer to the frontier, nor like those of the South, but it was characteristic of a widespread type. The larger and older seacoast towns in New England were more specialized and more commercial, but there, too, commercial, agricultural, and professional activities mixed easily. In Salem, Massachusetts, in 1771 one man in eight was listed as a merchant or shipowner. Yet the richest of them, Richard Derby, held half of his wealth in land, the other half consisting of one rum distillery, five and a half warehouses, one wharf, and some small ships. In equivalent towns in the South at that time, the rich were predominantly plantation owners, than whom, among agriculturalists, none was ever more commercial in spirit. In the South, as in the North, only about one in five whites worked for wages; the great difference, apart from slavery, was the larger fraction of small farmers in the South—perhaps two in every five whites— many of them subsistence farmers, in whom, undoubtedly, the commercial outlook has little room for practice.

A last illustration of the hypothesis that broadly speaking the United States was a nation of businessmen in 1800 comes from considering the character of the Constitution-makers. Today's picture of the Framers is still colored by Beard's theory that they were businessmen, and that the Constitution represented a victory of businessmen over the farmers, especially the yeoman farmers of the Appalachian uplands. But the meticulous analysis carried out by Forrest McDonald shows that, as usual, the facts were infinitely more complex and, in summary, distinctly otherwise. Very broadly, thirty-four of the fifty-nine delegates were lawyers, eighteen were farmers, and seven were merchants. These categories, however, are misleading. If one looks at how the delegates earned their livings, rather than at occupational labels, a different picture emerges. Thirteen of the lawyers had country practices, involving mainly farmers and land; and nine of the thirteen were farmers themselves. The next largest slice of lawyers, ten, were officeholders. Eight were mercantile lawyers; and three, though lawyers by training, did not practice law. If one now shuffles the men into the "interest" groupings suggested by Beard, it turns out that the primary interests of twenty were in land (though about thirty owned and operated farms), those of thirteen were in commerce, those of twelve were in public office, and those of the rest were scattered. If the categories are jettisoned, the intermixture of business becomes clearer still. Charles Pinckney, of South Carolina, is a notable instance. Extremely successful as a lawyer, he married the daughter of a prominent merchant, owned plantations and slaves, and speculated in public securities—as did half of his fellow delegates. Rufus King, of Massachusetts, was the son of a farmer who kept a store on the side; his wife's father was president of the New York Chamber of Commerce; and he practiced law in Newburyport. William Paterson of New Jersey had as his father an Irish immigrant peddler; he was a lawyer, a part-time storekeeper in a small way, and bought a large agricultural estate. George Mason, of Virginia, engaged on an equally large scale in trade and tobacco planting. And among the hundreds of delegates to the state ratifying conventions, something similar prevails; whatever their principal occupation or status, many were businessmen or did the things that businessmen do.

It now becomes easier to see how businessmen rose to the top of American society—not only in the sense that wealth gave them confidence that they were on top, but also in the sense that the citizenry accorded them the highest honor available to a democracy, election to principal public offices. It was not so much that men of business were preferred because they were men of business, but that candidates were not disqualified by a career in which business-like activities had been a part. Candidates were elected for their various qualifications, sound and spurious; and so many businessmen were present that many of the preferred candidates were bound to be businessmen. Moreover, businessmen of the era before 1860 were not categorically different from Americans in general. They were slightly specialized, sometimes more successful, versions of what many Americans aspired to be and counted on becoming. The United States enjoyed no magical harmony of interests; on the contrary, it experienced, as every political community does, endless disharmonies and numerous bitter clashes; but it suffered from few deep cleavages, and its hottest political passions were reserved for the matter of slavery.

The rise of businessmen was facilitated also by the absence of an aristocracy, or rather of an aristocracy that could effectively repress businessmen. Aristocracies did form in the United States. Old families, transmitting hereditary fortunes, came to enjoy inherited respect, though the sphere of influence of any aristocratic family was seldom wider than a state, and as the aristocracy of one state seldom married with that of any other, this restricted their national influence. But the northern aristocracies did not reject their commercial antecedents, even if individual members became poets, patrons, or sybarites. And although southern aristocrats began to feel that trade is base, the power of southern aristocracies to impose any view on the nation waned as the electoral preponderance of the free states increased, and ended with the Civil War. To most other Americans, self-made men must have seemed more sympathetic, more easily understood, and more readily emulated than the refined and therefore less approachable descendants of self-made men who claimed merit by birth rather than by the personal achievements that most Americans understood or valued. Refinement is not, in America, the key to eminence. It consistently loses any contest with vitality and energy, which is not surprising since vitality was what brought Europeans from stable societies into the American stir. Moreover, refinement resembles laziness, which Americans have always, for the same temperamental and economic reasons, despised or feared.

Not everyone has cheered the rise of American businessmen. It is easy to cull great scrapbooks of sayings—from the sermons of Puritan divines, poor men's letters, the manifestoes of Philadelphia cordwainers, political speeches, and philosophical essays—that voice criticisms of businessmen. But they do not negate the presumption that in a free society people get largely the results they want. Particular attacks on businessmen do not change the fact that businessmen rose prior to the Civil War in the United States because they embodied the common aspirations and symbolized the working life of most Americans.

II

It is easier to understand how businessmen came to be accepted as natural leaders of American society than to explain how they managed to retain that position despite all that they and others did to destroy it.

Criticisms of businessmen are to be found in all periods of American history and emanate from every social group, including the businessmen themselves. The difficulty is to know what such criticisms really mean. For a start, in an active democracy sporadic criticism does not imply deep disaffection and does not, in fact, disrupt the social order. Criticism of businessmen is not revealing if, as was the case, every social group and every occupation was constantly subjected to criticism of similar intensity. Frontier farmers were regularly castigated as boorish, lazy, superstitious, and envious. Country gentlemen and plantation owners were condemned for pride, ostentation, and libertine luxury. Lawyers were constantly portrayed as shifty, tradesmen as mean and grasping, politicians as corrupt, and teachers as hypocritical. All orders of American society and any number of individual men whose actions touched on public life were exposed to the unbridled language, the lack of courtesy, which set the tone of public controversy in the

United States and which can be correctly appreciated by the observer who understands American manners as expressing general irreverence rather than specific hatred. If businessmen came in for their share of casual malice, it would be wrong to interpret this as profound "social criticism."

Other sorts of criticism may seem deeper. What of the regular reminder to Puritan congregations that since no man can serve both God and Mammon, industriousness might be lauded, but money-grubbing must surely be punished? This view persisted, and the Protestant Evangelicals went on saying the same thing throughout the first half of the nineteenth century. Their critique, as Perry Miller summarized it, "accused the business spirit of having 'done much to produce this lamented declension of vital piety.' As might be expected—while foreign observers found it amazing that pastors dared so to preach to rich parishioners—ministers regularly denounced as the great source of iniquity among the people their 'haste to be rich,' and included Benjamin Franklin's method of 'the steady, industrious, persevering course.'" Criticism this certainly is, persistent and perhaps deep-seated, but it did not attack the high status of businessmen, even when said to the businessman's face. It attacked, rather, an attitude toward wealth, as contrasted with work, that might have been shared by any American, whatever his occupation. Greed is not a special prerogative of businessmen; but—by a poetic convention that dates back to ancient times, when perhaps it had some foundation in fact— businessmen were the symbolic personification of greed. In America it was commonly said, and with a certain sense of pride in this bit of harmless wickedness, that all Americans were greedy. Irreverence, rather than moral fervor, colors Washington Irving's famous line on "the almighty dollar, that great object of universal devotion throughout our land."

Other, more specific objections to business, can also be misleading. Consider this:

There seem to be but three ways for a nation to acquire wealth. The first is by war. . . . This is robbery. The second, by commerce, which is generally cheating. The third by agriculture, the only honest way.

It seems blunt enough: Business is generally a cheat. The passage, however, comes from a pamphlet written in his advanced age by Benjamin Franklin, the archetype of the successful American businessman—rags to riches, early to bed early to rise, and all.

It would be melodrama to interpret the passage as showing that after Franklin retired from business into statesmanship, he felt a deep revulsion against his misspent youth; his autobiography, written not much later, reveals the unimpaired pride he felt in his business career. What this passage illustrates, instead, is a traditional doubt that perpetually plagued businessmen and everyone else, and still does. The doubt is that there must be something wrong about commerce, because the merchant profits even though he does not *make* anything. Farmers make things, and carpenters make things, but businessmen earn by merely buying and selling; the merchant is a middleman, and the middleman is a parasite. This doubt, this superstition, is natural in simple agricultural societies and is hard to shake off. It underlies the saying that business consists of selling things you do not have to people who do not want them; it underlies Galbraith's picture of the private sector in an affluent economy.

That Franklin could express it shows that this doubt about the social utility of business is quite distant from a conviction that businessmen, especially former businessmen, are not fit to govern a decent society. In any case, the effectiveness of the doubt as social criticism began to wane because of a fundamental change that took place in American business during the nineteenth century. When Americans said "businessman" at the beginning of the century, they saw in their minds a merchant in a shop or counting room; when they said it at the end of the century, they were more likely to imagine a manufacturer—that is, a maker of things. This change was recognized, and as a matter of pride, by businessmen. Their older organizations, starting in the eighteenth century, called themselves chambers of commerce; the trade organizations that emerged at the end of the nineteenth century called themselves associations of manufacturers. Why manufacturers should have been assimilated into the category of "businessmen" is a special puzzle in the history of ideas. The consequences of this arbitrary act of classification are considerable. If, for instance, manufacturers and merchants had been grouped instead under the heading of "entrepreneurs"—one fair way of summarizing the basic economic similarity between these otherwise different activities—then it might have occurred more readily to Americans that independent farmers also fit that category, since they—like shopkeepers and factory-owners—risk their capital in enterprises and decide what to buy and sell. But that is a separate question. As it turned out, the new view of business as being connected with manufacturing did tend to quash the indictment that business is unproductive and therefore parasitic.

On the other hand, the displacement of "Commerce" by "Industry" exposed businessmen to a new and much more serious order of criticism. Industry means factories and employees. The scale of the social transformation that resulted is suggested by the statistics. In 1800, only one free man in four was an employee; in 1900 a majority were. From a nation of businessmen, the United States turned into a nation of employees.

It is not likely that a citizenry of wage-earners would accept the general authority of employers as readily as businessmen of one sort accepted the dominance of businessmen of another sort. Nevertheless, despite this apparent hazard, this conflict of interests, businessmen have survived among the leaders of American society—so much so that among the contenders for the presidential nomination in 1968 were the former president of an automobile manufacturing firm, the grandson of an oil refiner, the former president of a camera company, and the son of a shipping magnate, not to mention the former operator of a radio station and present operator of a commercial ranch.

A number of things explain how businessmen were able to weather the criticisms levied at them during the century after the Civil War. They were accused of victimizing their workers by using Pinkerton men to shoot down strikers and by putting women to work in sweatshops and firetraps; of corrupting city bosses and Cabinet secretaries in order to fill their pockets from the public purse; of cheating small investors with watered stock and financial trickery; of driving small competitors out of business and using their monopoly power to exact tribute from consumers; of grossly displaying their wealth, of atrocious taste and moral apathy. These accusations were sometimes well-founded, often vastly exaggerated; but they were neither conventional nor abstract. They expressed sharply felt antagonism, directed against fairly concrete persons. They were, in short, serious attacks against the ordering principles of American society at that time. Nevertheless, the skeleton of that society remained unchanged.

It survived, in part, because the main attacks were not aimed at "Business" in general, but at quite specific varieties of businessmen. For instance, the Granger movement in the 1870's attacked the railroads and grain merchants on the argument that about

WILLIAM LETWIN

60 per cent of the market price paid for wheat in New York
ended in the pockets of the leeches, leaving the smaller share
for the midwestern farmers whose honest toil had raised it. As this
argument may be construed to express a profound principle of
natural justice (rather than a profound misunderstanding of a
complex economic system), as the force of the complaint is vastly
exaggerated by the practice among historians of calling the
Granger campaign an "Agrarian Revolt," and as "The Railroads"
are regularly misconstrued as having been the essential form of
"Business" at the time, the whole affair has been seen as an assault
on the foundations of "Capitalism." It was nothing of the sort.
Rather, it was a demand for a specific, limited reform. Practically
nobody proposed that the railroads be nationalized, and the
Grangers would have been the last to tolerate any collectivization
of their own private enterprises. What was wanted and ultimately
accomplished was regulation of railroads, regulation in keeping
with the narrow doctrine that railroad owners, like innkeepers or
ferrymen, follow a public calling and benefit from grants of privilege, rather than the broad view that private enterprise is un-
acceptable. The most telling feature of the episode is that the movement was successful in the long run because it was supported by
the large number of businessmen—manufacturers and merchants
—who, as shippers, were as keenly interested as any farmer in low
freight rates and nondiscriminatory service.

In much the same way the antitrust movement between 1885
and 1914 can be misinterpreted, and has been, as an assault on
businessmen launched by other economic groups—farmers,
workers, and writers. The facts are quite otherwise. Part of the
movement derived from a vague and old sentiment against monopoly, a sentiment of which businessmen were at times the most
intense spokesmen, as for instance when they campaigned during
Jackson's Administration against the restrictive practice of charter-
ing corporations by special acts of legislation rather than under
the auspices of general acts. Part of the movement derived from
quite specific complaints against the practice of certain trusts.
Among the most persuasive complainants were smaller businessmen
who had been damaged by the aggressive behavior of Standard
Oil Company, the American Sugar Refining Company, or some
other one of the handful of huge national firms created around
the turn of the century. These giants were not "Business," but
"Big Business," and it was no great intellectual feat to attack them

while endorsing "Business" and taking measures to protect the position of "Small Business."

Theodore Roosevelt's stance on the trust question is revealing. He had always distinguished "Big Business" from "Business," and he came to distinguish between "Good Trusts" and "Bad Trusts," finally directing his rhetoric against an even narrower group, "malefactors of great wealth." His program adhered closely enough to a declaration he made when coming into office: "I intend to be most conservative, but in the interest of the big corporations themselves and above all in the interest of the country I intend to pursue, cautiously but steadily, the course to which I have been publicly committed again and again," a course of suppressing certain inimical practices. One of the early results of this policy was the destruction of the Northern Securities Company. Some businessmen wondered where this might all lead, but Elihu Root managed to persuade fellow members of the New York Union League Club that Roosevelt, far from being dangerous, was "the greatest conservative force for the protection of property and of capital in the city of Washington." And this judgment was endorsed by businessmen, who continued to support Roosevelt, at times somewhat reluctantly, but often with an enthusiasm that has failed to be noticed by historians.

The social history of business during the reform period has been misconceived in three characteristic ways. One school of historians rests its case on two undisputed facts: that the main reforming statutes—from the Interstate Commerce Act in 1887 to the Clayton Antitrust Act in 1914—were voted in by large majorities of both parties, and that those statutes did not in practice convert American society into something fundamentally different from what it had been. Historians of this persuasion conclude that the failure of these "anti-business" laws to expel business from its commanding height can only be explained by a deliberate conspiracy: Congressmen, the executive, the judges, and the businessmen colluded to create an illusion of reform. It was all mere window dressing. "They" never intended to satisfy the demand for reform that welled up from below, but only to fob it off with empty gestures.

Another school, the school of democratic optimism, has argued that since government was dominated by businessmen and administered by their supporters and confidants, and since the reforms instituted by government were "anti-business," the only possible explanation is that the supporters of business were forced to act against their will. Documentation for this view takes the form of quotations from businessmen who opposed the reforms, and quotations from reformers, who were not businessmen, urging the reforms. There are many such quotations, and the hortatory conclusion implicit in the works of this school is that the people can curtail the power of the business oligarchy by democratic action. This school or attitude was by far the most popular among historians writing between about 1930 and 1950.

A third school, more recent, portrays the history of reform in terms of the rise of state capitalism or "political capitalism." Their argument is that government, which was in the hands of businessmen and their adherents, carried out the so-called "reform" measures because businessmen finally recognized that instead of resisting the intervention of government, as the doctrine of *laissez faire* had urged them to do, they should put government to positive use as a means for imposing the social arrangements that suited their own economic interests. It is to the credit of this small but growing group of historians that they have looked much more carefully and patiently than their predecessors had at what businessmen said and did. And they have found that, on the whole, businessmen invented, advocated, or at least rapidly recognized the usefulness of each main measure of reform. Their more careful research shows, as one should have predicted, that businessmen disagreed among themselves about political questions, but that the majority or substantial minorities supported the statutes, policies, and administrative mechanisms of reform.

Only one further step is necessary to arrive at what I should consider the correct view of the matter—that is, to recognize that the attitudes of businessmen toward reform corresponded pretty well, at most times, to the attitude of most Americans of all classes, occupations, and political outlooks. A token of this is the pre-eminence among the Progressives of George Perkins, a Morgan partner. His adherence to reform was not an idiosyncrasy, but only the best-known instance of a position taken by other merchants and industrialists. Another token is that the philanthropic activities of businessmen like Carnegie and Rockefeller supported undertakings of a sort that all Americans have endorsed. In short, businessmen were able to retain their position of general leadership in American society chiefly because no fundamental cleavage of outlook between businessmen and the rest ever became a hard-set presumption of American life. It seemed for a moment that this might happen during the Depression, when "Business" and "Republican" almost turned into synonyms, and the majority of other Americans appeared to be becoming perpetual Democrats, perpetually frustrated by the Supreme Court. That impression was superficial, for while some businessmen were vilifying Franklin Roosevelt as a traitor, many others were eagerly taking advantage of the cartel arrangements authorized by the N.R.A., the hot-oil rules, and other economic policies of the first New Deal. Business has probably never been regarded with less favor in the United States than it was during the Depression years. This can easily be accounted for, partly by the intractability of some businessmen, their insistence that they alone knew the cure for depression, but probably much more by a widespread sense that the economy would not have collapsed if the businessmen, who had been its leaders, had been fit for that responsibility. But the balance was redressed during World War II. Since then businessmen have so indoctrinated themselves and one another in the new gospel of social responsibility and have so visibly followed it that little criticism remains to be heard. There are murmurings, to be sure, condemning the whole of bourgeois civilization; and from the mitigated left rise troubled remarks about the private sector of our civilization (including the military side of the public sector). From various other corners stem complaints against the particular dangerousness of cigarettes, automobiles, and smog. Yet on the whole, American businessmen enjoy as much public confidence now as they ever have before.

III

Nevertheless, despite his triumphant survival during the past century, the American businessman is now expected to vanish into extinction. The three forces expected to bring about his demise are The Managerial Revolution, The Technological Revolution, and The Planning Revolution. It is a common impression that this will happen, and it may turn out to be true. But if so, it will be because too many people believed this to be inevitable, even though in fact there is nothing inevitable about it.

The Managerial Revolution is supposed to eliminate the businessman since many business firms are controlled by salaried managers rather than by owners. As a result—so goes the hypothesis advanced by Berle and Means in 1932 and restated by Galbraith in 1968—large corporations are no longer run with the objective of maximizing profits, for profits benefit owners rather than managers. Instead, the managers use their power to maximize their own goals at the expense of the multitude of powerless shareholders. Managers aim to aggrandize themselves as individuals and to maintain the integrity of the organization or, more concretely, to make life more comfortable for themselves as a group. The whole psychology of business is therefore changing beyond recognition. Risk-bearing, enterprising proprietors are being displaced—will soon have been extinguished—by corporate bureaucrats who, since they neither risk anything of their own nor profit from taking successful risks, always incline toward lazy mediocrity. And so, predicts the theory of Managerial Revolution, the economy will stagnate while executives grow sleek and stuffy.

The Managerial Revolution is a theory extrapolated from the single presumed historical fact that management has been increasingly divorced from ownership. That instances of this divorce exist is obvious. The du Pont Company, which once belonged to a man called du Pont, now belongs to hundreds of thousands of men, not to mention countless other thousands who have taken on and put off ownership during a hard morning's work with their stockbrokers. The only question is whether enough of this is happening to justify a state of nerves about the uncharted seas into which History is bearing us. The answer is clearly no.

For one thing, the divorce is not a new thing. Management and ownership have been separable functions since business began. They were separate in ancient commercial ventures where dozens of men jointly owned a ship sent to voyage for years under the sole management of its captain. So were they separate in the relation, old as time, of lord and steward, and in the relation of sleeping partner to managing partner, which financed much of industry during the nineteenth century.

Secondly, to speak of this as divorce begs the question. It might just as accurately be called marriage. If social arrangements have been devised for cooperation among specialists, so that he who is lucky enough to own capital can get help from a man skilled enough to manage it, so much the better. But of course this is just where the supposed crux appears: How will the owners keep the managers in order? How will they be able to tell whether the managers are acting as good stewards should? The problem is much milder than has been thought. Shareholders, no matter how small and stupid, can generally tell whether their stocks are paying dividends or rising in value, and they display a low commercial cunning in getting rid of stocks that do not pay dividends or capital gains. The prices of such stocks thereby fall, which makes them attractive ultimately to raiders, renovators, and nascent empire-builders. By this simple mechanism, managers who are noticeably inefficient often find themselves out of office, replaced by managers who have been more attentive to the profit-seeking intent of owners. So it comes about that executives fare better as owners profit more.

Bureaucracy has certainly come into the large corporations—though not into the several million other businesses within the American economy. Bureaucracy carries with it a danger that men will rise to the top not because of their substantive skills as, say, makers of automobiles, but rather because of their political skills in climbing hierarchical ladders. If such political experts could stay at the top, despite being poor at their real work, then they would ruin their organizations as productive units—this is the fear of the Managerial Revolution theorist. But the fear is unreal so long as the stock market remains fairly free, for the power of owners to walk out on an inefficient but entrenched management is enough to keep executives generally in good order. And the evidence of the American economy suggests that the process has worked reasonably well. The biggest bureaucracies—those of General Motors, Standard Oil of New Jersey, The Bank of America, even A.T.&T.—have provided rather efficient management. The lesson of history seems to be that an increased amount of managerial bureaucracy need not destroy the vitality of American business.

It is reassuring also to observe, from recent studies of executive incentives in the United States, that today's managers show the same vigorous appetite for income and wealth that spurred yesterday's businessmen to bold progress. Moreover, the earnings of executives, especially their earnings in the form of stock options, tend to turn the successful executive into an owner himself, thus giving him a powerful incentive to harmonize his interests as manager and owner; in other words, making him act like a traditional entrepreneurial businessman.

The Technological Revolution is supposed to be eliminating the businessman by replacing him with technical experts. An increasing share of the national income is produced by complex machinery and processes that can be understood intimately only by scientists and engineers. It follows, say the proponents of this view, that only scientists and engineers can manage those industrial processes. Businessmen will thus be excluded by their incapacity to understand the work they pretend to manage. This view—among whose many prominent proponents were Weber and Veblen and are, at this moment, Crossman and Galbraith—rests on a thorough misunderstanding of what experts do and of what businessmen do.

Consider a simple technical problem—how to package pills for retail sales. They might be packaged in light cardboard boxes. These would be cheapest, but the pills would deteriorate most quickly in them and they would be most prone to damage in shipping, besides being fairly unprepossessing in appearance. The pills might also be packaged in glass bottles—the next cheapest method—allowing for the tightest seal. This packaging would be less prone to damage in shipment and best from the standpoint of appearance. The third and most expensive choice would be plastic bottles, intermediate as to tightness of seal, quite unbreakable, middling as to appearance in the eyes of consumers.

The respective roles of the technician and the businessmen in solving this problem epitomize their relation with respect to any business problem. The engineer knows the various qualities of materials. He knows how to find out from reference works or by fresh research the relative probability that packages in the various materials will be damaged by various sorts of handling. But nothing in his training or experience as an engineer enables him to say whether it is more desirable to have a cheap package, a tight package, an unbreakable package, or a pretty package. In fact, his training and experience equip him in just the opposite way. He can solve problems *after* the criteria of success have been specified, after somebody has said to him: "Design the least breakable container that can be produced for 5 cents (assuming an output of 10,000 per day), and keep pills fresh for not less than twelve months." An engineer knows how to work to engineering specifications; he even knows something about how to translate a collection of loosely stated ends into moderately precise specifications. But he knows nothing, as expert, about which ends ought to be preferred.

The function of the business executive is to state the ends that will define the engineer's effort. This is the manager's work, ideally and in fact. He comes by this function not because of his formal education—for no formal education can enable him to tell whether to emphasize the cheapness of the package or its durability. Nor does the manager acquire any proper claim to his function by virtue of experience in carrying it out. Rather, the businessman does that job precisely because somebody must do it, and the name typically given to the man who makes those arbitrary decisions within a private firm is "executive," or "manager." The ultimate justification for any man who takes the responsibility of arbitrarily deciding the detailed objectives of an organized effort is that he does this well or bears the main consequences if he does not. Businessmen—proprietor-managers—therefore are extremely useful to a society. If they make mistakes, they lose their own money; and if they make too many mistakes, they lose along with all their capital their power to make mistakes. 1693599

It may be said, of course, that a capitalist economy judges correctness or error in the choice of the detailed goals of production by the base criterion of profit, though it might be retorted that base profit merely reflects the democratic and therefore laudable mechanism of consumer sovereignty. But that difficult discussion can be left to one side, for the need to choose the detailed ends of production is just as pressing in any non-capitalist economy, and it has an irreducible element of arbitrariness. Socialist pills also have to be packaged, and a socialist engineer is not a bit better able to design the "best" package until somebody else prescribes the specifications, the specific criteria that define "best." That is why no society whatsoever can get along without business managers.

This simple conclusion is often obscured by an ambiguity in the term "engineer." A man may be an "engineer" either in the sense that he was trained in engineering and experienced in it or in the sense that he now practices that particular skill as his principal occupation. Thus, although more American business executives than ever before are scientists and engineers, it is also true that no business executive is a scientist or engineer—for insofar as his work is to make certain arbitrary decisions, his technical education and experience have no direct relevance whatsoever.

Although this line of reasoning is enough to refute the notion that The Technological Revolution will do away with business managers, it may be worth mentioning another consideration. In any effort that requires the collaboration of human beings, disagreements occur from time to time. Sometimes the disagreements can be resolved quite easily by the contestants; sometimes, for emotional reasons, this cannot be done easily, especially when the issue has arisen over a question of taste or irrational preference. In a polity such questions are identified as political and are resolved by political processes, among which is arbitrary decision by executives. In any other organization, such disputes are equally political in essence and are resolved, in the end, by somebody who is called a manager. Experts are not, as experts, able to make arbitrary decisions; indeed, the only point in having experts is that they are supposed to be able to reach rational, non-arbitrary decisions. But since every community must be able to decide certain questions which can only be decided arbitrarily, no community can do without managers. There is no way of getting rid of managers.

The Planning Revolution was designed in the first place to supersede businessmen with expert public servants. In the early, severe variety, of which Russian central planning was the prototype, all productive units were subjected to the control of a central headquarters, whose decisions were executed in each firm by public functionaries. In the later, gentler variety, of which the best-known specimen is French indicative planning, businessmen are not eliminated. They continue to manage their own concerns, as private agents rather than in the guise of public servants; but their larger entrepreneurial decisions are guided, limited, coordinated, and in some essentials dictated by the planning apparatus—a complex centralizing machinery within which businessmen play a part, but whose critical decisions are taken by civil servants, the legislature, and the government. In both varieties, despite the different amounts of coercion that they entail, the same premise pertains: that the economic decisions reached by independent business firms result in an outcome that is less efficient and less just than would result if all those decisions were subordinated to a set of targets determined centrally and politically. The deeper premise is that the public good can only be achieved by the action of public authorities.

Since planning seems, on this view, to be linked with the higher justice and the greater rationality, many have deduced that the upward march of civilization would sooner or later make central planners of us all. Is this an inescapable tendency, such that reasonable men ought to accept it with the best possible grace, whatever their private preferences might be? So it seemed, only five years ago, after England and France and India had joined many other countries in installing non-communist central planning, and when, for all one could tell, the United States was left alone to bring up, reluctantly no doubt, the tail of the procession. Today, the evidence looks different. Many Social Democrats in Western Europe have lost their enthusiasm for planning; and many countries within the Communist bloc have been making considered retreats from central planning. They are re-establishing a place for decentralized independent management. They have recognized that managers cannot successfully be eliminated, even from a system where many ultimate choices are made by experts and politicians at the center.

Yet although planning in the full sense no longer seems certain to overtake us, a shadow of it remains in current American discussion of the "Social Responsibilities of Business." This centers on the assertion that because business now affects the public more than ever before, businessmen must take into account *all* the effects of their actions, for if they do not do so voluntarily, they will be made to do so by force. It moves toward the conclusion that the businessman is being transformed, willy-nilly, from the swashbuckling privateer that he once was into a sort of public servant.

The assumptions of this view are realistic. American economic life has long been developing in the direction of increasing interdependence. This is due, in part, simply to crowding. The smoke exuded by any factory is now more likely to dirty the neighbors' curtains—because factories, like everything else, now have more neighbors at their shoulders. It is due, besides, to the growing complexity of economic life, which increases the number of cooperative links that tie each productive unit to the others.

Only the conclusion is at fault. The result of increasing interdependence, admittedly, is that in making certain decisions the businessman now needs to take more side effects into account. Those side effects are an inescapable concomitant of interdependence. But their extent can be exaggerated. In some instances, the side effects may be massive, so much so that the "incidental" may outweigh the "essential"; the external net costs or net benefits of some firms and of some productive activities may exceed the market value of their "output." Nevertheless, although this is possible and in some instances even probable, there is no reason to think that it is general in the American economy. Moreover, there is no way to get rid of the side effects. They can be dealt with in many ways—by installing smoke-suppressors on chimneys, moving smoky factories to down-wind locations, levying taxes on smoky factories, or installing air conditioners in places affected by smoke. But even if all the businessmen in the land were turned into public servants or technical experts, the side effects would still be there. Planning is one way to make decisions about them, but it appears to be a costly one. Development of a sensitive conscience in private businessmen is another way, also costly, especially if businessmen neglect their businesses in order to become irresponsible quasi-public benefactors. Another way is to continue improving the clumsy, familiar system that deals with problems piecemeal by regulations, taxes, private suits, and private agreements, operating within a general framework of public policy.

History, therefore, does not prove that the American business-man is on the way out. Nor can it prove that he will continue to enjoy the high esteem that American society has usually accorded him. But whether he survives as a recognizable species or becomes extinct, the work he does will necessarily have to be done by someone. The function of making ultimate arbitrary choices in production cannot be eliminated. As long as men disagree at all about their preferences, and as long as their knowledge and fore-sight are in the slightest degree imperfect, there will always be a need for managers, whatever they may be called and no matter whose interests they are thought to be serving.

ALFRED D. CHANDLER, JR.

The Role of Business in the United States:
A Historical Survey

FOR A paper on the historical role of business in America to provide a solid foundation for discussions of the present and future, it must examine a number of questions: Who were the American businessmen? How did they come to go into business? How were they trained? How broad was their outlook? And, of even more importance, what did they do? How did they carry out the basic economic functions of production, distribution, transportation, and finance? How was the work of these businessmen coordinated so that the American economic system operated as an integrated whole? Finally, how did these men and the system within which they worked adapt to fundamental changes in population, to the opening of new lands, resources, and markets, and to technological developments that transformed markets, sources of supply, and means of production and distribution? The answers to these questions, as limited as they may be, should help to make more understandable the present activities and future capabilities of American business.

The Colonial Merchant

The merchant dominated the simple rural economy of the colonial period. By the eighteenth century he considered himself and was considered by others to be a businessman. His economic functions differentiated him from the farmers who produced crops and the artisans who made goods. Although the farmers and artisans occasionally carried on business transactions, they spent most of their time working on the land or in the shop. The merchant, on the other hand, spent nearly all his time in handling transactions involved in carrying goods through the process of production and distribution, including their transportation and finance.

The colonial merchant was an all-purpose, non-specialized man of business. He was a wholesaler and a retailer, an importer and an exporter. In association with other merchants he built and owned the ships that carried goods to and from his town. He financed and insured the transportation and distribution of these goods. At the same time, he provided the funds needed by the planter and the artisan to finance the production of crops and goods. The merchant, operating on local, inter-regional, and international levels, adapted the economy to the relatively small population and technological changes of the day and to shifts in supply and demand resulting from international tensions.

These men of business tended to recruit their successors from their own family and kinship group. Family loyalties were important, indeed essential, in carrying on business in distant areas during a period when communication between ports was so slow and uncertain. Able young clerks or sea captains might be brought into the family firm, but sons and sons-in-law were preferred. Trading internationally as well as locally, the merchants acquired broader horizons than the farmer, artisan, and day laborer. Only a few of the great landowners and leading lawyers knew the larger world. It was the colonial merchants who, allied with lawyers from the seaport towns and with the Virginia planters, encouraged the Revolution, brought about the ratification of the Constitution, and then set up the new government in the last decade of the eighteenth century.

The Rise of the Wholesaler, 1800–1850

During the first half of the nineteenth century, although the American economy remained primarily agrarian and commercial, it grew vigorously. The scope of the economy expanded as the nation moved westward into the rich Mississippi Valley, and as increasing migration from Europe still further enlarged its population. Even more important to American economic expansion were the technological innovations that occurred in manufacturing in Great Britain. Without the new machines of the Industrial Revolution, the westward movement in the United States and the migration to its shores would have been slower. These innovations reshaped the British textile industry, creating a new demand for cotton from the United States. Before the invention of the water frame, the spinning jenny, the mule, and then the power loom, cotton had never been grown commercially in the United States, but by 1800 it had become the country's major export. The new plantations in turn provided markets for food grown on the smaller farms in both the Northwest and Southwest. The growth of eastern commercial cities and the development of the textile industry in New England and the middle states enlarged that market still further. The titanic struggle between Great Britain and Napoleon obscured the significance of these economic developments, but shortly after 1815 the economy's new orientation became clear.

The merchants who continued to act as economic integrators had the largest hand in building this new high-volume, regionally specialized, agrarian-commercial system. The merchants of Philadelphia, Baltimore, and New York took over the task of exporting cotton, lumber, and foodstuffs and of importing textiles, hardware, drugs, and other goods from Great Britain and the Continent. Those in the southern coastal and river ports played the same role in exporting cotton and importing finished goods to and from the eastern entrepôts; those in the growing western towns sent out local crops and brought in manufactured goods in a similar way. At first the western trade went via rivers of the Mississippi Valley and New Orleans. Later it began to be transported east and west through the Erie Canal and along the Great Lakes. To meet the needs of the expanding trade, the merchants, particularly those of the larger eastern cities, developed new forms of commercial banking to finance the movement of crops, set up packet lines on "the Atlantic Shuttle" between New York and Liverpool to speed the movement of news and imports, founded specialized insurance companies, and helped to organize and finance the new canals and turnpikes that improved transportation between them and their customers.

These innovations enabled the merchants to handle still more business, and the high-volume trade in turn forced the merchants to alter their functions and, indeed, their whole way of life. They began to specialize, becoming primarily wholesalers or retailers, importers or exporters. They came to concentrate on a single line of goods—dry goods, wet goods, hardware, iron, drugs, groceries or cotton, wheat or produce. Some became specialists in banking and insurance and spent their time acting as managers for these new financial corporations.

Of the new specialists, the wholesalers played the most influential role, taking the place of the colonial merchants as the primary integrators and adaptors of the economy. More than the farmers or the retailers, the wholesalers were responsible for directing the flow of cotton, corn, wheat, and lumber from the West to the East and to Europe. More than the manufacturers, they handled the marketing of finished goods that went from eastern and European industrial centers to the southern and western states.

Moreover, the wholesalers financed the long-term growth of the economy. Enthusiastic promoters of canals, turnpikes, and then railroads, they provided most of the local capital for these undertakings. They pressured the state and municipal legislatures and councils (on which they or their legally trained associates often sat) to issue bonds or to guarantee bonds of private corporations building transportation enterprises. At times they even persuaded the state to build and operate transport facilities.

The wholesalers also encouraged the adoption of the new technology in manufacturing. In Boston, the Appletons, the Jacksons, and the Cabots financed the new textile mills of Lowell and Lawrence. In New York, the Phelps and the Dodges started the brass industry in the Connecticut Valley, while in Philadelphia and Baltimore wholesalers like Nathan Trotter and Enoch Pratt financed the growing Pennsylvania iron industry. They not only raised the funds for plants and machinery, but also supplied a large amount of the cash and credit that the new manufacturers needed as working capital to pay for supplies and labor.

Although the wholesalers made important contributions to early-nineteenth-century economic life, they played a less dominant role in the economy than had the colonial merchant of the eighteenth century. The economic system had become too complex—involving too many units of production, distribution, transportation, and finance—for one group to supervise local, inter-regional, and international flows. Nonetheless, the wholesalers had more influence in setting prices, managing the flow of goods, and determining the amount and direction of investment than had other groups—the farmers, manufacturers, retailers, and bankers.

As the economy expanded, the recruitment of businessmen became more open than it had been in the colonial period. At the same time, the outlook of even the most broad-gauged businessmen grew narrower. Family and family ties became less essential, although they could still be a useful source of capital. Businessmen began to place more value on personal qualities, such as aggressiveness, drive, and self-reliance. Nor did one need any lengthy training or education to set up a shop as a wholesaler. Because of their increasing functional specialization, this new breed of wholesalers rarely had the international outlook of the colonial merchants. Not surprisingly, they and the lawyers and politicians who represented them saw their needs in sectional rather than national terms—as did so many Americans in the years immediately prior to the Civil War.

The Rise of the Manufacturer Before 1900

By mid-century the American agrarian and commercial economy had begun to be transformed into the most productive industrial system in the world. The migration of Americans into cities became more significant in this transformation than the final settling of the western frontier. Immigration from Europe reached new heights, with most of the new arrivals staying in the cities of the East and the old Northwest. By 1900, therefore, the rate of growth of the rural areas had leveled off. From then on, the nation's population growth would come almost wholly in its cities.

The second half of the nineteenth century was a time of great technological change—the age of steam and iron, the factory and the railroad. The steam railroad and the steamship came quickly to dominate transportation. In 1849 the United States had only six thousand miles of railroad and even fewer miles of canals, but by 1884 its railroad corporations operated 202,000 miles of track, or 43 per cent of the total mileage in the world. In 1850 the factory—with its power-driven machinery and its permanent working force—was a rarity outside the textile and iron industries, but by 1880 the Bureau of the Census reported that 80 per cent of the three million workers in mechanized industry labored in factories. And nearly all these new plants were powered by steam rather than by water.

America's factories made a vital contribution to the nation's economic growth. By 1894 the value of the output of American industry equalled that of the combined output of the United Kingdom, France, and Germany. In the next twenty years American production tripled, and by the outbreak of World War I the United States was producing more than a third of the world's industrial goods.

As manufacturing expanded, the wholesaler continued for many years to play a significant role in the economy. The period up to 1873 was one of increasing demand and rising prices. The manufacturers, concentrating on building or expanding their new factories, were more than happy to have the wholesalers supply them with their raw and semifinished materials and to market their finished goods. In addition, wholesalers continued to provide manufacturers with capital for building plants, purchasing equipment and supplies, and paying wages.

After the recession of 1873, however, the manufacturer began to replace the wholesaler as the man who had the most to say about coordinating the flow of goods through the economy and about adapting the economy to population and technological changes. The shift came for three reasons. First, the existing wholesale network of hundreds of thousands of small firms had difficulty in handling efficiently the growing output of the factories. Secondly, the manufacturer no longer needed the wholesaler as a source of capital. After a generation of production, he was able to finance plant and equipment out of retained profits. Moreover, until 1850 the commercial banking system had been almost wholly involved in financing the movement of agricultural products, but about mid-century it began to provide working capital for the industrialist. Commercial banks also began to provide funds for plant and equipment, particularly to new manufacturing enterprises.

The third and most pervasive reason why the manufacturer came to a position of dominance resulted from the nature of factory production itself. This much more efficient form of manufacturing so swiftly increased the output of goods that supply soon outran demand. From the mid-1870's to the mid-1890's, prices fell sharply. Moreover, the large investment required to build a factory made it costly to shut down and even more expensive to move into other forms of business activity. As prices fell, the manufacturers organized to control prices and the flow of goods within their industries. If the wholesalers would and could help them in achieving such control, the manufacturers welcomed their cooperation. If not, they did it themselves. In most cases, the industrialist came to play a larger role than the wholesalers in integrating the economy.

The wholesaler was pushed aside in transportation before he was in manufacturing. Railroad construction costs were high, and after 1849 when railroad expansion began on a large scale, the local merchants simply could not supply the necessary capital. Modern Wall Street came into being during the 1850's to meet the need for funds. By 1860 the investment banker had replaced the wholesaler as the primary supplier of funds to American railroads.

In the 1850's and 1860's the railroads also captured many of the merchant's functions. They took over freight forwarding in large towns and eliminated the merchant by handling through traffic in many commercial centers along the main routes west and south. Indeed, during the 1860's the railroads had absorbed most of the fast freight and express companies developed earlier by the wholesalers in order to use the new rail transportation. By the 1870's the coordination of the flow of most inter-regional transportation in the United States had come under the direction of the traffic departments of a few large railroads.

The first manufacturers to move into the wholesalers' domain were those who found that the wholesaler could not meet their special needs. These were of two types. The makers of new technologically complex and relatively expensive durable products quickly realized that wholesalers were unable to handle the initial demonstration to the consumer, provide consumer credit, or ensure the repair and servicing of the products sold. Thus manufacturers of agricultural implements, sewing machines, typewriters, cash registers, carriages, bicycles, or, most important of all, electrical machinery and equipment created national and even international marketing organizations well before the turn of the century. So did the second type, the processors of perishable goods requiring refrigeration, quick transportation, and careful storage for their distribution —fresh meat, beer, bananas, and cigarettes.

Once the pioneers of both types of enterprises—the McCormicks, the Remingtons, George Westinghouse and Charles Coffin, the Swifts and Armours, the Pabsts and Schlitzes, Andrew Preston and James B. Duke—had created their widespread distribution networks, they began again to eliminate the wholesaler by doing their own purchasing. They could not run the risk of stopping complex fabricating or assembling processes because they lacked critical parts or materials. Some integrated backwards even further, doing their own purchasing by building or buying factories to manufacture parts, controlling their own iron, steel, or lumber, or obtaining their own refrigerated cars and ships.

The manufacturers who produced standard commodities that might be distributed easily through the existing wholesaler network were slower to move into wholesaling. Even though the pioneering firms were demonstrating the economies resulting from a combination of mass production and mass distribution, most manufacturers had to be pushed rather than enticed into a strategy of vertical integration. They did so only after they failed to meet the oppressive pressure of falling prices by the more obvious methods of price control through trade associations, cartels, and other loose combinations.

The railroads pioneered in developing ways to control prices in the face of excess capacity and heavy fixed costs. During the 1870's, the railroads formed regional associations, of which the Eastern Trunk Line Association was the most powerful. By the 1880's, however, the railroad presidents and traffic managers admitted defeat. The associations could only be effective if their rulings were enforced in courts of law, but their pleas for legalized pooling went unheard. Indeed, the Interstate Commerce Act of 1887 specifically declared pooling illegal. As a result, the American railroad network became consolidated into large "self-sustaining," centrally managed regional systems. By 1900 most of American land transportation was handled by about twenty-five great systems informally allied in six groupings.

Where the railroads had hoped for legalized pooling, the manufacturers sought other ways of obtaining firmer legal control over the factories in their industries. They began personally to purchase stock in one another's companies. After 1882 when the Standard Oil Company devised the trust as a way of acquiring legal control of an industry, companies began to adopt that device. The holding company quickly superseded the trust as a more effective and inexpensive way of controlling price and production after 1889, when New Jersey passed a general incorporation law that permitted one company to hold stock in many others. The Supreme Court's interpretations of the Sherman Antitrust Act (1890) encouraged further consolidation in manufacturing. Court decisions discouraged loose combinations of manufacturers (or railroads) in any form, but (at least until 1911) appeared to permit consolidation of competing firms through a holding company if that company came to administer its activities under a single centralized management.

In many cases these new consolidations embarked on a strategy of vertical integration. Where the railroads formed "self-sustaining" systems to assure control of traffic over primary commercial routes, the manufacturers attempted to assure the uninterrupted flow of goods into and out of their production and processing plants. John D. Rockefeller and his associates at Standard Oil were the first of the combinations to adopt this strategy. The Standard Oil Trust had been formed after associations in the petroleum industry had proven to be, in Rockefeller's words, "ropes of sand." Legal control of the industry was followed by administrative consolidation of its refineries under a single centralized management. In the mid-1880's, the trust began to build its own distribution network of tank farms and wholesaling offices. Finally, after enlarging its buying organization, it moved in the late-1880's into the taking of crude oil out of the ground.

The examples of Standard Oil, the Swifts, the McCormicks, and others who had by-passed the wholesaler, the rulings of the Supreme Court, the memories of twenty years of declining prices resulted between 1898 and 1902 in the greatest merger movement in American history. Combinations, usually in the form of holding companies, occurred in nearly all major American industries. Holding companies then were often transformed into operating companies. After manufacturing facilities were centralized under a single management, the new consolidated enterprise integrated forwards and backwards.

At the same time, retailers who began to appreciate the potential of mass markets and economies of scale also moved to eliminate the wholesalers—although they did so in a more restricted way than the manufacturers. The mail order houses (Sears, Roebuck and Montgomery Ward), which turned to the rural markets, and the department and chain stores, which looked to the growing cities, began to buy directly from the manufacturers. By the turn of the century, some large retailers had even bought into manufacturing firms. As a result, wholesalers' decisions were of less significance to the operation of the economy than they had been fifty years earlier. Far more important were the decisions of the manufacturers who had combined, consolidated, and integrated their operations and the few giant retailers who had adopted somewhat the same strategy.

As manufacturers replaced wholesalers as key coordinators in the national economy, they became the popular symbol of American business enterprise. The industrialists and the railroad leaders were indeed the reality as well as the symbol of business power in the Gilded Age. The recruitment of this new dominant business group remained open, at least for a generation. As had been true earlier for the wholesaler, aggressiveness, drive, and access to capital or credit were prerequisites for success. Lineage or specialized training were less important, but some technological know-how was an advantage. Although the manufacturers' horizons were more national and less regional than the wholesalers', they came to view the national scene from the perspective of their particular industry. They and their representatives in Washington tended to take positions on the major issues of the day—tariff, currency, immigration, and the regulation of business—from an industrial rather than a sectional or regional viewpoint.

It was not long, however, before the needs of the manufacturers and their response to these needs altered the recruitment and training of the nation's most powerful businessmen. The increasingly high investment required for large-scale production made the entry of new men and firms more difficult. The emergence of the vertically integrated enterprise limited opportunities still further. By 1900 it was becoming easier to rise to positions of business influence by moving through the new centralized managements than by starting a business enterprise of one's own. This pattern was already clear in the railroads, the nation's first modern business bureaucracies.

The Dominance of the Manager Since 1900

Although the twentieth century was to become the age of the manager, the growing significance of the manager's role in the operation of the American economy was not immediately apparent. Until the 1920's manufacturers and their assistants concentrated on rounding out their integrated enterprises, creating the internal structures and methods necessary to operate these business empires, and employing the managers necessary to staff them.

At first, external conditions did not seriously challenge the new enterprises. Population trends continued, and heavy migration from abroad sustained urban growth until the outbreak of World War I. During the war, migration from the rural areas to the cities increased. At the same time, impressive technological innovations, particularly those involved with the generating of power by electricity and the internal combustion engine created new industries and helped transform older ones. The continuing growth of the city, the expansion of the whole electrical sector, and the coming of the automobile and auxiliary industries made the first decades of the twentieth century ones of increasing demand and rapid economic growth.

The initial task of the men who fashioned the first integrated giants at the beginning of this century was to build internal organizational structures that would assure the efficient coordination of the flow of goods through their enterprises and permit the rational allocation of the financial, human, and technological resources at their command. First came the formation of functional departments

—sales, production, purchasing, finance, engineering, and research and development. At the same time, central offices were organized, usually in the form of an executive committee consisting of the heads of the functional departments. These offices supervised, appraised, and coordinated the work of the departments and planned long-term expenditures.

By the late-1920's the pioneer organization-builders at du Pont, General Motors, General Electric, Standard Oil of New Jersey, and Sears, Roebuck had developed new and sophisticated techniques to perform the vital coordinating and adaptive activities. They based both long- and short-term coordination and planning on a forecast of market conditions. On the basis of annual forecasts, revised monthly and adjusted every ten days, the companies set production schedules, purchases of supplies and semifinished products, employment and wage rolls, working capital requirements, and prices. Prices were determined by costs, which in turn closely reflected estimated volume of output. The annual forecasts took into consideration estimates of national income, the business cycle, seasonal fluctuations, and the company's normal share of the market. Long-term allocations were based on still broader estimates of demand. After 1920, the managers of many large corporations began to include in these allocations the funds and personnel needed to develop new products and processes through technological innovation. From that time on, the integrated firm began to diversify. The Depression and World War II helped to spread these methods, so that by mid-century most of the key industries in the United States were dominated by a few giant firms administered in much the same way.

Their managers considered themselves leaders in the business community and were so considered by others. Yet they differed greatly from the older types of dominant businessmen—the merchants, the wholesalers, and the manufacturers: They were not owners; they held only a tiny portion of their company's stock; they neither founded the enterprise nor were born into it; and most of them had worked their way up the new bureaucratic ladders.

Even to get on a ladder they were expected to have attended college. Studies of business executives in large corporations show that by 1950 the large majority had been to college—an advantage that was shared by few Americans of their age group. Like most of those who did receive higher education, these managers came primarily from white Anglo-Saxon Protestant stock. Once the college man with his WASP background started up the managerial ladder, he usually remained in one industry and more often than not in a single company. That company became his career, his way of life.

As he rose up the ranks, his horizon broadened to national and international levels. Where his firm diversified, his interests and concerns spread over several industries. Indeed, in some ways his perspectives were wider in the 1950's than those of most Americans; nevertheless, because of his specialized training, he had little opportunity to become aware of the values, ideas, ambitions, and goals of other groups of Americans. He had even fewer direct contacts with farmers, workers, and other types of businessmen than had the wholesaler and the manufacturer.

The dominance of the large integrated enterprise did not, of course, mean the disappearance of the older types of businessmen. Small business remained a basic and essential part of the American economy. The small non-integrated manufacturer, the wholesaler, and retailer have all continued to be active throughout the twentieth century. The number of small businesses has continued to grow with the rapid expansion of the service industries (such as laundries and dry cleaners, service and repair shops not directly tied to the large firm); with the spread of real-estate dealers, insurance agencies, and stock brokerage firms; and with the continuing expansion of the building and construction industries. Throughout the century small businessmen have greatly outnumbered the managers of big business. The former were, therefore, often more politically powerful, particularly in the local politics, than the latter. Economically, however, the managers of the large integrated and often diversified enterprises remained the dominant decision-makers in the urban, industrial, and technologically sophisticated economy of the twentieth century. Their critically significant position has been repeatedly and properly pointed out by economists ever since Adolph A. Berle and Gardner C. Means wrote the first analysis of the role and functions of the modern corporation in 1932.

In many ways, the managers were more of an elite than the earlier businessmen had been. Even though this elite was based on performance rather than birth and played a critically constructive role in building and operating the world's most productive economy, its existence seemed to violate basic American democratic values. At the same time, its control of the central sector of the American economy challenged powerful economic concepts about the efficacy of a free market. After 1930, the managers came to share some of their economic power with others, particularly the federal government. Nevertheless, they were forced to do so *not* because of ideological reasons, but because they failed by themselves to assure the coordination and growth of the economy, the basic activities they had undertaken after 1900.

Until the Depression, the government had played a minimal part in the management of the American economy. The merchants had used the government to assist in financing internal improvements that they found too costly or risky to undertake themselves, and the manufacturers had called upon the government to protect them from foreign competition. Small businessmen—wholesalers and retailers—had joined farmers and workers to use the government to regulate the large corporation, but such regulation did not deter the growth of big business nor significantly alter the activities of the managers. Before the Depression, the government had developed few means to influence consciously the over-all performance of the American economy, the major exception being the creation of a central banking system in 1913.

The Depression clearly demonstrated that the corporation managers alone were unable to provide the coordination and adaptation necessary to sustain a complex, highly differentiated, mass-production, mass-distribution economy. The coming of the Depression itself reflected population and technological developments. Legislation in the 1920's cut immigration from abroad to a tiny flow. After World War I, migration from country to city slowed. Meanwhile, new industries, particularly the electric and automobile industries, reached the limit of demand for their output permitted by the existing size and distribution of the national income. At the same time, improved machinery as well as the more efficient management of production and distribution meant that in still other industries potential supply was becoming greater than existing demand. By the mid-1920's prices had begun to decline. Only the existence of credit helped maintain the economy's momentum until 1929.

Corporate giants, like General Motors, General Electric, and du Pont, fully realized that the demand was leveling off in the 1920's, but they could do little more than maintain production at the existing rate or even cut back a bit. When the 1929 crash dried up credit and reduced demand, they could only roll with the punch. As demand fell, they cut production, laid off men, and canceled orders for supplies and materials. Such actions further reduced purchasing power and demand and led to more cuts in production and more layoffs. The downward pressure continued relentlessly. In less than four years, the national income was slashed in half. The forecasts at General Motors and General Electric for 1932 indicated that, at best, the firms would operate at about 25 per cent capacity.

The only institution capable of stopping this economic descent appeared to be the federal government. During the 1930's it undertook this role, but with great reluctance. Until the recession of 1937, Franklin D. Roosevelt and his Secretary of the Treasury still expected to balance the budget and to bring the end to government intervention in the economy. Roosevelt and his Cabinet considered large-scale government spending and employment only temporary. When Roosevelt decided in 1936 that the Depression was over despite high unemployment, he sharply reduced government expenditures. National income, production, and demand immediately plummeted in 1937. The nation then began to understand more clearly the relationship between government spending and the level of economic activity, although acceptance of the government's role in maintaining economic growth and stability was a decade away.

World War II taught other lessons. The government spent far more than the most enthusiastic New Dealer had ever proposed. Most of the output of these expenditures was destroyed or left on the battlefields of Europe and Asia. But the resulting increased demand sent the nation into a period of prosperity the like of which had never before been seen. Moreover, the supplying of huge armies and navies fighting the most massive war of all time required a tight, centralized control of the national economy. This effort brought corporate managers to Washington to carry out one of the most complex pieces of economic planning in history. That experience lessened the ideological fears over the government's role in stabilizing the economy. This new attitude, embodied in legislation by the Employment Act of 1946, continued to be endorsed by Eisenhower's Republican Administration in the 1950's.

The federal government is now committed to ensuring the revival of investment and demand if, and only if, private enterprise is unable to maintain full employment. In 1949 and again in 1953, 1957, and 1960, the government carried out this role by adjusting its monetary and fiscal policies, building roads, and shifting defense contracts. The continuing Cold War made the task relatively easy by assuring the government ample funds. The new role has been defined so that it meets the needs of the corporate managers. The federal government takes action only if the managers are unable to maintain a high level of aggregate demand; it has not replaced the managers as the major coordinators in the economy, but acts only as a coordinator of last resort.

The Depression helped bring the federal government into the economy in another way. During the late-nineteenth and twentieth centuries, workers, farmers, and (to some extent) retailers, wholesalers, and other small businessmen had formed organizations to help them share in making the economic decisions that most intimately affected their well-being. During the 1930's, when the managers were having difficulties in maintaining economic stability, these numerically larger and more politically influential groups were able to get the federal and state governments to support their claims. Through government intervention many workers acquired a say in determining policies in wages, hours, working rules, promotions, and layoffs; farmers gained control over the prices of several basic commodities; and retailers and wholesalers increased their voice in the pricing of certain goods they sold. Nevertheless, the Wagner Act, the Agricultural Adjustment Acts, the Robinson-Patman Act, and the "fair trading" laws did not seriously infringe on the manager's ability to determine current output and to allocate resources for present and future economic activities.

The growth of organized labor during the twentieth century indicates much about the economic power of the large corporation, for this politically powerful group has been able to impress its will on the decisions of corporate managers only in a limited way. Until the Depression, labor unions had little success in organizing key industries dominated by large, managerially operated enterprises. Even during its first major period of growth at the turn of the century, the American Federation of Labor was not successful in the manufacturing industries. From the start, organized labor's strength lay in mining, transportation, and the building and construction trades. In the manufacturing sector, the Federation's gains came not in factory but small-shop industries, such as cigar, garment, hat, and stove-making and ship-building. During the first quarter of the twentieth century, organized labor acquired its members in those industries where skilled workers achieved their goals by bargaining with many small employers. (The railroads were the exception.) The geographically oriented operating structure developed by the American Federation of Labor unions was admirably suited to this purpose.

Precisely because the craft union had grown up in industries where the factory and the large integrated enterprise had never been dominant, the American Federation of Labor found itself in the 1930's unable to organize, even with strong government support, the mass-production, mass-distribution industries so basic to the operation of the modern economy. To unionize these industries required the creation of a structure to parallel the structure of the large integrated enterprise and a program that appealed to semiskilled rather than skilled workers. The AF of L failed to meet this challenge. Only after "a civil war" within the ranks of labor and the creation of a new national labor organization, the CIO, did the automobile, iron and steel, nonferrous metal, rubber, electrical machinery, and other key industries become fully unionized.

During the great organizing drives of the late-1930's and immediately after World War II, union leaders rarely, if ever, sought to gain more than a voice in the determination of wages and hours, working rules, and hiring as well as promotion and layoff policies. Even when they asked (unsuccessfully) for an opportunity "to look at the company's books," union spokesmen did so primarily with the hope of assuring themselves that they were obtaining what they considered a fair share of the income generated by the firm. The critical issue over which management and labor fought in the years immediately following World War II was whether the managers or the union would control the hiring of workers. The unions almost never asked to take part in decisions about output, pricing, or resources allocation. With the passage of the Taft-Hartley Act of 1947, the managers obtained a control over hiring which has never been seriously challenged. Nor have any further inroads into "management's prerogatives" been seriously proposed.

Since 1950, business managers have continued to make the decisions that most vitally affect the coordination of the economy and the pace of its growth. They have also continued to have a major say in how the economy adapts to external forces generated by population movements and technological change.

Population movements in the 1960's present a different challenge than they did before the 1930's. Migration from abroad has remained only a trickle and that from the country to the city has continued to drop. The move to the suburbs, the most significant post-Depression development, has expanded the urban sprawl and undermined the viability of the central city. The resulting problems are, however, more political and social than economic. Whether government officials are better trained than corporate managers to handle these new problems is open to question. If the business managers fail to meet these new challenges, the government will obviously have to do so.

Meanwhile, technological change has maintained a revolutionary pace. Through their concentration on research and development of new products and new methods of production and distribution, corporate managers have been trained to handle the processes and procedures of technological innovation. The large corporation has so "internalized" the process of innovation that this type of change is no longer simply an outside force to which businessmen and others in the economy adjust. Here the expertise of the business manager covers a broader field than that of governmental or military managers. In most of the costly government programs involving a complex technology, the development and production of new products have been turned over to the large corporations through the contracting process. The federal government does, however, supply the largest share of funds for research and development. Thus, even though the business manager continues to play a critical part in adapting the economy to technological change, government officials are in a position to determine the direction and the areas in which research and development will be concentrated.

This brief history of the role of business in the operation of the American economy suggests several tentative conclusions. From the beginning, it seems, businessmen have run the American economy. They can take the credit and the blame for many of its achievements and failures. They, more than any other group in the economy, have managed the production, transportation, and distribution of goods and services. No other group—farmers, blue-collar workers, or white-collar workers—has ever had much to do with the over-all coordination of the economic system or its adaptation to basic changes in population and technology.

Over the two centuries, however, the businessman who ran the economy has changed radically. Dominance has passed from the merchant to the wholesaler, from the wholesaler to the manufacturer, and from the manufacturer to the manager. In the last generation, businessmen have had to share their authority with others, largely with the federal government. Even so, the government's peace-time role still remains essentially a supplementary one, as coordinator of last resort and as a supplier of funds for technological innovation.

In the past, businessmen have devoted their energies to economic affairs, giving far less attention to cultural, social, or even political matters. Precisely because they have created an enormously productive economy and the most affluent society in the world, the non-economic challenges are now becoming more critical than the economic ones. There is little in the recruitment, training, and experience of the present business leaders—the corporate managers—to prepare them for handling the difficult new problems, but unless they do learn to cope with this new situation, they may lose their dominant position in the economy. As was not true of the merchant, wholesaler, or manufacturer, the corporate managers could be replaced by men who are not businessmen. To suggest how and in what way the managers will respond to the current challenges is, fortunately, not the task of the historian. Such analyses are properly left to social scientists and businessmen.

This article is an outline of a study of the history of American business that the author is undertaking with generous support from the Alfred P. Sloan, Jr. Foundation.

RICHARD H. HOLTON

Business and Government

GOVERNMENT REGULATIONS of business are pictured, perhaps not in-accurately, as being so pervasive that most major decisions in the large firm must be reviewed for consistency with federal law and administrative regulations before they are carried out. Corporate plans for advertising campaigns, for mergers and acquisitions, for changes in employment practices, for new stock issues, for changes in the manner of computing and reporting earnings, for pricing to different groups of customers—all can raise questions that the management must put to its legal staff.[1]

Although businessmen are inclined to date the great intrusion of government into business from the days of Franklin D. Roose-velt's tenure in the White House, the role of government in business life was by no means insignificant before then. Before 1890 government intervention in the form of protective tariffs and subsidies was clearly intended to promote business. Although much of the legislation since the Sherman Antitrust Act of 1890 has had a different emphasis, business spokesmen often overlook the many ways in which, even now, government promotes and assists business. The government's monetary and fiscal policies are designed to keep employment and incomes (and therefore profits) at high levels; depletion allowances, subsidized construc-tion programs, the mail subsidy, and other policies are also of positive assistance to business.

Restrictions on business behavior are designed to improve the functioning of the system; thus, the loss of some freedom of action for some parties ideally represents not a net loss of freedom, but rather a gain for the system as a whole.[2]

Debates on business-government relations will long be with us, but in recent years the antagonism seems to have been di-minishing. Indeed, on some issues, especially the problems of the cities, business and government are working more closely together than ever before. The extent of the *rapprochement* should not be overstated, however, since much of the business community lies outside the world of the more enlightened corporations.

Evolution of Business-Government Relations

Until the late-nineteenth century, legislation was designed, on the whole, to encourage business and commerce. After the War of 1812 it was clear that the new nation could not rely on the Old World as a source of manufactured goods, and protective tariffs were enacted to promote the growth of American industry. Government also subsidized business directly, especially the transportation industry. The canal system was developed during the 1830's and 1840's in part through government subsidy. In the 1860's and 1870's massive land grants promoted railroad development, and some 130 million acres were given away by the federal government—establishing a railroad empire twice the size of New York, New Jersey, and Pennsylvania combined. This action perhaps set a record (in one sense or another) for government support and encouragement of business in the United States.

Government regulation of business in its present pattern probably dates from the passage of the Interstate Commerce Commission Act of 1887 and the Sherman Act of 1890, which were responses to changes that had taken place in the twenty-five years following the Civil War. Not only was there rapid industrial development in the eastern part of the country and in the Midwest, but the agricultural West grew markedly in economic and political strength. The farmers and ranchers of the Midwest and West became increasingly suspicious of the railroads and the financial interests of the East. Discriminatory freight rates infuriated the farmers, yet were directly attributable to ruinous competition among the railroads. The Interstate Commerce Act of 1887 attempted to solve these problems by setting up the Interstate Commerce Commission to regulate freight rates and other aspects of competition in the transportation field.

At the same time, collusive agreements to soften competition and predatory tactics to drive rivals out of business led to the Sherman Act of 1890. It was becoming increasingly apparent that competitive behavior had to be policed in some degree. The Food and Drug Act of 1906, the Clayton Act of 1914, and the Federal

Trade Commission Act of the same year were all designed to set up "rules of the game" for competition. World War I brought an end to this first major wave of regulatory legislation.

The business prosperity of the 1920's, marked by relative calm in business-government relations, was smashed by the stock market crash and the ensuing Depression. New federal agencies—the Securities Exchange Commission, the Federal Communications Commission, the Civil Aeronautics Board, and the National Labor Relations Board, to cite a few—imposed new requirements on American business. The public, at least as represented by the President and the Congress, viewed the Depression as evidence that all does not necessarily go well in an economy following the 1920's version of a *laissez-faire* policy. From the passage of the I.C.C. Act until World War II, much legislation supportive of business was enacted; the recitation of regulatory bills above should not cause one to overlook, for example, the Hawley-Smoot Tariff of 1930 or the depletion allowance provisions in the federal income tax.

World War II again brought a cessation of significant new restrictive legislation, and the 1950's witnessed for the most part only relatively minor modifications of regulatory statutes already on the books. The Celler-Kefauver Act of 1950 amended the Clayton Act and significantly increased the power of the federal government to prevent mergers considered contrary to the public interest. In the 1950's and 1960's, government regulation of business was modified by court decisions and administrative interpretations, with little new legislation.

A Taxonomy of Business-Government Relationships

The current status of business-government relations can be clarified by considering four categories of government policy. One consists of measures to maximize the rate of growth of the economy and, thereby, reach and maintain full employment. A second is directed at the performance of markets—the market for goods and services, for capital, and for labor. A third set of programs is designed to redirect resources toward agreed-upon social goals, such as improved housing and education. Finally, certain government programs are directed toward correcting for "external diseconomies," such as environmental pollution. Since segments of the business community have complained about the rationale of these policies and the implementation of them, each group of policies warrants brief examination.

Government and Economic Growth

The first half of the 1960's has been especially notable because of the implementation of a set of neo-Keynesian policies designed to promote economic growth and employment. Illustrative are the investment tax credit of 1962, aimed at increasing aggregate demand by stimulating the demand for new capital equipment, and the 1964 tax cut, passed to offset a budgetary deficit. It is a sobering thought that the effective translation of Keynesian economics from the printed page into action required more than two decades, although the landmark Employment Act of 1946 at least recognized the role of government in the employment problem. After eighty years of steady expansion, the number of former doubters who have been persuaded of the virtues of the so-called "New Economics" is now impressive. The federal government has recently encountered difficulty with the "fine tuning" of the economy through fiscal and monetary policy. Its efforts to design and carry out a combination of policies to reduce unemployment, especially in the ghettos, but to avoid at the same time an uncomfortably high rate of inflation have been frustrated, in part, by pressures generated by the war in Vietnam. These problems do not, however, signify failure of the so-called New Economics; indeed, they would not have been encountered had the New Economics not been successful.

The business community's slow acceptance of modern theories of taxation and expenditure stems from a deep suspicion of government spending in general and is reinforced by its concern about a growing national debt. Yet society as a whole, as reflected in the Congress of the United States, has now made the judgment that policies designed to facilitate continuing economic growth and low unemployment are definitely in the public interest. An expanding economy can more easily adjust to problems of technological change and shifts in demand than can an economy that is limping along with 6 or 7 per cent of its work force unemployed. Such structural difficulties as regional unemployment or discrimination in hiring can be corrected more readily if the system as a whole is dynamic rather than static. In an atmosphere of economic expansion, risk-taking by new entrepreneurs as well as by established firms is more attractive, and technological change is accelerated. Social problems requiring new government expenditures can be more comfortably financed in a context of growth. Furthermore, the business community itself is a prime beneficiary of high employment policies, since profits suffer more in a recession than do the other shares of the national income. And partly because a growing number of businessmen are aware of this phenomenon, the resistance to monetary and fiscal policies designed to maintain a high rate of economic growth will surely continue to diminish over time.

Government and the Performance of Markets

The many regulatory laws that have been enacted since the I.C.C. Act and the Sherman Act have been a sore spot with most businessmen over the years, yet the business community does, on the whole, agree that it would be a mistake to abandon such government regulation. Business executives may have suggestions for modifying either a law's language or interpretation, but few would call for its repeal. Businessmen do, however, complain about overzealous bureaucrats who allegedly have an inadequate understanding of the real world of commerce and therefore fail to realize the full consequences of their actions. In private, if not in public, discussions, it is agreed that regulatory legislation has helped to keep the competitive environment in the United States considerably livelier and healthier than it would otherwise have been. Contrasts with the cartelized industries in Europe underscore this point.

The individual firm may well find it difficult to live with the regulatory legislation as it is enforced. The legislation is usually rather vague, and its interpretation is left to the regulatory agencies and to the courts. Interpretations can and do shift as new faces appear on the regulatory commissions and on the courts of law. The absence of clear, reasonable, and consistent guidelines in the antitrust area, for example, is a continuing problem for the individual firm, although the complexity and diversity of individual situations preclude significant departures from the case-by-case approach.

Economists evaluate the state of competition in the market by looking at the conduct and performance of market structure. By the crudest measure, competition appears to be eroding in the manufacturing sector of the economy; the percentage of manufacturing assets held by the two hundred largest manufacturing companies in the country rose from 46.7 per cent to 55.4 per cent between 1950 and 1965.[3] Yet examination of the conduct and performance of the individual industries suggests to many that these markets are, in a sense, highly "competitive." Although economic concentration is high in them, they exhibit the innovation and efficiency that one would expect from firms trying to best one another in the market. Anti-competitive behavior is difficult to ferret out and to prove except in instances of blatant collusion, such as the electrical equipment conspiracy of the 1960's.

Over the last few years the market for consumer goods and services has received unusual attention. The position of Special Assistant for Consumer Affairs has been established in the Office of the President; "truth-in-packaging" and "truth-in-lending" legislation has been passed; automobile safety has been the subject of more regulation; and product warranties are being reviewed. At first glance, it seems paradoxical that the consumer's problems in the market place should draw such comment precisely when the average consumer is better off than ever before, judging by disposable income per capita. Furthermore, the body of consumer legislation on the books before the new wave of concern was perhaps as comprehensive and as effective as that to be found anywhere in the industrial world. Perhaps the issue surfaced at this particular time only because its apparent political appeal was accidentally discovered; or perhaps the concern of an increasingly sophisticated public about advertising and merchandising practices finally grew to some critical mass.

The technology of consumer goods is increasingly complex. More and more features of goods and services cannot be judged intelligently by the typical consumer. The rate of technological change may be increasing, and sellers' marketing tactics are becoming more imaginative and (at least in part) confusing.

The so-called "professional consumers" argue that the average consumer has too little information at his disposal to make an intelligent decision. The defendants of the *status quo* reply that ample information is available, but that few consumers use it. Both sides may miss the important point—namely, that the consumer faces an increasing need for an *efficient* information system.

The simplest models of competitive markets assume that buyers and sellers have perfect information about the options open to them. Since information is not costless, any improvement in the efficiency of the informational process should make competition more effective. Given the multitude of decisions that must be made in, say, the supermarket, proliferation in package sizes makes it extremely time-consuming for the consumer to compute values in terms of price per ounce or per pound. Although there are obviously other important components of an item's "value," price per ounce or pound is presumably a major one for the consumer. If we believe what we say about the desirability of the competitive process, we should not oppose measures designed to make that process more efficient. In practice, of course, the problem is not so simple, since the proposed "truth-in-packaging" measures may increase manufacturing costs or inhibit development of better packaging.

Business commonly responds to the demand for more regulation in consumer markets by contending that competition and the legislation already in effect amply protect the consumer. A retailer or manufacturer who does not satisfy his customers will lose them. This argument assumes, however, that the buying public learns rather quickly which sellers do the better job, yet in many cases the learning process is slow and imperfect.

The consumer may learn to judge his suppliers fairly rapidly if the item is bought quite frequently, if the quality and performance characteristics of the item are either apparent at the point of purchase or immediately after the item is used, and if the rate of technological change is slow, relative to the frequency of purchase. Certain items bought weekly in the supermarket might well meet all three of these conditions, but many goods and services do not. For example, automobile tires are difficult for the individual consumer to evaluate because they are bought so seldom and are subject to relatively rapid technological change. And how quickly does one learn whether Company A or Company B offers the best casualty insurance coverage for a given premium? One rarely files a claim, and the differing circumstances of each claim make it difficult for the consumer to judge whether or not some competing company would provide better service on that claim. Hearsay evidence and advertising provide additional information, but both sources are imperfect. Competition is reduced to rivalry among selling and merchandising techniques, with little relation to qualitative differences in product. When the learning process is slow and imperfect, a brand may prosper not because it is the "best buy," but rather because it is "best merchandised."

Differences in the frequency of purchase, the susceptibility to objective measurement of quality and performance, and the rate of technological change lead to important differences in the nature of the competitive discipline imposed on sellers in the markets for consumer goods and services. In some markets the consumer can assess the value of a good or service, while in many others he must rely largely on information provided by the seller. The model of the competitive economy assumes that all consumer markets are of the first sort; in markets of the second type, consumer satisfaction might not be maximized simply because the consumer is not fully aware of the alternatives. It is interesting to note how often opponents of further government rule-making for consumer products cite the markets for high-frequency items, usually those encountered in supermarkets, as evidence of the proper functioning of consumer markets.

The federal government's regulation of the market for goods and services may well be shifting away from *intermediate* markets (markets in which goods are bought by firms) toward consumer markets. Given the rapidly growing varieties of goods and services available, the imaginative new marketing techniques, and the increasing technical complexity of consumer goods, consumers will have less time and less relative ability to judge the quality of their purchase options. This situation would seem to call for more rule-making by federal agencies in the area of consumer goods and services. If the analysis above is correct, the recent legislation regarding packaging, disclosure of financing charges on consumer purchases, and tire standards is but a harbinger of things to come. The present concern about the welfare of the nation's poor people serves to reinforce the pressures for consumer legislation since poor people are, for a variety of reasons, least able to evaluate properly the purchasing options they face.

Further regulating activity may also be expected in the capital market, where innovations were especially notable during the 1930's. The Securities Act of 1933, the Securities Exchange Act of 1934, and related legislation were clearly a reaction to the speculative excesses of the 1920's. The resulting improvements in the quality and quantity of information available about individual companies, coupled with such safeguards as penalties for manipulation of stock by insiders, have been largely responsible for the marked difference in the role of the equity capital market in the United States and other industrialized countries. Although corporate financial officers can criticize the burden of detailed corporate reporting to the S.E.C., there can be little doubt that federal regulation of capital markets has been essentially salutary.

The complexity of the modern corporation in the United States and certain institutional features of our capital markets are raising new questions, however, about the efficiency of the country's capital allocation mechanism. The informational requirements imposed by the S.E.C. help investors make better investment decisions. The quantity of information on all publicly traded equities is so great that the individual investor needs a screening device to select essential information for his consideration; the community of brokerage firms, investment advisory services, and ancillary institutions provides this service. But the growing importance of corporate and conglomerate firms has made this screening more difficult in recent years.

The conglomerate is in some ways comparable to a mutual fund that is not required to report on its portfolio, since it need not report its financial results by division. Consequently, the prospective investor does not know whether the corporation's total performance reflects some mix of good and bad records among the divisions or whether all components of the firm have performed in a comparable manner. Two conglomerates conceivably might file identical reports with the S.E.C., yet one might be far more dependent on the profits from one or two divisions than the other. Were this information known, it could make one corporation more or less attractive to the investor than the other. If this is the case, the capital market does not work so well as it should, and the growing concern about the components of the conglomerate may well lead to further regulation.

This question is related to a second—namely, the role of the corporation in making investment decisions on behalf of its stockholders. Corporations are major capital-generating machines. They retain and invest roughly half of their after-tax earnings. One can ask whether society would utilize this reinvested capital in any different pattern if all corporate earnings were paid out to stockholders who would then have the option of buying new issues of equity stock offered by firms in need of additional capital. Under such circumstances, the steel industry, for example, would be forced to go to the equity market to raise capital for any expansion not financed by the cash flow from depreciation charges. It is difficult to imagine that stockholders would not reinvest their earnings differently than the corporations are presently doing on their behalf. It may well be, however, that investment decisions under the present system are better informed and hence more productive for society as a whole than they would be with a 100 per cent pay-out rule.[4]

Regulation of the labor market seems to have been singularly stable in recent years. The basic labor legislation of the 1930's, as modified by the Taft-Hartley Act of 1947 and the Landrum-Griffin Act of 1959, seems quite durable. The National Industrial Relations Board faces a continuing stream of cases, it is true, and further refinement of acceptable practices can be expected. But no major legislative changes in business-government relations affecting the negotiating process seem imminent.

Instead, attention will continue to be focused primarily on the wage-determination process as it affects prices and the price level. Under conditions of high-level employment, employers bargaining on an industry-wide basis are able to pass wage increases onto buyers through increases in prices more easily than when the level of aggregate demand is low. The Kennedy Administration's attempt to institute voluntary wage-price guidelines was relatively unsuccessful. The guidelines policy was weak largely because it lacked sanctions and favorable public sentiment. The individual parties in bargaining situations have considered the cost of compliance with the guidelines too high. This has been more true of those situations involving local contracts than of the major industry-wide contracts. Unless mandatory wage and price controls are instituted, the country might not be able to lower unemployment to 3 per cent without generating an uncomfortably high rate of inflation.

The nation's effort to find jobs for the hard-core unemployed promises to lead to modifications of business-government relations in the unskilled and untrained labor market. Federal minimum wage legislation and minimum wages under existing labor contracts discourage employers from using workers whose productivity is so low that the applicable minimum wage is not recovered. Pressure appears to be mounting for tax incentives or direct subsidies to employers hiring the hard-core unemployed. This may well be the next major innovation in business-government relations in the labor market if an adequate control and enforcement mechanism can be devised.

Government and the Redirection of Resources

Business-government relations extend well beyond the regulatory legislation designed to improve market performance; much (if not more) business-government contact stems from government policy designed to alter the pattern of the nation's resource use. The government accomplishes some redirection of resources by purchasing goods and services that would not otherwise be produced, such as military weapons systems. It also redirects resources without becoming a buyer—for example, by levying tariffs.

Business objections to redirection of resource use are milder than the feelings about the regulation of market behavior. The steel industry does not seem to object to tariffs on steel as a form of government intervention. Many business leaders may speak out for free trade, but few cite specific tariffs or quotas as an unwarranted government intervention for fear of alienating suppliers, customers, or others in the business community. The Federal Reserve Board of Governors and the Treasury influence the level and structure of interest rates, thus serving not only to redirect resources toward or away from housing and investment goods, but also to control the level of aggregate demand and hence the price level. Objections to high interest rates, even from the housing industry, seem to be couched in relatively understanding terms. Business-government relations in the defense sector of the economy are such that President Eisenhower warned the public about the military-industrial complex as he was leaving office.

The federal government's influence on the resources engaged in research and development in the nation is especially clear. About two thirds of the R & D expenditures in the country are federally financed.[5] Government dollars are underwriting the defense and space R & D work. The R & D budget of the Atomic Energy Commission assures that the country is spending far more to develop nuclear power than to improve coal utilization. The government-financed R & D work in universities and in nonprofit organizations is drawing talent away from other areas. The growing concern about present social problems is causing a modest alteration in the predominant pattern of the last decade, but as yet the redirection of funds is not significant. As R & D efforts lead to new products and processes, the development of business is furthered along the lines of those products and processes. Thus, government decisions about R & D financing can definitely influence the pattern of industrial growth.

Government can also shift the pattern of resource use by means of tax incentives or subsidies. In terms of funding, this method of control lies between the tariff, which requires little expenditure, and R & D programs in space exploration and defense, which necessitate great outlays. The maritime subsidies, the subsidization of the feeder airlines, and the oil depletion allowance are illustrative. Here, too, business objections to government intervention in the market place are mild despite the increased public expenditures or loss of revenues that these programs entail.

Governmental programs redirecting resource use are not subject to the intense and continuing criticism that business brings to bear on efforts to regulate market performance. Perhaps because certain industries clearly benefit from government intervention to direct resource allocation, the individual businessman hesitates to object publicly to such programs. He is more likely to restrict his criticisms of government policy to those areas in which business can present a more united front.

Government and External Diseconomies

Some costs of production are not borne by the firm, but shifted to the public at large. In the economist's terms, these costs are generally known as external diseconomies. For example, a paper mill may deposit untreated waste into a stream because that is the easiest and cheapest means of disposal. The costs arising from the pollution of the stream—the value of the lost recreational benefits and the increased cost of purifying the water downstream for drinking purposes—are costs or diseconomies that the general community must bear. Programs designed to correct for these diseconomies might be viewed as redirecting resource use, but certain diseconomies are becoming so important that they warrant special attention.

Air and water pollution are of growing concern, and new programs and controls are being designed and introduced, especially at the state and local government level. Expenditures to improve urban transportation can be considered an attempt to offset at least some of the diseconomies of urban agglomeration, diseconomies that arise because firms have found it desirable to operate in the central city.

Business Influence on the Governmental Process

Prior to the turn of the century, the influence of the corporate community on the legislative process in Washington was scandalous. A number of senators and congressmen were known to be "in the pocket" of one corporate group or another. The Senate of 1889 was called the "millionaires club," and the railroads in particular could count on reliable spokesmen. The Tillman Act of 1907 and subsequent legislation have attempted to outlaw corporate financial contributions to campaign funds. Corporate funds can, nevertheless, be used for certain types of campaign activity, and corporate officers are often expected to make contributions to pooled campaign funds. Thus the corporate community, if not the individual corporation, can make its financial importance felt in particular campaigns.[6]

The growing complexity of the federal government has forced the corporation to shift some of its attention from the election process to the day-to-day operations of legislative committees and executive agencies. A firm's representative in Washington— whether he be a full-time employee or an attorney retained to keep his ear to the ground as well as to represent the firm in actual legal proceedings—is expected to maintain continuing contact with key individuals in the government bureaucracy and in Congress. These relations are not limited to Cabinet officers and chairmen of selected congressional committees. The staff director of a legislative committee or a career civil servant several echelons down in an executive agency might be more important in the lobbyist's network of information and influence.

Within the executive branch, the Department of Commerce would appear to be the most logical spokesman for the business community, paralleling the importance and influence the Departments of Labor and Agriculture have for their constituencies. But for a variety of reasons it is not. Its major bureaus perform service functions that have little to do with the policy matters of greatest interest to the business community. The corporate executive may be most concerned about the award of public contracts or about actions taken by the Internal Revenue Service, the Antitrust Division of the Department of Justice, the Federal Trade Commission, the S.E.C., the N.L.R.B., and the other regulatory agencies. The Department of Commerce cannot bring much influence to bear on these agencies since most of its twenty-seven thousand employees are in such agencies as the Weather Bureau, the National Bureau of Standards, the Bureau of the Census, the Patent Office, the Bureau of International Commerce, and the Economic Development Administration. The Business and Defense Services Administration, which consists largely of industry specialists, is a spokesman on certain industry problems, but never has enough money or expertise to be particularly effective. Furthermore, on numerous issues the business community is so divided that the Department of Commerce finds it difficult to take a strong stand.

There is evidence that the trade association is playing a relatively less important role in Washington than it played a generation ago. On some issues the association finds disagreement among its own members; it is often short of funds, which limits the talent it can bring onto its staff; and the key men in government are likely to shun association executives with an obvious ax to grind. At the same time the major corporations have adopted a "do-it-yourself" approach to representation in Washington. The increase in government contracting alone now justifies a corporation's having a Washington office with a full-time representative. Direct access has reduced the corporation's reliance on the trade association.

The Washington representative may play two roles—that of the marketing specialist skilled in arranging sales to government agencies and that of the lobbyist. The two roles often overlap: The cocktail party and reception staged by the Washington office when the company president is in town will include as guests not only selected congressmen and senators, but representatives from customer agencies as well.

The Washington lobbyist is a popular target for contempt and criticism, but his power to influence legislation has probably been exaggerated. The communications media have converted Washington into a goldfish bowl, and the congressman or presidential appointee who is a lackey for one interest group or another must be prepared at any moment to be exposed by a zealous columnist. Thus, the threat of adverse publicity disciplines the recipient of the lobbyist's influence.

The lobbyist who survives in Washington performs a useful

function in the governmental process. Given the chronic shortage of staff to generate the information and analysis needed to deal with any particular policy issue, the government official often welcomes the lobbyist's contribution. The lobbyist is disciplined in the exercise of this informational power by the knowledge that his opponents in the particular struggle will also be offering information and testimony to defend their views. If he presents a weak or misleading case to a congressman, the congressman may well refuse to see him again. Since contacts with the right people are the representative's stock in trade, he dares not alienate the people through whom his influence on public policy becomes operative. He is forced, therefore, to become a more useful part of the government process than he might otherwise be.

Although the business lobbyist's influence in Washington is limited by the fear of adverse publicity or the possibility of losing valuable contacts, this influence is clearly substantial. Furthermore, over the last decade or so the corporate community has become conscious of the importance of public relations as a means of generating public support for business, thus laying the foundation for more effective lobbying. The new emphasis on business cooperation with government in the solution of social problems may well serve to reinforce this support. Although the net impact of this public relations effort may be impossible to assess, the public acceptance of, if not explicit enthusiasm for, the large corporation would seem to suggest that the effort has been successful. It has surely helped to establish a more sympathetic environment for business in Washington.[7]

Big Business, Small Business, and the Smaller Governments

Discussions of business-government relations generally cover only the relationships between the giant corporation and the federal government. The business community is typically pictured as "*Fortune's* 500" largest firms. Little study has been accorded the relationship between small business and government or between business, large or small, and state and local governments.

The rhetoric of today's corporate chiefs about the social responsibilities of business and the importance of closer cooperation between business and government is heartening, but this is probably not the voice of business as a whole. Of the 3,293,000 non-agricultural enterprises in the country in 1963, about 3,114,000, or 95 per cent, had fewer than twenty employees. Not quite 40 per cent had no employees at all.[8] The owner-managers of these small firms have been growing further apart from the corporate executive in recent years, and the business-government *rapprochement* one perceives is limited to the large corporate sector of the business community.

The top operating official of the large corporation may now be more sympathetic with the federal government first because of his necessary interest in the health of the economy. He watches the forecasts of the Gross National Product with considerably more care and interest than does the local retailer, insurance broker, or real-estate agent, who believes his firm's performance depends primarily on his own prowess rather than on the G.N.P. By contrast, the corporation with operations across the country is more closely tied to the national indices. The corporate leader is also especially concerned about what is now commonly called the "corporate image"; it is important for the corporation, as represented by its top management, to demonstrate concern about the problems of the country and (publicly, at least) to take a constructive attitude toward their solution. The small businessman may want to be known as a good citizen of the community; but, being less visible, he is not under the same pressure as the chief executive of a large firm.

The top echelons of the modern corporation are filled with men who have come to know Washington, while Washington is still a dirty word to the small businessman. Flattered by an invitation to a White House breakfast with other corporate leaders, the executive finds himself impressed by the President's problems. When presenting testimony for his firm before a congressional committee, he may be exposed to some reasoned rebuttals, but he may also find himself shifting his position or at least appreciating the need for compromise. If he himself has not served on a special committee set up by the President, a Cabinet officer, or the head of one of the regulatory agencies, he knows people who have. Moving in this milieu, he can scarcely avoid developing sympathy for the nature and magnitude of the problems in drafting public policy. He may even take a tour of duty in Washington himself and emerge with a higher regard for the efficiency and dedication of the career civil servant.

The suburban automobile dealer, the owner of the local lumber yard, or the local attorney is denied this depth of contact with

Washington. To him government appears as the source of a steady demand for reports to be filled out and taxes to be paid. Since he signs these reports himself (he may even complete them without assistance), he is much more aware of them than is the corporate executive whose staff performs this function. The local business-man's impression of the efficiency of the civil service is colored by his contact with state and local government offices, where efficiency of management is probably below that of the federal government offices. Thus, his image of waste in government may vary substantially from that of the corporate official.

The small businessman's attitude toward government may be reinforced by his resentment over government salaries. The cor-porate president with a salary several times that of the top govern-ment officials is at least spared the bitterness of the small business-man who sees himself living no better than some civil servants who, in his view, enjoy a good income without the worries of entrepreneurship.

Finally, the small businessman may have less time to participate in government. He must be his own specialist in everything, and he is often too busy to do well the various functions he should perform in his business, to say nothing of taking time for outside activities. An exception must be made here for the small business-man whose business or professional position is strengthened by public exposure. Thus, the insurance agent or the real-estate broker may reason that the publicity associated with running for election helps his vocation, and that political life multiplies his contacts.

If these observations are not overly wide of the mark—they all deserve more qualification than has been entered here—certain conclusions may follow. First, business-government relations may be improving if one considers only the top executives of the *"Fortune* 500" and the leaders of the federal government. The countless small businessmen in the country, less exposed to Wash-ington than the corporate leaders, may still be as unsympathetic to the programs of the federal government as ever.

This difference in attitude toward government becomes clear if one compares the tone of the articles and editorials in *Nation's Business,* the monthly magazine of the U.S. Chamber of Com-merce, and the speeches on business-government relations given by the top executives of the major corporations or the articles in *Business Week* and *Fortune.* As a rule, the latter are much more likely to recognize the grounds for cooperation and to make constructive and realistic suggestions. *Nation's Business,* by contrast, caters to the views of the owners of small and medium-sized businesses (who account for most of the Chamber of Commerce membership) and still employs the anti-New Deal rhetoric of the Roosevelt era. Thus, the *rapprochement* between business and government may not reach far into the ranks of business.

A second conclusion may be warranted. The major corporation is not so deeply involved at the level of state and local government as at the federal level. There are exceptions, of course: The large public utility, regulated by the state, is interested in state legislation affecting utility rates; the major insurance company watches the state legislatures' debates about insurance rates; the nationally known manufacturer planning a new plant deals with local officials about zoning regulations; and in some states a handful of corporations are so dominant that they, perforce, play an influential role in the state capital. But the large corporation is primarily concerned with the policies of the federal government. Its influence at the state and local level is typically less significant. Although the top executive in the company may exhort the troops to become involved in politics, the rising young executive in the company is not likely to wield much power at the state and local level. He is struggling up the corporate ladder and has limited time for politics. More important, he is transferred so often that he cannot build a solid political base from which to be effective. Thus, business influence on state and local governments may be primarily the influence of the owners of the medium-sized and small firms, while the business influence on the federal government may be much more heavily weighted toward the views of the major corporations.

If this line of reasoning is defensible, it suggests that the state and local governments are not so likely as the federal government to obtain the help of business in the development of new and imaginative programs for solving particular social problems. To the extent that business influences public policy—and other influences, of course, may often dominate—the state and local government will opt for minimizing taxes and expenditures and avoiding new programs. Competition among states and local jurisdictions in offering a good "business climate" for new industry reinforces this tendency. Thus business interests most influential at the state and local level, those most concerned about keeping government activity to a minimum, may by their inaction force policy designs to surface in Washington rather than in the state capital or in city hall.

REFERENCES

1. For documentation of the common business view of the role of government in the business environment, see Francis X. Sutton, Seymour E. Harris, Carl Kaysen, and James Tobin, *The American Business Creed* (Cambridge, 1956), especially Ch. 9. Different capitalist ideologies are discussed in R. Joseph Monsen, *Modern American Capitalism, Ideologies and Issues* (Boston, 1963).

2. See Paul A. Samuelson, "Personal Freedoms and Economic Freedoms in the Mixed Economy," in Earl F. Cheit (ed.), *The Business Establishment* (New York, 1964), pp. 193-227.

3. Statement of Dr. Willard F. Mueller, Director, Bureau of Economics, Federal Trade Commission, before the Select Committee on Small Business, U.S. Senate, March 15, 1967, p. 50.

4. A mild version of an undistributed profits tax was actually enacted in 1936. For a discussion of the nature of the debate, see Arthur M. Schlesinger, Jr., *The Politics of Upheaval*, Vol. 3 of *The Age of Roosevelt* (Boston, 1960), pp. 505-509.

5. Richard R. Nelson, Merton J. Peck, and Edward D. Kalachek, *Technology, Economic Growth and Public Policy* (Brookings, 1967), p. 46.

6. For a review of the status of this question, see Edwin M. Epstein, *Corporations, Contributions, and Political Campaigning: Federal Regulation in Perspective* (Berkeley, 1968). The author argues that corporations should be permitted to spend corporate funds for election purposes if such expenditures are subject to proper reporting and publicity requirements.

7. See V. O. Key, Jr., *Politics, Parties, and Pressure Groups* (fifth edition; New York, 1967), pp. 93-96; and Harold Brayman, *Corporate Management in a World of Politics* (New York, 1967), especially Ch. 5.

8. Bureau of the Census, *1963 Enterprise Statistics*, Part I, Table 8.

ROBERT T. AVERITT

American Business: Achievement and Challenge

THE ECONOMICS of developed countries is commonly divided into two parts. The newer and perhaps better known of the two divisions is called macroeconomics, or sometimes Keynesian economics. The "New Economics" of the Kennedy-Johnson Administration flows directly from this macroeconomic Keynesian base. As the name implies, macroeconomics takes as its frame of reference the economic system as a whole. The twin objectives of macroeconomic policy are maintaining a high level of employment (usually defined as between 96 and 97 per cent of the labor force employed) and reasonable price stability.

From the macroeconomic point of view, the most important prerequisite for a well-functioning economic system is the maintenance of full employment over a long period of time. If the economy is less than fully employed, the goods and services that could have been produced by idle workers are forever lost. Unemployed men and idle machines produce nothing, and yesterday's foregone production opportunity can never be regained. Today's living standard is still suffering from the machines not built during the 1930's. Unlike the national debt, yesterday's unemployment does indeed pass its burden on to future generations. Since it is estimated that increasing employment by 1 per cent can increase output by about 3 per cent, a relatively small gain in employment can pay rich dividends.

If labor can remain fully employed for a considerable period of time, output as measured by the Gross National Product will show rewarding growth. The additional goods and services will be reflected in higher real profits and wages, allowing both labor and business returns to advance without doing so at each other's expense. And when additional laborers are difficult to find, discrimination in hiring begins to disappear. If almost all who seek work can find it, the distribution of income becomes more equal. Even without federal programs directed specifically at poverty, a fully employed economy will gradually pull an increasing fraction of the population from deprivation.

A rapid rise in the level of employment may be accompanied by an increase in industrial prices. Yet even here the major villain is not a high level of employment, but frequent *changes* in employment levels.[1] A perpetual prosperity maintaining high employment tends to minimize price rises in the industrial sector because most manufacturing output comes from firms with high overhead costs. When the demand for output falls, the firm's total costs do not fall proportionally. Idle machines continue to depreciate; much of the specialized labor force must be retained if the fall in demand is assumed to be temporary; and the volume of clerical work is only loosely related to short-run fluctuations in sales. When competition is not keen, businessmen may be tempted to *increase* prices if volume falls, as steel firms did during the 1950's in an attempt to maintain profits in the face of falling sales.

The lesson of macroeconomics is clear and persuasive. There is an optimal level of employment in an industrial economy. When the economic system operates below that level, potentially available goods and services are lost, poverty becomes more prevalent and intractable, prices will not fall far, and some may even rise. Above the optimum level, inflation becomes unmanageable, leading to price imbalances and problems in the balance of foreign trade. In short, our economic system is a finely tuned mechanism that operates well only within a rather narrow employment range.

The second branch of economic theory and policy enjoys a somewhat longer history, but a diminished contemporary reputation. Microeconomics differs from its counterpart by taking the consumer, and not the economic system, as its fundamental point of reference. The defining goal of macroeconomics is the maintenance of the optimum level of output and employment; the criterion of success for microeconomics is the maximization of consumer choice. Seen from the microeconomic perspective, the function of an economic system is not to operate at its optimum peak, but to maximize the satisfaction that consumers enjoy from the goods and services produced at all levels of operation. Since every man is the best judge of his own satisfactions, any policy that expands individual choice is a gain, and all contractions of the individual's ability to choose are undesirable. Microeconomists provide no ideal prescription for the good society save that men must be free to choose.

To be sure, society must impose certain restrictions on choice. Addictive narcotics may be outlawed because their consumption can in time reduce the user's ability to make further choices. Some minimum level of schooling may be required because literacy expands the individual's ability to make meaningful choices. Children in particular must be protected from making choices today that will impair or drastically restrict their range of options as adults. But microeconomics is based upon the fundamental assumption that men must be free as consumers to make the maximum number of meaningful decisions. Where possible, the consumer's options should remain open.

The Structure of the U. S. Economy

National economies can be classified in a variety of ways, but the simplest and perhaps the most useful method separates the developed economies from the underdeveloped ones. A per-capita income of $500 is most often used as a convenient dividing line between advanced economies and their less affluent, but far more numerous, fellow nation-states. Low income, however, is only a visible result of underdevelopment. To reveal something of the underlying structure of poverty and affluence, one must divide the economic system into sectors.

A primitive breakdown groups economic activity in three broad categories—agriculture, industry, and services. Although quite crude, such a division illuminates one striking difference between rich and poor nations. In less-developed regions, the overwhelming majority—three quarters or more—of the labor force finds employment in agriculture. By contrast, farming provides economic support for less than 6 per cent of the work force in the United States. The highly productive U.S. farmer is far outnumbered by his nonfarm countrymen, an invariable indication of the American economy's advanced state.

A more extensive taxonomy might also provide categories for mining, construction, manufacturing, transportation, communication, trade, finance, and government since an advanced, affluent economy will possess substantial productive capabilities in all of these sectors. Any developed economy is characterized by a close structural interdependence. Although no national economy can hope to be wholly self-sufficient in resources, advanced nations are usually able to supply the bulk of their domestic demand for manufactured goods. They tend toward economic self-sufficiency, while the underdeveloped nations tend toward dependence. Most of the world's wealth and income is generated in the highly diversified economies of the United States, Western Europe, Japan, and the U.S.S.R., and these areas have in common a relatively complete economic structure.

A mature, developed economy provides the potential for producing almost infinite combinations of goods and services, although full employment near the total quantity of production is under a stringent short-run limitation. In an advanced economy, the possibility of structural flexibility and resource mobility between sectors reaches its maximum. The contemporary U.S. mix of goods and services produced and the industrial configuration that supplies them are now matters of considerable choice. If consumers in an underdeveloped nation decide to consume more washing machines, refrigerators, or electric stoves, their increased demands will merely increase the price of the particular good. To consume more, they must usually import either the goods or the machinery for producing such goods. Both require foreign exchange, a medium in short supply. To purchase more industrial goods, poor nations must sell more raw materials or agricultural products and thereby earn foreign purchasing power. When a wide range of varied productive capacity is available, as in the American case, shifts in consumer preferences can more easily be reflected in a changing combination of goods and services produced. In the very long run, consumer choice is facilitated by a nation's advancing into the ranks of the developed. Only in developed nations can consumers make their demands felt with minimum friction. In a poor nation, the incomes of most consumers are so meager that consumer choice and its physical limitations are of small importance; yet even those few with incomes well above the subsistence level are restricted in their choices.

The activity most often missing or severely undernourished in the economies of nonindustrial countries is manufacturing. Wholesaling, retailing, construction, agriculture, mining—these are major identifiable activities in underdeveloped regions, although they may be primitively performed. The United States clearly has a developed economy because it relies heavily on manufacturing for its income and employment. Manufacturing firms account for about one third of the country's total output, employ one quarter of its workers, and pay one half of its corporate income taxes. Economic growth and prosperity are not exclusively confined in the short run to those nations that have or are rapidly building substantial manufacturing capacity. A few countries with a poorly articulated manufacturing sector can, at least for a time, experience a rising demand for their products and a favorable trade balance. Booms in rubber and petroleum, for example, can temporarily foster local prosperity substantially devoid of manufacturing. In the long run, however, manufacturing is crucial in maintaining the flexibility essential for compensating for shifts in domestic and foreign demands.

Just as manufacturing is critical to economic viability, so certain segments of manufacturing are central to the manufacturing complex.[2] Economic activities outside manufacturing are also unquestionably important to the prosperity of the U.S. economy, and most are essential to it. A high level of industrial interdependence is characteristic of a developed economy, but manufacturing sets the rhythm for movements in output and employment in trade, transportation, communication, and mining. Indeed, so central are domestic manufacturing and the modern services supporting it that growth in the industrial sector of poor countries is often equated with economic development. Like all developed economies, the United States relies heavily on manufacturing for its income, employment, and export earnings.

The Business Organization of the U. S. Economy

Neither manufacturing nor any other economic activity is self-organizing. Business firms are the nerve system controlling production. All business firms incur costs by purchasing inputs, receive revenues from selling an output, and seek to conduct their affairs in a manner that results in a profit. Little else that is meaningful can be said about business firms without dividing them into classes.

Can American firms, large and small, be classified by the product they produce? In an advanced economy many industries produce goods that are relatively close substitutes. Industry lines blur as substitution possibilities multiply. Most large American businesses no longer try to adhere to strict industry or product lines. Product diversification has been and remains a prime corporate goal for large companies. Industries become more difficult to define in a developed economy, as firms are less interested in maintaining their industrial integrity.

During the past fifteen years a new kind of big business—the pure conglomerate—has emerged. Two prominent examples are Litton Industries and Textron, forty-fourth and forty-ninth largest U.S. industrial firms, respectively, in 1967. Litton began in electronics and Textron in textiles, but neither now belongs to a specific industry. Litton and Textron have grown rapidly through conglomerate merger, acquiring a variety of business organizations in widely divergent fields. Pure conglomerates provide an extreme case of diversification and exemplify a tendency prevailing throughout the large corporate sector. Textron, for example, is strongest in manufacturing, but produces goods ranging from poultry products to helicopters.

While industry lines blur in an advanced economy, national boundaries remain firm. Does nationality offer a guideline for classification? Referring to a large firm as American, French, British, or Japanese still says much about its cultural style, but little about the location of its markets or productive facilities. The pace at which the larger American corporations are becoming international has accelerated during the last two decades. A single world capital market, centered in New York, has been emerging since 1958. And as a national market for finance facilitated the national expansion of large firms in the 1890's and 1900's, so the internationalization of finance has abetted the international spread of U.S. firms. The major American firms in automobiles, rubber, machinery, chemicals, electrical equipment, nonferrous metals, electronics, and petroleum are wholly international undertakings.

Firms can be grouped according to the character of their internal organization. Thus, most large corporations are distinguished by administrative decentralization, vertical integration, geographic dispersion (national and international), and product diversification.[3] Firms are conventionally classified by economists in terms of market structure—whether they are highly competitive, monopolistically competitive, oligopolistic, or monopolistic. Since the more competitive firms are assumed to have a higher output and lower prices, the economics profession has a strong predilection toward competitive markets, and thus toward relatively small firms. The professed purpose of most antitrust laws is to enforce competition on as many markets and firms as possible. But diversified firms may operate in many kinds of markets—some highly competitive, others less so. The economist's conventional theory of the firm is, in fact, only a theory of the product.

Surely no division of American business is more meaningful than the one separating large and small businesses. So important is this cleavage that Congress established a Small Business Administration to aid firms lacking preponderant size. A numerical dividing line—based on number of employees or volume of yearly sales—is useful in classifying the business community. One can, for example, develop a demography of small business. Changes in the number of small firms are highly correlated with variations in Gross National Product, employment, and population. Small firms multiply in a predictable fashion as the economy grows. So persistent are trends in the birth and death rates of small businesses that mortality tables have been constructed for their population. Their infant mortality rate is high. Only one third of all small, newly established firms live to age five; about one fifth survive to age ten; but after the treacherous first ten years have passed, the survival rate becomes quite high.[4]

The Twin Economies of the Business World

Using differences in size as a touchstone, the business portion of the U.S. economy can be divided into two distinct, though interconnected, systems. The large-scale component is made up of enterprises with national or international operations. Such organizations do not depend on a single locality nor, in most cases, on a single nation for markets, factor inputs, or finance. Most of these firms achieved their extensive size in one of the key manufacturing industries or in mass retailing, but few are now confined to their industry of origin. With small but significant exceptions, they are highly diversified. They provide an organizational center for a cluster of associated firms.

Large-scale enterprises use more capital per worker than do their smaller rivals.[5] A large cash flow and an excellent credit rating combine to facilitate the financing of labor-saving capital equipment, while strong unions exert continual pressure for wage increases. Usually oriented toward research and development, if only for defensive purposes, they are prepared to innovate new products from time to time. Their ultimate growth potential is unlimited, given an expanding economy in the U.S. and Western Europe. So long as their management remains competent and flexible, these firms grow when the U.S. economy grows. If American prosperity falters, they may be able to expand in foreign markets. Although the antitrust laws circumscribe their direction of growth, and their financial and managerial assets limit their *rate* of expansion, their ultimate size is bounded only by management's ability to preserve a viable internal structure. I call this network of firms the *center* economy and refer to the firms comprising this economy as center firms. Firms in this center economy are important throughout the manufacturing sector, and their presence is especially visible in key industries. Should nineteen of the leading American business organizations divided among the electrical, farm machinery, aluminum, copper, rubber, and automobile industries suddenly disappear, six of our key industries would virtually vanish.

The other business system in the U.S. economy is populated with comparatively small enterprises, most of which are local in orientation. They thrive where the market for their output is severely circumscribed. Management revolves around one or a few individuals. Most of these firms are craft-oriented, labor-intensive, and less efficient in terms of output per man-hour than center firms; single-plant firms are common. A few are pioneering enterprises established to innovate a new product, but the majority have little interest in research and development. Medium- and long-term money is, for them, a scarce commodity. Their growth prospects are precarious and restricted so long as they retain their present character; any significant expansion would necessitate restructuring the firm's internal organization. These smaller firms comprise the *periphery* economy.

Many periphery firms serve as economic satellites to the center economy. These supporting firms are of two types: backward or forward satellites. Backward satellites supply center firms with inputs, and forward satellites channel the center firm's output toward the final user. In the automobile industry, for example, a host of machine tool firms depend on sales to auto manufacturers, while franchised dealers serve as forward satellites.

Backward satellites usually cluster close to their purchasing center firms. Their principal output provides a minor input to the center firm, and their minimum economic size is well below that of the center industry. Prime government contracts typically go to center firms, which then subcontract part of the work to backward satellites. Satellites are operationally integrated into the activities of center firms, but fall outside the large-scale corporate hierarchy. "Floating" satellites are dependent on sales to an industry dominated by center firms, but are not beholden to a single center firm. "Attached" satellites are tied by contract, tradition, or personal contacts to a single center firm or, perhaps, to a small group of firms. In rare cases, center firms use divisions of other center firms as satellites, creating a situation of countervailing power.[6]

Another set of periphery firms forms the center economy's "loyal opposition." Sometimes called the competitive fringe, the loyal opposition is composed of relatively small, nondominant businesses producing competition for center enterprises within their home industry. The loyal opposition typically surrenders the power to make price decisions on common products to center firms. The loyal opposition is sometimes disloyal, however. When price stabilization is disrupted, loyal-opposition firms are usually the disrupters; where nonprice competition predominates, the loyal opposition is the primary representative of price competition.

Loyal-opposition firms are of two pervasive types. A *pioneering* loyal-opposition firm relies upon the innovating abilities of its scientist-entrepreneurs. Well known in the electronics field, such small firms flourish near technical-academic centers that have a banking community inclined toward risk-taking. Loyal-opposition pioneers are notoriously deficient in merchandising experience, a weakness often fatal in markets blanketed by center-firm expertise. Yet a few—Varkian, Thiokol, Hewlett-Packard, Polaroid—have known spectacular success. A more common type of loyal opposition challenges center firms in their strong markets without relying on pioneering. The U.S. economy is far-reaching enough to allow room for a few, well-run periphery firms selling a single line of center-dominated products nationally or serving a large regional market.

The third periphery firm group might be called "free agents." They are free of center-firm affiliation, formal or informal, and occupy the interstices of the economy. They fill in the cracks and crannies in the continuum from raw material processing to finished manufacture to retailing, or they provide small-scale services. Most free agents are small, local firms, suffering the many disadvantages accompanying limited size in an increasingly mobile national market.

Splitting a business system as diverse as the American one into two categories, center and periphery, obviously compresses reality, but emphasizes ideal business archetypes or conceptual forms that are approximated by numerous contemporary organizations. The ideal center firm has a long planning horizon, enjoys financial permissiveness or the absence of major financial restraints, and has a scientific orientation. A mutually adaptive relationship exists between the progressive center firm and its economic environment. By means of advertising and the creation of new products, an innovative center firm may influence the specific channels through which demand flows, although more fundamental factors determine the general direction and magnitude of consumption trends. Dynamic center firms help structure the economy by their reaction to the economy's structural evolution.

Many large American firms do not fit our ideal center firm because they are constrained by a vested interest in existing techniques, a fixed commitment to the *status quo*, or an excessive concern for costs already sunk in existing products and processes. The railroad and steel industries, to name only two examples, are famous for their large but lethargic organizations. Yet even these laggards are eventually forced to embrace a newer technology. Large size is a necessary, but not sufficient condition for the ideal center firm. Economic size must be combined with an alert and creative management. Growth to a certain size does, however, seem to provide an impetus for resourceful management. A big firm is rich in assets and high in social visibility. The portfolios of pension funds and educational institutions are composed of its stock certificates. When scholars discuss business and American society, their frame of reference is most often the center economy, and many Americans believe that the economy would fall apart were this strategic center to give way.

The Technical Anatomy of the U. S. Economy

Three groups—unit and small-batch production, large-batch and mass production, and process production—represent the dominant kinds of production technique. Unit and small-batch production prevails where the market is severely limited. It includes products made to fit customer requirements (large electrical generating equipment, dies from the machine tool industry) and the production of prototypes (experimental aircraft and automobiles). Largely craft-oriented, it utilizes either the traditional craftsmen, such as tool and die operators, or the newer professional craftsmen in engineering, physics, and chemistry. The craftsmen's talent determines the efficiency and productivity of the unit and small-batch operation.

Production schedules are based on orders received, and development is the firm's most critical function, making the production operations difficult for management to speed up or control. Work proceeds at a pace set by the craftsmen; salesmen in these lines sell ideas and technical potential, not a standardized product. Labor output per man-hour is usually low by manufacturing standards, and cost per unit is inevitably high. Prices are established by what the market will bear, intensity of competition being the critical determinate of price levels. Unit and small-batch production is an inviting field for small firms. It thrives where demand is largely segmented or radically fluctuating, but it also flourishes at times in areas of heavy demand, such as construction, medical care, and education. When demand in these areas grows quickly, prices show rapid acceleration.

Under large-batch and mass production, standardized products made on a moving assembly line are characteristic. Large-batch and mass production is not directly based on orders received, and management carries on relatively long-range planning. The firm's short-run success depends on a full use of productive capacity, lowering costs through greater output. Long-run profits may depend on product development and advertising. The sales staff has scant technical knowledge and sells whatever the firm produces. Formal and elaborate management systems are useful in maximizing output while minimizing per-unit costs. Skilled craftsmen are replaced with unskilled workers, who in turn can be displaced by capital equipment. Those skilled workers who remain perform maintenance on the plant and equipment. In large-batch and mass production, unlike small-batch production, management and labor are separated by the wide disparity in their educational and social backgrounds. Prices are usually determined on a cost-plus or "break-even point" basis.

Process production is characterized by materials that can be made to flow through the production network without the artificial aid of moving belts or conveyors. Originating with the manufacture of liquids, gases, and crystalline substances, process production is now spreading to the making of steel, aluminum, and engineering parts. Radio, television, and similar communication devices are a form of process distribution, as they depend on a flow of electronic signals transmitting a service rather than a good. Because initial capital costs are extremely high under process techniques, the barriers to new firm entry are considerable. A mass market for every firm is essential to efficiency; but if plants can be operated full time at near capacity levels, the unit costs of capital and labor can be dramatically reduced. The firm's most critical function is marketing, because low unit costs depend directly on high sales volume. Firms plan for the very long term, and management by a committee representing various technical talents is the norm. Committee decisions are usually reached after an exchange of information and an evaluation of data. Most routine work is performed by machinery, with tense, taxing work occurring only during infrequent machinery failures. Worker morale is usually high, and personnel relations are comparatively easy.[7]

American Economic Evolution

Like any system of classification, our division of production into three types involves oversimplification. It is, for example, particularly difficult to draw a fine line between mass and process production. Both are defined by standardized products that flow through the production sequence. Yet throughout our various classification schemes the direction of historical progression is clear.

The American economy has moved from a heavy dependence on agriculture toward an emphasis on industry, and is now shifting toward the service sector. The business system has evolved from a pattern of small firms managed by owners who work alongside the hired help, to the corporate stage where ownership is separated from control, to the present form with firms that are not tied to their mother industry nor solely dependent on the domestic economy. Having been freed from the life cycle of specific human beings, center firms are now seeking, through conglomerate diversification and international markets, to outstride the bounds of the depression-prosperity cycles of specific products, industries, and national economies.

Firms in the center are generally adept at utilizing the more advanced productive modes. These mass and process production techniques require large quantities of capital, but they hold the promise of enormous outputs at low costs per unit when fully employed. Several important goods, including housing, and virtually all services are produced in industries outside the center orbit. Here technical change is usually less rapid, with the cost of labor comprising a larger proportion of the charges against each item. Hence, if consumer demand is to be served and inflation attacked in a perpetually prosperous economy, mass and process techniques must make further inroads into those craft-oriented services where demand grows most rapidly. (These include education and medicine.) The associated movements of business organizations toward the ideal center type, toward mass and process modes of production, and toward the humanizing services of medicine and education carry a major impetus for further economic and social advances in our mass-consumption society.

The Center Economy and American Economic Development

The United States was not the first nation to industrialize, nor has its rate of industrialization remained the greatest. Nevertheless, although England began the Industrial Revolution, and Japan and the Soviet Union have shown ingenuity in accelerating their rate of advance, the United States has witnessed the greatest triumph of industrialism. Industrialization is the key to its affluence, with production shifting from agriculture to industry. The developing center economy has played a critical role in facilitating this transformation. By moving the productive process in key industries up the technical hierarchy to large-batch output and then to mass and process production, center firms have met a rising industrial demand with products manufactured at falling real costs per unit.

Economists have long known that the wages of labor depend on labor's productivity—the market value of the output each man produces in an hour. The productivity of workmen, in turn, depends largely upon the quantity and quality of the capital equipment at their disposal. When supplied with equipment capable of both speed and precision, workers may be expected to yield plentiful results. Wages will reflect this high productivity, particularly when the workers' union constantly presses management for adequate wage compensation. Thus, the center firm, well supplied with capital, exerts a wage pull on the best workers outside the center orbit.

The firms of the center economy are organizational mechanisms pragmatically designed for harnessing society's most efficient productive methods. When economic development through industrialization was of overriding social importance, they were strategically situated to bring the country's scattered national resources to bear on solving problems of considerable magnitude. U.S. industrialization might well have progressed with smaller personal fortunes and fewer financial scandals had government been willing to risk its control over the transformation; yet the goal of industrialization has been served effectively by the expanding and maturing center complex. What do these giants now have to contribute to us and to future generations? Can such a business system, having shaped and been shaped by industrialization, still serve us well in a post-industrial society?

The Center Economy and Full Employment Growth

Writing nearly a century ago, John Stuart Mill pronounced: "It is only in the backward countries of the world that increased production is still an important object."[8] Modern macroeconomics has proved Mill incorrect. An industrial economy functions best when it is fully employed, and the system cannot remain fully employed unless production expands. The American economy cannot stand still, and without growth it will decline. If a mature industrial system is to work well, it must have *controlled* growth, and it is here that the center economy offers help. A smoothly operating industrial system demands planning as well as flexibility, and the organization of key industries by center firms provides the islands of planning that give shape, stability, and direction to the system.

The federal government provides, typically through the Department of Commerce, a continuing supply of economic data—the raw material of planning. On this informational base, center firms build tentative production and investment plans for the next four or five years. Since a large portion of all new investment is performed by center firms, the regularization of investment at the center furnishes a major nongovernmental economic stabilizer. Wrong decisions penalize specific firms, but do not cripple the economy so long as other firms plan wisely.

Government's macroeconomic function is to control the level of economic activity, boosting it when unemployment becomes excessive and slowing it when inflation threatens. With its visible seat of economic power, the center economy is a useful organizational structure through which the economy's pivotal sectors can be influenced. While trying to prevent inflationary wage and price increases in 1966, Secretary of Labor Willard Wirtz lamented the absence of center firms in the construction industry:

Last year, it was steel, aluminum and maritime wages. The year before, it was automobiles. This year, it's construction. And construction is a very different matter from what we had to deal with in those other industries. In steel, for example, you talk with Abel [President of the Steelworkers] and you talk with Blough [Chairman, U. S. Steel Corporation]. There's no such center of gravity in the building trades.[9]

The progress of American production from the late-nineteenth century to the present makes it clear that the emergence of the center economy was thoroughly consistent with the nation's economic development. The 1960's have shown that the business community's present shape is not a brake on contemporary growth. Although the existing business configuration has its undeniable faults, they are not fatal to the realization of macroeconomic goals.

The Business System and Consumer Choice

But what of microeconomic objectives? How does business fare when viewed from the consumer's vantage point? Economic growth generates higher incomes, and consumption patterns do not remain unaffected by this increase in income. "Men first feel necessity, then look for utility, next attend to comfort, still later amuse themselves with pleasure, thence grow dissolute in luxury."[10] So wrote the Italian philosopher Giambattista Vico in the early-eighteenth century. Surely Vico's first two observations are correct. In poor countries men do indeed feel necessity first and then look for utility. As affluence spreads, many move from comfort to pleasure and luxury. But American consumers are spending more on health and education as well. Individuals choose between a new car or college for their children, yet such choices are strongly conditioned by relative prices, and prices are in turn influenced by costs reflecting the mode of production.

In the present economy, the American consumer is confronted with a choice between the heavily advertised, mass and process produced goods of center firms and the ill-advertised, craftsmen-produced services of, for example, health and education. The result is a price disparity that strongly favors the expenditure of income gains on goods, even when these yield satisfactions below additional health and education. Our imbalance in production techniques threatens us with a society where comforts accumulate while human potentialities decay. (The price of a college education includes the foregone earnings of the learner, a sum comprising about half of the total costs of the education.)

Many Americans are vaguely aware that their lives are not suf-

ficiently enriched by their expanding affluence. The truly rewarding life seems forever too expensive. New cars with more accessories
or television sets with color and automatic tuning are freely available to those with money. Yet safer transportation, cleaner air and
scenery, creative schools where a child can develop his peculiar
talents, and hospitals that treat patients as more than medical statistics seem beyond the reach of all but the very rich.

It is tempting to seek the remedy from government. Surely new
laws can make travel safer, air and water cleaner. Moreover, most
of the country's schools and hospitals are public institutions. A major challenge of the post-industrial society is to make the production and distribution of public goods more responsive to consumer
demand. Many of the things that governments produce are primary
for the good life. In a wealthy society, their quality and variety are
important.

When the heavy influence of disparities in labor productivity
is underscored, consumption choices come into sharper focus.
Automobiles and television are woven into our lives in part because
they are subsidized goods. The roads we travel are provided "free"
by government; we are not charged for polluting the air with carbon
monoxide. Nor do we, as consumers of commercial television, pay
the full cost of TV production. Our addiction to the auto and the
television set can be partially explained by our not paying the full
cost of their use. But, equally important, automobiles are mass
produced, while TV programs are process distributed. We might all
prefer live professional theater, but a mass living standard rests
upon mass production and distribution, with the personal services of
talented craftsmen reserved for the few.

Consumers can make their preferences felt only when price
disparities are not extreme. For services as well as goods, the key
to lowering unit costs is found by supplementing expensive labor
with generous quantities of capital. But can the services ever be so
mechanized? Is the rising demand for education doomed to push
up education's price when compared with more easily mechanized
goods? Educational television and programmed learning have thus
far offered disappointing results. But as the first automobiles were
but horseless carriages with the added disadvantages of noise and
frequent failure, so today's educational hardware is just a replica
of the most mechanical teacher. We must rethink the entire educational process before mass education can be individualized. Learning does, after all, take place within the learner. What indispens-

able function does the teacher perform in relation to him? What is the essence of human learning, and how can it be aided by non-human devices? Future innovations are difficult to predict, and, like the automobile, they may significantly alter our social patterns. But the American past indicates that only volume production can continually reduce prices; low-cost and mass output requires partial substitution of non-human for human inputs, a technique thoroughly familiar to center firms.

In a mature industrial economy, the microeconomic goal of giving maximum reign to consumer choice should rival our concern with maintaining the system's macroeconomic vitality. The center economy does not serve well if it distorts choices through advertising and concentrates the potential of mass output on a limited range of products. Numerous center firms are now moving into the education and health industries. If business can play a major role in meeting the expanding demands in these areas at reduced real cost, it will have found a renewed place in the new society.

REFERENCES

1. William G. Bowen and R. A. Berry, "Unemployment Conditions and Movements of the Money-Wage Level," *Review of Economics and Statistics*, Vol. 45, No. 2 (1963), pp. 163-72.

2. See *The Dual Economy* (New York, 1968), pp. 38-45, where I define the distinguishing qualities of key manufacturing industry, concluding that these key industries are located in the machinery, iron and steel, non-ferrous metals, transportation equipment (including automobiles and aircraft), chemical (especially industrial), rubber, petroleum, electronics, and instruments sectors.

3. Alfred D. Chandler, Jr., *Strategy and Structure: Chapters in the History of Industrial Enterprise* (Cambridge, 1962).

4. The demography of small business is discussed in Edward D. Hollander *et al., The Future of Small Business* (New York, 1967), Chapter 7.

5. U. S. Senate, Committee on the Judiciary, Subcommittee on Antitrust and Monopoly, *Economic Concentration, Part V* (U. S. Government Printing Office, 1966), p. 1897.

6. The theory of countervailing power is given in John Kenneth Galbraith, *American Capitalism* (Boston, 1962).

7. Joan Woodward, *Industrial Organization: Theory and Practice* (London,

1965), is an excellent study of technical production types and their importance for the internal management of firms.

8. John Stuart Mill, *Principles of Political Economy*, Vol. 2, Book 4 (fifth edition; London, 1878), p. 338.

9. *Forbes*, Vol. 97, No. 7 (April 1, 1966), p. 17.

10. Quoted in A. Robert Caponigri, *Time and Idea: The Theory of History in Giambattista Vico* (London, 1953), p. 196.

ELI GOLDSTON

New Prospects for American Business

IN THE mixed economy of the United States the traditional function of big business has been to produce, distribute, and sell material goods. That business has performed this function better than most other segments of our society have performed their functions is probably more commonly recognized abroad than at home. The element of U.S. society most envied by other countries today is its industrial and commercial management, an envy that even extends to the Soviet Union and its satellites.[1]

Although American business has been developing the most efficient production and distribution system in history, our religious, academic, and government leaders have not achieved a consensus on the sharing of our national income so that poverty does not flourish amid affluence. Until a clear majority of Americans recognizes the gravity of our social problems and makes sufficient funds available to cope with them, no leadership can accomplish very much. But given the determination and the funds, any number of approaches might work. Moreover, the newer attitudes we need are becoming common among big business leadership, and private business can now be drawn into participating in the solution of many current social problems.[2]

I predict that American business will increasingly supply many of the physical goods and the services we have obtained, at least since the New Deal era, from public sources. Already there is a perceptible and accelerating shift of the administration of proposed solutions for public problems from government bureaucracies to private business enterprises. This superseding of public administration will come through an enhanced attractiveness of these problems as viewed with the traditional profit motivation of business. The entrepreneurial thrust, if encouraged, guided, and controlled by the public agencies of our society, may represent the only permanent solution to the urban problems that have clearly overtaxed the capacity of our public agencies. It offers the best hope that the deprived and neglected parts of our society can be swept into the mainstream of our economy. Of course, instead of the carrot of profit motivation, we could try the stick of punishment or the persuasion of moral exhortation to involve business in social issues. Historically, however, there has been no permanence in the plea or in the stick—only the carrot endures.

These predictions run quite counter not only to the more common notion (shared by an approving left and a deploring right) that big government will learn industrial management and take over business roles, but also to the ethical belief that private profit motivation cannot be used to attain social goals.

It is useless, in any event, to deplore the expansion of an alliance between industry and government. The alliance is already with us in the so-called "military-industrial complex," which is performing very well the task of arming a technological society. But the tools to guide this kind of an alliance must be perfected so that a maximum of social benefit is achieved. We must develop appropriate and controlled incentives that will enable business to deal with such public problems as low-income housing and education; we must find a way to make certain that what is good for business is good for the country. It is often assumed that housing for the poor and schools are "non-market products" that must necessarily be provided by government. Certain products and services must be supplied to all in an ordered society and cannot be metered and charged for—for example, police protection and sanitation. But some of the job can be contracted out to private firms, and there are fewer "non-market products" than post-New Deal history leads many to assume.

Handwringers would do well to consider that our cities may never have been so effectively run for the benefit of the majority as at the turn of the century when political bosses in cahoots with utility magnates made City Hall thoroughly responsive both to the prosperous resident and to the working-class citizen. The working man was properly recognized as a source of both political power and business profit. There was no talk *then* of alienated voters. And those who criticize business for past reluctance to become involved in social problems, or even to investigate the opportunities for doing so, might compare its performance with that of public agencies. For example, Kenneth Clark has said that business offers the best hope for leading us to racial peace, because "business is the least segregated, least discriminatory, most fair of the areas of our society—better than education, religion, unions or government."[3]

This essay will attempt to describe some characteristics of modern big business as they appear to a participant; to indicate how those characteristics will make increasing business involvement in our current public problems quite probable; and to suggest some ways in which such involvement can be encouraged and controlled. The essay does not intend to argue that the profit motive of itself will lead business to socially responsible actions, although it does suggest that professional management of a major firm tends to take a broader and longer view of profitability than the personal owner of a small enterprise. Goal-setting is a public, political function, and it may be more difficult to agree upon goals than to accomplish them once agreement has been reached.[4] My thesis is only that agreed-upon goals may best be realized by using a carefully calibrated system of incentives for private firms. I suggest that the business apparatus is a better social instrument than many realize for two reasons, which appear on the surface to be contradictory: First, net profit per share is more important to professional managers than many current theorists assume, and, second, the concern of big business executives with the social responsibility of business is more genuine than many current critics believe.[5]

Some Characteristics of Contemporary American Business

Observations about business by one immersed in it may lack the breadth and depth of a scholarly inquiry and, above all, its historical perspective.[6] But without endorsing the discredited barnyard aphorism that only a hen can judge a good egg, perhaps an active businessman can add some new knowledge of business to what is usually reported by academic observers.

My comments will apply principally to big business—business with substantial public stock ownership. Small, proprietary businesses are an important element in the American economy, but they are not likely to be significant in changing the way business generally participates in major social problems. I believe my observations should, however, be pertinent over quite a range of business sizes. Just as styles and manners tend to drift out from Cafe Society or the Jet Set through society columns, so the structure, staffing, procedures, and objectives of *Fortune*'s 500 Largest Industrials spread through the business press to the rest of business. A wise government will make use of this "trickle-down" theory and try first to get the business "influentials" or "opinion leaders" to accept new programs.[7]

Big business firms today often differ from the customary descriptions of American corporate enterprise in a number of ways: ownership, structure, exposure, motivation and measurement, character of decision-makers, objectives, and product. I will emphasize the factors that make for greater participation by private firms in solving social problems.

Ownership. The degree of separation between owners and managers of modern big business has been overstated. So has the alleged ability of incompetent or unaggressive management to survive and even to perpetuate itself by selecting its successors. The number of shareholders in United States corporations has risen from about 6.5 million to over 24 million during the past fifteen years. Those economists who feel that a corporate manager can turn his back on stock prices and no longer feel any real pressure for earnings performance should try coming home to find that the cleaning woman who owns ten shares of his company's stock wants to know if she should buy more. They should try going to a cocktail party that develops into an impromptu shareholders' meeting or attending a dinner party where the hostess has the cleaning woman's question—except that, in addition, she plans to report on the stock to her investment club.

The firms where unaggressive management can relax are typically ones where a founding family is still powerful enough to keep control and affluent enough not to press for profit maximization. Except in such firms, ownership is proving to be an increasingly strong influence on management. Repeated successes in unseating poor managements by "takeovers," "overhead tenders," and "forced mergers"[8] have demonstrated that the owners of a contemporary American business more often than not insist on and can demand growing profits. "Performance-minded" investment trusts have speeded the process, for they no longer automatically vote with incumbent management or sell off their stock. Instead they look for, follow, and even back "raiders" in undervalued situations, convinced that nothing can be bought so cheap as a company under poor management about to be replaced.

Banks are still occasionally reluctant to finance "overhead tenders," but they have raised their sights from the days when it was assumed that about $500,000 for expenses and $50,000,000 in capital was the absolute maximum a "raider" could raise. Managements are no longer safe behind these financial limitations, as witness the takeover of United Gas by Pennzoil in 1966 largely by the use of bank loans. United Gas management, owning 3.3 per cent of a market equity of $442 million, was not safe.[9]

Both the number and value of tender offers have increased spectacularly. In 1960, there were 25 tender offers with a total value of $186 million. By 1965, there were 75 with a total value of $951 million, and 1967 went well over the $1 billion mark. In the first six months of 1968, the 1967 total was exceeded. Not only shareholders, but institutional lenders and public creditors are intent on profitable performance, and they may bring quiet but considerable pressure, the existence or true nature of which is seldom publicly revealed. Those economists who believe that size and inertia provide a safe moat for an incompetent but incumbent management should follow Hodson's "Beauties Between the Balance Sheets" or *Finance Magazine*'s "Wolves of Wall Street," which list companies selling below break-up value. Watching the names of the listed firms disappear suggests that the moat is loaded with amphibian sharks who are not above crawling out to devour those they are intended to defend.

Structure. The degree to which large enterprises can once again be personally directed is not yet fully appreciated. With modern technology, a business enterprise can truly be the shadow of one man. Communication is instant, so rapidly improved that it is difficult to realize that as recently as 1929 even the President of the United States did not have a telephone in his office. Personal transportation makes it possible for any executive group to be assembled anywhere in the world within forty-eight hours. Data-handling technology applied to budgeting, forecasting, accounting by profit centers, and control by variances brings small and early deviations quickly to the attention of top management. The applications of business simulation with third-generation computers permit the choice of policies to be isolated in a small top-management group working on long-range planning and leaving operations to carefully watched line managers. The clearer separation between policy and operations permits the elimination of vast clerical staffs and the accompanying middle management, making the corporate apparatus more responsive and personalized. This separation also heightens concern with profit in both policy and operating decision-making; objectives and reasons for decisions cannot remain fuzzy under modern procedures.

Exposure. Greater disclosure requirements by the S.E.C., the growth of security analysis as a profession, and broader public stock ownership have combined since World War II to create what many corporate managements regard as well-nigh indecent exposure.[10] Also of importance have been continuous expansion of commonly accepted accounting principles, increasing detail of reports to regulatory authorities, and the stock exchange dictum: "If in doubt, announce it." Together these forces have released an unprecedented flow of business data, all making up the public performance scoreboard.

Security analysts of brokerage firms, institutions, and mutual funds hammer on the doors of management requesting interviews and pressing invitations to speak at their weekly meetings in forty-one cities. Since 1948, the number of security analysts has increased from 1,600 to 11,000, so that there are almost five full-time students for each of the 2,296 companies listed on all United States exchanges. Their findings appear in *The Wall Street Transcript,* a trade publication whose circulation has gone from 500 in 1963 to 7,500 in 1967, and their judgments are summarized in the *Wall Street Journal,* whose circulation has increased from 56,500 in 1945 to over 1 million today. The number of "owners" has also soared, which greatly increases the attention given to all these materials. No manager can publish a report bare of progress and can assume that he is sunning on an isolated beach where his nakedness will be unnoticed.[11]

Motivation and Measurement. As management feels ownership influence more and more and as its exposure increases, it will be even more concerned with the public scoreboard that records the market value of stock and the price-earnings ratio. This will be reinforced by the trend to greater stock ownership among managers themselves. Managers have become owners in varying degrees—to some extent by ordinary purchases, but more often through stock options granted as a performance incentive. At present, 860 companies listed on the New York Stock Exchange (two thirds of the total) have stock option plans. A recent study indicates that within this group the median number of shares authorized under the plans equals nearly 3 per cent of the outstanding stock. Although this is a modest percentage of the total market equity of a company, it usually represents a substantial percentage of the total net worth of management.

For the new manager, the lure of personal financial gain is thus linked to that of publicized good performance; he seeks good results for reasons both of personal gain and of team pride. He realizes a significant part of his compensation through market appreciation and therefore tends to appraise his own performance, even if his functions are non-financial, by the stock exchange scoreboard that operates from 10:00 A.M. to 3:30 P.M. each market day and displays the market opinion of the management team to which he belongs. One should think of big business in the United States as something like a highly competitive professional sport in which the players have intertwined desires for greater personal wealth and for team victory. The teams are organized and guided by coaches who, like athletic coaches, must be smart enough to understand the management of people and the changing rules of a complex game, but also simple-minded enough to regard winning as being terribly important. Government planners might usefully study American professional baseball players.

Character of the Decision-Makers. Today's typical top-management decision-maker has had advanced professional business education after an A.B. in economics, engineering, or accounting. He is pragmatic and goal-oriented to earnings per share, but he also shares the middle-class American notions of team competition, fair play, observance of the rules of the game, rewards calibrated to results (with some modest recognition of length of service), and the ability of the individual to make himself into pretty much what he wishes. He has a stern regard for honesty and for the importance of paying one's own way. He looks on taxes as an expense and would no sooner think of cheating on them than of cheating a supplier or customer. But he considers taxes an important and controllable expense and is interested in exploiting all proper allowances, deductions, and exemptions. This well-trained, law-abiding, profit-motivated entrepreneurial administrator, fully in command of his own operations, can easily be guided by a government that understands him and the game he is playing.

The memory of the electric equipment price-fixing case and of General Motors' clash with Ralph Nader is too recent for me to suggest that all professional managers fit this description. But such incidents, which put the machinery of business decision into an opaque box for idealistic bright college graduates, are less likely to happen when some of these young men, with a fresh concept of the role of business in society, mature into top business leadership. I am not suggesting that violations of law or morality will cease or that private enterprise can be moved by social concern to do the uneconomic. Nor will business decisions be based upon uncertain and unquantifiable concerns about the impact of a general urban crisis on a particular firm. But an atmosphere of understanding and commitment can be developed so that reasonable incentives will work.

Objectives. With the clear focus of business on a public scoreboard where growth in earnings per share is the major criterion, it is easy to understand that earnings growth has become the consuming objective of American business. Four major areas are seen today as places for substantial growth in sales which, it is hoped, will be carried down from higher sales to the real objectives of higher earnings.

1. *New or More Products to the Existing Market.* Color television, electric toothbrushes, and home humidifiers have been developed and made into necessities; and now second cars, vacation homes, and larger freezers are likewise becoming essential. Marketing, advertising, and selling become even more important as the existing market tends to become saturated, and managers look to new markets and new activities.

2. *New Markets Abroad.* Companion essays in this volume consider this trend. (See especially Michel Crozier's essay.)

3. *New Markets Among the Emerging Poor.* Many businessmen who would be inclined to oppose generous relief, a guaranteed minimum wage, or a negative income tax be-

cause of Charlie Wilson's "hound-dog philosophy" and their own Horatio Alger upbringing[12] are now beginning to support such proposals. To a considerable extent the civil rights movement has made us all more conscious of the needs of the less affluent. But business also sees the promise of a vast new market. Indeed, one of the major marketing interests at the moment is the analysis and segmentation of the Negro market on the theory that no single group in American society will increase its effective total purchasing power more quickly and to a greater extent.

4. *New Activities Once Considered the Province of Government.* The wider opportunities for business growth and profit in areas beyond its conventional operating spheres are just now being realized.

Product. Encouraging a wider ranging view of the business arena is the new "free form" or "conglomerate" enterprise. There is a recently developed idea that top management is really producing not physical products, but financial results. Under this banner, space companies enter the insurance field; investment trusts take management positions in heavy industry; and aircraft companies become comfortable partners of meat-packing firms. More and more, and somewhat to the dismay of the analysts who helped to set the trend in motion, categories of American business are becoming hazy.

If the foregoing picture of the major characteristics of contemporary business is fairly accurate, strong forces are pushing business to face the major problems of our society, and ways exist to encourage and control business participation. Today's highly professional manager, eyes focused on profit performance, operating with excellent controls and within strict rules in the glare of a public scoreboard, needing growth opportunities, and not limited by conventional business boundaries, may be the most promising recruit for solution of the crises in our public services.

The Problems—A Municipal or a Business Solution

Population is concentrating around cities and demanding more and better municipal services. Thus the public problems that business may help to solve are primarily urban ones. Local government will not compete for the task in part because it cannot perform today many services it undertook when the core cities were prosperous. During the first six months of 1968, for instance, garbage remained uncollected for almost a month in New York City and Memphis; classrooms lacked thirty-five thousand teachers in Florida after that number resigned; and snow from a storm lingered eight weeks on the streets of Boston. Everywhere there is a threat of a paralysis of municipal services. It is not surprising that the existing municipal organizations have proved totally inadequate to handle the immense new needs. Only a thin line remains of the talented manpower from the Depression class of public employees. Antiquated and inadequate physical plant and equipment cannot be modernized because urban problems grow more rapidly than urban revenues, particularly in the old core cities.

The obstacles to improvement in the municipal sector seem hopeless in the short run. A direct, public tax rate permits no such comforting concealment or sugar-coating of costs as is possible in private commerce or even in federal funding. People seem unwilling to pay municipal taxes for goods they willingly purchase in the private market: The home owner cheerfully landscapes his house, but grudgingly pays the city for trash removal. Part of the psychological problem is that the pleasure of shopping is absent when the tax is compulsory and the service is non-competitive. Moreover, the tax bill usually does not connect the tax to be paid with the services received. Of course, where the majority rules, an itemization reminds the minority of the imposition; some have, for example, calculated the portion of their Federal Income Tax that goes for military purposes and tried to pay only the balance.

Easy solutions to the fiscal problems of the core city will not be found. It cannot realistically recapture by annexation the tax base that has fled to the suburbs. Suburban municipal costs have themselves been rising. Even federal grants in aid to municipalities may be opposed in Congress due to increasing black domination of the government of core cities.

As a result of insufficient funds and inability to attract talented people, local public agencies have little of the freedom of action available to business in its progress toward more efficiency. In trash and garbage disposal, police and fire protection, traffic control, mass transportation, water and sewage services, local public agencies expend little of the research and development effort that business so effectively and rewardingly applies to its problems. Because government services are not sold and other measurements of value are difficult, the cost cannot be matched against value to measure performance.[13] (How much better are the police now? How much cleaner are the streets?)

The lack in government of profit pressure or any other effective scoreboard is reflected over a period of time in the personality patterns of personnel recruited, retained, and promoted. Anyone who has worked, on the one hand, with door-to-door salesmen and, on the other, with passenger railroad employees knows there are a tone and a style to the staff of an organization that attract similar types and repel opposites. Over the years, from top to bottom, an institution develops a pace and tradition that can be changed only by bringing in new people at key spots. There is a business maxim: "If you can't change a man, change the man." It is astonishing how rapidly a bureaucratic structure can respond to a carefully articulated and communicated change of philosophy accompanied by shifts in key posts. This was most dramatically demonstrated in government by Robert McNamara's transformation of the Defense Department.

Such an accomplishment is usually easier in business than in government for three reasons. The goals of business are simpler and can be expressed in a single figure—net profit. The staff of business has usually been taken from a less bureaucratic and seniority-minded group of people. And the power to hire and fire is less affected in business than in government by considerations other than efficiency. But no one would be rash enough to claim that business can always manage better than government, particularly when the output of a government operation can be quantified and checked for efficiency. For years the federal government ran a better utility at Bonneville than Consolidated Edison did in New York City. But the appropriate acknowledgment of this came from business itself with the appointment of a man from Bonneville to head the new management at Consolidated Edison. In short, the demand for everything from trash disposal to better public schools is unlikely to be met by present municipal governments, and business is unlikely to overlook the resulting opportunity to make a profit.

One question will be whether the total cost to the public of a business solution will be more when not only a profit, but incentives including tax benefits are included. The experience has been that the ability of business to assemble the resources to do a job rapidly and without the constraints of government has generally produced a lower total cost, as in the current turnkey public housing experiments. Of course, in some municipal functions efficiency and economy may be of less importance than a feeling of fairness (justice can be too speedy) or concern (police car cruisers are pretty impersonal).

Incentives and Controls

Assuming that the government and the rest of non-business society have reached some agreement on the nature of a problem and the solutions to be sought, business involvement requires some evidence that the goals are feasible and that a reasonably certain profit can be expected. A sales campaign will still be required to persuade business leadership to direct capital and effort to this particular opportunity. For present purposes we will assume that our goals are agreed on and will consider the incentives and controls useful to involve business in the solution. Of course, the assumption of agreed goals is enormous. According to the Kerner Commission, for example, the race problem requires a society-wide change of priorities.

Moral exhortation and mild social pressures will get a few small contributions and some attendance at meetings from businessmen, particularly if no major capital commitment or significant diversion of executive attention is ultimately expected. Public approval may be gained, relations with federal agencies cemented, and some sense of participation provided—all with no diminution in potential earnings per share. Many firms that have responded to the program of private Job Corps management or "hard-core" unemployment contracts have been moved by such reasons. There is also the incentive of fear—the realistic recognition that our cities, and with them our urbanized society, might simply fall apart. But these reasons do not suffice to attract the commitment of substantial capital or top executive manpower. One must, therefore, turn to the basic profit motivation of business and its increasingly public scoreboard. Not an oral moral whip, but an enticing economic carrot will make the stubborn business animal get started.

The continuing problem is to offer the appropriate form of incentive, to make it obvious, and to guard against abuse. For one thing, it is necessary to calibrate the incentive so that it will be enough to attract the less efficient firms without creating too great a bonanza for the more efficient. The so-called "F.H.A. 608 Scandals" resulted to a large extent from incompetent adjustment of incentives rather than dishonesty, but the public and political reaction was just as bad. Another requirement is to make the incentive clear and certain enough to attract entrepreneurs, but murky enough so that the costs do not set up a legislative barrier to their approval. Whether it be percentage depletion for the oil industry, less than 100 per cent F.H.A. mortgages on values that include allowances as well as costs, or export credit guarantees, public and legislative agreement seems to require disguising the fact of the subsidy and its extent. (All of these may seem undemocratic; but perhaps some such finesse is necessary to make workable a democratic system for the reconciling of conflicting interests.) Andrew Shonfield has labeled a similar finesse in French planning a "conspiracy in the public interest,"[14] and American political theorists occasionally talk of assigning unpopular functions to such less visible bodies of government as commissions. A political cry of "making a profit out of poverty" could discourage perfectly legitimate business participation in social problems.

The enticing economic carrots that may hasten business entry into public problems may be of four varieties, all designed to compensate for conditions which otherwise would make a reasonable profit unlikely:

Guarantees and Insurance. The evaluation of business risk always includes an allowance for the uncertainties involved, especially the worst, or so-called "down-side risk." By mortgage insurance, export credit insurance, disaster-risk insurance (such as the nuclear explosion provisions of the Atomic Energy Act), the federal government has traditionally provided guarantees, found them politically acceptable, and indeed sometimes profitable, as in the case of F.H.A. Often a guarantee not only reduces the interest cost of money, but makes it available at any cost. An advantage of guarantees is that usually more of the processing is kept in private hands than with direct government loans.

Tax Benefits. Most incremental corporate income is taxed at about 50 per cent. This means that a tax reduction of $1 (such as the present investment credit) is equivalent to $2 in pre-tax earnings. Reciprocally, a deduction of $2 from pre-tax income is equivalent to $1 post-tax. Because consolidated tax returns on unrelated business operations are permitted, high income corporations can defer taxes (in effect borrowing at no interest) through tax incentives which, like accelerated depreciation, move expenditures forward into pre-tax costs. They can also get indirect permanent subsidies by tax reductions that do not affect the tax basis of assets.

Subsidies. Although direct cash subsidies may theoretically be better social policy than tax benefits and the other less obvious methods since the legislator has a clearer picture of what he is doing and the voter has a clearer picture of what his legislator is doing, they seem to be less politically acceptable. One acceptable direct subsidy of vast importance has been reduction of debt service cost as a way to attract private investment. This can be accomplished by providing loans with time conditions that would shock conservative bankers (no down payment, terminal balloon payments, and so forth) and by lowering interest rates. In a typical $1,000,000 housing project, such changes in debt service requirements eliminate the need for $300,000 "front money" and also reduce yearly principal-interest payments from $84,000 to $39,500. At the same time they provide significantly greater tax deductions for unrelated income of the investors.[15]

Contracts and Franchises. A final form of incentive is the long-term contract or perpetual franchise. Just as private utilities have needed such long-term arrangements to finance their plants, cities will have to grant such arrangements for the trash removal and other services they require if they hope to persuade business to adopt the high level of technology and heavy plant investment that will bring efficient service. In the franchise, of course, there will be need for regulation of rates and services, but concepts and techniques are well established for this. Long-term public housing leases and rent supplement contracts are now being used to open low-income housing as a market for private investment.

Those who doubt the effectiveness of the first three incentives should review the history of the industrial bond financing now available in almost all states. The more industrialized states, after denouncing Arkansas and Mississippi for using it to attract industry, finally passed enabling legislation in self-defense.

Just as important as incentives, however, are the controls that not only make the incentives politically and socially acceptable, but also regulate the extent of business participation. Controls can, for instance, vary the relative advantages accruing to business from providing mass transportation as compared with middle-income housing, thereby setting the scale of business interest in each. Much of our present central-city crisis derives from an F.H.A. policy of encouraging housing expansion into new subdivisions without concurrent provision for the social consequences.

The most effective controls for economic incentives will, obviously, also be economic. The Japanese, for example, control their economy by making use of what we would regard as a tradition of insolvency. The major industries pay out large cash dividends and finance fixed plant expansion with short-term commercial bank borrowings that cannot be paid when due. The banks show these debts as relatively short-term assets and pile up against them short-term liabilities, including those to the central bank. Any failure of the central bank to renew and extend its short-term loans creates pressure throughout the economy. This provides the financial policy-makers of government with a control apparatus which can be tuned with the precision of a transistor radio and as quickly adjusted and readjusted. Allowing for the greater financial strength of American firms, our government is not using imaginatively enough the characteristics of American business firms to direct the significant force of business toward critical social problems. One, of course, returns to the problem of goals and means. The timing of the 1968 tax increase was delayed in Congress despite business and Presidential support. It was not the means that were lacking; it was the will.

A basic problem in the control of the public activities of business is the prevailing distrust of business enterprise and the misunderstanding of its operation. The result is the type of over-detailed regulation through which the I.C.C. produced stodgy railroad management with little encouragement to innovate and market effectively. The recent rejuvenation of railroad management has been spearheaded by lawyers turned professional managers who have simply outmaneuvered the regulatory bureaucracy by a legalized patrogenesis permitting diversification and escape of the non-railroad operations from I.C.C. regulation.[16] To control big business, performance should be post-audited rather than cumbersomely prescribed in detail in advance. The difference is comparable to the difference between a bureau for advance censorship and a system of punishments for clear abuses of free speech.

Even with post-auditing, incentives for superior performance should be provided to make use of the drives for profit and competitive success basic to our business society. There is much to be learned about how business can be employed for social purposes from McNamara's Defense Department "target pricing." If regulation is to become more pervasive, the interplay of business and government should be designed so as to bring out the best in each.

A novel method of incentive and control might be to require expansion of the simple profit scoreboard of business to include an annual public accounting of its performance in other directions: growth in minority group' employees, reduction in pollution, improvement in safety records, or encouragement of employees to use mass transportation. In some areas, the competitive team spirit of American business might be enough by itself. (To understand American business you must follow not only Berle to Burns to Galbraith, but also Tinker to Evers to Chance.) In other cases economic incentives could be scaled to these achievements, and companies could be given rewards for high grades on the scoreboard in integrated employment and minimal pollution. With these built-in rewards, security analysts should be on the watch for firms with high marks of this kind, recognizing that these companies are working toward compensation for the costs of clean air and clean water, which are too often hidden now. There are also ways to educate the public about the costs of these desirable and necessary activities.[17]

Those inexperienced with group leadership often fail to realize that even a poorly conceived scoreboard can have a dramatic effect. Compare a group of boys tossing a football with two sides playing a scored game of football. Consider the substantial increase in judicial output that Justice Vanderbilt, of New Jersey, accomplished by publicizing a scoreboard of cases awaiting decision by each judge. His monitoring made it less of a nuisance to decide a case than to explain delay.[18]

Perhaps even a social audit could be developed. Some firms presently' have management consultants review them at intervals just as they provide for annual executive health checkups. To the extent that security analysts could predict social diseconomies that might become internalized costs, they would tend to regard better citizens as the better investment.[19] Such social accounting will never have the force and precision of the market mechanism and the profit motive, but it will make incentives and controls much more effective.

Altogether, it is inconceivable that a society which has been able to develop through years of technical and political processing such an intricate structure of federal taxation cannot also devise effective systems of incentives and controls to lead business in and out of problem areas.

Examples

Three examples of business participation in social-problem areas may offer a guide to the future: the economic miracle of Puerto Rico; the experience of private enterprise in low- and middle-income housing; and current experiments in training and hiring "hard-core" unemployed. The last two examples show the current expansion of business into areas until recently considered public. The first example shows the research, political leadership, as well as the incentives and rules that government must provide if it wants business involvement.

The Economic Miracle of Puerto Rico. The dismal Negro ghettos in the core cities of the United States today are almost gardens of health and prosperity compared to the American colony of Porto Rico in the 1930's. No one who has first read Rexford Tugwell's descriptions of the island he went to govern and then visited modern San Juan and the remainder of the Commonwealth of Puerto Rico[20] can be pessimistic about what an aroused society can accomplish in connection with the Negro and Puerto Rican ghettos in the United States. Today Puerto Rico has one of the highest rates of industrial growth in the world, outpacing the European Common Market. More than twenty-four hundred industrial plants are humming. Thousands of workers are trained by vocational schools in thirty-one trades. (American vocational education could learn a great deal from the Puerto Rican example.) The labor force, numbering 807,000, includes tens of thousands of skilled workers. Over five thousand United States executives live and work happily in Puerto Rico. So effective has the development of opportunities there been that the population movement to the mainland has slowed substantially and a net return to

Puerto Rico is anticipated in the near future. (Does this not suggest that some industrialization of the agrarian Negro in the South might relieve the pressure on the urban North?) Puerto Rico has become the largest per-capita customer of the United States.

Three things brought about the remarkable change: a feasible development plan, a charismatic political leader, and a solid program of well-publicized incentives for business. The original development plan depended largely on government action with a detailed control of private company participation. From 1940 to 1947, the development effort was attempted almost entirely through government ownership and operation of new factories. Over $20 million in investment brought only two thousand actual and potential jobs. With an estimated need for one hundred thousand jobs, government capital of $1 billion would have been needed, and that could not have been raised. The government's role consequently was shifted from actual operation of industry to promotion of private industry. Beardsley Ruml, one of the mainland's shrewdest financial and tax minds, joined the planning, introducing a new approach that featured the ingenious interplay of federal taxes, expenditures, and benefits, an approach which our decaying cities will soon have to establish in relation to state and federal agencies. Munoz Marin provided the political leadership; Teodoro Moscoso adjusted the interplay of government incentive with imaginative administration; and free enterprise firms provided the motive power to propel an impoverished colony into a prospering commonwealth.

To persuade mainland industry to come to Puerto Rico was not easy, nor quickly accomplished. There was an illiterate, Spanish-speaking work force, untrained, undisciplined, and unfamiliar with the urban-industrial way of life. The extra cost and time of two-way ocean freight protected even higher-cost United States domestic producers against island competitors. There were limited funds for promotion, problems of distance and communication, government red tape, and few United States managers who relished an assignment in Puerto Rico.

But the government administrators sought out U.S. firms that needed to expand and sold hard the fact that low labor costs plus tax exemption offered substantially higher profits than were possible on the mainland. Even the location of plants was guided by the scale of incentives. Benefits were provided in three scales, giving extra advantages to firms moving into particular undeveloped areas.[21]

David F. Ross provides insight into the philosophy of this second and hugely successful phase of the development plan:

Leaders of governmental programs to improve the lot of suffering humanity are likely to be men of high ideals and high moral standards, with pronounced egalitarian tendencies. In most situations, they like to have private capital and enterprise participate in the programs which they sponsor because they need all the help they can get; but they see no occasion for more than a 5% or 10% return being earned on private investment.

Puerto Rico's experiment clearly shows the sheer driving force of human avarice as an inducement to investment.

It is hard to watch a man of wealth get away with 50% when his employees are making ends meet with $15 or $20 a week; but it is the size of the pie, much more than the way it is sliced, that determines the fate of the masses. With 5% or 10% the pie stays small; with 50% it grows; and soon the employees are getting twice what an equal division of the original pie would have brought them.

Greed is not a pretty motive, but it works, and the promoters of progress cannot afford to disdain it unless they are prepared, both philosophically and financially, to rely exclusively on governmental enterprise and capital.[22]

Our core-city problems are like those of the former Colony of Porto Rico or any other underdevelped area. Core cities need export earnings. No matter how much the ghetto poor take in one another's washing or establish local restaurants or set up papa-and-mama stores to retail to their neighbors, economic progress will not be possible. The ghetto residents lack income to buy and capital to invest. Outside business must employ them to make products that will be sold to the more affluent outside world. Outside investment must rebuild the housing. But, just as securing foreign investment in the Commonwealth of Puerto Rico required a plan, leadership, and publicized incentives, getting business into our urban ghettos will require much more than oratory.

The Experience of Private Enterprise in Low- and Middle-Income Housing. A pioneering example of a sound government approach to improving a ghetto housing inventory is the Federal Housing Administration's 1968 rehabilitation program in the Roxbury-Dorchester section of Boston. In two related programs, with slightly different types of incentives, the F.H.A. has enlisted private developers in the complete renovation of almost three thousand dwelling units within less than one calendar year. This is the nation's largest and fastest low- and middle-income housing rehabilitation project. It is designed to bring, in well under twelve months, one of every seven Negro families in a rapidly declining city area out of deplorable substandard housing and into thoroughly modernized dwellings. The 221(d)(3) program is used, under which the Federal Housing Administration underwrites 90 per cent mortgage financing. This, combined with the 10 per cent "builders and sponsors profit and risk" provision of the agreement, reduces the front money requirements substantially.[23]

The principal incentive to private involvement in the first of these rehabilitation programs is rent supplements. The government assumes that a tenant can afford 25 per cent of his income for rent and makes up to the landlord the difference between this figure and the "economic rent" that must be charged to return a reasonable profit under the F.H.A. formula. In this case, the private developers borrow money at the going mortgage interest rate against the security of a lease at rents that, taking into consideration the federal subsidy payments, will meet the mortgage requirements.

In the second program, the Boston Urban Rehabilitation Program (with the acronym of "BURP"), the profit opportunity to the developer comes through F.H.A. mortgage loans at 3 to 3½ per cent, which lower the fixed charges of the projects. This makes possible quite low rentals and creates an attractive business opportunity in apartment rehabilitation. Here the tenants are expected to pay the full "economic rent," which, of course, is at a rate approved by the F.H.A. Some units are being leased at these rents to the Boston Housing Authority in the leased-housing program under which the B.H.A. makes up the difference between the F.H.A. rent schedule and what low-income families can afford.

My company is participating in these two programs as a limited partner of various developers, thereby taking an ownership interest in more than two thousand units being rehabilitated. The decision to become involved in this way was made quite as much in response to the financial and marketing opportunities as to moral exhortation to corporations for help in solving the urban crisis. As a part owner, we are able to specify gas for heating, cooking, and water-heating in the rehabilitated units, thus creating for our subsidiary, Boston Gas Company, its largest single sales gain in recent years.[24] To make gas thoroughly competitive with any fuel in the cost-conscious low-income housing field, the Massachusetts Department of Public Utilities permitted the company to apply its lower, public-housing rate to these programs. For the investing parent company, the opportunity to use real-estate depreciation as a tax deduction provided another incentive. Together the revenue to the Gas Company and the tax benefits to the parent created the economic carrot that made our entry into the critically necessary low-income housing field reasonably justified on a financial basis. The combination of government incentives plus investment by us provided all of the profit potential, working capital, and motivation required to move this vast program into rapid execution by the various developers. We are training a group of Roxbury residents for later participation in the Model Cities Program by sponsoring almost two hundred units with them; but without the federal incentive programs and the participation of several non-ghetto developers, the rehabilitation program would have had to be done entirely by the government and would have taken years, if it were done at all.[25]

Our experience with the BURP program has been somewhat less profitable, but somewhat more exciting and satisfying than a good many other matters to which our executives might have directed their attention. The important lesson, however, is that a reasonable enough opportunity for profit was presented. Our firm was able to consider the project as a major business task rather than as a secondary civic assignment or a hobby for a couple of executives. There was not enough profit to compensate fully for top executive attention to complex social controversies, but there was at least enough profit to bolster executive concern about the social problem with a sense of business purpose.[26]

Current Experiments in Training and Hiring "Hard-Core" Unemployed. My third example is the move to enlist industry in attacking the problem of urban "hard-core" unemployables announced in President Johnson's Economic Report of February 1, 1968:

This year the Federal Government is also seeking a new partnership with private industry to train and hire the disadvantaged. I believe this partnership can succeed—and must—in providing work opportunities for every American who wants a job and who will make reasonable efforts to prepare himself to hold it.

In a subsequent message to Congress, President Johnson proposed a $350,000,000 partnership to put five hundred thousand "hard-core" jobless to work in fifty cities over the next three and a half years. He also set up an alliance of businessmen with Henry Ford II at the head of a fifteen-man board. The heart of the program is to reimburse business for the "extra costs" of training and hiring the unemployed selected by the government.

The "hard sell" given to the program, the concern of the business community for the subject, and the economic incentives have already been strong enough to elicit a meaningful contribution from the private sector. In less than six months, the five hundred thousand job openings had been promised. In one sense, this program faces an easier task than the one Puerto Rico confronted. Though these unemployed are equally untrained and undisciplined, most of them have some familiarity with the urban-industrial way of life. However inadequately, they also speak English, the language of American industry. But the Puerto Rican example may not exactly fit the problem of our urban ghetto jobless. For one thing, the Puerto Rican poor, despite skin color gradations throughout the population, considered themselves as part of the nation. The current complication of poverty in America by racial issues was not present. There also is a major difference in motivation and morale between a peasant eking out a living on a marginal farm and an urban loafer long unemployed. To some extent the Puerto Rican industrialization took poor farmers in without passing them first through urban slums. But enough of the urban poor were reached in the Puerto Rico miracle to give hope to President Johnson's program.

We return again to the distinction between social goals and techniques for achieving them. The basic problem is whether society is prepared to spend as *much* as it takes for as *long* as it takes to succeed in such a program. The projects to date (several buttressed by federal procurement contracts granted on a noncompetitive basis) have suggested that many people can be made employable fairly promptly, but also that the goal of a society where substantially all the able-bodied are mentally and emotionally ready for work may be far too high for accomplishment with the present poverty generation. In any event, much more is being accomplished much faster by the government-business coalition than was being accomplished by government alone.[27]

Some Present Trends

The three examples discussed are not sports. They represent a current American trend to involve private enterprise in public matters. Without doubt the controversial "military-industrial complex" is a tempting model and an example of how business may be willing and able to take over many functions previously considered public responsibilities. Few government arsenals and shipyards remain as producers of modern weaponry. The extent to which the system has changed since the days when government plants produced the major war machinery is put in sharp relief by any suggestion that the government might have built its own missile and anti-missile systems.

Just as the government stopped much of the designing, building, and repairing of its own ships when war vessels became merely containers for a vast quantity of electronic gear, perhaps the extent of public management of education will change as schools increasingly contain advanced educational equipment. General Learning (made up of Life and G.E.), Raytheon Education Co., R.C.A.-Education, and other industrial firms are already planning to penetrate the public education field through teaching machines and the related software. Until these major corporations saw education as a marketing opportunity, there was little hope that their skills might find application in editing higher education materials. Unfortunately for the commercial expectations, the 1967-68 school year, the first in which many of the new complexes participated, was troubled by reduced federal grants and widespread teacher strikes, which led many school boards to continue with the old textbooks and equipment.

Michael Harrington and others have warned of the social dangers in the creation of an "educational-industrial complex," but the shortcomings in the present method of public education have themselves been the subject of comment. The Coleman Report, the second-largest social study in our history, suggests that almost all our conventional wisdom about high schools is wrong: Class size seems to make little difference except at the extremes, peer motivation by classmates seems to be more significant than teaching quality, and so forth. Others question the validity of long summer vacations in a society where youth is no longer needed on the farm. Still others cite as evidence of the stagnation of our present system of education the absence of experimentation and the lack of interest in cost-effectiveness studies, in mechanizing routine work, or in improved evaluation of performance. There is, of course, a social decision to be made on the content of education, but no one would argue that our present public school is doing as good a job as could be done with the hardware and software now available.

It is inconceivable that the sales energy of American business cannot penetrate this complicated and conservative market and, in doing so, make public education not only more efficient, but also more effective. Perhaps in this way some of the educational accomplishments of the business community, such as the outstanding work several firms have done in upgrading uneducated employees,[28] and educational techniques developed in business-managed Job Corps centers can be spread to the public schools and receive increased community support. Many corporations are already running major educational operations. G.E. spends $40,000,000 annually on educational support and training programs. In any given year, one out of every eight G.E. employees attends a training program of some kind.

It is often forgotten that many municipal services—such as fire and police protection—were originally supplied cooperatively or commercially. When core cities were occupied by middle- and upper-class citizens, municipalities could afford to supply these services. With the current core-city situation, there is a growth again of private firms in many of these areas because of the deterioration of municipal services. Crime prevention is one of the "high multiple" growth favorites of the financial community. Almost $1.2 billion is now spent annually for protection service from companies such as Pinkerton's Inc., The William J. Burns International Detective Agency, Inc., and the Sonaguard Alarm system for homes and automobiles. Expenditures for protection have been growing at well over 10 per cent annually in recent years.

The first signs of similar developments in other "public" areas are also appearing. Already a number of firms have set up "Environmental Departments," mostly to sell hardware for pollution control to factories forced into such control by municipal regulations. In some cases, however, they are merchandising detection services and systems to municipalities. Chemical New York Trust

Company recently signed a contract to handle the processing of mailed payments of New York traffic fines. The State of California has already employed some air-space firms to apply systems analysis to city management. I.T.&T., with its continuing expansion into car rental, hotel operations, and so forth, is the prototype of the service firm with great flexibility in direction, capacity, and overhead—perfect for involvement in services previously run by government. Such firms frequently have little in bricks and mortar and no inventory. Their strength is in their perspicacity in anticipating trends well in advance of competition. An increasingly high percentage of our Gross National Product is spent for services. In the last decade alone, the dollar volume of spending for services increased 85.4 per cent as compared to 67.7 per cent for the G.N.P. as a whole. As consumers demand more services, our municipal and state governments will not be able to finance or to supply them. Commercial service firms will increasingly be the suppliers, either directly to the consumers as in special protection services or by government contract as in the Job Corps Centers.

Perhaps HUD and H.E.W. should, like Defense, be contracting out not only some R & D and hardware purchases, but also part of their operations. HUD has just set up an Office of Business Participation to be headed by a systems planning executive from I.B.M. with the announced purpose of developing ways in which the government, by taxes and other incentives, can encourage business participation in rebuilding slums. Stouffers Foods Corporation already operates the food operations at four colleges and universities, and the Tishman Realty & Construction Company has built and is operating dormitories at two colleges. Other nonprofit institutions are shedding administrative functions to service corporations. Might not education be better served if Berlitz or other specialized firms were to operate the language laboratories of many public high schools? Some of the complex problems of serving a technical and urban society require a greater specialization of manpower than most government bureaucracies can hope to maintain.

With growing employment and income, a potential market will develop to attract business into further involvement with the problems of the urban ghetto. In this way the Negro may be brought into the mainstream of American society, as business dramatically raises its current estimate of twenty-three million Negro consumers with about $30 billion a year to spend. If this income doubles in five years as a result of all the efforts to improve the Negro's economic status, no other market in this country will be growing so fast. For the first time, business today has begun "segmenting" and analyzing this emerging market. It finds, for example, that forty-four of every hundred Negro households use seven or more bars of toilet soap a month, as compared with twenty-three of each hundred white households. This means, for example, that in Detroit, where Negroes make up 20 per cent of the five million population, they constitute 30 per cent of the heavy soap users. This piece of marketing information is significant to soap companies in planning their mix of advertising media, their use of Negro advertising models, their choice of distribution channels, and their reputation as non-discriminating employers.

It is not only personal income of the Negro population, but also the rise of Negroes to positions where they can affect nonpersonal purchasing decisions that matters. Can any vendor of police and fire equipment, parking meters, or voting machines fail to consider in his marketing plans (no matter how bigoted he would prefer to be) that Cleveland and Gary have black mayors and that similar black control of City Hall is predicted within five years for Chicago, Philadelphia, Baltimore, Oakland, Berkeley, St. Louis, and Detroit? It does not require refined sociological research to note the differences in actions and ultimately in attitudes when the feared stranger becomes a customer.

On the international level, it should be noted that Litton Industries has contracted with the Greek government to help develop tourism, industry, and agriculture in Crete and the Western Peloponnesus. Litton proposes to attract $150,000,000 of foreign capital over twelve years while the Greek government organizes $90,000,000 of public and private money. Litton Industries also has similar arrangements in Portugal and Turkey, and Northrop Corporation has contracted with Iran to revamp irrigation and transportation systems.

Meanwhile increasing attention is being paid to business participation in social problems in the conferences where businessmen exhort and educate one another and gradually arrive at a consensus on "business policy." These meetings and recent courses and research at the Harvard Business School and elsewhere on "social responsibilities of business" and "business and urban problems" are signs of the things to come. Thus one of our most important bankers has proposed: "Business must move from the defensive to the offensive and begin pushing the boundary line between the public and private sectors the other way. Both business and society stand to gain from the doctrine of socio-commercial enterprise."[29]

For 80 per cent of the world's population, the central problem remains that of producing enough material goods for minimum comfort or even survival. For the United States, however, the most optimistic hopes for nineteenth-century technology have been fulfilled. Thus our central problems are to devise a more just distribution of our increasing quantity of material goods; to meet the demand for a better quality of life by expanding vastly the service sector of our economy and by controlling our technology; and to develop a consensus on these and other social values and on their relative priorities. Big business presently foresees in these American problems vast new markets for products and services. Building materials, construction equipment, and contracting services will be needed to rebuild the slums. Teaching machines, classroom materials, and textbooks are required for an expanded and improved educational system. Chemicals and machinery are needed to cut pollution. Fertilizer companies look at backward parts of the United States and underdeveloped nations. Drug firms see expanding sales in disease prevention and population control.

These markets cannot be served by a system of municipal and state government units. As the nation becomes more urbanized and the core city becomes a less significant part of the metropolis, the areas of municipal and state authority increasingly lack any real relationship to the problem areas and service areas. No one would want the federal government to take over all our government functions. An appropriately motivated and guided business structure is able to meet these needs, and every indicator suggests that this development is already well started. It could result in a new and beneficial interplay between the social concern of government, the scholarship of the university, and the know-how of big business.[30]

References

1. It is not our technology so much as our managerial capacity to make early and extensive use of innovations which has been found difficult to copy.

See Michel Crozier, "A New Rationale for American Business," in this Volume.

2. Herbert Marcuse and J. K. Galbraith, among others, would say that our industrial capitalism has so shaped popular attitudes as to make business, in a sense, responsible for the present unfortunate priority of popular goals. My own view is that the newer attitudes of big business leadership would be found more acceptable, at least to Galbraith, than the attitudes of small business or of rank-and-file employees. The appointment in many firms of a "Manager of Urban Affairs," a new rung on the management ladder, reflects the higher priority already being given by top managment.

3. *Nation's Business* (October, 1967), p. 69.

4. It should be emphasized that I am not suggesting that the selection and formulation of social goals can be achieved without a political process of resolving conflicting interests. Such a process takes into account certain social costs and social benefits that will be irrelevant to the profit calculations of the business manager until government controls make them part of his internal cost accounting. For example, a political decision favoring cleaner air made effective through regulation of smokestack emissions might be met by installing expensive control devices or by burning more expensive fuel. Such political control internalizes for the plant manager (and for his customers and owners) as an operating cost the former social diseconomy of air pollution. It does leave the particular cost equation to local solution, including the possibility of closing the plant as no longer capable of profitable operation even after deduction of "sunk costs."

My suggestion is that cleaner air will be achieved more quickly and cheaply by a free enterprise society in which administrative decision-making is decentralized and profit motivated. Such an entrepreneurial society concurrently creates a new growth industry of environmental control firms. It tends to reach the social goal sooner than a society that operates through a centralized government program with comprehensive and detailed plans. This thesis is particularly well developed in Gerald Sirkin, *The Visible Hand: The Fundamentals of Economic Planning* (New York, 1968).

5. See Richard H. Holton, "Business and Government," in this volume.

6. The historical essays of Chandler and Letwin, herein, suggest that the past role of business may be so different from the role of big business in the future that in our society of accelerating change, a rear-view mirror may be less useful than a speedometer.

7. Consistent with this strategy, during 1968, Mrs. Henry Ford II was one of the pace-setters for women's high-style clothing while her husband was assigned by the White House to head the National Alliance of Businessmen in seeking jobs for "hard-core" unemployed.

8. These terms do not have precise definitions, but, in general: a "takeover" is a replacement of management by market purchases of stock, possibly

including a proxy fight; an "overhead tender" is a public offer to purchase control without the recommendation of management that the offer be accepted; and a "forced merger" is voted against the wish of the submerging management. A "defensive merger" is a hasty corporate marriage contrived to foil one of the foregoing.

9. The Pennzoil takeover of United Gas was one of the first "overhead" tenders involving a large amount of borrowed funds. Since then there have been a number of others including, in 1967, the Ling-Temco-Vought takeover of Wilson with a management owning 1.3 per cent of a total $111 million market value of equity. L.T.V. also made a bid, although an unsuccessful one, for Allis-Chalmers, which had a market value of equity totaling $221 million (of which management owned 0.4 per cent). Transamerica Corporation acquired control of United Artists Corporation, which had a market equity of $146 million, again with management owning only a relatively small 16.5 per cent. Paul Revere Insurance acquired control of and later merged with Avco; the latter had a market equity of $305 million prior to the tender, with management owning 2 per cent of the outstanding stock. During May, 1968, L.T.V. probably set a record (at least to date) for a non-competitive offer, tendering $425 million cash for 63 per cent of the stock of Jones and Laughlin Steel. The market value of J. and L.'s total equity prior to the offer was about $650 million.

In these and other cases, the acquisition of relatively large minority interests by tenderers usually placed them in a position to force through a subsequent merger of the two companies.

As the number and size of tender offers has increased, competition among tenderers has accelerated. During 1967, it was not unusual to see one tender offer or merger agreement immediately followed by a competing bid from another company. For example, both Reliance Electric and Emerson Electric went after Dodge Mfg.; United Utilities and Kaneb Pipeline both sought to acquire Kansas-Nebraska Natural Gas; Rockwell Standard and Indianhead competed to acquire Draper Corporation; and three companies—Dillingham, City Investing, and Seeburg Corporation—went after Rheem Mfg. One battle gaining wide publicity has involved Crane and American Standard seeking to outbid each other for Westinghouse Air Brake. In the latter case, the highest bid so far is $230 million for equity that had a market value of $180 million prior to the initial bid. Allis-Chalmers has also been the subject of successive offers since L.T.V.'s failure, including most recently one by City Investing.

Another emerging trend seems to involve small companies going after much larger ones. Thus Lowe's Theatres ($100 million equity) offered $439 million of its convertible debentures for Commercial Credit ($351 million of equity, before the tender).

Among the companies where lenders, trade creditors, and other outsiders have brought pressure to bear for management change or merger are Curtis Publishing, Chrysler Coporation, Douglas Aircraft, T.W.A., and Wheeling Steel.

Some have challenged this Darwinian theory of tender offers because so frequently a growing smaller firm is absorbed in an agreed merger, often in part to provide the larger company with a management team. Statistical research by D. A. Kuehn has not proved conclusive as to British experience: *Stock Market Valuation and Acquisitions: An Empirical Test of One Component of Managerial Utility* (Warwick Economic Research Papers, University of Warwick; Coventry, England, 1968). The fact that good managements are frequently invited into consolidations is no reason why bad managements should not fear being invited out. In his *Theory of Managerial Capitalism* (New York, 1964), Robin Marris regards the possibility of tender as an important discipline on management. The practice of stock tenders was earlier and more widely used in England. Its full impact has yet to be felt in the United States.

10. On the other hand, some critics feel that the S.E.C. accounting rules, like a teeny bikini, require the exposure of much that is interesting while permitting the non-disclosure of all that is vital. This criticism is made especially of consolidated reports for different divisions.

11. The later discussion of disclosed social accounts proposes that S.E.C. financial disclosure techniques be extended further as an instrument of social control.

12. At a Detroit Press Conference, Secretary of Defense and former General Motors head Wilson said: "I've always liked bird dogs better than kennel-fed dogs myself—you know, one who'll get out and hunt for food rather than sit on his fanny and yell." *The New York Times*, Oct. 13, 1954, p. 14. One example of how myth replaces fact even when the documents of literature are available is the metamorphosis of Horatio Alger's heroes from lucky farm boys who came to the city and saved the daughter of the boss from drowning to endlessly working junior executives who grew up in the city and never would have taken time off to go to the beach.

13. It should be noted that federal recruiting continues to attract more able people than state and municipal recruiting, and that policy-planners are more attracted to government service than are executives. These trends add to the feasibility of federal funding of centrally determined policies to be spent by local government on projects carried out by business firms. There is a problem as to how far a popular democracy can go before the finesse becomes a "credibility gap." An aristocratic tradition of decision by the elite makes an easier background than a republican idea of delegated authority.

14. Andrew Shonfield, *Modern Capitalism* (New York, 1965).

15. To illustrate some of the direct subsidies that are accepted but little understood, consider the attraction of 221(d)(3) as opposed to conventionally financed projects to investors and resulting benefits to tenants. The following table summarizes the acquisition and rehabilitation costs together with financing.

$1 MILLION REHABILITATION MODULE
80 Units

Cost:

1. Acquisition of Land and Bldgs.	$ 320,000
2. Rehabilitation⁽ᴬ⁾	680,000
3. Total Cost	$ 1,000,000

⁽ᴬ⁾ Includes $618,000 Cost and $62,000 Builder's and Sponsor's Profit and Risk Allowance

Financing:

4. Mortgage	$ 900,000
5. Equity: Waived Profit and Risk Allowance	62,000
6. Cash Front Money	38,000
7. Total Financing	$ 1,000,000

Note that rehabilitation cost includes the 10 per cent ($62,000) builder's and sponsor's profit and risk allowance. This is a mortgageable cost; and if it is "waived" (to the equity left in by the developer), only $38,000 of cash equity is required. By comparison, the same project with conventional financing might be eligible for only a 70 per cent, $700,000 mortgage loan, in which event the developer would have to put in $300,000 of cash equity.

Also, a federally insured project may be eligible for a below market interest rate loan, bearing interest at 3 per cent, and repayable on a level debt service basis over forty years. On the $1 million project, total debt service would be $39,500 annually. By comparison, the interest rate on a conventional loan today would be about 7 per cent, repayable over twenty years; annual debt service would then total $84,000 on the $1 million project. The difference between these debt service figures works out to over $550 annually per apartment unit and becomes significant to low-income tenants when the annual rent amounts to only $1,350.

Besides benefits to tenants in the form of lower required rental payments to cover expenses and debt service, developers stand to benefit materially from tax shelter created by the project. The $1 million project would probably have a depreciable base of $888,000 (exclusive of $50,000 value of the land and the $62,000 profit-and-risk fee, both non-depreciable). Straight-line depreciation over thirty years would average only $29,600 annually. For tax purposes, however, the project is eligible for accelerated depreciation, which in the first year would amount to $53,000. The result of depreciating a project on this basis is to create substantial losses for tax purposes—particularly in the early years of the project—which investors may deduct from other taxable income, thereby reducing cash tax payments.

The next table summarizes the total cash flows from the project to a corporate investor in the 48 per cent tax bracket. (This example assumes that the project generates sufficient cash to pay annual dividends to the owner up to the legal limit of 6 per cent of "book" equity.)

Year	Tax Loss	Tax Saving 48% Rate	Direct Cash Distributions	Cumulative Cash Gain
Original Investment		-	-	$(38,000)
1	$28,000	$13,400	$6,000	(18,600)
2	24,500	11,700	6,000	(900)
3	21,000	10,000	6,000	15,100
4	17,600	8,400	6,000	29,500
5	14,500	6,900	6,000	42,400
Total—				
10 Year	-	-	-	90,700*

* Assumes sale after tenth year and payment of capital gains tax.

Often projects will generate insufficient cash to make full dividend distributions. Declines in cash earning power and resulting increases in tax shelter will, however, be about offsetting.

In this example tax savings and direct cash distributions are sufficient to recover the entire investment in two years and create a 240 per cent net gain over the entire ten-year life of the project. A conventionally financed project might create about the same amount of tax shelter although the $300,000 investment would not be recovered until much later, if ever. See Robert Kennedy, "Race and The City: The Slums and Community," *To Seek a Newer World* (New York, 1967), p. 18, for a full discussion of tax incentives and low-income housing.

16. Railroads that created their own parent holding companies and thereby diversified include: Illinois Central Industries (Illinois Central R.R., 1962); Kansas City Southern Industries (Kansas City Southern R.R., 1964); Northwest Industries R.R. (Chicago and Northwestern R.R., 1967); Santa Fe Industries (Santa Fe, 1968).

17. In addition, perhaps an affirmative demand for investment in the securities of a socially responsible firm would develop among the students and church members who presently are purely negative in demanding the exclusion from investment portfolios of the securities of firms who are known to discriminate in employment or to deal with South Africa.

Indeed, just as this essay went to the printer, our company received the following letter from one of the major women's colleges:

"We hold 5,000 shares of common stock of your company in our investment portfolio.

"In this connection, we would like to know what action your company has taken to help solve current racial problems, either social or economic. In this increasingly questioning age, we want to be in the position of having this type of information at our disposal.

"I hope very much to hear from you on this matter."

18. Arthur T. Vanderbilt (*Selected Writings of Arthur T. Vanderbilt*, Vol. 2. [Dobbs Ferry, 1967], p. 98) reports that the same judges doubled their productivity in three years following procedural changes.

19. The idea of social accounting is developed more fully by Andrew Shonfield, in *Business in the Twenty-First Century*, in this volume.

The report of the President's Council of Economic Advisors might usefully incorporate the social indicators being developed by H.E.W. as an example for business annual reports.

20. Just as black nationalists now prefer "black" to "Negro," the word "Puerto" has been substituted for "Porto" by the Commonwealth.

21. Similarly, Robert Kennedy had suggested special benefits for ghetto investments. *To Seek a Newer World*, pp. 39ff.

22. David F. Ross, *The Long Uphill Path* (San Juan, 1966), p. 177.

23. See Note 15.

24. Our sales slogan was "When you BURP, think GAS."

25. The BURP program description and some of my comments in an earlier draft of this essay have been carefully reviewed and slightly revised after publication of the Solow-Galbraith-Marris-Solow controversy on the economic theory of corporate behavior in the Fall, 1967, and Spring, 1968, issues of *The Public Interest*. It is particularly interesting that the Marris low-rent suppositions (p. 45 of the Spring, 1968, issue) are almost precisely the circumstances of the BURP program which I describe and that both the Solow comments (p. 51) and the Marris theory fail in this particular instance of "empirical testing." Both our entry into BURP and the great interest from other major corporations in our activities were the result of a growing managerial determination to find ways to make socially beneficial undertakings reasonably profitable. They resulted from neither a careful selection of the most profitable possible application of time, effort, and capital, nor a concern with expansion of sales or assets. Because of its social benefits, the project was regarded as a challenge to the ingenuity and professional capacity of the professional manager. It did, nevertheless, require just the sort of adequate, but not excessive government incentive tailored to the particular circumstances which I suggest earlier.

26. *Fortune* Magazine, in its issue devoted to Business and Urban Crisis (January, 1968), editorialized:

"What it comes down to is this: the public, and many government officials at various levels have now eagerly embraced the idea that private corporations have a unique capability for dealing with the cities' problems. But many in government, and indeed many businessmen, have not yet perceived that we need new institutional arrangements to help corporations use that capability as well as they might. It will not do to pretend that we can create all the jobs and houses we need simply by appealing to the profit motive. Nor will it do to pretend that corporations can make major investments in the cities on a nonprofit basis.

"What kinds of arrangements are called for? Several possibilities come to mind. In some cases, presumably, tax incentives and subsidies might be appropriate when there is no other way to get major corporate involvement. Another possibility would be to allow competitors to form industry councils, with immunity from antitrust action, so that all could engage in 'public service' operations from the same competitive base. Some kind of immunity from stockholder action might also be considered. Corporations, and their individual officers and directors, should be freed from concern that any special efforts they put forth will entangle them in court with stockholders. We need a great many more working relationships between our executives, our local planners and government officials, and our universities. In fact, we might well try to evolve a concept of our top managers as a major unused national resource—a resource from which society might expect a lot more. The possibility of a management 'tithe' for public service is an intriguing one.

"If we really are looking to business to provide some leadership in the cities, what may be needed most of all is a change that will require no new laws, but simply some new attitudes. It is a change already taking place in a good many business communities; its main symptom is a sudden intense feeling of *involvement* with the city on the part of businessmen. It is this sense of involvement that sent James Roche, the new chairman of General Motors, on a pilgrimage to Lansing to lobby for open housing; and got Henry Ford II to go calling personally on a Negro activist in the Detroit slums. Large and beneficial consequences can be expected as more and more business leaders act on the idea that the city is not just a place where one works and, possibly, lives—but is the major component of America" (p. 128).

27. A growth industry is developing in firms that specialize in the hiring and training of dropouts and other hard-core unemployed. Many firms, including my own, have used such professionals not only to raise the motivation level of prospective hard-core employees, but to prepare present employees to work with the new type of recruits.

28. Note the following extract from the 1967 Annual Report of Corn Products:

"Corn Products also entered the 'knowledge business' with three small but promising affiliations . . . . MIND, Inc., was set up as a subsidiary following demonstrations of its effectiveness in a pilot project of the National Association of Manufacturers at our plant in Argo, Ill., in 1966. MIND provides an innovative system to help undereducated persons acquire reading, writing, and arithmetic abilities needed for employment and advancement. MIND clients include business firms and community and government agencies.

"We invested in Information Science Incorporated . . . . The company's basic business is the application of computerized systems for matching human resources to job opportunities and availability. These techniques serve not only the undereducated whose needs are to find employment after acquiring basic skills, but also professional, executive and technical personnel sought by client companies.

"Corn Products also acquired an interest in Information Management Inc. [which] . . . specializes in the design of computer information systems for operations and management control in business and government.

"All of these ventures in the 'knowledge business,' including MIND, present opportunities for meaningful and profitable participation in the effort to solve problems that increasingly affect our social and economic environment both here and abroad. We intend to expand our search for ingenious and productive approaches to the efficient use of human resources in this era of unprecedented social change."

29. George Champion, "Creative Competition," *Harvard Business Review* (May-June 1967), p. 67.

30. This essay has been greatly improved by the thoughts, suggestions, and criticisms of O. F. Ingram, J. de Varon, H. V. Eggers, H. N. Finkelstein, the late W. L. Glowacki, M. Lach, G. A. Rothrauff, Jr., S. H. Scheuer, R. E. Tracy, and R. W. Weinig.

RAYMOND VERNON

The Role of U. S. Enterprise Abroad

FOR NEARLY a century, U. S. scholars have been analyzing the interplay between U. S. enterprises and the environment in which they operate. Sometimes the emphasis has been on understanding the effect of enterprise upon society; sometimes it has been the other way around. But as a rule, whatever the emphasis, "the society" has usually been the United States itself.

The impact of United States enterprise upon foreign countries, however, is large and growing. And although there may be pauses in the process from time to time, there is every reason to suppose that the impact will grow larger still. Between 1946 and 1967, the investments of United States companies in foreign subsidiaries and affiliates rose from $12 billion to $55 billion, more than a four-fold increase. During the same period, the assets of the corporate sector in the United States increased at only half that rate. Of the $55 billion or so invested directly by U. S. enterprises in overseas subsidiaries, about 65 per cent is located in the more advanced countries of the world—that is, principally in Western Europe, Japan, and the white nations of the British Commonwealth.

For the most part, the foreign investment of U. S. firms appears in industries that are dominated by a relatively few large enterprises. Petroleum, chemicals, machinery, and transportation equipment are heavily represented; food processing and tobacco also are very much in evidence; but such industries as textiles and furniture are not. There are a few industries, such as the computer industry, in which U.S.-owned firms actually have dominated in the economies of foreign countries, but dominance of this sort has been exceptional. Still, because of the emphasis on the dynamic industries, the subsidiaries and affiliates of U. S. enterprises have had an impact upon the national economies of their host countries that often was quite out of proportion to the size of the investment. To understand the nature of some of these effects, however, an introductory word or two on the character of the corporate entity itself is necessary.

The Corporate Entity

The corporation of the twentieth century, one has to be reminded from time to time, is a revolutionary institution, endowed with powers of an extraordinary kind. For many centuries, true to the doctrine of mortmain, the jurisprudence of Western nations had resisted the creation of institutions that might have the power to control property over prolonged periods of time. Accordingly, as recently as two centuries ago, corporations were a rare and special thing. Most performed their assignments under charters that severely constrained their length of life, their functions, and even their size. When corporations were created to operate overseas, as was the case of the British East India Company and the Massachusetts Bay Colony, they were thought of as instruments of the Crown itself, brought into being for a limited purpose to support the Crown's objectives (or the objectives of the Crown's favorite subjects) and deriving their claim to continuous life from the link to the Crown.

Not until the middle of the nineteenth century did some jurisdictions, pushed by populist pressures, begin to permit the creation of corporations under general enabling statutes, and not until some decades later did limitations on size, life, and purpose begin to disappear. As a result, for almost the first time, it was possible to envisage a business entity that possessed immortality. Being immortal, the corporation became independent of the finite life cycle of its entrepreneurial creator. It could attract professional managers whose commitment was to the survival of the organization, and it could stretch its credit-worthiness and its supervisory reach beyond the limits that any individual businessman could hope to attain. For an ambitious and gifted few, those endowments offered unparalleled opportunities.

By the end of the nineteenth century, the big public corporation was ubiquitous in American life. Most American corporations, of course, still were fairly small; and most of them continue to be small to this day. But the big corporation dominated the domestic industrial scene. What is more important for the purpose of this essay is that the big corporation was the principal vehicle for direct overseas investment in subsidiaries and affiliates.

Within a few decades after the big corporation had become commonplace, some basic implications of its appearance were being widely recognized and debated. The enduring aspect of the big corporation was its bureaucratic machinery—more enduring than the stockholders who nominally "owned" its assets, the creditors who loaned it money, the customers on whom it relied. Once a corporation was large enough to generate a public market for its securities, the umbilical tie to its stockholders and debt-holders was weakened; those who provided the capital could come and go, attracted by an opportunity for profit or repelled by the fear of loss. A few quixotic characters among the stockholders might enjoy the practice of nipping at the heels of the corporate bureaucracy; in an exceptional case or two, the heads of the bureaucracy might even be pulled down. But these rare cases were not to be parlayed into the illusory notion that the stockholders greatly affected the behavior of their enterprises.

By the 1950's, still another implication of the evolving corporate structure began to be articulated. Increasing size in the corporation had been leading to increasing specialization of its parts. Increasing specialization meant increasing division of function. Inevitably, those attached to a given function tended to see the objective of the corporation in terms of that function. Accordingly, production engineers gauged success in terms of plant performance, comptrollers thought of adherence to the budget as the supreme virtue, and salesmen applied gross volume increases as their yardstick for success.

What effects did these developments have upon the goals and performance of the large corporation? Let me pause here to warn the reader that the question is not a casual one. Among economists, the response to that question is widely used to classify the respondent according to whether he is Muslim or Hindu, Russian Orthodox or Old Believer.[1] I need only say here that the view of the large corporation from close up usually gives the impression not of an organism single-mindedly devoted to maximizing the firm's profits, but of a group of cooperating semi-independent forces with distinguishably different goals. To be sure, every element in the coalition makes appropriate obeisance to the firm's profit-maximizing objectives, and no element is likely to take any action that would imperil the existence of the firm. But each will resist having its own functions cut back or obliterated in the interest of the firm as a whole. And the growing strength of any one element will almost automatically stimulate the creation of a defensive alliance of the other elements, devoted to the objective of restraining the growing unit. The coordinating mechanism at the apex may occasionally impose decisions of a dictatorial sort, but it is also concerned with maintaining "loyalty," "incentive," and "initiative" over the long run and is usually prepared to accept a less-than-optimum compromise in a particular situation in order to keep the principal members of the team in play.

Just as the simple Darwinian model of the firm as a profit maximizer seems somewhat at variance with the behavior of the large modern enterprise when viewed from close up, so also do other time-honored concepts seem out of place, including the concept of unambiguous national identification. Most sovereign states will permit the corporations created under their laws to own other corporations or to be owned by them. Each parent, sibling, or offspring in the group may have its own juridical identity, its own assets, and its own liabilities. Accordingly, the "firms" that are heavily engaged in foreign investment actually consist of a group of corporations of diverse corporate nationality.

It would be an error, however, to regard such firms as a consortium whose units are simply drawn along national lines. Foreign business now generates a considerable part of the total income of large U. S. parents. Although few yet obtain as much as half their total income from this source, a figure of one fourth or one fifth is fairly common. Accordingly, the tendency to regard such business as a normal, undifferentiated part of the total business of the corporate system has been growing rapidly.

It is true, of course, that the non-U. S. managers in these corporate groups are usually assigned to subsidiaries located in their home countries. But there are some signs of growing fungibility of personnel. Managers recruited in the advanced countries outside the United States are being invited from time to time to serve in third country subsidiaries. Occasionally, they are being allowed to mount the main career ladder of the corporate system to its summit, including key positions on the staff of the U. S. parent.

Even more important as indications of the integrative process are the changes that seem to be going on in the internal structures of the corporate systems. There was a time when such systems tended to lump the business done outside the United States indiscriminately in an "international division," separated from the mainstream of the system's affairs. The international divisions, however, are now giving way to new organizational structures— structures that eliminate the domestic-international dichotomy and group the firm's business by product or market or both.[2]

Members of the coalition, therefore, do not draw the distinction between the U. S. market and other markets with anything like the old clarity. Their nationality as individuals may still be unambiguous; the national identity of the subsidiary to which they are attached may be clear; but their interest in the coalition may be best expressed in terms of a product or a market that is not conterminous with a set of national boundaries.

That fact has a bearing on how the participating units in a multinational enterprise see their relationship to the sovereign states that have bestowed nationality upon the unit. Note that the inclusion of many corporate nationalities in a single corporate group means that the group can be exposed quite directly to the pressures and commands of more than one sovereign, with each such sovereign taking the position that it is addressing its commands to its own nationals. Thus, the parent of an Asian subsidiary of one of the world's major oil companies may be commanded by the U. S. government to embargo oil to Communist China, while the subsidiary is being commanded by the Asian government to supply that oil. But the establishment of such corporate systems of national personalities in many jurisdictions also increases the capability of such systems to withdraw from any given jurisdiction. If the pressures imposed on one of its units by a local government are costly, the corporate system can divest itself of the onerous nationality. Such a step may sometimes be a bit painful, particularly if it requires the corporate group to withdraw from an especially attractive market or to give up a particularly cheap source of raw materials, but it can be done.

How does one predict and describe the overseas effects of entities endowed with the powers and purposes I have just outlined? It would be difficult enough to generalize if the firm were a simple profit-making entity. As the product of a complex coalition, the firm's behavior is even more difficult to fathom. But one does see certain regularities, and these regularities are worth some attention for what they may reveal about the underlying forces. Let me turn first to the less-developed areas, then to the advanced countries.

The Less-Advanced Countries

In order to appreciate the forces that shape and constrain the role of the foreign investor in the less-developed countries, one has to begin by turning back the clock about one hundred years. This will require the reader to think of the corporation once again in its pristine state, at a time when its involvement in foreign investment was principally for the purpose of securing a cheap source of raw materials for the home market.

Until a few decades ago, most of the producing activities of foreign enterprises in Africa, Asia, and Latin America were limited to the simple purpose of raw material extraction. While most of these areas were colonial, some were independent. From the viewpoint of the independent governments, foreign investments generally were quite consistent with national objectives. In those years, any effort to extract significant quantities of minerals or agricultural products for export usually involved large amounts of capital and high risk. Few local entrepreneurs were prepared to take the risk, especially if the sale of the product demanded access to foreign markets. Therefore, the opportunity cost to the economy of granting permission to foreigners to exploit the resource was generally thought to be low; at the same time, the value to the country of receiving benefits early rather than late, given the high social discount rates in such areas, was usually rather considerable.

It is not unreasonable to raise the question whether the payments of foreign investors to the oligarchs of those early days should be classified as "benefits." Using the yardstick of current national objectives, my guess, applicable to most periods and most countries, is a slightly hesitant, slightly qualified "yes." Infrastructures such as roads, rails, and power plants, designed primarily to support the foreign investor's activity, tended as a rule to support the growth of the internal economy. Training that was needed to build up a class of minor supervisors and technicians contributed in the end to a pool of manpower for the essential modernizing activities (including, in some cases, the revolution) of the developing country. In those early days, to be sure, the lion's share of the prospective rewards was earmarked for the foreigner. But the history of such investment is littered with the bleached bones of many enterprises; and, taking the failures with the successes, it is not clear that the investment was handsomely rewarded.

While a persuasive historical case can be made that the foreign raw material investors in the less-developed countries usually contributed to social and economic change, one must also candidly recognize that many of these investors tried repeatedly to block the political expression of that change. Change meant uncertainty. At best, it meant re-establishing disrupted lines of communication with a characteristically *dirigiste* governmental apparatus; at worst, an end to the opportunity to do business inside the country.

The transition to the modern era of relations between foreign raw material investors and less-developed countries took place partly in the interwar period. The political structure in many less-developed countries was beginning to change. At the same time, the three essential ingredients originally provided by the foreign investor in the raw material field—capital, technology, and markets—no longer seemed quite so indispensable to the host. After the first injection of capital, any added funds usually came from the earnings of the operation itself. After the first introduction of technology and organization, the mystery of operating a producing enterprise seemed less and less opaque. Only the marketing problem lay beyond the apparent capabilities of the local economy; and even this aspect of the business was not quite so overwhelming as it had once seemed.

Accordingly, as concession terms were negotiated and renegotiated, the bargaining goals of the less-developed countries were repeatedly raised. During this period, the Chileans managed to double their relative share of the rewards in copper mining; the Venezuelans laid the basis for a 50-50 split of profits in petroleum; and the Mexicans allowed their negotiations with the oil companies to break down, leading to the nationalization of the foreign properties. When the new African and Asian nations became independent after World War II, they took some of their cues from the negotiated results and the attendant ideologies of Latin America.

By the early 1960's, host governments had managed in some cases to impose levels of cost and taxes on foreign raw material investors that were so high as genuinely to cut into the investors' profits. More than that, there was an increasing disposition on the part of host governments to become involved in the day-to-day business activities of the foreign enterprise. In some cases, foreign investors were regularly required to justify their production, pricing, and marketing policies. In other cases, taxes and other payments by foreign investors were taken in the form of a share of output and were marketed independently of the foreign tax-payer. In still other cases, foreign investors were being required to set aside portions of their output for buyers designated by host governments. The prerogatives of business management, once the clear and undisputed preserve of the foreign investor, began to be shared.

As far as some foreign investors were concerned, these developments were annoying, but they were not fatal. The strategy of the business still suggested the wisdom of maintaining a controlled supply of raw materials. For other investors, however, some of the advantages of overseas raw material investments were badly impaired by the new developments. At some point, one could picture the investor moving across a watershed, to a point at which he saw advantages in divesting himself of the remaining elements of his raw material control. This would not occur unless the sources of supply had become sufficiently diverse so that buyers no longer felt imperiled by the lack of a tied source of supply. At some point, however, foreign producers of some commodities would presumably be content to become arms' length buyers, dealing with their erstwhile host government on the basis of open market prices.

It is doubtful if a change of this sort will occur suddenly and dramatically. Basic strategies of large companies change sluggishly at best. In a stable oligopolistic industry, no one is likely to take the risk of such a change unless there are signs that the others are moving in the same direction. Even a small move in the indicated direction, however, will be sufficient to create new tensions between the host governments and the investors. However desirable it may have seemed to the host governments to be "free" of the tutelage of the investors, they are unlikely to shoulder the task of developing their own properties and marketing their own product without a certain amount of initial fear and recrimination. Still, the nettle may be seized, and if it is, the era of the foreign private investor in the sale of major raw materials may gradually give way to new arrangements in which the foreign investor's role is greatly subordinated.

Foreign investment in manufacturing facilities in the less-developed areas, however, is quite another matter. For such investments, the foreign investor's bargaining position cannot be said to have declined; the capital, the technology, and the markets

that foreign investors have to offer continue to be vitally important to the less-developed countries. If a single generalization
were justified, one would have to say that the negotiating position of foreign-owned manufacturing enterprises in the less-
developed world was being strengthened, not weakened, with
time. But let me elaborate this conclusion at once, in order to reduce the risk of error.

Most decisions by foreigners to establish manufacturing facilities in the less-developed world have been acts of reluctance,
defensive steps forced on the investor because of the threat that
import restrictions might cut him off from an existing or potential
market. Confronting the threat in a state of ignorance and uncertainty, the investor has usually tried to make the smallest possible financial and organizational commitment that was required to
counter the threat; he usually preferred to establish packaging and
assembly plants, for instance, rather than plants that produced
their own components. Once the investor took the plunge, experience suggests, his perception of the risk and the opportunity involved
in his commitment sometimes changed; with facts replacing
ignorance, his projection of the likely outcome improved and his
willingness to accept commitment expanded. In any case, persistent pressures from the host government usually obliged the
investor to deepen his commitment. Little by little, therefore, investors turned to using domestic materials rather than imports and
domestic skilled labor rather than expatriate technicians.

Local reactions to the presence of the foreign manufacturer
enterprise in the less-developed countries have been predictably
ambivalent. As seen through the eyes of the local private sector,
the foreigner who is producing a superior version of an existing
local product is patently "unfair." If he is elbowing the local product aside by heavy advertising, this is even more objectionable.
On the other hand, if he is engaged in some non-competitive
venture, such as the assembly of automobiles, his potential demand for locally manufactured parts may be more important to
local business than his pre-emption of the automobile market. In
that case, the political strategy of local business is generally directed at exploiting the existence of the foreign facility as a buyer.

As a rule, governments in the less-developed countries would
prefer to acquire the capital, the technology, and the markets
that they need without conceding ownership to foreigners. But,
alas, the harsh reality of the bargaining process usually determines

the outcome. In the process of bargaining, countries with large internal markets are in a stronger position than those with small markets; foreign investors, for instance, will generally have a larger interest in India than in Malaysia, despite the less hospitable climate of the larger country. A country in a weak balance-of-payments position is handicapped by comparison with one in a strong position, witness the recent history of Brazil and Mexico. And the nation aspiring to the acquisition of advanced technology is in a more difficult position than one requiring simpler processes.

Whatever the bargaining position of the foreign investor and the host government may be at the outset, however, it tends to change over time. Technology that once was new and esoteric, such as that embodied in petroleum refineries, eventually becomes available to the less-developed country in the form of packaged plants for sale on a turnkey basis. Markets that once were small and insignificant, as far as the foreigner is concerned, eventually become glittering prizes. So some elements in the host government's bargaining position seem to strengthen.

At the same time, however, the governments of less-developed countries confront new needs. As their economies grow and become more complex, their technological requirements, their capital needs, and their exporting aspirations change as well. Each step forward exposes such countries to a need for technology, capital, and markets that can weaken their bargaining position in relation to the foreigner.

Two tendencies in particular have reduced the less-developed countries' capacity to drive a hard bargain. One has been a growing emphasis on the development of exports of manufactured goods. Until a few years ago, most local manufacture was intended for import substitution, and less-developed countries had barely any interest in exports. Many adopted a regulatory approach reflecting the conviction that exports are principally a "vent for surplus," not a normal purpose of domestic production. (The officials of one large developing country, for instance, were reported refusing to allow an international company to export some of its locally-produced automobiles, asserting stiffly that the local production facility had not been built "solely for the convenience of the company.")

Now that the less-developed countries have decided to push the export of manufactured goods, only a few have been willing and able to take the early Japanese approach to export promotion

—an approach compounded of heavy government subsidies, large promotional efforts abroad, and persistent study of foreign markets. Lightning solutions have been sought, and lightning solutions demand an alliance with someone who knows about market opportunities abroad. Outstanding in this regard is the foreign investor, especially the investor whose corporate structure encompasses many countries.

Another recent development that may have impaired the negotiating position of the less-developed countries is the emergence of regional market schemes, notably the projects for development of the eleven-country Latin American Free Trade Area and the five-country Central American Common Market. The establishment of such a market presents its members with new opportunities of selling to other countries and with new threats of competition in home markets. Accordingly, some members are prepared to offer special incentives to attract foreign firms into their economy, especially firms that already know a good deal about the markets of the other less-developed countries in the regional grouping.

The continuous change in the negotiating position of the foreign investor creates an atmosphere in which some uncertainty and risk seem always present. While numerous proposals aimed at altering the atmosphere have been made, few of them seem likely to produce the desired result.

Perhaps the most persistent proposals of all are those that look to some kind of partnership between the foreigner and local interests. The partnership concept is embodied in various legal forms, such as management contracts, licensing arrangements, "coproduction" schemes, and joint ventures. No one can deny that such partnerships may indeed be useful for some purposes, such as propitiating the local business and political interests that are in command at the time of the foreigner's entry. But it is unwise, even dangerous, to assume—as is so generally assumed in less-developed areas—that where inherent conflicts of interest exist between the economy of the host country and foreign investor, such partnerships lead to policies that are more favorable to the host country.

Consider, for instance, some aspects of the financial relations between foreign parents and their local subsidiaries. There is a widespread assumption in less-developed countries that foreign parents draw profits out of their wholly-owned subsidiaries at a rate that is higher than if the subsidiary were a joint venture. But the fragmentary evidence that exists so far suggests a much more complex pattern, rather more at variance with the assumptions than consistent with them. Parents seem inclined to take a more relaxed attitude toward wholly-owned subsidiaries than toward joint ventures when fixing their royalty, price, and dividend policies. And when the facilities of the international enterprises in less-developed countries begin to be more widely used for export purposes, as I think they will be over the next decade or two, I anticipate that parent companies will assign a larger export role to wholly-owned subsidiaries than to joint ventures.

There is an important generalization to be drawn from the export market illustration, a generalization that sums up the dilemma that confronts a less-developed country when framing a policy with regard to foreign direct investment. The problem as seen by such a country is to secure the benefits that can be provided by a unit of a powerful international organization operating in the local economy, but at the same time to retain the benefits of continued control over the national economy. As long as the local unit is not closely integrated with the rest of the international system of which it is a part, the system may not see the weakness of control as being serious. But once the unit is deeply integrated with the international system, as is unavoidably the case if the subsidiary is to act as a supplier of outside markets, the conflict in objectives becomes sharper and clearer. The dilemma is even more evident in the case of foreign-owned enterprises in the advanced countries.

The Advanced Nations

Although U. S. parent companies have not been surprised to encounter an ambivalent and reserved reaction to their investments in countries like Mexico, Nigeria, and India, they have not been quite so well prepared for a similar reaction in nations like France, Germany, and Britain. Even a superficial glance at the history of international investment during the past century should have conditioned them for the reaction. That history included the rise and fall of U. S. life insurance companies in Europe before 1905, the Canadian and European worries over the ebullience of U. S. manufacturing investment before World War I, and the restrictive measures applied in various European countries between the two great wars. But few U. S. businessmen had had any firsthand experience with those events.

When foreign-owned subsidiaries representing a large multinational system have appeared in an advanced country, the local business community has tended to react in much the same way as its counterpart in the less-developed countries. Local businessmen have been quite content to accept new sources of complementary business, but they have bridled at the threat of rough, undisciplined competition. The sense of threat has been accompanied by a touch of resentment as well, because the competitive strength of U. S.-owned enterprises is usually felt to be based on "unfair" advantages of various sorts, arising out of their size and their international spread.

The sense of alarm among local businessmen over the intrusion of U. S.-owned enterprise has been due, in my opinion, not only to the seemingly unlimited strength of the new competition, but also to the relative unpredictability of the way in which that strength might be used. Uncertainty is intolerable for businessmen accustomed to tight, familiar, protected markets. Unpredictability in a prospective rival generates great psychic pain. The sheer unfamiliarity of local businessmen with the behavior patterns of a new participant—especially a new participant introduced into a market characteristically organized on an oligopoly basis—has created raw nerves and heightened tensions.

The governments of advanced countries, like those of the less-developed nations, have had rather more complex reactions. With varying degrees of support and conviction, practically all governments have responded sympathetically to the complaints of the local private sector. On the other hand, most governments are prepared to acknowledge that the subsidiary of a foreign-owned enterprise may be helpful to the economy if its output represents products or processes of an advanced type. If the British electronics industry needs miniaturized circuits to keep it competitive in world markets, then that production capability must be introduced in Britain even if the Americans are the main producers. If the ailing French farmer needs a commercial outlet for his green peas that is capable of processing and packaging the peas under tight quality controls, then that difficult skill must somehow be brought to France even at the cost of tolerating Anglo-Saxon enterprises in the country.

Up to World War II many advanced countries were prepared

to entertain the possibility that their national economic and security goals could be achieved even if they retained a certain amount of economic isolation and austerity. Those that believed such a course to be possible felt no need to encourage the flow of capital, ideas, and specialized goods across their boundaries. But most of the advanced countries have now concluded that they cannot follow the isolation course—that their interests lie in fostering a large-scale exchange of goods, capital, and ideas with other countries. Behind that judgment there probably lies another—the judgment that the modern state needs so many highly specialized inputs of skill and materials that no one nation can possibly hope to provide efficiently all its needs from within its own borders. These judgments and the policies accompanying them have led to a swiftly growing exchange of manufactured goods among such countries. The growth has generated a self-supporting circle of consequences, vicious or benign. A high level of trade means a high degree of opportunity, but also a considerable degree of threat. So the international enterprise, itself the source of the threat in many cases, also becomes the instrument of the rejoinder.

Still, governments in the advanced countries are visibly reluctant at times to accept foreign-owned subsidiaries. While recognizing that the subsidiaries of foreign companies may bring advantages to the economy, host governments fear that the advantages may be just as summarily withdrawn. An international manufacturer, having found that a subsidiary no longer fits very well into its global strategy, can begin to shrink the activities of the subsidiary and to transfer them to some other location; or, having decided that the profits generated by the subsidiary can better be used elsewhere, he can quietly draw off the surplus funds for use in another country; he can even drain off local brains for employment in another part of the international structure.

The same sort of governmental worry exists with respect to the enforcement of national policies. Governments have a nagging concern, not without foundation, that local subsidiaries attached to foreign parents have considerable flexibility in expanding or contracting their money balances and inflating or reducing their stated profits. They may not exercise that freedom to the detriment of the local economy, but the very existence of the choice is a source of unease. Constantly in the mind of the monetary and fiscal authorities is the question whether they are capable of applying their respective policies to these local subsidiaries.

Finally, host governments are concerned about the extrajuris-dictional reach of other governments. From time to time, such governments are brought up short by the realization of the naked power that other governments feel capable of exercising over such subsidiaries. Controls over U.S. capital export command that the parents direct subsidiaries, despite the non-U.S. nationality of the subsidiaries, to withdraw funds from local banks in the host coun-try and to ship them "home" to the United States. U.S. trade controls prevent the German subsidiaries of United States com-panies from shipping advanced electronic gear to the Soviet Union. While the pressure may sometimes be made to run in reverse, from subsidiary country to host country, the reverse flow is not thought of as the dominant one.

Some of the worries of governments on these lines may be ill-founded, but some are obviously thoroughly justified. The re-search of my colleagues will eventually illuminate some of these murky corners, suggesting just how seriously issues of this sort are to be taken. Meanwhile, however, a few points can be made with reasonable assurance.

Governments are right to assume that the affiliation of a sub-sidiary with an international group must have some significant effect on the subsidiary's capabilities and behavior. Where govern-ments may be in error is in assuming too readily that the subsidi-ary is a puppet on the end of a string, incapable of conditioning either the nature of the command it receives or the response it provides. Recall that the multinational corporate group embraces a coalition. The Vice President for Europe, as long as he exists, presides over a domain that he feels committed to protect. The desire of the coalition to retain the loyalty and participation of the Vice President for Europe is likely to restrain it from imposing its collective fiat, even if the action seems to make sense from a profit-and-loss point of view.

Nor should one underestimate the capacity of widely dispersed subsidiaries to resist the instructions of the center, whenever those instructions seem stupid or threatening. The subsidiary possesses facts the center cannot hope to have and alternatives of which the center cannot be aware. How extensively the subsidiary exploits its advantage in order to protect itself depends on the cultures, habits, precedents, and personalities that are involved. But the folklore of multinational enterprises, like the history of military ventures and Soviet planning, is full of anecdotes in which remote agencies in the field managed to have their way over the blind-folded center.

Whether this propensity for independence will continue to exist in the future, however, is less evident. As communication and travel grow easier, the give and take between the center and its subsidiaries will mount in volume. In the course of time, a more conscious and more fully articulated global strategy will emerge. At the same time, however, there will be greater opportunity for individual subsidiaries to negotiate with the center for exceptions and deviations from the battle plan.

One other change in the future relations of parent to subsidiary seems plausible. Parents have no desire to imperil the future of their subsidiaries; in particular, they have no desire to act as a conduit for commands to the subsidiary emanating from the parent's government if such commands would place the subsidiary in jeopardy. Accordingly, if the threat of such commands should grow, parent companies will have an increasing incentive to create international organizations along lines that reduce such risks. While yet seeking to retain the option of a coordinated global strategy, parents may look for formal relationships that do not subject them to the onus of transmitting harmful official commands. Relationships of this sort will demand new forms, but the history of corporations eloquently suggests that such forms can be devised if the incentive is strong enough.

With the collapsing of time and distance, therefore, the ambiguities, compromises, and accommodations among the elements that make up the multinational enterprise may grow just as rapidly as the integrating forms and coordinating plans. It is important to recall, however, that the compromises and accommodations will not be organized primarily on national lines. Instead, as I noted earlier, the disputants involved are likely to associate their interests much more with products or functions or with geographical units that bear no correspondence to national boundaries. The dialogue inside the coalition will turn on the issues that would concern certain peripatetic members of an international fraternity, not schizophrenic nationals torn between loyalty to master and loyalty to state.

A Glance Ahead

Several pages earlier I set myself the task of exploring the impact of the foreign investments of U.S. enterprises upon the economies of their host countries. Repeatedly, the discussion has come back to one basic point: That sovereigns feel the need for the resources that multinational enterprises have to offer, but are loath to give up the national control that may be involved in securing those resources.

A second point has also figured prominently in the discussion: that although the enterprises involved are usually thought of as U.S.-owned, their identity is likely to become more and more ambiguous in national terms. Commingling human and material resources of many nations, formulating problems and solutions on lines uninhibited by national boundaries, multinational enterprises may not be easy to classify in terms of national association. That fact is neither necessarily harmful nor necessarily helpful to the countries in which the units of such enterprises are located. But it is a new possibility that one must weigh in projecting the future reactions of nations. How ought one to appraise its significance?

My first guess is that long after any such development has become evident to the detached and uncommitted bystander, its existence will be steadfastly denied both by the nation-states and by the enterprises involved. There are certain deep-seated and tenacious forces that compel both governments and enterprises persistently to refuse to recognize any such tendency.

Consider the state of mind of intellectual and political leaders in the countries where foreign investment is located. As a general rule, they cannot bring themselves to believe that the objectives of U.S. parent companies abroad and those of the U.S. government are not intimately and continuously coordinated. There are endless illustrations that can be drawn upon to bolster the conviction—from the landing of the Marines at Vera Cruz to the enactment of the Hickenlooper amendment to the foreign aid legislation. Moreover, opinion leaders in foreign countries are aware of the intimate ties that usually exist in their own home countries between their governments and "their" enterprises operating abroad, ties that effectively restrain independence of action on the part of either side. Attempts to impart to such a well-conditioned audience the full flavor of the ambiguity, conflict, and independence that shape government-business relations in the United States are overwhelmingly likely to fail. Evidence that the ambiguity may be growing is unlikely to have much impact.

Nor are the agencies of the U.S. government itself much more disposed to entertain the possibility of increasing ambiguity. Each such agency has its needs and objectives in the foreign field. Some, like the Treasury Department and the Commerce Department, are eager to enlist the "voluntary" or statutory cooperation of firms in such programs as increasing U.S. exports, controlling the flow of capital funds, restraining trade with Communist China, and so on. Such agencies can scarcely contemplate with equanimity the view that the subsidiaries of U.S. parents abroad may not be unreservedly available in the future to serve national ends.

Finally, the firms themselves may be reluctant to recognize and articulate the subtle changes in identification that are suggested here. Conditioned to the view that national identity is absolute and unequivocal, they will be loath—understandably loath—to confront overtly the implications of an uncertain and ambiguous identity.

But my guess on this critical point may prove wrong, so I proceed to a second. If the nations and enterprises concerned should explicitly recognize the growing change in the character of multinational enterprises, I see no reason why such a response would reduce the tensions. Mere recognition will not reduce the expectation that there are to be rival efforts by sovereigns to influence or control the subsidiaries of U.S. parent corporations. Nor will sovereigns draw much comfort from the fact that multinational systems look with equal favor on the use of the personnel and capital of all countries. Assume, for instance, that young Frenchmen are eligible to climb the career ladder of General Electric to its summit and that French investors are eligible to buy G.E. stock. One should not expect these facts to gladden the heart of France; indeed, quite the opposite may occur. Such internationalization, useful and well-intentioned though it might be, is not responsive to the real worries of the French government; and, being unresponsive, it is likely to do no more than generate complaints of a new sort, such as assertions about a growing brain drain of managerial talent and a growing drain of capital funds.

Both the national sovereign and the multinational enterprise are likely to exist side by side for a long time. If one accepts that fact, then the reduction in tensions between them is probably a useful and constructive aim. How can such tension be reduced?

Some elements of the problem are less tractable than others. It is hard to see, for instance, what one can do about the skittishness of the local business community over the putative strength of U.S.-owned subsidiaries. That skittishness may well be justified to some extent. On the other hand, it may be possible to deal with other sources of the tension, notably the fact that the subsidiaries are subject to the commands of more than one sovereign state. The subsidiaries have a stake in avoiding a situation in which they receive conflicting demands from different sovereigns and the sovereigns have a stake in ensuring that the multinationality of the enterprise is not used by other states for purposes that contravene national objectives.

There are three main approaches to the problem. For some stated purposes, governments can agree on the limits to which they will extend their jurisdictional reach, so that conflicts of jurisdiction are reduced; or they can agree on the application of uniform codes, so that conflicting standards are less common; or they can surrender up their sovereign powers to the ministrations of some super-power. A recent agreement among OECD member countries, undertaking to consult in the application of national antitrust laws wherever important interests of another member country are involved, represents an embryonic application of the first approach; the standard bilateral tax treaty, coordinating the application of national tax laws, is conceived in the spirit of the first two approaches; proposals for a "world-wide corporation," chartered and monitored by some supranational body, are generated in the spirit of the third approach.

The areas to which these approaches most urgently need to be applied are those in which jurisdictional conflict seems most immediate and most pressing. These include the area of trade regulation, from the enforcement of antitrust criteria to the encouragement of concerted action among enterprises; the control of trade and payments in the alleged interest of national security; and the area of capital controls, epitomized by the U.S. capital export controls and the French capital import controls. One wishes he had the courage to add other subjects to the list: the subject of technology transfer within the multinational enterprise system, especially technology transfer involving sensitive military products, and the subject of restricting or enticing personnel in their movements within the multinational enterprise system. But efforts to deal with items of this sort might prove overly ambitious, at least in the early stages.

In all these fields, insofar as the first approach was involved, the issues raised would be roughly the same. Under what circumstances would each of the governments concerned agree to stay its hand in the application of national power? Under what circumstances would each of the governments agree to let the other reach out to apply its power? As a first step in answering these questions it might be useful to agree on the international legitimization of the Calvo Doctrine. That much-maligned principle, generated as a measure of self-protection by the beleaguered Mexicans during the 1920's, provides that in any dispute with a host government, no national entity may appeal to a foreign power to support its claims. One would have to go further, however. In the application of antitrust, for instance, governments might agree to exercise no more jurisdiction over the foreign subsidiaries of their domestic parents than they would exercise over foreigners that were not subsidiaries. In the application of trading-with-the-enemy statutes, governments might agree to relinquish altogether their indirect control over the foreign subsidiary.

This kind of approach clearly is not enough for all situations. The control over capital movements, for instance, would demand more than a mere drawing of jurisdictional lines and might lead one to think in terms of the second and third approaches suggested earlier. For some time to come, a step-by-step approach in each of the functional areas will be sufficient to absorb the energies and tax the ingenuity of those concerned.

Eventually, there will be a need to pursue the possible ramifications of the third approach, that of the supranational authority. The idea has a certain logical appeal, a certain attractive symmetry. Enterprises that are global in scope do seem to deserve a regime in which they are responsive to authorities whose scope is just as broad. At this stage, however, despite the discussions of world corporations, of world-integrating taxing authority, and of world-harmonized capital movements, there is almost nothing to suggest that the approach has immediate promise. But while awaiting the day when the approach seems propitious, there is much that can be done to reconcile the concept of the multinational enterprise more effectively with that of the nation-state.[3]

REFERENCES

1. For a characteristic polemic between economists concerned with the issue, see Solow v. Galbraith, *The Public Interest*, Vol. 9 (1967), p. 100.

2. This tendency is conclusively demonstrated by analyses performed by John Stopford at the Harvard Business School.

3. This article presents, in unelaborated and undocumented form, some concepts that are emerging from a study of multinational enterprises and the nation-state, financed under a grant from the Ford Foundation to the Harvard Business School. Four of my collaborators in that study—Professors J. N. Behrman, L. E. Fouraker, R. H. Holton, and Detlev Vagts—have been in regular communication with me on the subjects covered by this paper and have originated or stimulated many of the ideas that appear here. In due course, they will be elaborating and interpreting these ideas in their own ways, which may well be at variance with the version here.

NEIL W. CHAMBERLAIN

The Life of the Mind in the Firm

How DOES the contemporary business corporation affect the intellectual activity of those who compose it? Considering the number of people involved, such internal effects are hardly less socially significant than the external effects of business, which in many ways can claim to be the dominant institution of our society.

There are more than a million corporations in the United States, most of which are small-scale operations scarcely different in many respects from their counterparts of a hundred years ago. When we inquire into the impact of the *contemporary* business firm on its people, however, we are generally referring to those few large firms, frequently identified as the "*Fortune* 500," which are more distinctively of our times. The very size of these behemoths raises the question we are exploring. When thousands of employees are organized into an articulated system of production, what effect does this organization have on mental activity? What are some of the consequences of "scientific management" in its most recent forms—operations research, linear programming, PERT, simulation, systems analysis, and computer applications generally? Organization theory has carried the notion of functional specialization far beyond the analysis and synthesis of production processes to make it coextensive with the totality of the administrative process. What are the implications of this extension?

With size has come the bureaucratic necessity of piling layers of authority on top of one another, in hierarchic fashion, and the possibility of specialization within this layering. The large firm can afford to fragment some tasks, assigning the parts to various people, whereas the smaller company must impose the "whole" job on one individual. Such division of labor is one of the economies of scale.

The limitation on intellectual freedom that comes with specialization is double-edged. It is limited by the need for coordination among specialties. A specialist's own intelligence is subordinated to the requirement of compromise or synthesis with other minds. In effect, it makes the man who had previously operated on his own, euphemistically speaking, into a member of a committee under an authority-wielding chairman (however much the latter may draw on Theory Y or human relations principles). Intellectual freedom is also limited because the substantive field within which the mind can roam has been constricted; its license to operate encompasses a smaller territory.

A system that operates with numerous levels of authority constrains discretion at each subordinate stage. Each authority carrying the decision process one stage closer to action narrows the range of autonomy for the next stage in the sequence. Automated processes, both of production and data flow, may eliminate some of the need for human synthesis, but in doing so they simply substitute inanimate constraints on discretion for those formerly supplied by people. Individuals become part of a programmed sequence that exercises the same limitation on autonomy as the premises imposed by a manager-superior. The more extended and complex the corporation's operations, the more layers of authority are necessary to control the activity. The organizational imperative of coordinating one unit's specialized operations with the specialized operations of all other units reduces the permissible area of discretion.

This circumstance springs not from bureaucratic willfulness or obtuseness, but from the firm's having identifiable objectives. Each subunit, led by a subordinate official, has its own objectives—which are partially congruent with those of the larger system, but also partially divergent. The subunit focuses on its own specialized role in the system, and it understandably tends to exaggerate the importance of that role. A higher official, coordinating that unit with others, puts it in system perspective.

Moreover, the personal goals of those who direct the subunit necessarily differ from those of others within the system; at a minimum, they seek personal preferment over rivals from other subunits, regardless of who may be "better" for the company as a whole. The specialized roles and personal goals of subunits thus conflict somewhat with system objectives, and the discretion of those in charge of subunits must be limited in order to achieve the goals of the system as a whole.

An individual's intellectual initiatives are confined to the specialized and constrained sphere of discretion that the system permits him. If his role is that of a marketing specialist for a particular product, he is not free to let his imagination roam into production problems or matters of finance. He will be told that suggestions are always welcome, and that colleagues will be grateful for any ideas he may have to pass along to them, but he will quickly learn that organizational propriety is best served by confining his activity to his own bailiwick.

Moreover, the modern corporation operates in two time dimensions. There is first the present, an extended duration somewhat comparable to the economist's abstract conception of the short run, a period during which the company's principal assets are more or less frozen in form. The product line is given, as are the technology of the production processes, the marketing structure, and the sources of the continuous financing of ongoing operations. Marginal changes may be made in all these spheres of activities, but the corporation has been committed to major decisions from which it expects to derive a profit over the near term, perhaps a year or two. Within this period, the drive is for efficiency, and all operations are reduced to standard operating procedures that maximize profit.

The corporation also functions within the framework of the further future, when it expects to recast the form of its assets along lines that will preserve its profit position in the face of probable changes in products and production processes. These decisions involving innovations occupy the major attention of only a limited number of individuals and the limited attention of a larger number of others. Most of the employees of a firm spend most of their time being concerned with the short-run emphasis on efficient performance and standard procedures. This time focus is not more important than the future perspective, but it does dominate most of what a company does with its people's time.

Thus, in addition to the specialized role of individuals within the larger corporation, the efficiency preoccupation further constrains the play of the imagination. The large corporation specializes the functions of its people and then coordinates them to achieve machine-like efficiency. An individual who acts as a piston cannot be permitted to function as a flywheel if the system is to operate smoothly. So the life of the mind of the individual is restricted in the firm to prescribed movements and routines.

This picture is overdrawn to make the essential point, but if the rendering is accurate, only two escapes are possible for the man who wants more intellectual freedom. He can climb the organizational ladder to the headier reaches where more time is given over to planning the future, where efficiency concepts and standard routines are inapplicable, where imagination and insight command a premium. This escape is possible only for a limited number. The free spirit can, however, also escape to the outside. The organization man can accept his institutional routine only as a necessary part of his life. Serving his time by day, by week, by year, he can build his own interests outside his working life. His job is a cage from which he regularly escapes.

But surely this is a distorted picture. Every job imposes certain constraints on the individual; even the self-employed must make their activities conform to the demands of their customers. Any organization—not just the large corporation—expects its members to perform functional roles according to the script. But such functional requirements seldom so inhibit the individual that he cannot structure his job according to his own specifications in some degree. The person with a lively and probing mind will make more of his job than the individual who is passive and compliant.

The question then becomes whether there is something in the large modern corporation that halters its employees more than is true of the smaller and more informal firm. Is there a more active life of the mind in small business than in big business?

In certain significant respects largeness contributes to the intellectual vigor of the organizational climate, and big business is not always more stultifying than small. For one thing, bigness augments the potential for creative activity. To put it simply, an organization with great resources can undertake projects beyond the capacity of the small firm. There is no point in arguing the much debated issue of whether the largest corporations are the most innovative. Probably the weight of the evidence, though admittedly inconclusive, is that medium-size firms produce more new products and new technology. But that is only part of the story. Creative activity is concerned with more than invention. It includes the application as well as the creation of knowledge, the organization of vast projects, and the undertaking of major risks. The capacity to mobilize facilities on a grand scale opens up possibilities of doing things that otherwise might not be possible.

Ideas may breed in a company of any size, but making an

idea "commercial" often requires an organization that can supply manpower and funds during a period when there is little or no return, an action precluded to the small business. Telstar could not have been launched by a company with a few hundred employees and assets of a few million. Nuclear power plants were not pioneered by firms specializing in making dry cell batteries or small motors.

A large aircraft corporation can pioneer with bigger and faster jets in a way that a small producer simply cannot. There may be intense satisfaction in turning out a compact five-seater craft, but it can scarcely compare with the scientific, engineering, production, marketing, and financial challenge of making a three-hundred-seat airship a reality. In fields like aerospace and oceanography, there is room for thousands of small subcontractors to participate in specialized capacities, but only a large corporation can take on the incredibly complex task of integrating the totality of such operations and making the technical and social system work as a whole. Only large corporations can undertake projects that require large sums of capital investment and involve prolonged gestation periods or high risk. Without asserting that creative potential increases directly with size, one can suggest that breadth of opportunity can create a vitality in a corporate climate that is not possible where resources limit potential activity.

Although size is no guarantee of profitability measured as a rate of return on investment, it does tend to provide a larger absolute pool of earnings with which the large firm can play. Commanding positions in particular markets coupled with greater diversification of risk tend to make big business wealthy in any absolute sense. A smaller company may have a remarkable return on investment, but the dollar pool that it thereby accumulates is not likely to enable it to attract much attention. Thus, large and wealthy companies, like large and wealthy countries, draw off the brighter and more ambitious specialists from smaller and less affluent rivals—not all the "best brains," to be sure, but enough to turn the larger establishments into centers of excellence, well endowed with people and facilities.

Despite the restrictions imposed by corporate role, the individual in a big business is likely to find himself stimulated by lively colleagues to make the most of what his position has to offer. Indeed, they will probably push him to do just that, so that they themselves can perform their own roles more satisfactorily and satisfyingly. If this idealized conception frequently fails in practice (the stories are legion of ineffective individuals who are carried by large corporations and of others who have learned that a routine performance is all that is expected or even wanted), it probably remains true that the ideal is more closely approximated in large firms than in small ones.

Hence the paradox of the effect of an organization's size on the intellectual activity of its members: The larger firms tend to narrow the field of exercise of the mind, through specialization and a need for centralization that no amount of *de*centralization can ever fully overcome. But the larger firms also invigorate the play of the mind by creating opportunities for action that otherwise would not exist at all and by pulling together talented individuals who, at their best, can create a climate that makes the probing of even narrow areas of responsibility a challenging and perhaps even a pioneering endeavor.

Before concluding that these effects on balance neutralize each other, let us approach the problem from a different perspective.

Aside from government itself, the business firm is the dominant institution of Western society, and it is so significant primarily because it represents a form of specialization in the social system. If specialization tends to limit the life of the mind, then business dominance in our society tends to have that effect pervasively. A reasonable case could be made for the proposition that specialization has indeed become characteristic of Western life generally—in the universities at least as much as elsewhere—but there is a monumental difference between the specialization of fields of learning, none of which dominate our way of life, and the specialization of a form of activity (business) that does in fact dominate our total society.

Because this argument has been made in one way or another by critics whose socialist alternatives have been unpalatable to most Westerners does not excuse us from examining it on its merits. In its simplest form, it reduces to the thesis that it is a crippling limitation on the life of any mind to judge the quality of its play by the single standard of profit.

At a stage of economic development where existence presses hard on resources, and private control over those resources is widely diffused, such devotion to profit as a standard of efficiency is justified. Adam Smith has articulated that position eloquently—so eloquently, in fact, that his words are still being recited even though their relevance has been blunted. Our society is no longer hard pressed for its subsistence, and although economic power is still diffused, economic concentrations have developed in the form of large corporations, distributed throughout society like lumps of fat in a buttermilk batter.

Under such changed circumstances we cannot remain pre-occupied with private corporate profit as the ultimate standard by which to test the validity of the activities of the largest part of our population. It is still considered a high economic virtue that our major corporations behave like somewhat softened, but scrimping Scrooges or modest, but misanthropic misers—whose actions are governed only by the test of whether they are efficient in adding to a revenue stream and whose only purposes are limited dispersal to a limited stockholder clientele and reinvest-ment to maintain or augment the profit flow.

The life of the mind in the firm is hobbled and its vision is blinkered by the constraint to which the business institution is subject within the larger social system. The firm's specialized role is perhaps the greatest limitation on the role of the individual within it. This argument has little or nothing to do with the question of private ownership of the shares of major corpora-tions; that is a separate issue. The argument is concerned with the standards that apply to the conduct of those organizations which give our society its special character. If our major corpora-tions were wholly government-owned, but still applied only the profit-efficiency test to their operations, the result would be the same. The socialist approach provides no solution for this prob-lem; its ideology may be defended or attacked on other grounds, but not in terms of the intellectual freedom that it automatically accords to those who compose its principal economic agencies. There is much to be said for leaving control over our giant cor-porations in private hands—diffusion of discretion and power is a value not to be given up lightly—if we can broaden the standards by which we judge their activity, if we can free them from a test of efficiency more relevant to the past than to the present.

In speaking of a role not restricted by the pursuit of profit, I am talking about something more than the corporate handout to colleges and community chests. I refer to those activities that a company is particularly geared to perform, but from which it does not expect to reap any reward, on which it may indeed have to spend some portion of its own funds—activities like urban housing, slum reclamation, recreational developments, education and training programs not restricted to its own needs, cooperation with city, state, and federal governments in a variety of programs that could not otherwise be undertaken. The list is limited only by imagination.

We already have an excellent foreshadowing—in what many are doing to make the unemployables employable—of the expanded role that major companies might come to play. Some are partially compensated for their activities by the federal government, but most are using corporate funds as well, and some are wholly self-financing. (North American Rockwell, in Winchester, Kentucky, for example, has been training Appalachian rural people entirely at its own expense.) Most corporations are training these hard-core unemployed to fill jobs that they themselves expect to provide, even though this is an uneconomic way of recruiting. Some are placing their "graduates" with other companies. (Lockheed-Georgia, for example, does so on the premise that smaller firms in its area cannot afford to mount a similar training program on their own; New England Telephone runs a sixteen-week computer training program whose "products" it shares with other firms.)

Of course this present spate of activity may be only a visceral response to a temporary sense of urgency. Training unemployables may be this season's business fashion, although the indicators all point to an expansion, not a lessening, of such programs. The nature of the likely expansion is, I think, rather easy to chart. From basic vocational training for non-employees a number of companies have already advanced to the next stage—improving the literacy of their own employees. Enough have done so to make this area a promising one for a new breed of consulting firm that advises on programs or contracts for their administration. But beyond these educational elements lies the enormous field of adult education.

The notion of continuing or lifetime education has taken root in our society nourished in part by the multiple-career concept, in part by the rapid expansion of knowledge, and in part by a vague, but spreading desire for intellectual enrichment of our later years. As this demand grows, the principal resources for meeting it will be discovered within industry, particularly in the form of classroom facilities and instructors. Instruction covering everything from foreign languages to biophysics and every level from public school to post-Ph.D. can be provided—and probably can *only* be provided on the scale required—by our major corporations, particularly if they pool their resources.

It is quite possible to envision a future in which business firms will be recognized as educational institutions, supplementing the formal educational establishment, collaborating with high schools, community colleges, and major universities. There will, of course, be some direct advantages to companies from such programs, but to a considerable extent they will have to be accepted as non-profit activities designed to improve the quality of the society of which business is an integral part. Education is perhaps the most obvious field in which we can expect a social contribution from our corporations, but there are many other activities within the areas of existing or potential business competence that could be undertaken as not-for-profit operations.

Many people believe that to cast any doubt on the profit standard is to imply, as an alternative, a limitation of managerial direction, perhaps by government regulation. Others fear precisely the reverse: that managers would have excessive discretion to use corporate revenues for a variety of purposes not subject to any social sanction were the discipline of profit maximization removed. Professor Milton Friedman of Chicago and Professor Fritz Machlup, for example, question the desirability of giving managers the right to use corporate earnings in any way they see fit so long as it is not actually illegal. What would guide the managers' judgment, they ask, if the standard of profit maximization were diluted with other standards? Investments could be justified by managerial whim, so that scarce economic resources might be channeled into fruitless or quixotic adventures ranging from utopian communities to museums of vintage automobiles. Personal managerial philosophies would be free to find their expression in large-scale corporate grants to the arts, to technical education, to park development without respect to housing needs, or to housing development without respect to park needs.

The Friedman-Machlup argument has two separable strands running through it. If one is to reject it, as I do, it is worth disentangling the two. First, their argument is based on the proposition that because economic resources are by definition scarce, they should not be wasted, and their allocation should be strictly governed by a standard of efficiency. It is further contended that no standard of efficiency has proved so efficacious as unalloyed profit maximization.

Second, their case rests on the political principle that economic power should be decentralized to private hands, but that this devolution can be justified only by restricting the exercise of that power: hence the *specialized* economic role of producing goods and services for sale, under a *systematic* constraint of profit maximization. Whatever a manager can legally do in "turning a buck," or a million bucks, is socially sanctified as a valid and desirable exercise of power and discretion; anything else is suspect as *ultra vires*, beyond the firm's appropriate role in the system.

Both these defenses are highly questionable. Scarce resources have to be assiduously husbanded by a society on the edge of subsistence, but for a society in some state of material comfort other considerations are at least as relevant. Among these concerns is the life of the mind of its people. If material goods-producing institutions dominate the society, as they do ours, all those whose functional activities are involved in them are subjected to a way of life based on resource conservation—and this without respect to whether resource conservation has actually been tested by the profitability of our large corporations.

The necessity for binding managerial discretion within a tightly woven systematic web involves a matter of faith. Those who would keep the web intact are presumably reluctant to entrust humans with discretionary power. I confess to a greater optimism. The managers of our major corporations *already* possess discretionary power, and I should like to see the field for appropriate exercise of that discretion extended to embrace other activities than those with a profit potential. Such dominant organizations of our times as General Electric or Union Carbide should not be inhibited from a larger role in nonprofit areas. To the extent that we encourage a wider range of corporate activity, we are likely to encourage the accession to business of many of the more imaginative and idealistic minds among the young. I should be willing to take my chances on the kinds of programs that might emerge from those who see the corporation in larger terms. In recent months I have read statements of officials of the Xerox and Polaroid companies asserting explicitly that there must be more to business than the making of a product and a profit. They see the need for the large corporation to use its resources and its powers perceptively in integrating itself more closely with the society by moving on social problems that the front pages identify daily.

There may be irresistible pressures driving us in the direction of greater centralization of power in all organized activity—in governments, universities, businesses. But even if this should prove to be the case, the effects of this process may be partially offset by developing in private hands the capacity to undertake actions as yet associated only with government. It may be worth experimenting as to whether we cannot make ours a livelier, more creative, more daring society by invigorating the private corporate centers of power. We may, in time, develop new standards for judging the effectiveness of such institutions, but I should not want to postpone our experimenting until we have done so. The pace of change is matched too closely by impatience with the lack of change. The corporation is one resource we cannot afford to waste by chaining it tightly to the profit stake, while searching for another more suitable stake to which to anchor it.

Those large firms with their present ambiguous effects on the intellectual life of those who inhabit them have the greatest capacity to move in this direction. By loosening the specialized role of the firm itself, we can invigorate the intellectual climate within which the specialized roles of its employees are performed. Perhaps, indeed, we have become excessively infatuated with systems analysis, in which all the cooperating parts are judged by their efficiency in contributing to the performance of the system as a whole, the system conceived as a machine. Perhaps a more ragged system has its own values in social affairs, granting discretion to the parts to move with some unsystematic purposiveness of their own.

This approach would obviously de-emphasize the role of profit in corporate life, but to de-emphasize is not to abandon. As long as private enterprise prevails, some profit is essential to survival. Moving from the certain discipline of profit maximization to the more flexible standard of simply making a profit would not entirely change the game, but it would require some institutional modifications.

A lower rate of return on its investment will increase what a company must pay for its capital whenever it resorts to the capital markets to finance its growth, and it may have to resort to them more frequently than in the past if its retained earnings decline because of expanded not-for-profit activities. Stockholders who are disappointed because their shares fail to appreciate as rapidly as those of a more profit-oriented company may band together to turn out the incumbent management. Alternatively, if the profit potential of a firm is not fully realized, and this is reflected in a lower value of its shares, it exposes itself to possible assault by a raider bent on realizing the profits implicit in its assets. None of these are minor matters to those responsible for the conduct of a corporation.

Nor are they beyond solution if we are persuaded that there is social value in the effort. A reconsideration of the desirable restrictions on corporate acquisitions of other companies may be required: Perhaps corporate assets should not be used in the purchase of shares of companies in the size range with which we are dealing, with whatever exceptions seem warranted. Corporate taxation could be used to induce the wanted result—perhaps by a marked gradation past some percentage return on investment, perhaps by a lower rate for firms that have put at least some percentage of earnings into other than production purposes.

If there is the intent to encourage such broader corporate activity, we can find ways to protect companies that respond. We need not impose a new system on our corporations; we can encourage independent business action with *ad hoc* devices. In the process, we may find that not-for-profit corporate activity will take on as much glamour and excitement as corporate activity designed for profit, and that part of the challenge of the game will be to effect a satisfactory mix of the two. In such circumstances, the life of the mind in the firm will almost certainly be invigorated.

Skeptics are sure to retort that business firms—even those that are most public in their professions of social concern—do not now undertake as much in this regard as present law permits. To my knowledge, the limit of the 5 per cent rule has not been approached by any major firm. The skeptics ask why one should expect any change of behavior when business has so clearly expressed how it views its interest. They may be right. Business may not modify its social role, but the issue is not closed.

If we play the currently popular game of looking ahead to the year 2000, it is not so fanciful to picture General Electric and I.B.M., Ford and I.T.T., L.T.V. and A.T.&T.—yes, even U.S. Steel and General Motors—operating in two broad categories of activities: a profit-making sector in which they continue to exploit change and to probe the social environment purposively for ways in which to improve their earnings position; and a nonprofit sector in which they employ their organizational and productive talents, with appropriate political encouragement and tax incentives, to modify the social environment itself. Each would still decide for itself how much of the latter it would do, but public attitudes and facilitating legislation would presumably encourage bolder actions than are now typical.

The possibility that private companies would, without sanction from the electorate, come to dominate society under such conditions can be faced as a calculated risk. If business abuses its extended powers of initiative, these can then be clipped. Similarly, if big business demonstrates that it lacks the capacity to carry out this new social role, government can assume this function. But the social conscience and social consciousness that would be needed for business to be infused with a new vitality and made an intellectually more stimulating sphere of activity cannot themselves be legislated. They can only be achieved intentionally by the business institutions; at a point in time, enough must realize that to retain their dominant role in Western society they may have to shift their perspective away from profit as a single standard toward a broader set of social objectives.

MICHEL CROZIER

A New Rationale for American Business

THE LARGE corporation developed by American business seems to
be a uniquely powerful instrument for carrying on economic activity. This organizational construct has gradually come to embody
collective rationality for all industrial and post-industrial societies.
Whatever its shortcomings, its basic pattern of functioning cannot
be questioned within the present socio-economic framework.

Confronted with the extraordinary might of the American
economic machine in the early postwar years, Europeans long
refused to recognize the extent of their inferiority. Productivity was the first catchword used to hide management deficiencies.
It was assumed that European organizations would become as
efficient as their American counterparts when supervisors were
trained in new productivity techniques. This kind of training did
bring progress, but only insofar as it obliged superiors to reconsider
some of their methods. The over-all results were somewhat disappointing.

The advantages of a large market polarized attention during
the late-fifties. It was argued that European business would dup-
licate American efficiency as soon as it began to benefit from
large-scale opportunities and competition. Now that the euphoria
of the first benefits has receded, however, European leaders have
begun to recognize that this is not enough. Although European
economies have been helped in their development by these opportunities, European firms are still not so successful in utilizing the
possibilities of the Common Market as are the international branches
of American corporations. The Europeans now perceive the importance of large-scale productive units, and amalgamation has
become their new goal. Everywhere in Europe firms have begun
to look for marriage partners; in the countries with a tradition of

state intervention, leading businesses have been forced into amalgamation under dire pressure. But financial resources are an asset only if the organizational capacity to utilize them exists. Amalgamation may only succeed in building large aggregates that are no more competitive than the individual firms they replace.

After twenty years of escapism, the great confrontation brought on by general economic growth has forced Europe to acknowledge that the weaknesses of its corporations are not restricted to ancillary problems. Rather, they touch on the basic fabric of its social structure and intellectual methods. The first task must be to develop new tools for economic activities that will match the efficiency of the American corporation.

America's business superiority lies not in the resources of its firms, however immense those may be, but in the capacities of its corporations to create and develop efficient organizations rapidly, to recruit and employ able people anywhere, competing among thousands to maintain the necessary pressure and at the same time cooperating so that each organization can utilize its talents constructively. This is what makes American firms desiring to prospect the European markets attractive to European investors.

Thus, the most thoughtful business leaders in Europe study product lines decentralization, measurement techniques, government systems, and the basic rationale of American corporations in an attempt to understand the secret of American superiority; and Eastern European economic leaders tour the West to analyze the reasons why such a high level of rationality has been achieved and can be maintained in capitalist countries. Business management has become a profession in Europe, and new business schools are springing up everywhere.

But the present-day model of the American corporation—with its organizational know-how, its social structure, and its intellectual rationale—is not the ultimate organizational form for either American or European business. Europeans will have to invest much creative energy in adapting and rebuilding the American model to fit the European environment, while Americans will have to face up to new challenges and not become complacent. Such new challenges already exist and will eventually become so important that meeting them will tend to feed back on the basic institutions of American business life. We may already be on the eve of a new wave of changes that, although not spectacular, will certainly affect the basic rationale of traditional business.

The Coming Challenges of American Business

For decades, if not centuries, we have lived with the idea that business was a separate kind of calling, corresponding to a finite number of activities. We have also thought that business was primarily concerned with making money here and now and not with taking any responsibility in shaping the future. And finally most people have believed that business is a nationally circumscribed, regulated, and well-identified activity whose foreign involvement should be subordinated to national interests.

These self-evident truths are increasingly being called into question. Business is gradually entering fields hitherto forbidden to its methods and philosophy. One can already perceive the role it will have to play in long-range planning as a partner of state and city governments; and its foreign operations are expanding so rapidly that they will soon be a main source of new activities and thinking. New fields, new societal responsibilities, and new cultural environments will provide the basic challenges for American business in the next two or three decades. They will be its new frontier—the primary source of its renewal.

A generation ago, activities like teaching, caring for the sick, helping the poor, developing scientific research, or providing governmental services to a community could attract gifted men. They were supported by businessmen and sometimes even run according to business methods. But outside certain definite limits business methods were considered absolutely unethical, and to consider these activities as possible fields for business would have raised violent feelings.

Today we discover that education, health and welfare, community redevelopment, social and cultural area rehabilitation, and big science projects are the main concerns of a number of legitimate businesses. Such fields seem to attract many gifted people in the business world. Moreover, many people contend that the general acceleration of change characteristic of modern post-industrial society raises social problems that traditional public institutions are unable to solve. On closer scrutiny, these problems appear to be basically organizational—adequation of means to ends and ends to means, measurement of activities and control of results, rational programming and budgeting, organizational problem-solving, and the search for alternatives and competition at all levels. In all of these areas, the business corporation is the best organizational tool with which to locate the basic problem, experiment with pilot projects, and prepare for large-scale application. Whatever its former ignorance (or perhaps even because of this ignorance), business is able to bring revolutionary thinking to fields where it is most urgently needed.

It is important to notice that such a transfer of intellectual methods and organizational abilities has been possible because management techniques have become more and more dissociated from the content of the activities in which they are used. These methods have been intellectualized to such an extent that they can now be employed in the abstract. The introduction of management techniques into new fields where the mechanisms of the market do not exist shows how much progress has been accomplished in this direction. Once we are able to develop rationality by using artificial substitutes for traditional markets, we shall be able not only to rationalize new activities, but also to use this knowledge in traditional business activities.

It would be shortsighted to think that all these new ventures will merely result in business methods being duplicated in other fields. Many innovations and much ingenuity will be needed, and in the process of this transfer invaluable learning will be gained, both intellectually and socially. Already rather striking in this connection are the effects that large science projects have had on those firms associated with basic research. The traditional management tools have proved to be inadequate, yet management standards cannot be abandoned; as a result, new thinking has been elaborated. One can expect that a similar process will take place in the urban as well as in the social and educational fields. Dealing with such problems will involve business in a greater concern for psychological, cultural, and political factors. Business—or at least some of its most sophisticated elements—is now ready, I think, to accept such a challenge. If this is so, these new beginnings will represent the bench mark in the progress that American business makes in confronting its own complacency on such issues.

New Societal Responsibilities

The acceleration of change that is provoking business to invade new fields is also compelling society as a whole to project the consequences of present or anticipated trends in an attempt to help people prepare for and adjust to them. In the past such activities have been so highly conjectural that they have not warranted serious commitment, but much progress has now been made in forecasting. Moreover, the pressure of change itself demands that we move ahead in planning.

Planning has been anathema to the American business tradition whenever it has had discernible socialistic or bureaucratic connotations. It is clear, of course, that no progress can ever be made in the direction of planning if business must subscribe to the centralized machine-like system of a command economy, but this stage in the evolution of economic planning seems to be over. Modern and efficient planning consists first in foreseeing the consequences of a purposive social action and feeding back this knowledge to the decision-makers. Individual firms have already made great progress in this direction, and, in a way, planning is done on a larger and more efficient scale within the modern business sector of America that it is in Western European nations devoted to the ideology of planning. But the real challenge to America lies in the passage from planning by individual firms to public planning that will minimize structural as well as conjunctural crises.

This great challenge for American society and the American government will also be a major challenge for American business. The new scientific methods developed to prepare governmental decisions—cost-benefit analysis and planning programming budgeting systems—are basically substitutes in a non-market economy for the sophisticated rational calculation developed in business. Their use has already helped government and business people to find a new common language. Although the capacity of these two sets of people to cooperate on a realistic basis has been tremendously enhanced, progress in modern planning requires not only a common language, but also a new professional expertise and deep changes in the behavior of business management. The same trend that has made it possible to overcome rigidity within traditional, hierarchical corporate bureaucracies has to be duplicated outside them. Complex organized systems have to be devised to channel decision-making processes so that business decisions with general consequences for the community can be taken care of without hampering in any way the capacity of individual business units to initiate action and to compete with one another.

Broadly speaking, the capacity to maintain strict measures of results within a network of increasingly intricate systems constitutes one of the basic bottlenecks of post-industrial society. This challenge will have to be met if the rate of growth is to be maintained without entailing unbearable social and human costs. Success in this domain will, perforce, feed back on the governing practices and the philosophy of the business corporation, whose internal decision-making abilities can be enhanced to mobilize more human resources by means of sophisticated systems of decision-making.

The Challenge of a World Environment

American corporations have become more and more involved in their international connections. This trend is likely to accelerate because of the superiority of the American corporation's organizational form in solving the economic problems of post-industrial societies. Although this expansion in international operations is usually viewed only in economic terms, and difficulties are discussed at best in political terms, the problems it raises are more basic. The issue is, in fact, whether the great American corporations that tend to dominate world markets will become truly international organizations or whether they will remain basically national in orientation, thus fostering resentment and opposition all over the world. In order for American corporations to become truly international, they would have to dissociate their business methods—organizational know-how, measurement practices, job evaluation, and so forth—from their cultural background.

Americans have a natural propensity to believe that anything American is truly universal and that others have to adjust to their codes. Their economic and organizational practices are more universalistic than those of the Western European countries, but these are in many obscure ways still culturally bound—which might explain in part so many failures outside America. The present generalization of such experiences on a larger scale will be of decisive importance in discovering what is truly rational, and therefore necessary, and what is only a cultural legacy among an already burdensome corpus of principles and practices.

Cooperation among people of different cultural backgrounds in a world environment will also develop the capacity to mobilize resources and manage conflicting systems. An organization that can build efficient international teams will certainly have a greater capacity for problem-solving than a culture-bound organization.

Whatever its idiosyncratic shortcomings, each culture possesses a range of original thinking whose addition may significantly enlarge the scope of an organization's intellectual and experiential possibilities. U.S. corporations may not be able to meet that challenge, and they may antagonize the elites as well as the middle classes of the countries they enter. They may open up only enough to minimize possible resentment. But, in any case, their responsibilities for the development of a world community will be basic, and they will have to face that problem squarely.

Consequences for the Future of American Business

A simple view of these new challenges and the processes that will be developed to meet them would tend to minimize their impact. After all, the problems that will be raised are peripheral. New methods may be developed to solve them, but why should they affect the hard core of traditional business activities? This may be true for some time, but we are now aware of the swiftness with which innovations made in one field can be transferred to another.

One can argue, of course, that what is true for technical innovation has not as yet been true for organizational or managerial innovation. As early as the twenties, Pierre du Pont, Alfred P. Sloan, and a few leading corporation executives experimented with new management structures. The concept of the general office as opposed to the tradition of central management and the practice of divisional decentralization were already well analyzed at that time, but it took at least twenty years for this analysis to diffuse widely. But at that time managerial practices were still predominantly empirical; nowadays the development of research in the business schools and the growing intellectualization of organizational know-how have made business practices much more amenable to change. Moreover, the development of systems analysis and of the automatized managerial system has uncovered tremendous possibilities for new techniques and arrangements.

Managerial practices will continue to be reduced to more general abstract and intellectual operations, so that they can be universally applied to all kinds of collective activities. Moreover, new and more rational ways will be developed for handling perturbing human variables—social, political, and cultural—that had hitherto been ignored or controlled in an empirical way. Narrowing the indispensable hard core of managerial reasoning will enable business to eliminate the considerable constraints that presently exist, thereby allowing more tolerance in many fields and increasing the basic accountability of the individual. At the same time, a greater knowledge of the impact of relevant human variables will permit business to increase the rationality of its organizational systems and to tolerate deviant and idiosyncratic behavior as long as it does not hamper performing abilities.

More generally, American business will be led to reconsider some of its basic thinking about economic and social rationality. Especially at stake will be the balance between human relations and economic rationality, between the demand for participation and the necessity of innovation.

Human Relations and Economic Rationality

Teaching of organizational behavior in American business schools still evidences a curious dichotomy. On the one hand, decision-making is discussed according to a rigorous kind of economic rationality, but, on the other, human behavior is analyzed according to a completely different view that can be subsumed under the term "human relations rationality." This mode of teaching never recognizes that decision-makers are also influenced by human factors and that organizational men at every level of the hierarchy are decision-makers bound by the constraints of economic and organizational rationality.

As a consequence, considerations of human relations have always been subordinated to economic considerations. What we have learned in studying human relations has been used not to reform structures, but in an ancillary way to help people adjust. This procedure may be convenient so long as the general pressure of the environment and of competition makes it difficult to manipulate people and obliges management to bargain, but it is basically unsound and leads to the routinization of whole sectors of otherwise efficient enterprises.

Such an uneasy compromise disintegrates in fields like education, welfare, and rehabilitation, where human relations are the substance of the performance and not one of its means. If business is to cope successfully with such fields, it will have to face basic problems in integrating technical requirements and human wants. As soon as management principles are divorced from traditional bureaucratic practices, modern management will be able to integrate different kinds of rationality and to abandon the narrow kinds of synthesis that had previously been necessary to insure precise processes and performance measurement. This will lead to more open systems and allow free bargaining among more and more agents without jeopardizing the necessary rationality of the outcome. Such progress will gradually enlarge the scope of business philosophy and will be absolutely indispensable if business wants to deal with responsible prospective action.

The Problem of Participation and Innovation

A vast amount of human resources is wasted because of our inability to organize social systems that allow people to mature, express themselves, and participate. This inability does not seem to be detrimental to traditional U.S. business activities where efficiency is already so far ahead of the performances of the past or those of other countries. But it does already pose a great problem for science, where conventional management—whatever its advantages are in comparison to Malthusian bureaucratic structure—has proved a considerable failure. Furthermore this inability will become *the* central problem if business enters such human fields as education, welfare, and rehabilitation, for it is on these grounds that business will succeed or fail. New formulas will have to be elaborated; indeed, they have already been elaborated, and one can trust that they will not be confined to their original context. One may very well expect a rapid expansion of such techniques and practices as soon as experiences have been analyzed on a large enough scale. All the human and intellectual tools exist; only confidence and experience are lacking.

These capacities will be especially decisive in enabling people to adjust to change. Change has, of course, been the main time dimension of our society for a long while, and business corporations have developed the philosophy and the methods that help institutionalize it. Yet one has to recognize that change is still handled in a rather rigid manner and that one has been fostering and eventually requiring passive adaptation rather than positive involvement. Time and again research has shown that even if people do not resist change, they do not want to be involved.

This general climate of apathy may provide some useful slack within a society that needs some degree of stability, but it slows down development and will constitute one of the great challenges of the coming period when change is going to accelerate. Here again new experiences in peripheral fields may well be the basic testing grounds for the theories and methods that have been gradually elaborated from observations of organizational behavior and discussions of laboratory experiments. The general potential for innovation and growth will increase tremendously if we use all of these experiences to understand how to motivate people within a formal organization and within looser structures so that they can release much more of their own innovative capacities; and to develop ways of introducing on a realistic basis the human costs of all contemplated changes within the traditional game of business calculation.

A New Rationale

To manage collective activities efficiently, men have always been obliged to appeal to contradictory values and to order them according to some ambiguous rationale. Whatever the degree of development and the peculiar social order of society, there can be no efficient collective action without a minimum of competition, which motivates people to act, and without a minimum of cooperation, which makes it possible to maintain the regulation necessary for any kind of organization, institution, or informal system to survive.

The traditional values of American business have been competitive and individualistic ones emphasizing the basic right of any individual to enter the market on free and equal terms; this creed should not be understood as a rejection of cooperative values. The cooperative capacity of American organizations may have been greater even in their traditional period than it was in Europe, but cooperation was taken for granted in the United States. The rationale of American business at that time was profit and free enterprise, and its hero was the entrepreneur as empire-builder. Between the 1930's and 1950's, American business moved from competitive to cooperative values, from free enterprise to organization. Profit still remained a permanent part of its rationale, but the organizer replaced the empire-builder.

The last two decades have seen the emergence of a new and more complex hero, whose main capacities are less those of an organizer and more those of an expert in rational arrangements.

In a strange way, the rationale of American business has increasingly gone beyond business to become rationality itself. Profit has become a measure, still an indispensable one, but it is no more the end. The appeal of the new fields that are going to shape business in the next two decades will accentuate this trend, which may soon become the dominant one.

This process will have basic consequences, I would argue, for the place of business within American society, for American culture, and for its values. First, it will mean a considerable broadening of business perspectives and mores. Business will leave what had become, to some extent, its ghetto. It will no longer be able to exercise its past claim to direct and orient society, but it will be open in a simpler and more modest way to most problems of society. As a result, the antagonism between business and the rest of society will recede, and business will be reintegrated within the main flow of American life. Frontiers between business and other callings will be blurred.

Second, business will be the standard-bearer of the new drive toward more rationality. One can visualize a change in the trend that has been diverting the most gifted students away from business. This will not mean a reversion to the predominance of business leadership over society. Business will bring not direction, but method and the capacity to act. Business interests will probably be much easier to control and to keep in line than before.

Third, as soon as the trend for rationality has enough momentum, rationalizers and systems analysts will lose ground and give way to a new kind of hero—the creative discoverer—who will be able to discover new problems and to define them for the rational analyst.

These general changes will have a direct impact on American values. At the simplest level, one can safely argue that the traditional alternative—competition or cooperation—will be dealt with in a more sophisticated and comprehensive way. But at a higher level of speculation one would expect three new developments:

1. Creativity will emerge as one of the basic values, not in a grandiose and romanesque way, but as one of the usual reference frameworks in daily organizational choice.

2. Tolerance for individual idiosyncrasies will increase tremendously because of the need for creativity and the under-

standing of the circumstances that can help develop it, and because as more pure rationality prevails within organizations, they will be more able to tolerate deviance. Contrary to the traditional gloomy prediction of the numerous "organization men," conformity will be on the decline.

3. Men will have tremendous psychological problems in facing the pressure of a too-rational pattern of action according to which they will have to measure up clearly and without possibility of escaping to their actual size. In order to play the game of rational calculation on whose outcome one's own success and self-respect depend, one will not have to comply and be subservient, but one may have to face harsher stress. Being completely responsible for one's own success may raise more problems than result when one retains the possibility of shifting from the aggressive game of the success stories to the protective game of the unfortunate underdog.

For all of these reasons, I should expect growing tensions to develop within American culture and new opposing hedonistic values to emerge. These will be necessary to counter the dominant rationalistic values, which will not be mediated as they have been before by religious or secular needs.

R. JOSEPH MONSEN

The American Business View

IN FEW countries is business so central to the culture, traditions, and power structure as it is in the United States. The vision that businessmen have held of our society has been crucial in shaping this country into a modern industrialized nation. In fact, U. S. society can scarcely be understood without a knowledge of how businessmen view themselves and their environment. This essay will focus on three major business groups—the traditional businessman, the modern manager, and the small businessman—that are distinguished by their ideology as well as by their roles, values, and positions within society. Further insight into the business image may be gained from a discussion of the views of two non-business groups: the new generation and the intellectuals.

The Traditionalist's View

The traditional business view has its roots in the philosophical system of the eighteenth and nineteenth centuries. Although the values of materialism, independence, rationality, and achievement were not new when Adam Smith brought them together in 1776, they still provide the backbone of the traditional business image in the United States. While this philosophy is essentially one of *laissez faire*, it blossomed into Social Darwinism and the ideal of the self-made man in the last half of the nineteenth century.

Today, the traditional business view is held by those businessmen who, although unconverted to Keynes' New Economics, do not fall into the category of small businessmen. These men, along with many classical economists, commonly believe that in pursuing their own best interest they are also serving the best interests of the public. Thus, traditional businessmen contend that most problems of social welfare are best left to the smoothly functioning market to solve. Any government intervention beyond enforcing contracts and law and order is thought to upset the natural equilibrium of the market. Traditional businessmen argue that critics of *laissez faire* are overly concerned with the short run and its occasional market imperfections to the detriment of the long run. In their opinion the market will solve such problems as unemployment and inflation if it is left to work on the basis of supply and demand.

The Puritan ethic is closely linked with the traditional business view, and the virtues of hard work, thrift, and shrewd investment have to some extent been used to provide a moral justification for traditional capitalist behavior. Indeed, many scholars have argued that Protestantism and business are both compatible and reinforcing agents. The hard working, thrifty, shrewd, materialistic, and pragmatic Yankee businessman has represented the dominant image of the businessmen for much of this country's history.

That a businessman's success could be measured not by birth or social class, but by the distance he had traveled financially from his beginnings was in keeping with the egalitarian values of a mass democracy. Regardless of the bias in American literature, where the businessman is almost always an anti-hero, the business arena has been ideologically and philosophically consistent with the beliefs of a society of individual advancement based on merit. Businessmen feel strong needs for achievement because of the highly competitive business tradition as well as the strong success orientation of the American culture.

The traditional business view is often associated with the National Association of Manufacturers, the bulk of whose members are medium-sized, and often family-controlled, firms with under a thousand employees. Senator Wallace F. Bennett from Utah, former president of N.A.M. and head of a family-owned paint manufacturing firm, has often been regarded as a congressional spokesman for the organization. His voting pattern in the Senate has consistently been that of a conservative Republican. The N.A.M. is one of the major interest groups of business and one of the most influential conservative organizations in Congress, but its members held few top policy-making positions in the pro-business Administrations of President Eisenhower and President Johnson.

Challenges to the status and position of business are deeply disturbing to the traditional businessman. He naturally views with some alarm the infringements upon his prerogatives and status made by government, unions, and intellectuals—particularly in the area of decision-making—and considers such incursions to be attacks not only on himself, but on the capitalist system.

The traditionalist feels his views more and more under attack in our society. The Puritan virtues of capitalism are increasingly being called into question, and except for a relatively small group holding conservative political views, there are fewer and fewer new initiates to the traditional business ideology. In general, society has not accepted the traditional businessman's solutions to the social problems arising from competition, unemployment, social discontent, and the newer hedonistic values embodied in consumer credit and deficit financing. Thus, the emergence of a newer managerial group was provoked, in part, by the failure of traditional business to meet successfully many of these contemporary issues.

The Manager's View

J. P. Morgan's selection of Judge Gary to run the newly formed giant U. S. Steel at the turn of the century foretold a new era. In the early 1930's, A. A. Berle and G. C. Means pointed out that owner-managers, like Carnegie, were becoming less common as the heads of great corporations, and R. J. Larner has shown that the trend has continued to the present. In fact, the number of management-controlled firms among the two hundred largest industrial corporations nearly doubled between 1929 and 1963. While there are some ten million businesses in the United States, nearly 80 per cent of all manufacturing, mining, public works, transport, and commerce is carried on by less than a thousand large companies. One corporation alone, American Telephone & Telegraph, accounts for nearly 5 per cent of the nation's entire non-banking corporate assets—or more than the G.N.P. of all but eight or nine nations in the world. The dramatic growth of such giant management-controlled corporations, due in part to the great merger movements of this century, has produced a group of managers with a distinct view of business and the world.

The managers increasingly tend to have advanced degrees, to come from a broad spectrum of backgrounds, and to have worked their way up in the corporate bureaucracy. Mabel Newcomer noted in her 1965 study the rising number of men from lower economic backgrounds who are assuming top executive positions. This democratization is, in part, a result of the trend toward the large corporation, where opportunities for nepotism are more limited than they are in family-owned firms. Furthermore, education, rather than family or friends, has become the criterion for business advancement. Newcomer's study reported that 91 per cent of the top managers now have college training—a percentage ten times greater than that of the adult male population as a whole. One third of the executives had graduate degrees and 45 per cent of those executives having college degrees in 1964 held technical degrees. This shift toward an open, but highly educated and technically trained bureaucracy has been rapid, with the greatest changes having taken place in the last fifteen years. Moreover, the trend characterizes not only the largest corporations, but also the new and rapidly growing technically oriented small firms, where the managers are more closely related in outlook to large corporate management than to the small businessmen.

A growing need among certain businessmen to look at the economy and business more pragmatically resulted in the establishment of the Committee for Economic Development. The new managers' view may be considered non-ideological in the sense that their main concern is not with an established and formalized ideology—such as *laissez faire*—but with the achievement of corporate goals. Keynes' "New Economics" is no longer eschewed, as in the traditional ideology, but is regarded and used as a technique for managing the business cycle and reducing business risk through governmental monetary and fiscal policies. Thus the manager views the New Economics as a technique for increasing corporate viability.

Walter Heller, former chairman of the President's Council of Economic Advisors, has argued that, with the exception of the small businessman, all traditional business groups have been converted to the New Economics. He also contends that the Puritan ethic of the balanced budget has disappeared. His argument is not completely convincing, however. The relationship between government and big business depends largely upon the political skill of the chief executive as well as upon the pragmatic test of business profits, and many of the changes Heller sees in the traditional business outlook are the results of President Johnson's cordial relations with business and the longest sustained period of prosperity in the country's history. Since ideologies as old and deep as the traditional business ideology are not replaced in a few years, the tensions between the traditionalists and the protagonists of the New Economics will probably continue to be felt for some time in both ideological and congressional confrontations.

According to the new managers, corporate goals require the implementation of new analytic and administrative techniques to stimulate growth in total sales, to maintain cash flow, to dominate or control their market share, and to operate efficiently. Business administration has become increasingly technical. The institutionalization of innovation and product development to meet carefully planned growth rates and firm targets is only a part of the new operations research technique of management which utilizes mathematical and statistical tools of decision-making, such as linear programming, input-output analysis, and queuing and information theories. The view that these methods are *essential* to the decision-making process is important because it commits the firm to a *new approach to business.*

Although the federal government has been prevented from planning on a national scale for conservative ideological reasons, large firms—both traditional and manager oriented—have for some time regarded planning and forecasting as necessary business practices. Thus, large firms in the United States are separately and independently performing the planning functions carried out centrally by many European countries. The new managers, unlike the traditional businessmen, think of business techniques in non-ideological terms and therefore as being potentially applicable in other institutions, such as government. One need not be reminded that it was Robert McNamara who championed the use of cost-benefit analysis in government.

In general, the newest management techniques are most highly developed and extensively utilized in the largest managerially controlled and run corporations. Critics argue that this emphasis upon efficiency achieved by bureaucratic and computerized techniques has dehumanized the business firm. But the modern manager believes that the introduction of these techniques has brought about a new phase in the industrial revolution, and that those firms which lag behind in their adoption will neither grow nor remain viable— the basic objectives of the firm in the manager's view.

While there is no conclusive evidence, there are indications that managers of large firms are more aware of the social implications of their actions than they were in the past. Their increased social awareness may result, in part, from fear of stockholder or government suits. Beyond this, however, is the obvious willingness of many executives and corporations to admit that their own self-interest is served by acceding to governmental and public demands for the employ of minority-group members (particularly Negroes). Managers also see good reasons for corporations to become involved in attempts to solve the complex problems of the city. And corporate aid to educational institutions is likely to continue, if not increase, in the future. Thus, many corporations have come to engage in activities in the social area that once seemed controversial to them.

In contrast to the traditional businessman, the manager sees himself as a steward of the public interest. He thinks of his role as that of a mediator between the various and often opposing interest groups that make up the firm and its environment—stockholders, workers, customers, competitors, and the government. Such a role requires that he stress the values of cooperation, and organizational ability more than the traditional businessman would.

Studies indicate that factors other than profits are more closely correlated to management's own compensation—suggesting that the manager's incentive system does not focus sole or even predominant attention upon profit maximization. Furthermore, the manager sees government less as an opponent than as a partner. The professional manager envisages his role as an adviser to, and often a participant in, government—a very different view from that held by the traditionalists. Indeed, President Lyndon Johnson's success in dealing with the business community early in his Administration derived, in part, from his ability to make top business managers feel that they were being consulted and involved in the national decision-making process.

The increasing power of the professional managers as a group is one of the major business phenomena of this century. Former managers like George Romney, Charles Percy, and Robert McNamara have assumed prominent positions in the national government. The professional manager's power and status in society as well as his political opportunities have increased tremendously since the 1930's, with the emergence of large professionally managed and non-owner controlled corporations. Although many professional managers publicize their corporations, but remain anonymous themselves, the status accorded the chief executive of a major corporation enables him to enter public life easily if he has the desire and the talent. Nonetheless, the new manager's view of his public political role is generally apolitical in the sense that he sees his role as working with both Republican and Democratic Administrations. The manager generally believes that in most elections it would be detrimental to the corporation for it to take an open political position.

As an increasing number of large corporations have become international, more business managers have come to view the world as their market. Even though the exploration of foreign opportunities may inadvertently increase the sphere of American influence—often bringing charges of American economic colonialism —the American manager is motivated not by a nationalistic impulse, but by the possibility of expanding his markets. As a result of this broader world-view, he is now finding that major changes in operating procedures and organization are necessary to meet different market conditions, labor demands, tax laws, and interest rates. Thus, the multinational corporation is evolving into a new business form.

The Small Businessman's View

Small businessmen in this country represent a widely diversified group—ranging from the owner-manager of a small missile-component firm to the hardware-store owner, to the man who runs the corner grocery, the local restaurant, or the nearby real-estate office. Although the views of the small businessman are similar to those of the traditional businessman, basic differences stem largely from the comparative sizes of their organizations. Capital shortage and lack of trained management personnel plague the small businessman. Since he is often in service-oriented businesses, he has a close personal relationship with his customers and hence a strong customer orientation. The costs of government regulations—in terms of bookkeeping and accounting fees, for instance—are a heavy burden. Union wage settlements, generally negotiated between big business and big unions, seldom take his economic problems into account. He finds it difficult to pass on these increased costs to his customers because of his close relations with them. Furthermore, the small businessman lives with the constant possibility that he will be driven out of business or bought up by larger firms either to provide capital for necessary expansion or liquidity for his heirs to meet estate taxes. The small businessman is, therefore, one of the few risk-takers left in our society.

The independent outlook of many small businessmen has prevented them from organizing successfully on a national scale. None of the groups representing small business have memberships much greater than one hundred thousand; nor are they strong enough to carry much political weight in Congress. Thus, despite the number of people engaged in small business, their views and interests are seldom fully represented in Washington. These circumstances have engendered discontent and frustration among small businessmen and account, in part, for the highly emotional tone of their ideology.

The ideology of the typical small businessman differs from the traditionalist's only on a few major points: the economic division of interests between big and little business, a tendency toward more extreme political solutions, and a greater concern for law and order.

Although both the traditional and managerial business groups value education, the small businessman often looks at the intellectuals and the large universities with suspicion. He sees such places as Harvard, Columbia, and Berkeley as sources of the socialist ideas he opposes. Although he wants to send his children to college, he is often concerned that they study something practical and, above all, avoid being tainted by the socialist ideas he equates with big government, deficit financing, or Keynesian economics. These views stem, in part, from his generally lower educational attainments and the economic pressure to which he is subjected. In this century the small businessman has seen both his status and his power position erode in the face of better organized power groups. He thinks he is insufficiently compensated for the risks and pressures he must face.

Although there are still incipient entrepreneurs, particularly on the assembly lines, who long to have their own businesses, by no means all of the new business starts are initiated by "traditional" entrepreneurs. A recent study conducted by the University of Washington Graduate School of Business revealed that a substantial number of new businessmen were either "by-chance" types who got into business by some unexpected occurrence or "employment seeking" types who were motivated primarily by the need for a job. Thus the goal of owning their own business was not the primary reason many small businessmen entered business. Nevertheless, they recognize that small business provides one of the last opportunities for independence and individualism in a large, highly organized society. They also know the critical economic role small business plays in the service industries and the development of new products. Thus, the small businessman is disturbed all the more that his values, ideologies, and role are so seriously challenged today.

The New Generation's View

Many businessmen have become concerned recently over the younger generation's indifference or hostility toward business. Studies dealing with this issue have generated considerable data, but much of this information is conflicting. Concern about the interest of college graduates in business first developed in 1960 when the National Science Foundation conducted a survey of 1958 graduates and found that "the proportion of college graduates with the bachelor's degree finding employment in private industry [had] declined" since 1952, when a similar survey was made. In 1964 the *Wall Street Journal* reported a continuing trend among college graduates away from business careers in favor of teaching, scientific research, law, and public service. It noted: "At Amherst, it was reported that 48 per cent of its alumni are businessmen, but fewer than 20 per cent of its recent graduates have been entering business." Aroused by such statistics, a number of corporations decided to examine the matter themselves. In 1965 the Motorola Corporation made an extensive study which confirmed that fewer technically trained college students were seeking careers in business and industry.

Although such studies have resulted in predictions of an impending recruitment crisis, other data appear less pessimistic. Harvard College has reported "that a trend of nearly a decade has been continued in the Class of 1967. Every year since 1959 a slightly increasing portion of the graduating class has chosen further study in business administration." The immediate plans of the class indicated that 18 per cent intended to go into business at once—the same percentage as in 1964, but slightly higher than that of 1965 or 1966. The Harvard report also noted that "business schools seem to be drawing a higher proportion of honors graduates than in the past."

At Princeton, the director of Career and Study Services found that the number of students going into business had not varied between 1961 and 1966, remaining stable at 16 per cent. Fewer students were going directly into business, but a greater proportion were entering business after graduate school.

A survey of one thousand students on eighteen college campuses that was published recently in the *Journal of College Placement* revealed business to be the first choice of employment among students. Surprisingly, the small private company was strongly preferred over the large corporation—followed by the Peace Corps, educational institutions, self-employment, and the government. The enrollment figures for graduate business schools also indicate strong interest in business. Between 1960 and 1966, graduate school enrollment in business administration increased 101 per cent, compared to an increase of 71 per cent for all other graduate schools.

Students, at least at the graduate level, do not seem to be losing interest in business, but competition for technically trained college graduates from other rapidly growing sectors of the economy may be increasing during this period of sustained prosperity. Thus, the bases of concern over future business recruitment may be the greater demand for college graduates and the tendency for entrance into business to be postponed—rather than the hostility of a large number of students toward business.

Nevertheless, certain groups among the student population are openly critical, even antagonistic toward business. These groups, notably the hippies and the New Left, reflect in an extreme form the feelings of many young people. A Louis Harris poll taken in 1966 showed that only 9 per cent of the college seniors interviewed regarded business as "public spirited." Even 32 per cent of the seniors at business schools doubted that businessmen had the well-being of the country at heart. These views of business, although not so radical as those of the New Left, are scarcely comforting to business.

David Rockefeller reflected in a recent issue of the *Harvard Alumni Bulletin*:

I suppose young people have always had a tendency to feel that their elders have made a botch of the world. But this is the first generation I know of which has publicly proclaimed distrust of anyone over thirty. The cold fact is that many of today's young people regard me and my fellow businessmen as hopelessly corrupt. We are, in their eyes, so crippled by the compromises we have made in order to find a place in what they call "the Establishment" that we are no longer capable of recognizing the truth or acting upon it. . . . The answers that young people themselves supply to this question are not reassuring. On the extreme left, there are some who believe that American society is so evil it must be torn down—that destruction must precede reconstruction. Even among the more moderate majority of youngsters, there is a general conviction that American society stands convicted of not practicing the principles it professes.

Such a summarization of the views of the new generation, regardless of recruitment success, cannot be other than disturbing to the thoughtful businessman. It may portend an era of tensions and change for business and society in America.

The Intellectual's View

The intellectuals have emerged in this decade as a major power group in our society, affecting both student and public opinion as well as legislation. The attitudes of intellectuals toward business cover a wide spectrum from conservative, to liberal, to New Left positions.

The conservative view of business was debated most recently and extensively during the 1964 Presidential campaign. Milton Friedman, a former adviser to Goldwater, persuasively argues in *Capitalism and Freedom* that a larger role in our economy should be played by an unfettered market. He contends that business should be free to operate within an environment essentially unhampered by governmental interference. Where government must interfere—for example, to provide the money supply—it should do so by automatic and not discretionary methods. He believes that discretionary government economic policies almost invariably tend to overcorrect any situation, thus accentuating rather than dampening the peaks and troughs of the business cycle. In Friedman's view the government's major economic function is to see that the market place operates efficiently and without undue interference from any of the major interest groups—such as labor.

In *Up From Liberalism,* William F. Buckley, editor of the *National Review,* attacks J. K. Galbraith for his criticism of the automobile industry's wasteful use of resources in developing planned obsolescence. The individual, Buckley maintains, should be allowed to indulge his taste as he will—even if it means buying cars with tail fins. He argues that to prescribe for the public, as Galbraith and the liberals might prefer, is to reduce man's individual freedom. The conservative position is not the most popular among intellectuals in this country; nor is it greatly debated in intellectual circles. The controversy presently dividing intellectuals in their attitudes toward business is between the liberals and the so-called New Left.

The modern liberal in this country saw his first opportunity emerge during the New Deal of Franklin D. Roosevelt, and his greatest hopes rested in John F. Kennedy's New Frontier. Indeed, he played an important, even key, role in both Administrations. As a result of the Vietnam war, many liberal welfare programs were aborted during the Johnson Administration, creating serious tension and conflict within the liberal group. Thus, the liberal position, the largest and most dominant intellectual position in our country, is under fire from its own members, from conservatives, and from the New Left.

Arthur Schlesinger, Jr., a prominent exponent of the liberal position, has described American liberalism by saying that it is "humane, experimental and pragmatic; it has no sense of messianic mission and no faith that all problems have final solutions." This pragmatic quality of liberalism permitted Schlesinger, when he wrote a new introduction for his book *The Vital Center* in 1962 (originally published in 1949), to admit:

If I were writing the book today, I would give more emphasis . . . that American businessmen share with American liberals a basic faith in free society. I have more confidence now than then in the intelligence and responsibility of businessmen who have thought about problems of public policy; and I fear I allowed myself then to be beguiled to extreme conclusions by Joseph A. Schumpeter's brilliant but exaggerated argument that the processes of capitalism were inevitably destroying entrepreneurial initiative.

Schlesinger's change of attitude may be typical of a general shift in the liberals' position toward a much more positive view of business. As Schlesinger suggests, the liberal and the new manager are, if not one, at least close neighbors on many issues. Schlesinger finds that "the modern American capitalist . . . has come to share many values with the American liberal: beliefs in personal integrity, political freedom and equality of opportunity."

The liberal now seems to accept business as a responsible partner. "The State can do a great deal to set the level of economic activity by policies which at once will be stable enough to create an atmosphere favorable to private investment and adequate consumption and effective enough to prevent economic breakdown. Keynes and his followers have pointed out the great resources of fiscal and monetary policy." Such a statement could as easily have been written by a member of the C.E.D. as by Schlesinger. The center position of the American political spectrum which Schlesinger sees the liberals occupying is also occupied by the modern business manager.

J. K. Galbraith has further outlined the liberal's view of the relationship of business and government in his book *Modern Capitalism: A Theory of Countervailing Power*, where he contends that modern capitalism worked because government saw that each economic power group was balanced by another in a series of countervailing relationships. In some of his subsequent books, Galbraith has suggested that government use its power to solve business and social problems. In the *Affluent Society* he writes that another balance between private plenty and public want must be created to channel a larger amount of the national income into the public sector. In *The New Industrial State,* Galbraith continues his liberal argument that the ills of our business society can be cured by government's greater and more judicious control of the business firm.

The protagonists of the New Left make both Schlesinger and Galbraith seem more moderate than they appeared only a few years ago when they were debating the conservatives. The New Left is a small group. Although most of its members are under thirty, its intellectual spokesmen are older figures, such as Paul Goodman, Michael Harrington, and the late C. Wright Mills. Mills, who wrote *The Power Elite* in 1956, lumped the leadership of all major occupational groups into one elite, or establishment, that conjointly controlled the country. Paul Goodman and others on the New Left later rejected the total leadership of the society and its institutions. Goodman charges, *In Growing Up Absurd,* that business, for example, no longer offers most youth meaningful or satisfying jobs, because the profit motive has made both jobs and products profitable, but useless. Such extreme positions have created a major gulf between the New Left and business, as well as most liberal intellectuals.

The New Left views itself as a radical political group. M. C. Gettlemen and D. Mermelstein, writing in an introduction to *The Great Society Reader: The Failure of American Liberalism,* claim that "the old polarities are no longer valid. Traditional concepts— 'liberal' and 'conservative,' Republican and Democrat—contribute little to an understanding of contemporary American society. Instead, it is our conviction that Lyndon Johnson's Great Society can only be understood within a framework that contrasts it with a socialist alternative." Michael Harrington explains that "in essence . . . the New Leftists and the black militants were, for quite different reasons, proposing that a minority make a revolution." In *Toward a Democratic Left,* Harrington notes that "black power advocates and the white youth of the New Left . . . proposed [in 1967] minority strategies for the conquest of political power. . . . The radical white youth had a different, but similar, perspective [to that of the Black Power advocates]. All of the agencies of social change from the previous generation had been corrupted by affluence and co-opted by the Establishment." The New Left argues that business has taken control of both parties, and, as Harrington states, "the old liberalism . . . can even be used as a screen for corporate collectivism." Business's new interest in social problems is strongly challenged by the New Left. Harrington maintains:

What is menacing about this sudden outburst of corporate conscience should be clear. . . . Satisfying social needs and making money are two distinct, and often hostile, undertakings. If they are systematically confused, if social causes become big business, there are disturbing possibilities quite like the ones Eisenhower saw in the military-industrial complex.

Unlike the New Left, the liberals, who are dominant among intellectuals, are not opposed to the involvement of business in the problems of society. Rather, they criticize business's lack of social awareness and hope that the system can be made to work better by judicious government intervention. Despite some differences with business, liberal intellectuals appear to have increased their faith in business as a responsible partner in American democracy. This *rapprochement* between the liberal intellectual and the modern business manager could create new political alignments.

In perspective, the modern manager emerges as the dominant figure in American business. His views and methods are in the process of reshaping both business and society. The transfer of new analytical, administrative, and computerized techniques from business to the military, government, and, to a lesser extent, education is already changing and rationalizing these institutions and portends even greater transformations. The latest phase of the industrial revolution, exemplified by the view and techniques of the professional manager, is being carried abroad by the development of our largest firms into giant multinational corporations.

Although the professional manager's view will probably continue to represent the central thrust and direction of our society, the more conservative views (held by traditional and small businessmen) and the more radical positions (held by some students, intellectuals, and Negroes) will have their own impact and change society accordingly. For example, a more conservative monetary and fiscal policy may finally be pursued by the govenment due to the problems of the dollar and the views of traditionally oriented business groups. Moreover, increased state, city, and community decision-making will, I suspect, develop because of the demands of conservative businessmen, who are opposed to the large role of centralized government, and the pressure of minority groups for greater control of their local institutions. On the other hand, the demands of the New Left and other less radical students and intellectuals will cause many of our institutions to include students and minority groups in their decision-making structures. Despite such accommodations by society to the views of both more conservative and more radical groups, the force of the logic of the professional manager's new techniques and technology will maintain his role as the key figure in the shaping of our institutions. The economic as well as social and political consequences of the professional manager's view, therefore, is likely to be increasingly important in both domestic affairs and international relations.

LEONARD S. SILK

Business Power, Today and Tomorrow

I

MANY AMERICANS use the term "business power" pejoratively, implying a usurpation of the rights and liberties of individual citizens and an exercise of authority for selfish pecuniary ends. At the same time, there is widespread recognition that corporate power has had much to do with the economic growth, high living standards, and international strength of the United States. The basic question at issue is how the nation can preserve what is necessary and desirable of business power, but prevent its abuse.

Clearly, no one power element can control the nation on the full range of issues confronting it. The society is held together by a system of rights and duties—or, in Walter Lippmann's words, "a slightly antiquated formulation of the balance of power among the active interests in the community."[1] Within that somewhat precarious social order, particular interests ordinarily affect only those matters of specific concern to them. When people or groups cannot work out an adjustment of their dispute, public officials may intervene; if the officials fail, public opinion is brought to bear on the issue. Business executives are highly sensitive to the pressures of these other groups, particularly the government, and feel excessively controlled by governmental and public pressure.

Big business actually has less power today than it had in the 1890's and the 1900's, and big labor has more; but neither "dominates" the society. The New Deal years marked a decisive curbing of the power of business, and the post-World War II period witnessed a check on the power of labor. Similarly, we have seen a swelling of the power of the executive branch of the federal government, but there have been unmistakable signs recently that Congress is again asserting its power effectively.

How much power does American business, operating within this system of checks and balances, actually wield? The customary answer to this question usually offers a statistical table showing what proportions of Gross National Product, or of manufacturing, or of certain selected industries are owned by the largest American corporations. Comparisons are made between the size of American Telephone & Telegraph or General Motors and that of selected foreign countries or American states. These statistical measures are so familiar that they have lost their power to astonish and alarm. Robert Heilbroner, however, presents a fresh and awesome perspective by asking what would happen if the one hundred and fifty largest companies disappeared, by some selective catastrophe:

To begin with the nation would come to a standstill. Not only would the Union and the Southern Pacific, the Pennsylvania, the New York Central [the latter two have now merged], and a half dozen of the other main railroads of the nation vanish, leaving the cities to starve, but the possibilities of supplying the urban population by truck would also disappear as the main gasoline companies and the tire companies—not to mention the makers of cars and trucks—would also cease to exist. Meanwhile, within the nine largest concentrations of urban population, all activity would have stopped with the termination of light and power, as the utilities in these areas vanished. In addition, communication in all these areas would break down with the disappearance of the telephone company.[2]

But that would be only the beginning. Virtually all steel production would stop, as would the production of the bulk of chemicals, electrical machinery, cars, trucks, tractors, and other farm implements. The food processors would be gone, together with the cans into which they put the food. Distribution patterns would collapse, and a national credit debacle would ensue. The insurance companies would vanish with $500 billion in life insurance, effectively bankrupting a majority of American families.

But to state the matter in this way reveals the true limitations upon the power of these enormous enterprises. None of these companies is seen to have the right to starve the cities, bankrupt the country, or prevent an individual from getting or using a telephone. As the late Arnold Rose pointed out, power in the United States is diffused among government agencies, trade unions, farm blocs, civil rights groups, and individual citizens—all aware of their right to oppose and constrain the powers of great corporations.[8] There is more than symbolic significance in the spectacle of a crusading Ralph Nader bringing to heel the General Motors Corporation, the Ford Motor Company, and the Chrysler Motor Corporation, forcing them to recall hundreds of thousands of cars and spend millions of dollars. It should also be noted that Mr. Nader assailed the automotive giants with the help of a book-publishing corporation, the mass media supported by advertisers, the Congress, and the American legal system, which protected him from attempts of certain officials of the world's largest industrial corporation to harass him and invade his privacy in efforts to discredit him.

Nevertheless, it cannot be denied that large corporations do exercise considerable power over individual employees, suppliers, and customers, as A. A. Berle has recently observed.[4] But Berle contends that "these fascinating, frightening, and fantastic institutions will be strengthened rather than weakened by the application of constitutional limitations—and requirements of action—to them."[5] He predicts that a body of rules and doctrines will emerge to prevent or correct abuses of corporate power, such as discriminatory extension of consumer credit, the coercive effect of pension trust agreements, and the invasion of privacy arising from business "data banks."

The laws and procedures of a democratic society (particularly the "equal protection of the laws" guarantee of the Fourteenth Amendment) have already been brought to bear on what had hitherto been the private province of individual businesses with respect to the rights of Negroes and members of other minority groups. Although we are clearly moving in the direction of greater safeguards against the misuse of corporate powers, we still have a long way to go before we can be sure that businesses cannot curb the rights of individuals or punish them in ways that lie beyond the protection of the Constitution.

II

Large business corporations exercise great influence in American society most clearly in the form of market power—some degree of control over the prices they charge, the wage rates they pay, and the profits they earn. But this market power, though real, is limited by the checks provided by labor, farm groups, and other power blocs in the American system; by the Antitrust Division, the Federal Trade Commission, and other governmental regulatory agencies; and by traditional pressures of competition, foreign as well as domestic, inter-industry as well as intra-industry. Those powerful corporations (such as the big steel companies) that underrate foreign and inter-industry competitive pressures can still be badly hurt in the market place.[6]

Given modern technology and the economies of scale, however, some degree of corporate immunity from the pressures of competition is by no means an unmixed evil from the standpoint of the society as a whole. Monopoly power does seem to have its social uses. Fritz Machlup, an ardent champion of free markets and vigorous competition, concludes that large corporations, not subject to heavy competitive pressures and enjoying increased affluence and liquidity, are likely to increase their expenditures on investment in new plant development and new equipment, outlays for research and development, or support for pure science and higher education.[7] Moreover, it is the strong and profitable, not the weak and marginal, companies that can create jobs for unqualified Negroes, train them, and find ways to hold them to the labor force. How effective business can be in dealing with large social problems remains to be seen. There is, for example, good reason to worry that the so-called business power structure will prove to have insufficient control over the directly involved forces of urban America to deal successfully with the urban problem.

American business is rapidly coming to understand that cooperation among business, government, and nonprofit organizations is necessary if genuine solutions to complex social problems are to be reached. The old business ideology is fading, as more and more corporations recognize that "free enterprise" is not an adequate answer to all national problems. Many companies are, in fact, eager to work with government and community groups in the welfare and educational fields. Some observers cynically conclude that the heavy degree of corporate involvement in the work of government and society is only a kind of corporate fascism. Michael Harrington, for example, sees a "social-industrial complex" taking its place beside the "military-industrial complex."[8]

There can be no doubt that the alliance between large corporations and government may create problems of monopoly and privilege. In speaking of the emergence of the "military-industrial" complex, President Eisenhower cautioned:

This conjunction of an immense military establishment and a large arms industry is new in the American experience. The total influence—

economic, political, even spiritual—is felt in every city, every state-house, every office of the federal government. We recognize the imperative need for this development. Yet we must not fail to comprehend its grave implications. Our toil, resources, and livelihood are all involved; so is the very structure of our society.

In the councils of government we must guard against the acquisition of unwarranted influence, whether sought or unsought, by the military-industrial complex. The potential for the disastrous rise of misplaced power exists and will persist. . . .

It is the task of statesmanship to mold, to balance, and to integrate these and other forces, new and old, within the principles of our democratic system—ever-aiming toward the supreme goals of our free society.[9]

Adam Yarmolinsky contends that the "military-industrial complex" is not a conspiracy, but that "there are coincidences of interest among the military project officer who is looking for a star, the civilian who sees an opening for a new branch chief, the defense contractor who is running out of work, the union business agents who can see layoffs coming, and the congressman who is concerned about campaign contributions from business and labor as well as about the prosperity of his district."[10]

Eisenhower was, of course, voicing a conservative view not at all unwelcome to a sizable majority of American businessmen. Although some businesses benefit greatly from increasing military expenditures, many more regret that they are burdened with heavy taxes to pay for them. Most American businesses, including the largest, do not like the uncertainties, high taxes, government controls, and physical dangers that go with war; they do not want a permanent garrison-state economy. Their preference may be partly ideological, but it has also become profit-oriented, contrary to the traditional Marxist assertion that businessmen favor war as a guarantor of high profits. Whatever the past truth of this assertion may have been, both U.S. industry and Wall Street have clearly come to prefer peace to war, especially since the emergence of modern fiscal and monetary policies that have made it possible to keep the national economy at a high level of activity without the impetus of war.[11]

A significant number of business firms, heavily involved in defense production, continue to promote higher government expenditures in the areas in which they are operating, but such firms can be rather clearly separated from most American businesses, which prefer to operate in the private sector. Again the reason is primarily financial, rather than ideological. A statistical study of defense and nondefense-oriented corporations by Murray Weidenbaum finds that the stock market evaluates government-oriented corporations less favorably than market-oriented firms.[12]

This results, at least in part, from the inherent instability of the government market and the historical volatility of the fortunes of individual contractors. The relatively low payout ratio (the proportion of net income which is disbursed to stockholders in the form of cash dividends) may also have an adverse effect. Reflecting these factors, earnings of defense companies tend to be more fully discounted, as shown by lower price-earnings multiples—10.9 versus 20.6 for the period 1962-65. The results for 1952-55 were not substantially different. Similar investor reluctance toward government-oriented corporations is evident in the bond market. . . .[13]

With reference to the possibility of the disappearance of that line between the mature corporation and the state, the market at least seems to distinguish increasingly clearly between government-oriented and market-oriented corporations.[14]

Nevertheless, one can safely expect that many American industries—not only those in the defense or space fields, but also those in transportation, oil, steel, chemicals, communications, shipbuilding—will continue to seek privileges, subsidies, tariffs, and market protections of many kinds from government. Thus, it is always necessary to safeguard the interests of the whole society against the bids for special favors of individual companies or industries.[15]

III

Despite continuing pressures for monopoly, with or without the help or collusion of government, the possibility for a basically liberal and competitive economic system to survive has been greatly enhanced by the advances in economic theory and policy in recent years. The major weakness of the capitalist system has been its tendency to undergo wide swings from boom to bust. But the progress in economics since the Depression makes one fairly confident that a similar national and international catastrophe can now be avoided by monetary and fiscal policies. A serious question remains, however, as to whether we will use intelligently what economic knowledge we have. There is still considerable economic illiteracy among businessmen, politicians, and the gen-

LEONARD S. SILK

eral public. Political opportunism and narrow self-interest may frustrate the sensible use of economic policy for preserving an environment of full employment, so necessary to maintain an essentially free market economy.

Overwhelmingly, American business shrinks from government-sponsored central planning and coordination. Events since 1962, when interest in the French indicative planning was at its height in this country, have borne out Edward S. Mason's prediction that such planning would be rejected here chiefly because of the attitudes of Americans generally and of American business in particular.[16] Work on input-output models, in which a number of American companies are now participating, illustrates how little central government or business control there is over the entire process of allocation of resources and distribution of income. Even the attempt at getting some orderly over-all projecting and planning of federal expenditures done publicly has encountered strong resistance from the Johnson Administration. The recommendations of the President's Commission on Budget Concepts for detailed, long-range projections of federal outlays were tempered seemingly because of the Administration's hesitancy to commit itself to long-range plans.

Although there have been some important business converts to Keynesian economic policies ("the New Economics"), most businessmen, especially men with small businesses, have been confused and wavering in their support of flexible national policies to ensure economic stability. In their daily activity, the majority of American companies still seek to control the environment in which they operate not by an alliance with government, but by marketing efforts. Nevertheless, business support for compensatory policies does seem to be increasing, albeit slowly, as the successful outcome of the long struggles for the tax cut of 1964 and the tax increase of 1968 would indicate.

Risk and uncertainty remain the dominant characteristics of the business environment. American businessmen still worry continuously (if not quite so fearfully as in the pre-Employment Act of 1946 period) about the business cycle and its impact upon the sale of their particular products. The company economist's fundamental job is to predict (imperfectly) events over which his employer exercises little, if any, control.

Clearly, neither the federal government nor the business power structure is going to establish central planning, open or secret,

196

for the American economy in the near future. Indeed, the trend in the industrialized world among economists and government officials alike appears to be toward a greater appreciation of the role of markets in the effective allocation of resources.[17] In order to achieve greater efficiency and greater sensitivity to consumer demands, even the advanced Communist countries are struggling toward a reconstitution of markets and toward greater decentralization and autonomy in decision-making for producing units. Abram Bergson finds wide agreement today that "the proverbial claims of socialists regarding the economic superiority of their system over capitalism have not been vindicated."[18] In the future, he suggests, it will become even harder for the socialist economies to catch up because the capitalist countries will continue to improve the performance of their economic systems "through the further development of macro-economic forecasting procedures; the continued improvement in information available to businessmen on the state of the market and in their techniques of interpreting this information; and the further extension and improvement of accounting and other internal controls, with or without the use of computers."

IV

The market economy, as it has evolved in this century, evidently does not lend itself to the emergence of industrial dictators. It is now three quarters of a century since Henry Demarest Lloyd warned that "this era is but a passing phase" in the evolution of "corporate Caesars."[19] Robert Heilbroner argues that, instead of corporate Caesars, "we are left with a largely faceless group known as 'management,' whose names the public neither knows nor cares about."[20] J. Kenneth Galbraith agrees and suggests that corporate power has passed to a bureaucracy of technicians, "the technostructure."[21] The prediction of a technocratic takeover was first made, of course, by Veblen in 1919; he asserted that the "technologists" were discovering that together they constitute "the indispensable General Staff of the Industrial System" and could, "in a few weeks, incapacitate the country's productive industry."[22]

Heilbroner and Galbraith have, I think, somewhat overstated the case. Many board chairmen and presidents are far from powerless either outside or within their own organizations, and "the technostructure" does not make the most important business decisions or provide its own leadership in corporations. As I observe corporate behavior, organizational achievements or failures are more related to the performance of top management than to the technostructure.

American technologists are as far away today as they were fifty years ago from taking control of the American economic system or the corporations in which they are employed. Scientists or engineers customarily strive to achieve power within the business world by making themselves into *businessmen,* rather than by remaining technicians. One route that leads in the direction of genuine corporate power is through graduate work in business or executive training courses paid for by their employers, and schools of business administration endow their graduates not with the values of a new technological elite, but with the attitudes of the existing profit-oriented business management. Business management does not *fear* the technologists; it needs all sorts of specialists to solve problems not only of production, but of marketing, finance, and accounting and to cope with the corporation's labor, community, and government relations. Top management is pleased when a specialist shows that he is qualified for general managerial responsibility and has a highly developed sense of the importance of making money.

Business is, at the same time, certainly becoming more demanding intellectually, one reason for business's great concern about the state of American education. Nevertheless, as much as business today needs educated brains, it retains a certain wariness of "intellectuals," if one defines the intellectual (rather than the technician) as J. P. Nettl does:

There are three main components to the definition of an intellectual. In the first place, his concerns tend to be universal. He is not a specialist, but one for whom any specialist activity always relates to a whole. He thus necessarily trades in generalizations—at least his views and statements are always intended to be capable of generalization. Here the idea of the intellectual as the conscience of society becomes relevant. . . . Second, his concern, and therefore the validation of his activities in the eyes of others, is cultural. He is concerned with the *quality* of life. . . . Finally, an intellectual is always strongly concerned with social and political matters; better, his is a socio-political role.[23]

Intellectuals have often shown a flair for political power, but rarely an ability or a willingness to operate complex organizations, whether governmental, business, or labor. On the whole, business has done a better job than organized labor in attracting and retaining intellectuals as well as technicians. It has done this in part by rewarding them well and in part by granting them a relatively greater degree of freedom than do labor unions. As academic pay and perquisites have risen, however, it has become more difficult than it once was for business to attract intellectuals.

A number of thoughtful observers of the American scene have concluded that the era when creativity and innovation were centered in the world of business is now passing, and that the locus of power is shifting from the business world to other sectors of the society, especially to the universities and research centers. Daniel Bell, for example, writes:

Perhaps it is not too much to say that if the business firm was the key institution of the past hundred years, because of its role in organizing production for the mass creation of products, the university will become the central institution of the next hundred years because of its role as the new source of innovation and knowledge.

To say that the primary institutions of the new age will be intellectual is not to say that the majority of persons will be scientists, engineers, technicians, or intellectuals. The majority of individuals in contemporary society are not businessmen, yet one can say that this has been a "business civilization." The basic values of society have been focussed on business institutions, the largest rewards have been found in business, and the strongest power has been held by the business community, although today that power is to some extent shared within the factory by the trade union, and regulated within the society by the political order. In the most general ways, however, the major decisions affecting the day-to-day life of the citizen—the kinds of work available, the location of plants, investment decisions on new products, the distribution of tax burdens, occupational mobility—have been made by business, and latterly by government, which gives major priority to the welfare of business.

To say that the major institutions of the new society will be intellectual is to say that production and business decisions will be subordinated to, or will derive from, other forces in society; that the crucial decisions regarding the growth of the economy and its balance will come from government, but they will be based on the government's sponsorship of research and development, of cost-effectiveness and cost-benefit analysis; that the making of decisions, because of the intricately linked nature of their consequences, will have an increasingly technical character. The husbanding of talent and the spread of educational and intellectual institutions will become a prime concern for the society; not only the best talents, but eventually the entire complex of social prestige and social status will be rooted in the intellectual and scientific communities.[24]

Robert Heilbroner worries that the shift of power to the intellectuals and technicians may assume a nasty, authoritarian character before it eventually grows gentler and more humane. He fears that we may first experience a dictatorship of the intelligentsia and technicians: "There lurks a dangerous collectivist tinge in the prospect of controls designed for the enlargement of man but inherently capable of his confinement as well." Nevertheless, he believes that all advanced industrial states—the U.S.S.R. as well as the U.S.—must make way for "the scientific cadres, the social scientists, the skilled administrators, and the trained brains." Admittedly, says Heilbroner, the intellectuals and technicians have not yet "divorced their social goals from those of the society to which they are still glad to pay allegiance, and no more than the thirteenth-century merchants huddled under the walls of a castle do they see themselves as the potential architects and lords of a society built around their own functions. But, as with the merchants, we can expect that such notions will in time emerge and assert their primacy over the aims of the existing order."[25]

Herman Kahn and Anthony Wiener also anticipate a "shift from private business enterprise as the major source of innovation, attention, and prominence in society," as the work of society becomes increasingly concentrated in the government, the professions, the nonprofit private groups, and the like.[26] Zbigniew Brzezinski observes that "in the post-industrial technetronic society plutocratic pre-eminence comes under a sustained challenge from the political leadership which itself is increasingly permeated by individuals possessing special skills and intellectual talents. Knowledge becomes a tool of power, and the effective mobilization of talent an important way for acquiring power."[27] Brzezinski thinks that, unlike the revolutions of the past, the developing scientific-intellectual metamorphosis of society "will have no charismatic leaders with strident doctrines, but its impact will be far more profound."[28]

J. Kenneth Galbraith ends his *New Industrial State* with this manifesto: "We have seen wherein the chance for salvation lies. The industrial system, in contrast with its economic antecedents, is intellectually demanding. It brings into existence, to service its intellectual and scientific needs, the community that, hopefully, will reject its monopoly of social purpose." That new community—the "educational and scientific estate"—will wax in power, Galbraith contends, as the financial community wanes and "the trade unions retreat, more or less permanently, into the shadows."[29] Although some writers, such as Brzezinski, seem to think that the metamorphosis of society will be gradual and gentle and may not involve an actual push for political power by the scientists and intellectuals, Galbraith implies that they will have to mold themselves into a conscious, new political force:

The educational and scientific estate is not inhibited politically by the ties of organization. It is also growing rapidly in numbers. It still lacks a sense of its own identity. It has also sat for many years under the shadow of entrepreneurial power. A seemingly respectable measure of cynicism as well as a residual Marxism join in deprecating any political power not founded firmly on the possession of money. Yet it is possible that the educational and scientific estate requires only a strongly creative political hand to become a decisive instrument of political power.[30]

I do not feel that a realistic model of the structure of the society and the economy emerges from the speculations of scholars who prophesy the decline of American business as a central institution. Their prognostications greatly underestimate the flexibility and adaptability of American business. Their culture-heroes are anti-bourgeois, but there are paradoxes in the situation they describe. Business has great power today, but only as one important element in a pluralistic society. It is less dominant than either Marxist ideology or Post-Industrial Society reasoning would imply. The sustaining source of business power has been its ability to innovate and to keep developing.

It is incontrovertible that there are many intellectuals and specialists who are hostile to business. Others—in great number—work for business corporations and even invest in business enterprises. Stock ownership, for example, has risen enormously in America, even on university campuses and in research centers. As A. A. Berle notes:

Directly, there may be 23 million owners of stock in the United States. Indirectly, through pension and similar funds, some 30 or 40 million more Americans have a beneficial interest in the market value assigned by share quotations to the accumulated corporate assets—and a still more direct interest in the income generated and partly distributed by them.[31]

The capitalist system, as Father Harbrecht has said, "seems well on the way to digesting itself."[32] Already vast and rapidly growing sums of money are flowing into financial institutions out of the weekly and monthly pay packets of individuals and then moving into the market to buy up ownership of American industry. In 1955, all these financial institutions—such as pension funds, state and local retirement funds, life insurance companies —increased by $1.5 billion their purchases of common stocks of corporations; in 1967, these institutional purchases increased by $7.4 billion. In the year 1973, according to estimates of Scudder, Stevens, and Clark, an investment counseling firm, the new institutional demand for equities will climb by $13 billion. In addition, of course, as Americans' incomes rise, individuals will be buying more and more stock directly and through mutual funds. A huge bidding up of equity values over time appears in prospect. This growing involvement of Americans in the ownership of stock, directly or indirectly, is likely to have subtle but profound effects in strengthening the foundations of American capitalism. It will provide a kind of political barrier to moves by government that could seriously undermine business profits or growth. Will masses of affluent Americans be responsive to some future call that they unite to change the system radically, since they have nothing to lose but their stocks, mutual funds, and pension rights? It seems unlikely.

Moreover, one of the most striking trends of our time has been the extremely effective performance of American corporations as they have moved into international markets. The huge sale of Jean-Jacques Servan-Schreiber's *Le défi américain* is one indication of Europe's recognition of and concern over the remarkable drive of American business management. The Europeans do not lack scientific and technological prowess; on the contrary, as they themselves like to point out, Europeans did most of the basic work in such major fields as nuclear energy, antibiotics, jet propulsion, radar. The American business advantage comes from the application of significant ideas and discoveries; it has to do fundamentally with the capabilities of industrial management, engineering, finance, marketing—the willingness to take risks and the willingness (indeed the zeal) to change.

This is not a new phenomenon in America. The prophetic de Tocqueville wrote in 1835:

I accost an American sailor and inquire why the ships of his country are built so as to last for only a short time; he answers without hesitation that the art of navigation is every day making such rapid progress that the finest vessel would become almost useless if it lasted beyond a few years. In these words, which fell accidentally, and on a particular subject, from an uninstructed man, I recognize the general and systematic idea upon which a great people direct all their concerns.

This general and systematic idea gave rise to other characteristically American institutions: mass public education and a labor force that (though far from ideal, especially in old crafts) largely recognizes its own stake in technological progress. American business corporations have shown in recent years that they have not lost their creativity and adaptability, but increased them by their liaison with the learned world. The new intelligentsia is helping to change the style and mood of our society, but it is not producing a radical change in the structure of the society or the economy. Business will, I think, prove to be flexible enough to adapt to these shifts in style and mood. Indeed, American businesses have shown a remarkable ability to ride the trends of the times—to produce the instruments and tools of learning, loafing, calculation, reasoning, fighting, extending life and curbing fertility, traveling through space (inner and outer), or whatever it is the human race wants to do. Thus, it seems to me, the "research revolution" has increased rather than reduced the capability of American corporations to survive and grow.

A new element is becoming apparent in the growth process . . . one that is destined to have a powerful impact on the pace of economic growth in the future and, even more than that, on the structure of our society and the nature of our civilization.

That element, largely a postwar phenomenon but with roots that go back to the first industrial revolution, is industry's new understanding of the importance of regular, systematic investment in scientific research and development.

The principle and practice of making regular provision for the discovery and development of many new ideas, new things, is taking increasing hold in American business, though its use still varies widely from industry to industry. It is already an important factor; and in the future it is likely to provide the spur to growth that came in earlier periods from particular developments such as steam power, railroads, electricity, automobiles. In reality, this discovery of the process of discovery represents a new revolution, a deep-going extension of capitalism's growth process.[33]

The performance of American industry in the past decade would seem to justify such optimistic words.

At the same time, however, economic growth and technological progress also produce social stresses and strains that may in the short run appear to outweigh the beneficial effects of industrial advance. American business must prove that it can be just as adaptable and imaginative socially and politically as it has been industrially if it is to avoid having more serious curbs imposed upon its freedom of operation. A failure of business to help solve the outstanding social issues of our time would, indeed, bring about the demise of business power. As Berle puts it, "power will invariably enter and organize any situation threatening chaos or disorder."[34] There have been moments in the recent past when the United States has ceased to be a workable society. The breakdown of the society expressed most tangibly in riots, crime, and urban decay has, in fact, called forth the serious efforts of businessmen, whose deepest faith is that things must work, or, if they do not, that they must be fixed.

. To do the job that needs to be done, business must, however, achieve a new conception of its role in the society. In the past the essence of American business power has been ideological—that is, it has provided the value conceptions and set the limits upon what the nation is doing or trying to do. Those conceptions must now be made more humane and sensitive to the needs and aspirations of all people, but especially to those at the bottom of society. The ideological limits that have prevented us from using our matchless resources of energy and imagination for improving the quality of American life need to be widened. If business plays its full role in this effort, it will help the society to avoid chaos and stagnation, on the one side, and an excessive concentration of power in the hands of government, on the other.

REFERENCES

1. Walter Lippmann, *The Phantom Public* (New York, 1925), p. 100.

2. Robert Heilbroner, *The Limits of American Capitalism* (New York, 1966), pp. 11-12.

3. Arnold Rose, *The Power Structure* (New York, 1967).

4. A. A. Berle, *The Three Faces of Power* (New York, 1967), pp. 39-45.

5. *Ibid.*, p. 48.

6. See J. E. Meade, "Is 'The New Industrial State' Inevitable?," *The Economic Journal*, Vol. 78 (June, 1968), pp. 372-92.

7. Fritz Machlup, "Corporate Management, National Interest, and Behavioral Theory," *The Journal of Political Economy*, Vol. 75, No. 5 (October, 1967), p. 774.

8. Michael Harrington, *Toward a Democratic Left* (New York, 1968), pp. 84-109.

9. President Dwight D. Eisenhower's Speech to the Nation (January 17, 1961).

10. Adam Yarmolinsky, "How the Pentagon Works," *The Atlantic Monthly* (March, 1967).

11. See, for instance, "Dovish Wall Street: Intensification of War in Vietnam Now Causes Big Stock-Price Drops," *Wall Street Journal*, March 6, 1968.

12. Murray L. Weidenbaum, "Arms and the American Economy: A Domestic Convergence Hypothesis," *American Economic Review*, Vol. 58, No. 2 (May, 1968), pp. 428-37.

13. *Ibid.*, p. 435.

14. *Ibid.*, p. 436.

15. For an excellent current treatment of this theme, see Walter Adams, "The Military-Industrial Complex and the New Industrial State," *American Economic Review*, Vol. 58, No. 2 (May, 1968), pp. 652-65.

16. E. S. Mason, Presidential Address to the American Economic Association, "Interests, Ideologies, and the Problem of Stability and Growth," *American Economic Review*, Vol. 53, No. 1, Part 1 (March, 1963), pp. 1-18.

17. See Meade, "Is 'The New Industrial State' Inevitable?".

18. A. Bergson, "Market Socialism Revisited," *The Journal of Political Economy*, Vol. 70, No. 5 (October, 1967), p. 672.

19. Henry Demarest Lloyd, *Wealth Against Commonwealth* (New York, 1899), pp. 9-10.

20. Heilbroner, *The Limits of American Capitalism*, pp. 24-25.

21. J. Kenneth Galbraith, *The New Industrial State* (Boston, 1967).

22. Thorstein Veblen, *The Engineers and the Price System* (New York, 1921), quoted in Daniel Bell's Introduction (1963 edition), p. 16.

23. J. P. Nettl, "Are Intellectuals Obsolete?," *The Nation* (March 4, 1968), p. 301.

24. Daniel Bell, "Notes on the Post-Industrial Society," *The Public Interest*, No. 6 (Winter, 1967), p. 30.

25. Heilbroner, *The Limits of American Capitalism*, pp. 128-29.

26. Herman Kahn and Anthony Wiener, "A Framework for Speculation," *Dædalus*, Vol. 96, No. 3 (Summer, 1967), p. 720.

27. Zbigniew Brzezinski, "America in the Technetronic Age," *Encounter*, Vol. 30, No. 1 (January, 1968), p. 18.

28. *Ibid.*, p. 16.

29. Galbraith, *The New Industrial State*, p. 399.

30. *Ibid.*, pp. 294-95. Galbraith notes the difficulty of finding the right term to describe the large group associated with education and scientific research apart from that undertaken by the "technostructure"—that is the technicians and managers tied to business and industrial organizations. "In political discourse," says Galbraith, "they are grouped with writers and poets and referred to either as intellectuals or eggheads. The first term is too restrictive in its connotation and if not too restrictive, too pretentious. The second is insufficiently solemn. One should coin a new term only as a last resort; we have a great many words already and new ones always afflict the ears. Accordingly, I have appropriated and somewhat altered the usage of my friend Professor Don K. Price." *Ibid.*, pp. 282-83.

31. Berle, *The Three Faces of Power*, p. 31.

32. Paul P. Harbrecht, S. J., "The Modern Corporation Revisited," *Columbia Law Review*, Vol. 64 (December, 1964), pp. 1410-26.

33. Leonard S. Silk, *The Research Revolution* (New York, 1960), pp. 14-15.

34. Berle, *The Three Faces of Power*, p. 4.

ANDREW SHONFIELD

Business in the Twenty-First Century

ANY ATTEMPT to speculate systematically about the long-term future of business enterprise forces one to take a view about the evolution of the whole institutional apparatus of modern society. The corporation occupies a commanding position in that portion of the system which is most obviously destined to grow. And it can hardly grow in importance without jostling other established centers of power. How will they respond to being jostled? The answer will very largely influence the relations between the corporation and the groups on which it most intimately depends— the consumers of its products, the labor that produces them, the shareholders that own its property, and the government that intermittently interferes with the way in which the business is run.

A simplifying device is to think of these relations in the framework of the crucial confrontation between the corporation and the state—rivals in certain areas of activity, close collaborators in others. I use the term "state" here as a convenient shorthand for public authority in its most general sense—that is, to include both the courts and the smaller agencies of collective power which are subject in the last resort to the central government, but operate from day to day with a considerable measure of independence. One has the impression nowadays that the dialogue between the corporation and the state consists largely of a simple assertion by the former: "Anything you can do, I can do better." And the claim is widely conceded by the public, indeed by many of the servants of the state itself. This is a remarkable reversal of roles compared with two or three decades ago. The reversal is so complete that it is worth reminding ourselves of how the relative authority and efficiency of these two rivals used to be regarded in the 1930's and 1940's. The failure of business enterprise as an instrument of social progress was celebrated at length in America during the New Deal and later on in Europe in a spate of postwar legislation transferring vast quantities of industrial and commercial property from private to public ownership.

The disenchantment with private enterprise was more complete in Europe than it was in the United States. The popular antipathy toward it had a systematic ideological content of a politically respectable kind in European social democracy. There has never been any anti-capitalist movement comparable to this either in political power or popular respectability in the United States. So the European reversal of opinion is especially noteworthy. It seems likely that one reason why the corporation has been rehabilitated so rapidly in the face of the established prejudice against it is the general disappointment with the performance of the postwar state as the manager of economic enterprise.

Yet this, too, is strange on the face of it. State intervention in the economy since the Great Depression almost certainly represents the biggest single achievement of a nonmilitary character in the history of modern government. The advance of social welfare and the maintenance of an orderly and stable economic structure during a period of exceptionally rapid growth have demonstrated the capacity of the state in new fields of economic and social management. Why, then, is there so little popular sentiment, even among the socialists in Western Europe, in favor of any general extension of the role of the state as entrepreneur displacing the conventional business corporation? The answer is largely that the state, through the changes it has wrought in the economic environment during the last quarter of a century, has provided the corporation with a splendid opportunity to demonstrate its flexibility and responsiveness as an instrument for meeting people's changing wants. The agencies of the state have seemed, by contrast, to be ponderous and insensitive.

The following are some of the specific elements in the rehabilitation of large-scale business enterprise. First, it has managed to establish rather better personal relations with the consumers of its goods and services than has the state. It is true that the typical products of the two are different, and the public does not have much opportunity for comparing like with like. Still, the overwhelming impression emerges that the average consumer in an advanced Western country does not believe that he would secure better service for his personal needs if more of the things which he buys today were produced and sold by the state. The second point is related to this: It is that the large corporation, which had a bad reputation, sometimes bordering on the sinister, for pursuing a variety of restrictive policies during the period between the wars, has come to be seen as an exceptionally powerful instrument of innovation. It is not that it is more fecund than its rivals in generating important new ideas; its strength lies in its proved ability to convert ideas, especially in the field of technology, very rapidly into useful products. The contrary reputation, reflected in the writings of critics like J. K. Galbraith—that the chief talent of contemporary business is in the creation of frivolous desires whose satisfaction makes no significant difference to the sum of human happiness—has so far not dented the image of the corporation as a beneficent innovator.

The social position of the large corporation has also been improved by its well-publicized attachment to the techniques of scientific management. This is the opposite of the nepotism that was widely believed, on quite plausible grounds, to be an inherent feature of organizations in which the ultimate power was held by the owners of share capital. While the corporation management liberated itself from the tutelage of the owners of the business, it also set about establishing a closer and more amicable relationship with the organized labor in its employ. In a growing number of instances, the active participation of trade unions has been sought in the process of innovation. And the new kind of wage bargain recognized certain *prior* claims of the wage-earners on the extra income that the innovating corporation expected to obtain. Thus, the brute fact of ownership, which had for so long dominated the political debate, lost some of its portentous quality.

Instead, the issue has come to be seen to be about the form of organization of large-scale enterprise—the powers of the management, the rights of the employees, the relationship between the management and the owners, whether the latter are private shareholders, a government, or some mixture of public and private interests. The final element in the structure of respectability which the large corporation has successfully established for itself in the postwar world is its position in several countries as the active and willing partner of the state in the conduct of major national policies. Outside the Anglo-Saxon world, big business commonly held a position in the past which was recognized as being analogous to that of a quasi-public authority. But that did not mean that it was particularly amenable to the public interest as the government of the day defined it. The strengthening of governmental power, together with the taming of some of the primitive ideological urges of an earlier generation of big business, have provided the basis for the practice of economic planning in contemporary capitalist society. The dependence of the planners on bargains made with a comparatively small number of major enterprises in key sectors of industry has come to be increasingly recognized—on both sides. The small group of major firms in an industry, sometimes fewer than half a dozen, are also aware that their business operations may be profoundly affected, for good or ill, by the interventions of government in a steadily growing range of economic and social activities.

The Expansive Giants

Thus, while the large business corporation has a secure status as a powerful and reliable social instrument, its position still depends on acting in the role of junior partner to the state in the pursuit of certain public purposes. The next stage in this exploration is to ask whether there are any identifiable forces that would tend to enlarge the social authority of the corporation vis-à-vis the conventional agencies of the state. To do this, I propose to examine some probable trends in the future relationship between the large corporation and the other bodies with which it is, and will remain, in close day-to-day contact: the consumers of its products, its shareholders, organized labor, government in the forms of executive power and of judicial power.

The method is to discover what constraints and what opportunities for expansion of corporate authority each of these relations seems likely to provide. For this exercise a number of assumptions have to be made about the basic economic climate during the remainder of this century. My own can be briefly stated. They are based on an extrapolation of trends which have become increasingly marked in the past two decades. I assume that production will continue to grow, and that although there may be variations from year to year, the average pace at which it grows will not be less in the Western developed world than it has been so far during the 1960's. It might well be slightly faster. I also assume that there is no economic slump in this period and no large-scale war involving the present industrial world.

In these circumstances, the very big business corporation is likely to grow faster than the average business. The experience of recent years suggests that it may grow a great deal faster than its competitors, both in terms of the assets that it owns and of the labor that it employs. Allowing for the fact that the giant corporations tend to be more highly capitalized than the average, it is remarkable how much additional manpower they have managed to absorb during the 1960's. The *Fortune* Directory shows that General Motors, the world's largest employer with a current payroll of three quarters of a million workers, added 25 per cent more employees to its books between 1960 and 1966.[1] Ford more than doubled the number of its employees during the same period, and General Electric registered a rise of 40 per cent. These are the three largest manufacturing companies in the United States, measured in terms of numbers employed. Exceptionally among the giant corporate employers, U.S. Steel showed a decline during this period; but this was due to the special circumstance, also exceptional among big business enterprises, that its prosperity was dependent on the fortunes of a single industry which was growing very slowly.

It is not simply by the extrapolation of past trends that one is led to the conclusion that the very big will probably get a great deal bigger. R. Marris (in *The Theory of Managerial Capitalism*) has convincingly argued that the drive of professional business management in contemporary capitalist society is directed—once the minimum condition of "financial security" has been achieved—toward the maximum expansion of the gross assets which the particular corporate managers control. The growth of these assets is, on the evidence which Marris provides, a more compelling objective than obtaining the highest possible rate of return per unit of capital employed. The two motives are, of course, entirely compatible with each other in the long run; what is important to establish is that actual behavior in the short- and medium-range is more readily explained in terms of the pursuit of the maximum rate of growth of the individual company. Marris makes a further point which is relevant to the future balance of power between states and corporations. The managerial motive of expanding one's area of authority is, of course, not lacking among the servants of the state; but "the most fundamental difference between business firms and government departments," he says, "lies in the former's capacity for autonomous growth."

It is worth adding to this that changes in the technology of management, above all the use of computers of increasing sophistication as a tool of decision-making, have removed many of the traditional constraints on the size of organizations which can be efficiently run by a single board of management. A more subtle point is that modern techniques of social and political analysis, tracing the precise routes by which power and influence are exercised within organizations, provide the opportunity for the more efficient design of their structure. In particular, the hierarchical relationships, which are an essential feature of the corporate type of organization, can be modulated to serve the different purposes of the various types of decision and action in which the corporation has to engage. A less authoritarian structure, offering scope for considerable initiative on the periphery while maintaining even stricter control over essential matters at the center, is likely to be better equipped for the process of expansion by osmosis between the giant and the small firm.

Whether the outcome will be quite so dramatic by the end of the century as the situation foreshadowed by Professor H. V. Perlmutter—a world industrial landscape dominated by some two hundred "monster" enterprises responsible for the greater part of output—is more doubtful. At any rate, it is necessary to envisage some countervailing social and political forces to the unlimited growth of the giant corporation. It might take the form of a popular political movement with a power base among the smaller firms—among which there will be some with ten to twenty thousand people on their payrolls—appealing to a widespread anxiety about preserving alternative and more decentralized sources of economic power in society. Tax concessions or subsidies will surely be employed to help to secure the independence and prosperity of enterprises separate and different from the giants.

This separateness will be the more readily maintained in practice because the odds are that the giants themselves will not develop an appetite for takeovers and mergers that is either unlimited in volume or unselective in content. Two considerations will serve to illustrate the spontaneous restrictions on appetite that are likely to assert themselves. First is the minimum critical size that firms will have to reach before they become worthwhile takeover prospects for giant corporations, which are envisaged here as organizations with a million or more employees. There will be a natural anxiety about spreading the inevitably scarce resource of skilled managerial manpower too thin. The resources of management are used particularly heavily in the process of integrating relatively small enterprises, taken over by the giant, into the purposes and the way of life of the expanding corporation. The second consideration is simply that certain kinds of industrial mergers—for example, vertical integration of some manufacturing process to include a variegated retail outlet—are sometimes judged to be positively inconvenient. The big corporation may feel that it retains more freedom for maneuver in the process of profitable expansion if it avoids tying itself indissolubly to particular partners, either in the conduct of its sales strategy or in its buying of materials for processing. There is too little evidence so far about the long-term prospect for companies based on an indiscriminate policy of conglomerate mergers. It is too soon to argue on the basis of facts available that in modern business the crucial resource of good management can be generalized at short notice to any product or process in which the expanding giant corporation identifies the prospect of profitable operation. There is at least a suspicion, which remains to be disproved, that the management know-how of successful companies is more specific than that.

Corporate Customers

The contemporary business corporation, as Bernard Cazes has observed,[2] seems to be increasingly concerned to achieve a wider or longer-lasting contractual relationship with its customers than the traditional relationship represented by a series of isolated selling transactions. It tries to get the customer to commit himself to the firm, either as the purchaser of a whole range of products instead of a single item or as a regular buyer of a particular product or service over an extended period of time. The inducement offered to the customer is frequently some form of discount on the price, in return for providing his supplier with an assured outlet. Cazes connects this trend with the desire of the modern automated enterprise to plan its production on the basis of secure outlets. There is, I believe, a further motive connected with the evolution of a society oriented increasingly toward the provision of services that is likely to reinforce the trend toward commerce in the form of a commitment over time rather than an individual transaction.

Services that are repeatedly performed for customers tend to involve the enterprise performing them in an initial investment, sometimes of a substantial kind, for each one of its clients. It is of the essence of the kind of service that people in the urban societies of the second half of the twentieth century will increasingly require that they must be first of all reliable and, secondly, fast. Individual transport in cities is perhaps the most obvious case in point. It is hardly likely that the vast and crowded conurbations, which will contain the majority of the population of the industrial world by the end of the century, will be able to accommodate individually owned cars in town centers. People, who will be on the average more than twice as rich as they are today, will be willing to pay a great deal in order to be assured of 100 per cent reliability and promptness of their transport service.

The issue goes a great deal deeper than consumer preferences. The population in the twenty-first century will contain a greatly increased proportion of very old people in the age bracket eighty to one hundred years plus. These people will be much more vulnerable to the failure of services, such as the delivery of food at stated times or the repair and maintenance of household equipment, than the rest of the population. The guarantee of the prompt delivery of services in the crowded urban conditions of the year 2000 will present acute problems of organization, and it becomes apparent that there will have to be a new set of relationships between the service corporation and its customer, giving the latter more security and the former more power to ensure that services promised are delivered on time to those who depend on them.

The problem of the very old and vulnerable is a particular instance of a more general proposition about the service relationship between the corporation and its customers. It is, for example, barely conceivable that societies in which the majority live in high apartment blocks will tolerate an attempt by the elevator operators to stage a lightning strike. Moreover, corporations which have entered into guarantees to provide precisely timed services will have to be supported by whatever means public authority can command in their efforts to meet their obligations. It seems likely indeed that their employees, going about the provision of certain services, will be endowed with official public service status; they will need to have the right, in the last resort, to exercise police powers to cope with obstacles that impede them in fulfilling their tasks.

The process envisaged here would put the service corporation in its relations with the consumer on a footing analogous to that of an enterprise fulfilling a government military contract in time of war. Failure to fulfill commitments undertaken might lay the enterprise open to the penalities of the criminal law. The contract for certain kinds of services, like the contracts undertaken to supply a nation with equipment essential for its defense, will tend to acquire a special sanctity because people's lives will hang on its performance. By an extension, it is plausible to speculate that popular sentiment about inflicting severe discomfort on the helpless old will develop an intensity similar to that felt about cruelty to children. Corporations will be subject to exigent standards. But concomitantly their status as a social instrument will be enhanced. They will be recognized as performing certain services that are not different in essence from the public law functions of the police or other bodies clothed with the authority of the state. At the same time, the committed customers of the service corporation, with their long-standing contracts and their guaranteed price discounts, will have some of the benefits that go with membership in a consumer's cooperative. This sense of consumer participation is something the corporation may well wish to foster.

All this is based on certain assumptions about consumer preferences and about the future of the economic system. It is assumed that the conventional bias will be against the accumulation of more and better consumer durable goods and in favor of an uncluttered style of living—an offset to the crowded environment of the future—based on the reliable provision of services by outside specialist organizations. People living in city apartments will have shed any illusions about their ability to fend for themselves and will recognize unashamedly their necessary and constant dependence on what others do for them. Secondly, the consumer of the future will not have readily at his disposal the traditional remedy against the supplier of a poor or unattractive product—the transfer of his very next purchase to a competing supplier. It is in the nature of the case that the number of possible suppliers of certain kinds of services, involving the special priority attached to performance and the tight guarantees for the customer indicated above, will be limited. Only a small number of franchises will be granted, and consumers in some areas may find that no alternative supplier is anxious to compete for their custom.

Moreover, the cult of guaranteed service, in which the competitive struggle between firms will be considerably muted, will not be confined to corporations selling directly to individual consumers. It is to be expected that an increasing number of services vitally important to the inhabitants of packed and lively urban communities—such services as noise reduction, weather control, or getting rid of air pollution—will have to be arranged on a collective basis. Once a corporation has undertaken a contract of this sort, it will be difficult for a community to change quickly to a new supplier if it is dissatisfied with the results. Again, the corporation will be treated as having some of the attributes of a public law body.

It is worth noting that there is no reason why these personal and collective services should not be provided by publicly owned corporations. Public transport, electricity, and gas are commonly provided in this way in Europe. But there is no widely held conviction in Europe, emerging out of this experience, that public ownership provides a better guarantee of performance in these fields of economic activity than private ownership. In any case it is not the ownership issue which is regarded as being important, but rather whether the enterprise is conducted on the lines of a conventional business corporation. It is essentially because corporate enterprise is obsessed by the desire for growth that it organizes itself in a demonstrative fashion to please consumers and to cajole them into buying more.

Corporate Shareholders

As indicated earlier, the business corporation has acquired its enhanced status as a social instrument partly by liberating itself from an exclusive concern with the interests of its owners. In future the bond between management and shareholders is likely to be loosened still further. Managements, however, have hitherto found it convenient to be formally subject to the orders of private property owners. This enables them to speak to governmental agencies, when they make awkward demands on them, as the representatives of people whose personal property they hold in trust on the understanding that it will be employed in ways that yield a solid profit.

The trouble is that the traditional mythology of ownership has increasingly come to lack verisimilitude in a situation where the management is overwhelmingly concerned with the long-term destiny of a great corporation in society, while many of the share-holders whom it purports to serve are solely interested in the short-term impact made by the corporation on the stock market between the moment when they buy shares and the moment when they sell them. Few people would accept the argument that the managers of a company ought to concern themselves exclusively with maximizing the gains of this changing group of temporary holders of the company's shares. The whole notion of ownership in relation to corporate enterprise will have to be re-thought and put on a fresh basis if it is to be treated in the future as a persuasive element in guiding management policy. The prospect is that there will be increasing numbers of consumers and of employees with a long-term interest in the policies of the giant corporation, to which many of its legal masters will be indifferent.

A solution to this problem which has been suggested by Bloch-Lainé is that shareholders should be divided into two categories, the long-term and the short-term holders, and that voting rights should be wielded only by the former.[3] The suggestion is interesting because it points to the possibility of a new general system of legal rights based on time as a measure of the degree of commitment, whether of shareholder, consumer, or worker. It is not fanciful to foresee a fresh set of definitions centered on the duration of commitment replacing the simplicities, already somewhat archaic, of laws resting on the doctrine of absolute property.

With the different interest groups crowding in on company boards and asserting their rights to a say in management decisions, it may come to be something of a problem to reassert the claims of the owners. Their right to demand policies which will assure them of at least the conventional rate of return on their capital, plus a measure of capital appreciation, will no doubt be conceded. But beyond that, they may well have to struggle to be heard above the din of competing claims. In addition to the long-term com-mitted consumer groups and the long-service worker groups, the state itself may be expected to wish to assert its right to influence the management decisions of giant corporations and to do so at an early stage in board-room discussions. To achieve this purpose it will not need to go through the motions of becoming an actual shareholder, in the style of the "mixed companies" which are a familiar feature today of France and other West European coun-tries. If the techniques of selective intervention by the state in the industrial policies pursued by large corporations become, as seems likely, an established part of economic planning, then, as one British journalist has put it recently, the government will take on a position "almost akin to that of a large shareholder, even when it does not actually own any equity."[4]

It is possible, however, that a revival of the rights of mere ownership may be brought about by the institutional investors. Certainly the insurance companies and pension funds will be especially well placed, as time goes on, to assert their claim to influence the decisions of corporate management, as long-term professional investors representing a mass interest in achieving the highest possible level of profits.

Organized Labor

The corporation, with its considerable investment in each new recruit to its work force, will have an increasing interest in the immobility of labor. It is possible that the Japanese convention of lifelong engagement will come to be nearer the norm of labor relations in Western industrial countries than the traditional idea of a labor market from which a business draws its fluctuating manpower requirements from time to time. If it is going to be usual for a worker to be retrained for new jobs two or three times in the course of a working lifetime as old jobs become obsolescent, then the great corporation, which will itself be in the constant travail of adapting itself to new technology, could well provide the natural context for the re-education of people in new skills. The sheer size of the giant corporation should greatly facilitate the process of job-changing. Indeed, this facility may come to be one of the particular attractions of employment in this type of enterprise. The corporation for its part will have to apply substantial resources to the business of education. The degree of efficiency in retraining redundant workers, cutting the idle time between the cessation of an old job and the performance of a new one, will plainly have a significant effect on its own costs.

The performance of this kind of function is also likely to affect profoundly the personal feelings of a corporation's employees. No doubt the general sense of insecurity caused by rapid technological change will be mitigated by generous welfare payments from public funds, in the form of redundancy grants and finance for retraining. But it will, nevertheless, be felt to be a considerable advantage to be able to move securely into one's next job under a familiar management and in the shelter of the corporation in which one started one's career. How far will the new kind of corporate loyalty affect traditional trade-union attitudes? Paternalistic companies have sometimes, though less frequently in the recent past, set out to rival the worker's loyalty to his trade union. The question is whether the special function of the trade union in an advanced welfare state enjoying full employment—namely, the representation of sectional or particular plant interests—will be so important in the future.

But whether it is or not, there will certainly be a continuing need for the professional representation of organized labor in the policy-making bodies of the giant corporation. The form that this will take will no doubt vary from one country and one legal system to another. But in one way or another the outcome seems likely to involve something analogous to the present system of worker representatives on the Supervisory Boards of German companies. Trade-union power and influence may well come to be concentrated at this point in particular. Just as a corporation nowadays appoints outside directors from banks, insurance companies, and other businesses, so the "worker-directors" of the future may have the recognized function of reflecting the wider interests of labor in a given industry, including the interests of those employed in competing corporations or in smaller enterprises.

Relations with Governments

Having mobilized the mass loyalties of the consumers of its product and of its employees, the giant corporation may appear in certain situations as a formidable rival to governments. How formidable will depend in large part on the size of the government concerned. A giant corporation in the United States will obviously be differently placed in a power struggle with the federal government than in a contest with the government of a country like Denmark or Ireland. It is to be observed that an international corporation with a work force one million strong would be supporting a dependent family population equal to the present size of these nations. The value of the physical assets controlled by such a corporation will be greater than those belonging to a small nation—if only because national assets, unlike those belonging to a corporation, are to a large extent an accidental agglomeration, including barren mountains and heaths and awkward towns developed for forgotten purposes. The corporation's command of scarce and specialized skills is also much greater. It can, after all, pick and choose among a world population of talented specialists to man its top posts. The corporation, in short, will be in a position to bully some governments. And the latter will be vulnerable to pressure because they will be loath to forgo the benefits of high technology at low cost which local enterprises controlled by international corporations will be able to offer.

On the other hand, the giant corporations will be the target of powerful popular suspicion. Governments are bad enough, but at least they can occasionally be teased into articulate honesty by parliaments; corporations are harder to crack open. It is inevitable that there will be demands for much closer public surveillance of their activities than anything to which they have been subjected hitherto. With the progressive accretion of corporate power, the pressures for new forms of public accountability will grow. The corporation's claim to a large measure of privacy, in order to be able to conduct its competitive activities without being spied upon by its business rivals, will seem less and less tenable. The public service function of the great corporate enterprise, in effective occupation of a large chunk of the economic terrain, will be seen as the ultimate justification for the special privileges, and obligations, enjoyed by it in its relations with consumers and with the planning organizations of the government. In its early days the great corporation assumed some of the attributes of a robber baron—the moat and the thick fortress wall surrounding its activities, the right to sally forth without warning to destroy its rivals and to disappear again behind its postern gate without being stopped and questioned. By contrast, the symbol of the giant enterprise of the future, as of the bank of the mid-twentieth century, will be the glass wall. The change in banking architecture from the old model of a fortress to that of a public show behind well-protected but transparent windows illustrates the progression.

Some of the demands for accountability may be met by the devices outlined earlier. Consumer representatives in the boards of management may be expected to exercise a watching brief on prices and to impose a curb on the temptations arising from established quasi-monopolistic positions in certain industries and trades. The traditional threat of the dynamic new business challenging the sitting occupants to do combat with it will grow less credible as great corporate enterprises become firmly embedded in positions of trust at a number of key points in the late-twentieth-century economy. Indeed, it may quite likely come to seem wrong to allow them to be challenged by an upstart entrepreneur not carrying any comparable burden of public responsibility. Traveling light and therefore maneuvering fast in a competitive situation will be regarded as less of a virtue than it was thought to be in the small-business phase of early capitalism. That will not prevent the mythology of this earlier phase, which gave the great corporation so much more room for maneuver—so long as it could keep up the charade of being just another small man grown somewhat taller than the rest—from being the subject of nostalgic devotion by some corporate managers. And they will no doubt try to use the myth in their struggle against the tutelage of interest groups with special rights, like the consumers of their products or the workers in their plants.

Meanwhile, the state, in those places where states are strong enough to insist on their rights as guardians of the public interest, may be expected to press for a great deal more information. It will not be enough for a corporation to be able to show that it makes a reasonable average profit on its operations and does not charge excessive prices. It will also be held accountable for the efficiency with which it uses the factors of production at its disposal—land, capital, and natural resources—in particular lines of production. Since the scope for offsetting losses in one branch of production against gains in another will be enormously increased, it will be difficult to establish whether a particular management is, for example, making effective use of the additional manpower which is absorbed into some new enterprise or not. If, as seems probable, labor, especially skilled labor, continues to be in short supply in advanced societies by the end of the century, then organizations which are especially well placed to acquire this scarce resource in the market may well be called upon to show, by objective measurement of the performance of labor in their different enterprises, that the marginal product of labor is higher there than it would be if it were employed for some alternative purpose. In other words, the "opportunity cost" of the marginal labor supply of an enterprise would be measured against the value of its product.

The principle behind these techniques of measurement—which may seem impossibly complicated today, but which are likely to be developed rapidly in response to planning needs during the coming decades—is that the employment of a social resource like labor requires a social justification. Similar criteria will be applied to the use of capital. It could, for instance, happen that a giant corporation, which was able to obtain investment funds cheaply and was also economical in its use of labor, employed the capital in its business in a relatively wasteful manner. Finally, and most obviously, corporate enterprise has hitherto been able to use up natural resources, like land, water, and clean air, with little or no regard for the social costs of its operations. The bias of latter-day capitalism toward what Albert Hirschman has described so shrewdly under the heading of the "internalization of external diseconomies"[5] is likely to go a great deal further rather fast. And the intrusion of social costs and benefits into commercial calculations of profit and loss will make for large changes in the kind of enterprise which is deemed to be successful because it yields the highest net rate of return.

My expectation is that the large corporation will adapt itself to this change, but will do so with a struggle. Wherever it has the opportunity to escape from the trammels on entrepreneurial initiative imposed by social costings, organized consumer pressures, and workers' representation in management, it will. Its political power will not be negligible. It may be able to play one or more of the forces with which it has to contend against another. For example, a body of consumers might be mobilized in a dispute with the state about some costly government proposal concerned with the preservation of the environment for the benefit of people a generation ahead. Or circumstances might arise in which it was convenient for a corporation to enter into an alliance with the planning department of the government in order to press some unpopular decision on organized labor. I assume that corporations, in spite of the pluralistic character of their boards of directors, will not lose their distinctive persona. Indeed, it is to be expected that the giant corporation of the future will be even more anxious to give expression to its own individual style, doctrines, and traditions. Differences in the corporate culture of particular giants will no doubt become the subject of erudite works by learned scholars; and as these fine points are established, managers will stoutly proclaim their mission of defending the individual ethos of the organization entrusted to their leadership.

Nevertheless, there will be occasions when the giants will find it convenient to band together. They will all hanker for an environment away from centers of powerful government, such as the United States, in which they can flex their muscles without being constantly asked what they are doing. The natural escape route will be via the further internationalization of the enterprise. It is no secret that some U. S. companies which currently invest abroad are partly influenced by the escape motive. It may come to be argued in time that a country so powerful and nationalistic as the United States, with so large a domestic market, does not provide an appropriate headquarters for a truly international company. The export of capital may then be followed, as it has been already in the case of some big British companies, by the emigration of the corporation itself to a more congenial environment in a foreign land. Governments will be invited to compete for its favors.

At that stage of the power struggle between corporations and governments, the small states in Europe and elsewhere may, in turn, find a compelling motive for banding together, as the only means of imposing a due regard for the public interest on the footloose giant.

REFERENCES

1. See July 1961 and June 1967 issues.

2. Bernard Cazes, *Futuribles*, Vol. 5, No. 4 (Paris, 1968).

3. François Bloch-Lainé, *Pour une reforme de l'enterprise* (Paris, 1963).

4. Christopher Tugendhat, *Financial Times* (January 31, 1968).

5. Albert O. Hirschman, *The Strategy of Economic Development* (New Haven, 1959).

Part II

ELI GOLDSTON AND G. NEAL RYLAND

Preface

THE PREFACE to Part I by Stephen Graubard provides the reader with a sequential line of thought to help bridge from author to author. In this Preface to Part II, we attempt to slice the same material in a different plane in order to emphasize another pattern. (Editors as well as lumber mills can saw the same wood into planking or parquet.)

Our purpose is to summarize six recurrent themes raised in the original *Dædalus* articles (written in 1968) and then comment on how these perspectives have been expanded by the added essays. The added essays (written during 1970–1971) were sought out in part because there is a surprisingly narrow range of opinion and prediction among the eleven original authors on these six issues:

First, it is pointed out that "business" is too general a term for useful discussion. Historically, in America there has been a progression from merchant to wholesaler to manufacturer to manager as the dominant type of businessman. Important current differences can also be discerned when businesses are classified by product, internal organization, market structure, type of production, or size. In particular, Neil W. Chamberlain believes that classification by size brings out important questions because most of the more than one million corporations in the United States "are small-scale operations scarcely different in many respects from their counterparts of a hundred years ago." But on the other hand, Eli Goldston suggests that "just as styles and manners tend to drift out from Cafe Society or the Jet Set through society columns, so the structure, staffing, procedures, and objectives of *Fortune*'s 500 Largest Industrials spread through the business press to the rest of business." Other *Dædalus* authors also recognize that the traditional businessman and the small businessman follow influential and prominent business leaders but lag behind them. Thus, at any moment in time, these businessmen can be distinguished from the managers of the modern major corporations—in R. Joseph Monsen's words—"by their ide-

ology as well as by their roles, values, and positions within society."
But these managers are selected as the principal type of businessman worth studying to ascertain whether "business" is currently
changing in ways of major social and political significance.

Second, there is a consensus that private business will increasingly supply many of the physical goods and services we have
obtained, at least since the New Deal era, from public sources.
Robert T. Averitt applauds this movement "into the education and
health industries. If business can play a major role in meeting the
expanding demands in these areas at reduced real cost, it will have
found a renewed place in the new society." Michel Crozier concurs:
"Today we discover that education, health and welfare, community
redevelopment, social and cultural area rehabilitation, and big
science projects are the main concerns of a number of legitimate
businesses . . . the business corporation is the best organizational
tool with whioh to locate the basic problem, experiment with pilot
projects, and prepare for large-scale application." Andrew Shonfield
suggests that the public is quite ready to accept business into these
formerly government-occupied areas and, indeed, "many of the
servants of the state itself" will concede that the corporation can
perform the job better.

But William Letwin warns that this can be a costly process,
"especially if businessmen neglect their businesses in order to
become irresponsible quasi-public benefactors," and Alfred D.
Chandler, Jr., comments that "there is little in the recruitment,
training, and experience of the present business leaders—the corporate managers—to prepare them for handling the difficult new
problems" of cultural, social, and political matters. Richard H.
Holton predicts that this is an area where the small firms may
diverge from rather than follow the corporate executives. "The
rhetoric of today's corporate chiefs about the social responsibilities
of business and the importance of closer cooperation between business and government is heartening, but this is probably not the voice
of business as a whole." Leonard S. Silk worries "that the so-called
business power structure will prove to have insufficient control over
the directly involved forces of urban America to deal successfully
with the urban problem."

Even those who doubt the wisdom of explicit recognition of
"social responsibility" as a factor in business decision-making see
such forces as crowding, increasing interdependence, and the under-

mined viability of the central city pushing business toward it. And even those who favor corporate recognition of "social responsibility" recognize that "the intrusion of social costs and benefits into commercial calculations of profit and loss will make for large changes in the kind of enterprise which is deemed to be successful" (Andrew Shonfield). One proposal, Eli Goldston's, is that "the report of the President's Council of Economic Advisors might usefully incorporate the social indicators being developed by H.E.W. as an example for business annual reports." An interesting and to some a frightening suggestion is that firms taking on such social responsibilities and accountability might eventually be granted police powers so that their employees could cope with any obstacles to the performance of these responsibilities (see Andrew Shonfield).

Third, although the profit motive might be tempered by social responsibility, it will remain, along with risk and uncertainty, according to the authors, a primary force in American business. Except for Mr. Monsen and Mr. Chandler, none seem to accept the 1932 Berle and Means or 1968 Galbraith notion of managers ("techno-structure") who pay little heed to earnings per share. Mr. Letwin refers to the discipline of "raiders, renovators, and nascent empire-builders," and Mr. Goldston comments, "The firms where unaggressive management can relax are typically ones where a founding family is still powerful enough to keep control and affluent enough not to press for profit maximization." Several authors refer to stock options and the growth of ownership of large holdings by institutions as factors ensuring intense managerial attention to profits.

R. Joseph Monsen and Raymond Vernon suggest that in large firms there is a little less profit concern by management, and William Letwin stresses the need to distinguish the profit motive from greed. The most common attitude seems to be, however, in Michel Crozier's words, that "profit has become a measure, still an indispensable one, but it is no more the end."

Fourth, there is general concern with the impact of accelerating technology and of more comprehensive planning. These themes are less fully developed and none of the authors seem to fear that the technicians are about to take control from the business managers. Mr. Letwin does point out, however, that "the function of the business executive is to state the ends that will define the engineer's effort" and that when the man trained in engineering starts selecting the ends, he is not functioning as an engineer. The question of who ultimately sets business policy becomes critically important when private business supplants public agencies.

Several articles recognize that the firm's forecasting depends on the macroeconomic planning of the state. Mr. Silk makes the interesting point that "both U.S. industry and Wall Street have clearly come to prefer peace to war, especially since the emergence of modern fiscal and monetary policies that have made it possible to keep the national economy at a high level of activity without the impetus of war."

Fifth, the increasing internationalization of American business is recognized and Mr. Vernon analyzes this in some detail. Several authors emphasize that the American business advantage has not been based on technological superiority but rather reflects the enthusiastic application of industrial management to new ideas and discoveries despite the risks involved.

Sixth, although the scholarly *Dædalus* authors are favorable to American business and optimistic about its continued great importance and high prestige in American society, a number of problem areas are recognized, particularly:

1. The relationship of large American firms and of multinational enterprises to the sovereignty of foreign governments is an evolving crisis.

2. A number of articulate critics, such as Michael Harrington, fear a "social-industrial complex" will take its place as a powerful social force beside the "military-industrial complex" so that a sort of corporate fascism could develop from corporate involvement in the work of government and society.

3. Disaffection with some of the pressures and consequences of industrialization once some level of affluence is attained will increase the number of critics of business and also of those who reject it as a way of life.

In order to broaden out the eleven articles of the original *Dædalus* issue, the present editors concluded that it would be useful to ask some businessmen to explain from their viewpoint how they see American business life evolving.

Because the impact of transportation on our economy has always been a considerable factor, we sought out one of the lawyers turned professional manager who has abandoned the traditional style of railroad management. John P. Fishwick, President of the Norfolk and Western Railway Company, argues that the transportation industry under private ownership but with the government as a substantial partner can meet the new burdens being placed upon it. There are those, like Mr. Holton, who would suggest that the government has already set a record with the railroad industry "for government support and encouragement of business in the United States," but Mr. Fishwick no doubt reflects the attitude of the contemporary manager who is asked to meet the cost of new challenges with reminders of subsidies long ago given to his predecessors and spent. His essay runs somewhat contrary to the second original theme that business will push government out of many areas.

Max Clarkson, another active businessman, has attempted to put into practice in his firm much of the theory of organic management developed by Professor Abraham Maslow and his school of humanistic psychology. It is interesting to note the contrast between the structure of Mr. Clarkson's business firm and Mr. Chamberlain's description of the impact on employees of the modern corporation.

A third article, by a very successful business entrepreneur who has become a government administrator and politician, Howard Samuels, explores the currently controversial topic of black capitalism. There are economists who feel that the same techniques described for the development of backward areas by Mr. Vernon and others could be applied in the ghetto areas of the United States to good effect.

The optimism of Mr. Clarkson and Mr. Samuels as to internal business life and of the original *Dædalus* essays as to the beneficial effect of involving business firms in social problems has been challenged. Many independent observers question whether business can make good even on promises already made. They detect presumptuousness in statements suggesting that business can do what other agencies—namely governmental ones—cannot. Those who feel that elected American government has itself lost contact with popular needs and sentiment see no possibility that the private sector will respond even as well as government. This debate is joined by Charles DeCarlo and Wolf Von Eckardt. The former attacks business for its materialism and calls for new efforts by the corporation in the field of human rights and personal development. Mr. Von Eckardt's article concludes that the assumption of social responsibility by business will fail to solve America's problems. His attitude and vigorous language conflicts with Mr. Letwin's conclusion that "the balance was redressed during World War II. Since then businessmen have so indoctrinated themselves and one another in the new gospel of social responsibility and have so visibly followed it that little criticism remains to be heard. There are murmurings, to be sure, condemning the whole of bourgeois civilization; and from the mitigated left rise troubled remarks about the private sector of our civilization (including the military side of the public sector). From various other corners stem complaints against the particular dangerousness of cigarettes, automobiles, and smog. Yet on the whole, American businessmen enjoy as much public confidence now as they ever have before."

Charles S. Shoup, Jr., Robert A. Charpie, and Donald A. Schon enlarge upon the fourth original theme of accelerating technology and relate it to the second theme of increased social responsibilities. They recognize a failure of business to provide a proper environment for innovation, especially in the area of growing social problems, as the creative process becomes somewhat dampened by a structure organized for effective production and marketing. But they also feel that the traditional structure of business can be modified to stimulate that innovative process which is so vitally needed to develop the concepts and technologies as well as to provide the motivation needed to meet our present social challenges. They suggest that the development of a systems approach to social problems with the combination of business, educational, and governmental forces could be an important application of a modern business innovation to a social problem.

With the emergence of new perspectives on business, it is a great challenge to prepare business students who must apply their skills in a society which is developing a new scoreboard for business—a society in which profits alone will not legitimize the role of the business enterprise. John W. Hennessey's article explores some of the fundamental issues involved in the business-school curriculum and the present status of its transformation.

Where, then, do the original *Dædalus* perspectives on business and the somewhat enlarged viewpoint provided by Part II brings us? The large American corporations are going through a period of change that has separated them from the vast number of small businesses whose managers still pursue goals and philosophies that do not relate to current social issues and therefore no longer seem relevant to many young people. The managers of leading businesses feel challenged by a new awareness of community responsibility, and a new relationship between government and industry is evolving. The government is being seen as a partner in, rather than as a regulator of, business activities. It is yet to be determined whether this socially responsible large business will seem attractive to American youth.

Traditionally, economists have referred to two sections of the American economy, the public sector (federal, state, and local government activities) and the private sector (the domain of business, both large and small firms). This neat division is no longer valid as the activities of the large corporation become increasingly associated with government, not only in specific business transactions but also in the minds of the American citizens who have begun to expect social action from the large private firm. This public attitude is the outcome of having private industry produce goods and services for the government, perform such diverse functions as undertaking research and development for the government, and provide housing under government guarantees and subsidies. In addition, the corporation is a readily identifiable source of economic power which draws its labor force from within the community.

Suddenly, the large corporation has become a focal point for many groups who seek corporate "appropriations" or "funding," unconsciously using the terminology of government agencies and legislatures, in order to receive corporate gifts for a vast array of projects—social, educational, and cultural. Organizations and journalists keep score on the donation and participation records of these corporations as if they were public bodies. Citizens have been known to hang company presidents in effigy and march on corporate offices if they disapprove of certain corporate actions. (Mr. Von Eckardt tells of a public burning of gasoline credit cards to protest an oil company's actions.) When the modern corporate president takes office, he finds that he must deal with the citizens of the surrounding community as if he were its mayor as well.

Many corporations have undertaken large social responsibilities and have found that they are not necessarily incompatible with the traditional profit motive of the firm. The growing awareness of the importance of this new social interest has been recognized not only by the corporate manager but also by two groups traditionally considered to be rather detached in their consideration of business profits and growth potential: the Wall Street security analysts and the graduate students in business. These two groups have singled out firms that have recognized the importance of social action in

their corporate activity by seeking out those companies for investment of funds and careers.

Those firms that have either not recognized or refused to accept
their social responsibility tend to be the smaller, closely held corporations. Their method of operation and their managerial structure is so considerably different from the large corporation that it
is misleading to combine the two types as a single group for study.
Yet, there is evidence that when responsible spokesmen for non-
business interest groups talk and write about business, they fail to
differentiate between the large professionally managed corporation
and the small business.

The political power of these smaller businessmen, owing to sheer
numbers, far outweighs that of the larger firms, though in the field
of economic power, the opposite is true.

In this volume, one will read various opinions concerning
whether the modern business manager is meeting the emerging
social challenge. If one separates those opinions that deal with the
small businessman and those concerning the professional manager,
the question of social responsibility becomes clearer. The important
thing to recognize is that the business community itself is fragmented, so it is misleading to speak in generalities about what
business thinks or what business does. Just as some other traditional
voter patterns have disintegrated, the business bloc, if it ever existed,
no longer exists.

There has been an important change in attitude by the citizenry
and by business concerning the public role of private enterprise.
These essays attempt to define this change and suggest possible
areas of further action and future trends. In the Von Eckardt,
DeCarlo, and Clarkson essays, particularly, business is charged with
having failed in important aspects of its role as a human institution
devised to serve human needs. Can the collaboration between business and government toward social objectives be structured so that
there is adequate public control over private corporate power without impairing business' ability to adjust to change? Can organic
management and other social-science techniques produce jobs with
opportunities for creativity that will attract bright youth? The
majority of the authors seem to feel that big business is making
a reasonable response to such challenges while admittedly groping
for the best resolution of the conflict between social responsibility
and traditional purely economic objectives.

JOHN P. FISHWICK

A Railroad Executive Looks
at Transportation Needs

AMERICANS ARE the most mobile people on earth. Every year the average American travels 7,000 miles, and one out of every five families changes homes. Our transportation system has made possible the mass production and distribution of goods which have brought about an affluent society. Transportation accounts for about 20 per cent of the gross national product and 13 per cent of the average family's expenses. Thus, a healthy transportation industry is essential to economic growth and full employment. But our transportation system now finds itself unable to serve adequately the affluent and mobile society it helped to build.

Urban transportation is characterized by accidents, delays caused by congestion, lack of mobility—especially for the urban poor—inadequate parking space, air pollution, noise, and ugliness. In large metropolitan areas the commuter spends countless hours creeping to work, often in the same equipment but at a slower pace than his counterpart did forty or fifty years ago. The inter-city traveler finds the highways often crowded and always dangerous, the airports remote from the central city, the landing and takeoff delays frustrating, the buses slow and confining, and the railroads operating only a few passenger trains (and these often on tediously slow schedules with ancient equipment).

Freight transportation, although not so apparent to the public eye, is also in serious trouble. The transportation industry's capability has expanded greatly since World War II with the outpouring of public funds into waterways, highways, and airways. Nevertheless, our transportation system—if it can really be called that—is uncoordinated: intermodal transportation is slow, costly, and often unavailable; the separate modes are fragmented and some—most railroads, for example—are chronically poor. The transportation industry has had neither the organizational nor the financial strength to support the research, planning, and capital investment required to bring into being a balanced transportation system adequate for current needs.

Moreover, we must look forward to a steadily increasing population with growing demands for transportation of persons and goods. The demand for transportation will double in the next two decades. Unless something is done, our transportation system will move from inadequacy to crisis to chaos.

The United States has the economic capability to produce over a reasonable period of time a completely adequate transportation system if that is given top priority as a national goal. A nation that can send men to the moon can plan and construct a workable domestic transportation system, even if this requires new and exotic hardware and enormous investments. But how much of the nation's will and resources should or can be brought to bear on transportation problems when we are faced with other high-priority problems, such as war, national defense, law and order, inflation, poverty, civil rights, and pollution? This is what we must weigh, taking into account that transportation has a pervasive impact and the solution to its problems may help achieve other economic and social goals.

An essay of this length obviously cannot even survey all of the major problems confronting the transportation industry, but I shall attempt to paint with a broad brush a part of the transportation landscape and suggest what I think we should do to improve the picture. I am a railroader, so my viewpoint is doubtless biased. Nevertheless, no realistic solution can be found that does not face up to the railroads' plight, for they have become the ghettos of our transportation system.

Passengers

The average American drinks his orange juice and coffee and eats whatever else he has for breakfast without thinking of how or with what efficiency it arrived at his breakfast table. But when he walks out the door of his home, his awareness of transportation begins. The interlude between comfortable home and comfortable office is often filled with frustration, whether he drives his automobile, takes a subway or bus, rides a commuter train, or hires a taxi to an airport. What he remembers most about his family vacation is sometimes the hard drives or the wait at the airport. If he does much business travel, he knows that the toughest part of this is getting to his destination and back.

A Railroad Executive Looks at Transportation Needs

The job of moving people can be divided into three parts: movement within the central city, movement between the suburbs and the central city, and movement between cities. Private enterprise has generally abandoned mass transportation within the central cities. The city dweller has been unwilling or unable to pay directly the high costs that private companies would incur in providing such service. Moreover, without reasonable profits private enterprise could not develop the credit or incentive to make the capital expenditures required to expand and modernize mass transportation systems as the population of the central cities shifts and grows.

Even though publicly owned, most transportation systems within the central cities are inadequate because the central cities have not had enough financial resources or planning capabilities. Money, of course, is the key, for there is little incentive to plan if there is no prospect that plans can be carried out. Another complication is that mass transportation has been deeply imbedded in politics and has been part and parcel of many of the problems of the cities. Even if only existing kinds of equipment and technology are used, a massive infusion of funds is needed to improve the mobility of people within our major cities.

Some of the circumstances that led private enterprise to abandon mass transportation within the central cities are now being felt by those engaged in moving the suburbanites to and from the central city. Most suburbanites drive their automobiles to work; some ride buses, and in the larger metropolitan areas many ride commuter trains. With few exceptions, commuter trains cannot be operated profitably and some are being aided by payments from state and local governments.

The position of state and local governments with respect to commuter trains is comparable to that of the central city with respect to mass transportation: too little money and too little planning. As a result, while commuter operations continue, the equipment involved is nearly always of an antique variety. And it is even more difficult to obtain adequate funds and planning in cases of suburban transportation than in central-city transportation because a number of municipal and state governments are usually involved. Support of a commuter train from Connecticut to New York City, for example, involves agreement by a number of governments.

The federal government has taken small but significant steps to assist the states and cities with mass transportation problems. The Housing Act of 1961 provided loans for equipment and grants for demonstration purposes. The Mass Transportation Act of 1964 went further, providing a grant program for capital needs and continuing the transportation and loan provisions of the Housing Act. Primary responsibility for these programs was vested with the Urban Mass Transit Administration, formerly within the Department of Housing and Urban Development, but now under the Department of Transportation. Not all responsibility, however, was transferred to the Transportation Department; at this writing some five projects remain at Housing and Urban Development. The Transit Administration's problems, therefore, repeat a now-familiar refrain: fragmented effort, divided responsibility, lack of trained manpower for planning, and lack of sufficient funds.

It is small wonder, then, that inter-city passenger travel is overwhelmingly by automobile. The proportion of such travel by car has shown a slow, sustained climb and 88 per cent of all inter-city travel is by highway. Airline travel has also shown gains and comprises nearly 10 per cent of inter-city passenger travel. Increases in bus travel reflect greater use by group tours rather than individual scheduled trips.

Less than 1 per cent of inter-city travel is accomplished today by rail. Since 1958, the number of regular inter-city trains has declined from 1,448 to only 498 at the end of February 1970. The Interstate Commerce Commission has reported that significant segments of the last remaining long- and medium-distance inter-city rail passenger service will not survive the next few years without a major shift in federal and carrier policies. Faced with this prospect, the commission has asked Congress to determine the need and means for preserving a national rail-passenger system, and the railroads are asking for federal support of all long- and medium-haul passenger trains that cannot be operated profitably.

Solely from an economic standpoint, it seems likely that intercity passenger trains can be justified only between large metropolitan areas such as New York, Boston, and Philadelphia. The Penn Central's Metroliner, which operates between New York and Washington on a two-and-one-half-hour schedule, represents a cooperative effort between the railroads and the federal government to determine the feasibility of high-speed trains and to test the market in this area. This is a good illustration of how a modest amount of seed money, only $11.5 million, provided by the federal government, can produce an effort on behalf of the railroads which ultimately may result in a shift of a substantial volume of passengers from overcrowded airways and airports to underused railroads. But there are few other city-pairs between which similar trains could be economically justified. As a practical matter, the nation's policy with respect to long- and medium-distance passenger trains is likely to be determined by both political and economic considerations.

Meanwhile, our population increases, the large metropolitan areas become more crowded, and the demand for swift, comfortable, and cheap passenger travel within cities, to and from the suburbs, and between cities grows. The policy we are pursuing obviously must be changed. There must be a hardheaded systems approach to the problem of moving people in the kind of urbanized society we have developed.

Freight

The railroads are still the core of our freight transportation system. There are 73 Class I railroad companies with annual revenues of $5 million or more that collectively haul over 40 per cent of the nation's regulated inter-city freight. These are the survivors or successors of hundreds of companies which, following rivers and Indian trails, crossing mountains, and connecting cities and towns, ultimately formed a network which for decades had a near-monopoly of freight transportation. In the last forty or fifty years, however, with the coming of highways, the development of inland waterways, and later of cargo-carrying aircraft, the rail monopoly disappeared and the railroads were faced with the reality of change.

The railroads are ill-prepared to react to change. They have an enormous investment in fixed plant. One railroad could not, for example, change the gauge of its rails without getting all, or nearly all, the other railroads to agree. It has to build freight cars that can move over the tracks of all other railroads and couple with the cars owned by other railroads, private companies, and shippers. Moreover, since many rail shipments move over more than one line, no railroad has complete control of the quality or pricing of its products. Because railroads must act in concert, their basic organizations tend to be similar. No other industry, I believe, has such formidable deterrents to innovations in plant, equipment, product, and organizational structure.

Despite these handicaps, in recent years the railroads, as haulers of freight, have made a number of innovations that have improved their competitive position vis-à-vis other modes, especially trucks.

Alarmed by the steady decline of their share of inter-city freight business, they began to place less emphasis on operating convenience and more on shippers' needs. By offering the automobile industry a rack car that could haul 12 to 15 automobiles, their share of this business increased from about 10 per cent to 50 per cent over the period from 1958 to 1968. Encouraged by this venture, the railroads now provide a multitude of special-purpose cars designed to fit shippers' requirements. They have inaugurated unit trains which generally haul trainload lots from one origin to one destination. In short, they have become market-oriented rather than production-oriented.

Although this activity has allowed the railroads to hold their share of inter-city freight traffic at about 40 per cent or above since 1960, it has produced only a trickle of earnings, keeping the railroads afloat but floundering. Over the last ten years, the railroads' cash flow was only about 70 per cent of their capital investment, which, in turn, was only about 50 per cent of what railroad spokesmen say it should have been. Their return on stockholders' equity has averaged only 2.7 per cent.

A far more significant step, in the long run, was taken by the railroads when they inaugurated, about ten years ago, what has become a nationwide merger movement. This movement has brought into being two major rail systems in the South—the Southern and the Seaboard Coast Lines—and one in the East—the Penn Central. A number of other merger proposals are now pending before the Interstate Commerce Commission, and it would appear that within the next ten years the number of railroad companies will be reduced substantially. There should evolve a rail network comprised of perhaps eight to twelve major systems.

Railroads have attempted to justify mergers to their stockholders and to governmental agencies primarily on two grounds: cost reductions and better service. The mergers consummated thus far have produced some successes and some disappointments when measured by these standards. In the beginning of a nationwide rail-merger movement, moderate savings and moderate improvements in service are all that can be expected from the first few mergers. Only with the consolidation of scores of railroads and the formation of regional systems can there be a real breakthrough in cost reduction and quality of service.

Although rail mergers on a broad scale seem to be in the public interest, there is no clear national policy encouraging them. Railroads cannot merge without Interstate Commerce approval, and obtaining such approval is a tortuous and lengthy procedure. Even after I.C.C. approval is obtained, the merger is frequently delayed and sometimes blocked by federal courts, where, as the result of a schizophrenic national policy, the Department of Justice is free to oppose a consolidation that the I.C.C. has found to be in the public interest.

Under present policy, a transportation service performed by a small number of companies—each one limited to railroads, trucks, barge lines, pipelines, or airlines—is possible; a system comprised of transportation companies—each of which offers service by more than one mode—is impossible. With minor exceptions, railroads are prohibited from entering the truck, barge, and airline businesses. Truckers and barge lines can operate railroads and pipelines, but not airlines. There are no comparable restrictions on airlines, but as a practical matter it seems unlikely that the airlines will seek to become all-mode companies in the foreseeable future.

The 1969 chairman of the Interstate Commerce Commission, Mrs. Virginia Mae Brown, has predicted the formation of transcontinental rail systems. This seems, to me, to be inevitable but distant under present governmental policies. A case can be made, however, for changing the direction of the rail-merger movement into one involving the formation of regional transportation companies which would precede, or perhaps supersede, nationwide rail systems. This would require a change in national policy since, as I have indicated, intermodal mergers are presently not possible. A failure to consider this option now will result in a default decision in favor of nationwide rail systems.

The formation of transportation companies with intermodal components would help solve some troublesome problems. Railroads and truckers, for example, are engaged in keen competition for the transportation of goods, especially over medium distances. Putting aside private carriage, which is a significant part of the competitive picture, the I.C.C. is charged with the task of regulating the competitive pricing of both railroads and truckers. Conflicting views of railroads and truckers have always resulted in Congress' adopting compromise standards that satisfy no one. A transportation company providing service by both rail and trucks could avoid this dilemma. Whether a specific shipment moves by rail or highway, or a combination of the two, would depend upon considerations of cost and service. Economic judgment would replace government fiat.

Federal regulation of motor carriers has been less strict and comprehensive than that of railroads, and most water carriers have been largely exempt from rate and service regulation. Since 1947, federal, state, and local governments have spent $228 billion for highways, $7 billion for airports, and $12 billion for waterways. In 1969 alone, the federal government spent $6 billion for facilities used by these industries, but allocated only $24 million for experimental railroad projects. Unequal treatment of railroads—and sometimes other modes, though perhaps not to such a degree—was undoubtedly necessary to develop a competitive transportation system, especially one adequate for the national defense. In any event, it was, and is, national transportation policy. The question is whether this policy must now be changed in the public interest.

In weighing that question we must take into account not only today's needs but tomorrow's prospects. The efficiency of truck transportation is rapidly improving with expansion of the 41,000-mile interstate-highway system. By using a sleeper tractor, the drivers work four hours on and four hours off and can move over 1,000 miles a day, compared to about 50 miles a day for an average freight car. Moreover, single tractors are now hauling double and triple bottoms (two or three trailers instead of one) with cost reductions estimated at about 25 per cent. Trucks have already taken from the railroads most of the high-grade or packaged freight moving 500 miles or less. With improvement of highways and equipment, their circle of competitive advantage will no doubt widen.

Air cargo, although still relatively small, is growing at a rapid rate. Coming onto the scene now are the giant Boeing 747 and C-5A which will double the capacity of the typical aircraft now in service. These huge jets will be able to transport 110 tons of cargo over great distances at an average speed of 500 miles an hour. In the next two decades the air carriers may do to the railroads' long-haul traffic what the trucks did to their short-haul traffic in the post-World War II period.

A Proposed Plan of Action

The present plight of transportation has been brought about because neither the government nor the industry has responded promptly or adequately to changing conditions. In the short run, the problem is to preserve the transportation system we now have and prevent its further deterioration. For years the railroads' earning power and cash flow have been inadequate to maintain their properties, much less provide funds for research and development or modernization. This deficiency affects not only our transportation system but also our entire economy.

Government has recognized its responsibility to aid the railroads in providing commuter service. The question of whether government should support such service financially is no longer open. The issues are how much help should be given and in what form. Most of the funds to support commuter service are now provided by state or local governments. Because these governments are fragmented and financially weak, financial participation by the federal government through categorical grants, revenue sharing, or other means will have to be added.

Interstate passenger service is a heavy drain on the railroads' cash flow. All of this service that cannot be provided on a break-even basis should be discontinued or supported by the government. If the railroads were relieved of the financial burden of providing unprofitable passenger service, their net income would increase by about 40 per cent and their ability to maintain and modernize their facilities would be enhanced. It would not, however, be an adequate long-run remedy for the ills with which our whole transportation system is afflicted.

What we need is a clear new policy and an organization to develop a program to make that policy effective. Transportation must be viewed as a system, not as separate modes. It must also be looked at as a part of our complex society. This policy should recognize that transportation is a competitive business, that restrictions designed to regulate it as a monopoly are obsolete, that we cannot have an adequate transportation system so long as each mode must be operated separately and on a small scale, and that both government and the transportation industry should have the responsibility and incentive to develop a coordinated and efficient system. Laws and regulations inconsistent with such a policy should be changed. Government, particularly the Department of Transportation, should encourage coordination and innovation. This can be accomplished in a number of ways. For example, a standardized box or container that can be transported by rail, truck, air, and water has been developed and is now in widespread use. It promises to provide a major breakthrough in transportation costs and efficiency, particularly in international trade. In this country, research by the Department of Defense and its insistence on the use of containers in intermodal service have accelerated such development.

Much more research and development should be undertaken by the transportation industry. The airlines rely heavily on research done by the military establishment, and motor carriers and railroads have left research largely up to their suppliers. Such research has been mainly testing, rather than trying to find new ways to move people and goods. Government might assist in paying the cost of research projects beyond the industry's capability—projects which, if successful, would improve our transportation system.

But money is not the sole answer. Neither is a change in national transportation policy. The government cannot do the job alone; there must be an appropriate response by industry. Many people, apparently, think the transportation industry in general—and the railroad industry in particular—is largely responsible for its own troubles. They look upon railroad managers as men basically oriented toward operations rather than cash flow who view their companies as institutions rather than competitive businesses, still carry their watches on the ends of gold chains, and are more fascinated by the *status quo* than by the challenge of innovation. There is, no doubt, some basis for this view.

Prior to World War II, when the railroads had a monopoly of large volumes of traffic, their chief problems were in operations, and it was inevitable that management was largely operations-oriented. After the war, the railroads suddenly found themselves in a competitive business. They were handicapped in adjusting promptly to this change because they were financially poor, restricted by laws and regulations which were often obsolete, and limited in their ability to improve because of the need to make many kinds of changes and innovations on an industry-wide rather than on a company basis.

Regardless of how well they ran their individual companies, transportation managers were not successful, collectively, in running the transportation industry and making adequate plans for the future. With hundreds of transportation companies in existence, there have been years of bitter intra- and intermodal fighting, especially between railroads and truckers, which has effectively thwarted congressional action in adopting a new and workable transportation policy. As a result, while all modes have been fighting legislative and competitive battles, collectively they have been losing an industry war.

We have now reached the point in the economic life of the transportation industry, however, when there is hope for the elimination of historic rivalries and the beginning of a broad industry outlook. Mergers have reduced the number of fragmented companies in all modes and more mergers are certain to come. Innovations, such as containerization, are bringing economic pressures to bear, requiring the several modes to look at total transportation needs. All modes have financial problems and are looking for some escape from a hand-to-mouth existence. Most important, there is a growing realization that the public demands better transportation and will not put up much longer with an inadequate system.

I have faith that if government accepts the transportation industry as a partner in a common endeavor, the industry will show that it can fulfill its essential role. Both government and the transportation industry must demonstrate that they have the flexibility and capacity to adjust to rapidly changing conditions to produce an adequate system. Unless they can, the prospect that other complex problems can be solved through an alliance of business and government are bleak indeed.

Since this essay was written, in 1969, there have been several important developments in transportation, including the bankruptcy of the Penn Central and the government's action in authorizing Amtrak to operate the intercity rail passenger business.

MAX B. E. CLARKSON

Management Is the Development of People

THE TRAINING and development of people has become a major preoccupation of American management. Managements in companies of every variety are continually trying to close the gap between their needs for changing skills and increasing competence and the supply of trained and flexible workers. Tomorrow's growth is predicated upon the development of the people of today, a qualitative rather than quantitative situation which differs from that in the earlier days of industrial expansion, when the *number* of people and sums of capital were the most important ingredients of corporate growth. Those companies that are unable to recruit, train, and retain adaptable and productive people cannot expect to grow and prosper in the technological environment of the remaining years of the twentieth century. The interests of both society and business will best be served by devoting substantially increased attention and effort to the development of human potential. This effort will entail more than the expenditure of money; it will require radical changes in our systems of values—in the way we evaluate people in their working environment, regardless of the type of organization, and in the way we view the management function itself, regardless of product or service.

During the past decade, behavioral scientists have shown that truly effective business organizations are those that consider human resources to be their single most important asset. In the words of Rensis Likert:

All the activities of any enterprise are initiated and determined by the persons who make up that institution. Plants, offices, computers, automated equipment, and all else that a modern firm uses are unproductive except for human effort and direction. Human beings design or order the equipment; they decide where and how to use computers; they modernize or fail to modernize the technology employed; they secure the capital needed and decide on the accounting and fiscal procedures to be used.

Management Is the Development of People

Every aspect of a firm's activities is determined by the competence, motivation, and general effectiveness of its human organization. Of all the tasks of management, managing the human component is the central and most important task, because all else depends upon how well it is done.[1]

A new school of thought in psychology, neither Freudian nor behavioristic in its orientation, that began to emerge at the end of World War II, has come to be called "humanistic psychology," and is based on two major assumptions: that the essential nature of man is either good or, at least, not bad; and that man possesses a basic, almost biological, characteristic—the need to grow, develop, and reach his full potential. Therefore, developing people and allowing them to express themselves, elicits the fullest commitment of their positive nature; inhibiting and suppressing them causes deviant, negative behavior, detrimental not only to any organization but also to the individuals themselves.

These examinations of human behavior, the research, and the development of behavioral theories have taken place over the past thirty years. At the same time social psychologists have been examining the world in which we are living. They see it as complex and turbulent, where social and moral values and the structures of organizations and institutions are being challenged and reexamined. This reexamination has produced the belief that the organizations most likely to survive today are those that are essentially democratic and that cultivate their human resources in such a way as to remain adaptable, flexible, and self-renewing.

Carl Rogers, psychotherapist and resident fellow at the Western Behavioral Sciences Institute, La Jolla, California, says:

Whether one calls it a growth tendency, a drive toward self-actualization, or a forward-moving directional tendency, it is the mainspring of life. . . . It is the urge to expand, extend, become autonomous, develop, mature . . . the tendency to express and activate all the capacities of the organism to the extent that such activation enhances the organism itself. This tendency may become deeply buried under layer after layer of encrusted psychological defences; it may be hidden behind elaborate facades which deny its existence; but it is my belief that it exists in every individual, and awaits only the proper conditions to be released and expressed.[2]

Since its development, "humanistic psychology" has continued to thrive and expand, attracting to it not only other psychologists and behaviorists but progressive thinkers from all walks of life. In the words of Abraham Maslow, professor of psychology at Brandeis University and former president of the American Psychological

Association, humanistic psychology "suggests action and implies consequences. It helps generate a new way of life . . . furthermore, it is beginning to be used, especially in education, industry, religion, organization and management, self-improvement and therapy."[3]

While these theories were being developed and substantiated, major changes in management beliefs were taking place within business and industry. Although some management thinkers in the 1930's were becoming disenchanted with the current techniques of industrial engineering for handling human resources, World War II eliminated any need for management to concern itself with productivity and motivation. The war itself served as a powerful stimulus of productive behavior, and many of the basic rules of a competitive economy were no longer applicable. But after the war, with a changed world, a changed work force, and a rapidly expanding peacetime economy, management began to look again at the worker and at how to make him more productive. The 1950's saw the development of what has since been called the "human relations movement": If management would be nice to people, they would be productive. This quickly proved to be erroneous. Progressive managements discovered that they could not buy off their work force, and that the old paternalism, dusted off and brought out under the guise of "human relations," just did not work.

In the beginning of the 1960's, management search for a better way of utilizing human resources found some answer in the new humanistic psychology. Since that time the ideas of many leading behavioral scientists have had growing acceptance among management in a wide variety of organizations.

Thus, manpower development in an industrial, profit-making enterprise has become a natural extension of the research and theories of contemporary behavioral science. In a world of change, survival depends on releasing the full potential of the organization's human resources and on cultivating the organization's ability to learn to adapt and to continue learning. With the growing understanding of behavioral investigations, it is not surprising to find a company such as Graphic Controls Corporation trying to apply them in the most effective ways possible. Over the last five years, we have come to the conclusion that "management is the development of people" since man's most productive contributions can be achieved only through self-development. The survival and growth of an organization depend upon development and renewal of its creative human resources.

Management Is the Development of People

Graphic Controls Corporation was formed in 1957 by merging several small specialized printing companies. Over the years the corporation had always taken a strong interest in its employees, but to avoid the paternalism of the past we evolved a system of manpower development in order to integrate theories of the behavioral scientists with the principles of professional management. In addition to hiring professional personnel executives to coordinate the benefit plans and personnel policies for our several hundred employees in the United States and Canada, we embarked on a course of self-education by using the facilities and experience of the President's Association, an affiliate of the American Management Association, to provide a common language and a mutually satisfactory definition of the nature of management. The assimilation of the new scientific theories resulted in the development of a manpower development system, devised under the auspices of the Industrial Relations Department.

System of Manpower Development

All the parts of this system are related to one another, and no single part can be effectively undertaken without careful consideration of all other parts. Development activities, for example, cannot be evaluated without considering their relationship to corporate goals and personal objectives, any more than existing manpower can be reviewed without reference to corporate goals.

Manpower development is viewed as a cyclical activity that never ceases because development can never be complete. No sooner do we reach our objectives than we discover new ones, and new development needs arise. Corporate goals and individual objectives continually modify each other. No rigid time schedule, however, is imposed on the system's operations, since each organizational unit, under the supervision of its manager, is responsible for its own development activities. Any manager can consult the staff of the Industrial Relations Department for advice on implementation, planning, and evaluation of the results of training and development activities.

Definition of Corporate Purpose

Both the management and hourly development programs are administered in line with statements of corporate purpose and policy regarding manpower development at all levels in the organization. At Graphics Controls Corporation our statement of purpose contains no reference to the nature of the company's business; products and services change, but our purpose will not. The purpose of Graphic Controls Corporation is to achieve optimum profits by identifying and satisfying on a continuing basis the reasonable needs and demands of the people associated with the company, and by seeking the company's own best self-interest in its relations with others. The "people associated with the company" include employees and their families, stockholders, present and potential customers, suppliers, and representatives of government and industry.

Every employee must have an opportunity to learn as much as he can about his job and the corporation so that he can make a maximum contribution in his present job and aspire to higher levels of responsibility. By developing the abilities of people, growth and profitability for the corporation will be achieved. In accepting the obligation to create an environment in which each person can reach his full potential commensurate with his ability and ambition, the corporation recognizes its responsibility to expand at a rate sufficient to accommodate new aspirations of individuals as they develop abilities beyond the scope of their present positions.

In this way a cycle of growth is created: The corporation helps individuals develop their abilities, which, when expanded, cause the corporation to grow in order to accommodate them. This growth in turn forces employees to develop to meet the new requirements of the organization. If people are our most important asset, then we should not be afraid to give them precedence in our view of the corporate cosmos.

Manpower Development Policy

A manpower development policy statement describes the actual implementation of basic corporate purposes, the responsibility for which rests with each manager at his individual level. The policy statement stipulates that each division and department of the corporation is responsible for undertaking effective development activities necessary to provide the proper quantity and quality of manpower to accomplish established objectives for the present and the future. This includes a periodic formal review that suggests development activities necessary to enable each employee to perform most effectively and to reach a level in the corporation commensurate with his ability and ambition. These reviews should also help each manager to improve his techniques in counseling others. In addition, outside resources such as seminars, conferences, and night-school courses will be utilized as they relate directly to on-the-job learning situations.

Every business enterprise can be looked at as though it were, in part, an institution of continuing higher education—a small university in fact, to teach experienced and skilled employees the fundamentals of effective learning and training so they may train others. Communications, the exchange of such information and ideas, and coordination between managers at all levels and between all departments must be such that an atmosphere is created in which optimum opportunities occur for management development. A manager who is exposed to many areas of our operations has an opportunity to broaden himself and prepare for greater responsibilities of general management in the future. Effective results attained in the development of subordinates will be one of the criteria used in the evaluation of his performance. To facilitate the entire development program, the corporation, through the Industrial Relations Department, provides functional assistance to each division and department in the planning, conducting, and evaluating of development activities at all levels.

As in the activities of manufacturing and sales departments, all development activities must be evaluated continually and revised to meet changing conditions. Effective training and development takes time and costs money. For that reason, no training and development activity should be continued if it has not proved its value in contributing to the effectiveness of individual performance. Tradition and habit have no place in any sound development program.

The specific illustrations of manpower development and the structured system outlined here are realistic extensions of the theories of "humanistic psychology" and human effectiveness summarized earlier. We may eventually find that if we create the right kind of environment, growth and creative achievement will take care of themselves. In the beginning, however, because our corporation was faced with the task of deliberately changing our attitudes and methods of management, such a system, in which these ideas of developing human resources could be integrated, was essential.

In this system we wanted to take into account what the humanistic psychologists told us about the "layer after layer of defenses" that people build up in the course of their lives. One of these obstacles, unfortunately, is the belief that learning and growing are something you do "outside" work, away from your daily job. Young managers are still coming to us with the attitude that their "learning" is over now that they have finished their formal schooling, and instead they are eager to "get to work." Like old-fashioned rural fundamentalists who believed that "the Lord helps those who help themselves," we determined to create a system that identified needs for training and development and provided situations where people would experience external encouragement to develop. We hoped that once the process began again, once the inertia had been overcome, the individual would then take over the responsibility for his own development.

Thus, in applying the principles of growth and development, we want to make sure we are providing opportunities for those individuals who are motivated, as well as those who are not, to express themselves fully in jobs of increased responsibility and complexity.

Problems of Development

During the last five years, while we have been creating this system, both sales and profits have increased substantially. We have been able to attract and hold talented people who, by virtue of their own growth and development, have caused the corporation to continue to grow and expand. Although no quantitative measures are readily available to help us substantiate the effectiveness of our manpower-development system, we are reasonably convinced that it has contributed significantly to the continued growth of the organization. Our success, however, has not been without problems. Any organization—business, governmental, or nonprofit—will probably encounter similar difficulties when trying to deal creatively with the complexities of the human element.

In our system of management development we stress heavily the fact that each individual manager has the responsibility for developing those who report to him. By giving each manager this responsibility, we also abandon the idea of universal or corporate "control" over the corporate development program, with the results that in some departments we see managers neglecting their own development as well as that of subordinates. One solution to this imbalance is to empower the staff with the authority to *insist* that all managers cooperate with the corporate training programs. But "forcing" this kind of cooperation often means that people participate reluctantly, with little or no effective changes in behavior. Managers believe that their subordinates are being trained and developed, when in fact they are merely going through the motions.

Another solution is to live with the imbalance, a course of action we have chosen to follow. We continue, however, to attempt to influence those managers who are lagging behind in their understanding of our philosophy of development because we see this understanding as part of *their* development. Eventually we hope to create an entire organization where all managers in key positions take an active, enthusiastic interest in developing themselves and their subordinates.

Training and development efforts usually pay off only over a long period of time, and indeed there is always the risk that they may never pay off at all. Tough, hard-driving managers who want good economic results in a short period of time are often tempted to sacrifice the long-range benefits of development, as is the corporation, to reduce budgeted expenditures. To remedy this situation, individual managers are not directly penalized for the corporation's heavy investments in development activities, and their economic performance in meeting short-range objectives is not compromised. A similar budgeting arrangement is used for the training staff and necessary materials, although a portion of the costs associated with administering the program is allocated to various divisions of the organization. Here again we must live with any conflicts, readjusting the program constantly to seek a viable balance. Time is essential for training and development. Managers caught up in a busy schedule are too often afraid to spend the time necessary to develop themselves and their subordinates for fear that they will neglect their everyday activities. At the same time they realize that if they do not, their effectiveness will eventually be critically reduced. Managers who insist on doing or checking everything themselves harm their subordinates by not giving them enough responsibility and independent work in their department. This neglect in turn jeopardizes development, because they fail to prepare themselves to take on positions of higher responsibility and complexity.

Part of the solution lies in the overall structure of the organization. If responsibility for decision-making is pushed down to the lowest level appropriate to the situation, managers at all levels have more time to develop themselves and to find more challenging work for their subordinates. Each manager then discovers that he is able to delegate to others more of the duties and responsibilities of his own position, thus giving himself more time.

It must be remembered that training and development consist largely of what is done on the job and not off. Too much emphasis can be placed on "outside exposure." If the demands of meetings, conferences, and seminars become too pressing, the development and growth resulting from work experience within the organization may suffer.

One of the key aims of our entire development effort is to produce the kind of "self-motivated achiever" described by psychologist David McClelland. We spend large amounts of money and effort in our recruitment programs to find such a man, one who gravitates toward accountability and responsibility and is capable of working hard to achieve his own objectives and goals without much outside prodding. Although we like to think that we are an organization of achievers, as achievers grow in stature and move from lower levels of the organization to higher levels of management, serious problems arise.

At the lower levels people are rewarded for their ability to do things on their own. Although the achiever learns to work with other people, he relies most heavily on his own enthusiasm and commitment to the task; he becomes identified as a "guy who gets things done." As he is promoted to positions of greater responsibility and complexity, we begin to stress the importance of developing those that report to him. We caution the achiever not to do everything himself now; instead, he must delegate responsibility and work with his subordinates in order to develop them. This is often confusing to the person who has learned that success comes from "doing it yourself," and some managers never make the adjustment. Those who do adjust realize that achievement in their new role is simply of another variety, and it is extremely important that the organization recognize and reward this appropriate change in behavior.

Another problem area in any development program, one well investigated by Chris Argyris, is the "congruency of goals," that is, the meshing of individual goals and objectives with those of the organization. Since we need to establish an atmosphere of freedom to develop, we must also pay the price of the confusion and disorganization that result when individuals are not completely aligned with corporate goals and vice versa. Our statement of corporate purpose describes our intention to develop people so that they can reach levels in the organization commensurate with their abilities and ambition. If we accept this goal seriously, we must be prepared to pay a great deal of attention to what individuals want to do. At higher levels in the organization we often find that the desires of individual managers cause a serious reexamination of the nature of the corporation's business. Although every organization continually faces these confrontations, it seldom recognizes that this conflict exists between individual and corporate goals and can result in the departure of individuals who are not encouraged by an organization to state their personal ambitions.

To solve this problem we have tried to develop a democratic environment of participation and to define with each manager the proper guidelines for his management position—budget and control guidelines, position descriptions, plans and objectives, and areas of accountability and responsibility. In addition, we encourage our managers to renegotiate the boundaries of guidelines that surround their jobs if they feel the position description or budget allocations are not appropriate. We want managers at all levels to show a certain degree of what I call "controlled mutiny," to challenge the *status quo* in an active attempt to redefine their position in the organization. But to maintain order and consistency, managers must operate within the established boundaries and guidelines until agreement has been reached on the new and extended definitions.

We must allow individuals to influence the destiny of the organization, for only in this way will the organization grow as the result of their development. If we do not attempt to accommodate personal desires and ambitions as people grow and develop their capabilities, we will either lose their services or they will operate at less than full potential.

The self-motivated achiever has caused many problems for our organization. Because he often has an abrasive personality and is usually a perfectionist intent on reaching his goals and objectives, he is not always a good team man. He tends to cause conflicts and frustrations among fellow workers because he is intolerant of their weaknesses and inadequacies. The successful development of subordinates requires a fine sense of teamwork, the "supportive relationship" discussed by Likert. Yet because the achiever operates with such aggressive determination, manipulating others as mere tools to help accomplish a task, he often prevents a smooth teamwork atmosphere from existing. We are a long way from evolving effective solutions to this problem. At best, we must try to soften the abrasiveness and the aggressiveness of the achiever without dulling the determination and drive that are so necessary to our success as a corporation.

Part of our training and development efforts has been directed toward educating our managers to work effectively in a complex interpersonal environment. We must learn to create and maintain an efficient, supportive, teamwork environment at the same time that we develop individuals who are making truly unique contributions as a result of their achievement drives. Since both elements are essential to the ultimate success of the organization, we must also seek the best possible solutions to the conflicts that will inevitably ensue.

An environment of rapid dynamic growth is usually considered ideal for the development of people. A growing organization finds it easier to attract new people, and the ambitions of the present management group can more easily be accommodated when new and interesting challenges and opportunities frequently occur. But once an organization is geared to rapid growth, it becomes very difficult to handle any slowdown that is often necessary for consolidating and preparing for future cycles of growth. At such times managers, especially the younger men, often become disillusioned and frustrated, and we run the risk of losing them to other organizations. Although fast change can provide an exciting and exhilarating atmosphere, it threatens to be a destructive force if suddenly replaced by a period of retrenchment.

Another difficulty results when managers tend to develop habits that are appropriate for temporary adaptive situations but unsuitable for establishing stability. We find that those new divisions and departments that are in a continual state of flux often have difficulty assimilating new people because traditional patterns of operating procedures and systems have simply not been developed. New people find no firm guidelines, no well-developed systems by which they can orient themselves and apply their abilities to their new tasks. As a result, their flounderings often add to the confusion already associated with rapid change.

Many managers joining our organization are attracted by the challenging and exciting atmosphere that they see or feel around them. But what we sometimes find is that many of these men, once faced with specific risk-taking and challenging situations, begin to take refuge in fairly bureaucratic practices. One of our chief problems, therefore, is to distinguish individuals who have the true entrepreneurial spirit from those who cannot handle the rigors of actual challenge and risk-taking. Furthermore, although one aspect of job enrichment is the delegation of additional responsibility, as Frederick Herzberg, professor of psychology at Case Western Reserve University, claims, people often request increased responsibility only because they think this is expected. We have used the services of industrial psychologists to help our managers gain insight into themselves, their capabilities, and their real ambitions and drives.

Business must learn to develop and reconcile two different kinds of people—the manager and the administrator—within one organization. The creative manager, the entrepreneurial, Promethean spirit, seeks out situations characterized by inconsistency and change because he enjoys creating order out of chaos. Once this task is accomplished to his satisfaction, he tends to lose interest in the project and to seek other more exciting situations. The administrator, on the other hand, gravitates toward fairly rigid situations that require the qualities of patience and consistency. The administrator is not flamboyant or particularly creative, but he is of equal importance to any organization that desires cohesiveness or continuity.

Learning depends largely on the freedom to make mistakes. If we are sincere in our desire to develop managers by encouraging them to take risks and accept challenges, we must find acceptable ways to tolerate mistakes. But how far can the organization go in allowing mistakes? Can we afford to let a young manager try to install a system that we are absolutely certain will fail? Can we afford to let a new salesman learn at the risk of losing one of our key customers? Will that learning experience enable him in the future to produce enough customers to make up for the loss? In short, can we really afford to absorb mistakes with the hope of getting a greater gain in the future as a result of the learning that occurs on the part of the individuals involved? Too often, I believe, we prevent people from learning by being fearful of possible mistakes.

Again, although we have found no perfect solutions, the guidelines and boundaries of operation that we give managers help prevent any major mistakes from being made that might be damaging to the organization. Once boundary lines have been established, however, we must allow individuals to make mistakes within their areas of responsibility and to explore different courses of action so that we maximize the opportunities to learn.

Accountability and responsibility allow the greatest opportunity for people to develop. As a result of this system, however, individual managers may become autocratic and dictatorial—behavior anti-thetical to that necessary for development. Organizations, like any democratic society, must decide how far to extend an individual's freedom to propose and follow possibly destructive courses of action. I believe that accountability for results will inevitably help to correct any weaknesses resulting from managers selecting inappropriate styles of management.

For any organization emphasizing the development of people, open communications is an absolute necessity. Again, however, we are immediately faced with the question of how much information must be kept confidential, how much must be imparted to a select few, and how much can be safely distributed to the entire management organization. By establishing what we call a Management Center where managers of all levels are free to meet and talk about anything they want at any time, we hope to provide a solution. Top management is expected to respond to any questions with open and honest answers and at the same time can gain a better understanding of problems and situations in areas not under their direct supervision.

Even this arrangement can cause difficulties. For example, outside visitors, including financial analysts, often meet managers from all levels and disciplines in the organization. Although we risk giving out improper or incorrect information, we continue to support an open, candid atmosphere of communications as necessary for the development of people.

As a result of improved communications, a more creative atmosphere exists within the corporation and recruiting has been made easier and more effective. Although selection has become very careful at the upper end of the employment scale, increased confidence in our ability to train and develop people has made it possible to lower qualifications for positions that require relatively low skills. The implementation of thoughtful individual development activities over a reasonable period of time has enabled us to identify more easily those whose personal objectives and needs cannot be integrated with those of the corporation. Terminations become less arbitrary and painful, and counseling for other employment situations becomes more fruitful.

Exposure to the hypotheses, findings, and application of behavioral science in the fields of organization and motivation enables managers to understand their own role in a positive manner and has given them a much wider comprehension of behavior in general.

Management Is the Development of People

The promotion and transfer of subordinates have been much easier to effect, and development through challenge can now be accomplished on a more realistic and logical basis.

Conclusion

Our entire development system has been designed to enable people to become more productive and thus to insure the growth and prosperity of the corporation. Several more years of implementation will probably be necessary before specific, definitive examples of success can be used to persuade others to accept and apply behavioral theories in their own organizations. Many businessmen have consistently failed to understand that we are actively pursuing these ideas of manpower development because we firmly believe that the people in an organization constitute its single most important asset: They contribute the most to its profitability and productivity; to the invention, research, and development necessary for growth and expansion; to the reduction of costly behavior that hinders profitability; and to the successful exploitation of market opportunities and the fulfillment of our obligations to our shareholders.

Since we allow for the depreciation of physical assets, it is equally important to provide for the appreciation of our human assets, not because of paternalism or exploitation but because of our belief that this is the most effective way to achieve profitability and continued growth. Businessmen are becoming increasingly aware that the development of our full human potential is essential to solve the complex problems of a modern world. Only by changing systems of organization and management can we make self-actualization possible for all people at all levels of society.

REFERENCES

1. Rensis Likert, *The Human Organization: Its Management and Value* (New York, 1967), p. 1.

2 Carl R. Rogers, *On Becoming a Person: A Therapist's View of Psychotherapy* (Boston, 1961), p. 35.

3. Abraham H. Maslow, *Toward a Psychology of Being*, 2d ed. (Princeton, N.J., 1962), p. iii.

HOWARD J. SAMUELS

Black Capitalism:
An Investment in America

AMERICAN BUSINESS is often dynamic, progressive, innovative, and successful. At the ownership level it is also monochromatic—and the color is white.

Business has responded admirably in recent years to employment of blacks at the shop and clerical levels. It has made a conscious, though not wholehearted, effort to bring more blacks into middle- and even occasionally upper-management levels. But in ownership, business is still very much a white world.

Even the term "black capitalism" did not surface in the public dialogue as a national goal until the 1960's. Indeed, it has only been with the new development of black pride and independence that blacks themselves have begun to think very much about the potential of business ownership. The goal of educated and aggressive blacks has traditionally been to rise in the professions where entry was easiest—and no capital was required.

Business ownership is still not a primary goal for blacks, either individually or as part of the black movement. The goal is jobs and advancement. But demands for "a piece of the action" are growing as the number of blacks who are both qualified and motivated for the next step increases. Although black ownership is no panacea for ending economic inequality, it is an essential part of the mix—jobs, education, professional training, and entrepreneurship—if blacks are to take their place in the main channels of the American economy.

As a result of my experience in launching the Small Business Administration's "Project Own"—the first national program that spelled out a commitment to the development of black capitalism on a meaningful scale—I am convinced that dramatic expansion is both necessary and feasible.

Black Capitalism: An Investment in America

A Black Landscape

Certainly we are starting from a very low base. Estimates of how many black businesses exist are based on uneven data, but the best estimate is that less than 3 per cent of the five million businesses in the United States are owned by blacks and other minorities. And the "typical" black business described in an SBA study is basically a one-man retail or service operation. Only one black business out of ten employs more than ten workers. ("Black capitalism" as used in this article is a convenient term for all nonwhite businesses.)

It is easier to see the bleakness of the landscape in a given city. In Washington, D.C.—a city nearly two-thirds black—only 2,000 of the 28,000 businesses are black-owned, and one-fourth of those are beauty parlors or barber shops. In Newark, where more than half the population is black, only 10 per cent of the businesses are owned by blacks. In New York, one out of 40 whites owns his own business; only one out of 1,000 blacks do.

Rebuilding the Inner City

Development of a significant black business community should be an essential national goal. The central cities are suffering from a decline in their business vitality, and the ghetto areas will never be revitalized without black ownership. Although disbursement of the ghetto may be a long-term goal, it is *very* long term. The argument raised in some quarters that expanding black businesses in the inner city is merely "gilding the ghetto" instead of abolishing the conditions that create ghettos is specious. One does not preclude the other, and the timetables are totally different.

White-owned businesses are having an increasingly hard time surviving in the inner city—even begging the question of whether their survival is desirable. Yet there is good business to be done there, where incomes are rising faster than the national average. Given decent stores, blacks would prefer doing business in their own neighborhoods if only as a matter of convenience. Development of modern retail stores and service outfits in these areas is one of the growth possibilities for American business.

Construction is an area of great potential for the inner city. Annual volume of construction in the next ten years is expected to increase from $105 billion to $180 billion. This is a field where small firms predominate, and 200,000 new firms will be needed to meet this demand. There is already a base on which to build further black ownership. Ten per cent of the 250,000 self-employed in the industry and 7.4 per cent of the skilled craftsmen are black. If capital plus some other requirements such as bonding are provided—and they could be—black entrepreneurs could increase their share of this industry significantly. The current Housing and Urban Development Act, in fact, specifies that inner-city construction is to be carried out by residents of those areas to the maximum extent feasible.

In addition to its contribution to the gross national product, the development of a black business "class" would have the same stabilizing and upward-mobility impact in the black community that it had for other ethnic groups in the course of American social development. The small businessman is more likely to be involved in working for community improvement than the employed worker. He has more of a stake in the community; he cannot give up his job and move readily. In the course of business he has to learn how to deal with city hall, with banks, and with the power structure.

In terms of simple justice, development of black ownership is essential to give minorities a truly equal place in the American economy. Only through business is the accumulation of a capital base and real affluence possible—especially given the tax laws of this country.

The Potential

Today, the potential for development of a black business class is encouraging. Although there are few black graduates of Harvard Business School, there is a large number of blacks just below the ownership level who are ready for the next step—the black managers of white-owned stores, for instance, and the middle-management blacks of American corporations. No one really knows just how large this reservoir of talent is, but these potential entrepreneurs can be identified. A systematic program is required for providing the necessary capital and the skills needed to round out their business expertise.

The emphasis in development of black capitalism, in terms of immediacy, should be in the retail and service areas where prospects for success are far greater than in manufacturing. Here, the capital required for entry is relatively small. Auto-repair shops and garages can get started on capital of $10,000 to $30,000 under a franchise arrangement. Something like $10,000 will open a small radio-TV repair shop. Apparel stores require $25,000 to $40,000 while clothing accessories or small specialty shops can get off the ground with $5,000. In addition to the smaller capital requirement, retailing and services are the growth areas of American business today.

Although the potential is there, black capitalism will not flower on its own. The markets and the entrepreneurial base may be there, but two essential ingredients are still lacking—capital and management assistance. There is little capital in the black community. All the black banks in America, for instance, have only one-half of 1 per cent of the assets of the Bank of America. The more affluent blacks are largely salaried and professional people, with no large accumulation of capital. And white banks, until recently, have not been notably keen to make loans to black businesses.

A way must also be found to extend management assistance to potential entrepreneurs who may have, say, sales and marketing experience but need some knowledge of accounting and inventory. Since there has never been a black business tradition of any dimension, young blacks have not grown up in a business environment the way the sons of the European immigrants did, and have not accumulated any comprehensive business orientation.

Looking for a Way

How, then, is black capitalism to be developed? The answer begins with government leadership. The resources, the talent, and the drive are in the private sector, but unless these are channeled into a systematic development program, they will remain untapped.

The history of government efforts to foster black capitalism is skimpy indeed. The Economic Development Administration (in the Department of Commerce) made some effort to encourage black businesses, but that was incidental to its main purpose of revitalizing depressed areas, particularly rural areas. The Department of Commerce had a small experimental program in the mid-1960's dealing with dry-cleaning stores in Washington. In 1967 only $30 million out of a total of $800 million loaned by SBA (or with SBA guarantees) was going into minority businesses.

A national commitment, led by the government, is needed to take more risks and channel more resources into black enterprises from rug-cleaning establishments to electronics-parts manufacturing. It will require a four-dimensional approach:

Capital must be obtained from private financial institutions. Only they have both the money and the knowledge of business potential in the community to carry out a widely diverse lending program.

Management assistance must be mustered from the only place it is now available in an adequate supply—the white business community.

Potential black entrepreneurs must be identified and stimulated to enter the business world, where they have been conditioned to expect only barriers. This is a job for black organizations.

Leadership must come from government. Government must establish goals and coordinate efforts to find, train, and capitalize entrepreneurs. It must energize the banking and business communities—and be prepared to absorb a major share of the financial risk.

The program must be sweeping enough to excite the black community and convince it that the commitment will be sustained. Cynicism must be overcome. A half-hearted program designed to paper over a political campaign pledge would be tragic.

Let us consider each of these requirements in turn.

Capital. There will never be enough capital supplied by government in direct loans to make much of a dent. It must come from private banks. There are enough banks willing to do their part, given adequate guarantee against undue risk. Banks in the big cities recognize both the growing markets and the growing business potential for themselves in cities where the customers increasingly are black.

Making loans to minority businesses, however, must be done on a different basis than regular business loans. There is no getting around the fact that the risk is higher. The expectable loss rate for regular bank loans is less than half of 1 per cent. SBA, which was created to provide capital for riskier ventures, has a regular loss rate of about 3 per cent. With minority enterprises, SBA's experience is that a loss rate of about 12 per cent can be expected. That will come down as the black community gains more business experience, but it is a fact of life now.

This approach—consciously taking larger-than-usual risks on loans with government absorbing the extra risk—is what I call "compensatory capitalism." It is an attempt to make up for historically shortchanging the black community in business affairs. It is no different in principle from the funds channeled into "compensatory education" under existing federal programs for improving ghetto schools.

In this way, the cost to the government is small. Most of the funds invested will show a return. The businesses stimulated in many cases will be net additions to the gross national product—such as home-service businesses where there is now a shortage. Black capitalism may be the least costly of all programs aimed at improving the standing of the black man in the American economy.

Within the banking community, some attitudinal changes are necessary if the banks are really to respond fully. Commitment from the leaders in banking is the start, but the crunch comes at the loan desk. Loan officers are trained to think cautiously. Their performance is judged by their superiors in terms of low loss rates, and too few loan officers have any personal experience for judging black applicants. A number of banks have responded to this problem by designating special loan officers (sometimes black but not always) to handle this business. Some banks have set up systems whereby a loan application from a minority businessman cannot be turned down without being reviewed by a top officer of the bank.

Management Assistance. Obtaining capital is in many ways the easiest part. Minority entrepreneurs need some expert management assistance to get over the first hurdles, and the best help is likely to come from businessmen already experienced in the industry. Organizing such assistance is a role for government. Plans must be formulated for organizing on an industry-by-industry basis. Supermarkets, clothing stores, dry-cleaning establishments, nursing homes, and auto dealerships are examples of proliferating businesses where the leaders can be called upon to participate in an organized drive. Trade associations provide a ready-made vehicle. On the whole, however, volunteers are not a reliable source of management assistance. It may be that a system of paid management consultants needs to be developed as part of a black-capitalism program.

Developing Entrepreneurs. The third requirement, after capital and management assistance, is finding and developing the potential owners. The help of black organizations is needed to identify those who have some business experience, ambition, and drive and to bring them into the business process. Some of the best potential, incidentally, is among the militants. Their aggressiveness and desire for independence are great assets. In a few cities, excellent black business organizations already exist, such as Detroit's ICBIF and Chicago's Economic Corporation. Organizations like the Urban Coalition, Urban League, and CORE can be utilized, and have been with considerable success.

The Leadership Role. Finally, the leadership to bring all these pieces together must come from government. The woeful unfamiliarity with the black community is a dimension that must be improved if any government agency is to function successfully as organizer and catalyst of a black capitalism program prodding the banks, stimulating management assistance from business groups, working with minority orgnizations, and helping individuals prepare and process loan applications.

There is no one best way of developing black capitalism; it is a field ripe for innovation. One idea that merits intensive consideration is to develop a national organization—similar to the National Alliance of Businessmen which organizes industry to find jobs for the hard-core unemployed—as the instrument for carrying out the "government" role of coordinator and catalyst. A national business organization utilizing government guarantees, training grants, and so on could establish a unit in every major city headed by a prominent businessman and professionally staffed. It could serve as "packager" to put loan applicants, loans, and management assistance together. It could work closely with government and yet be the real focal point for community action. Above all, what is now important is that the government identify black capitalism as a major national goal, organize a program that will stimulate the capital and talent of the private sector, and demonstrate a significant and continuing commitment. It is time to end the white-on-white coloration of American business ownership.

CHARLES R. DeCARLO

Business and the Quality of Life

WE ARE swimming through a sea of business bureaucracy, with some companies operating for profit, some as nonprofit but private, some as quasi-public, but all operating as chartered agents of the state, with their own organizational life and their own role in the psychological mosaic that is our materialistic culture.

This materialism that is America has a special quality, and our life is suffused with its consequences. It represents a flowering of progress and technology which is rooted in the materially conditioned philosophy of pragmatism. From its first days, the Republic has paid attention to things and to the concrete; there has been little room for the metaphysical or speculative philosophy. In the days of the frontier, and later in the days of industrial expansion, the thing at hand was always of more concern than the speculations of the mind. Early colleges may have trained the ministers and teachers, but the doers and changers of society went into the practice of law and the mercantile world. In both the tradition of law and mercantile practice, property and things were the ground plane upon which the system of values was conceptualized. Property rights under the powerful impress of a pragmatic science of technology were soon extended and amplified to include not only ownership of immediate and local things but ownership of opportunities distant in time and space. The individual owner (later to be expanded into the corporate entity), extending and consolidating his property and aided by the frontier myth of rugged individualism, became the model of the successful economic man. Faced with the enormous opportunities the rich land offered, business and technology grew like a weed feeding on knowledge. We grew far beyond Bacon's dictum that "knowledge is power" to convert knowledge and technology into prime movers and engines of power.

"Success breeds success," "what works is right," and all of the other maxims of the hardheaded pragmatic world became our faith.

But in the philosophy of pragmatism, the strain of instrumentalism sounds a dominant note. Instrumentalism's conception of seeing ideas as instruments for action fitted perfectly the pragmatic nature of the individual, private-property, free-enterprise system. In this spirit colleges were founded, as in the Land Grant Act, for the purpose of achieving the useful application of knowledge. The growth of our great state universities and technical schools was in this tradition of applying knowledge and ideas for the transformation of the material world. And if ideas are instruments for action and solving problems, a kind of dualism follows that leads to the organization of knowledge in terms of problems to be solved. By this process there has been a continuous adjustment of the functions of knowledge and technological process to the ever-arriving edge of new opportunities presented in the market place. In the pragmatic world, the pursuit of knowledge became the key to unlocking the next industrial opportunity. It is only natural that in the last decade we should have come almost full circle in this dualism between knowedge and action with the creation and naming of a new industry—the knowledge industry.

American public and private educational systems are in the grip of this instrumentalism. In large universities and professional schools, knowledge is organized in terms of problem areas. Institutes are formed to assemble knowledge and ideas around specific programs and processes. Within the schools, at all levels, knowledge is packaged, quantified, and almost weighed out on a pound-by-pound basis in a credentializing rat race. David Riesman and Christopher Jencks in their volume, *The Academic Revolution*, sketch out the hierarchy in American education which is dominated at the top by recruitment requirements of the business and professional establishments.

But one of the consequences of materialism is the fact that, as it is successful, it gluts its own markets. For materialism, which is built upon the idea of individual property rights and individual consumption, must ultimately be bounded by the number of hours and days, the amount of energy, time, and spatial movement the individual can undertake. Thus in our economy, in order to guarantee more individual consumption, we must have a brilliant scheme of planned obsolescence and an increasing devotion to converting frivolous desires to urgent needs.

Until recently only the crank, the socialist, the outsider questioned the virtues of progress, technology, entrepreneurship, and the other ideas of the business society. It was easy for most to accept the idea of business providing products to individuals. This clearly raised the standard of living and gave an increasing abundance to our lives. However, we began to be vexed in instances where business provided services to more than the individual, or affected other individuals in providing such service. With such situations came the beginnings of social control. Public utilities and other bodies that come under state and federal regulations are demonstrated attempts to solve the problems associated with providing something other than that which can be individually owned and individually consumed. The necessity for social control has been aggravated as American business develops increasing refinements in science and technology—refinements that bind us closer together and make of us a systematic society. For example, I cannot afford to take the time, money, or training necessary to fly myself from New York to California, nor to grow food, nor to build the house that I need. Therefore I am drawn into a network of electrical power, transport systems, news-media distribution systems, educational systems, and so forth. And each of these services is organized as almost separate subgovernmental units. The New York Port Authority, the Air Traffic Control System, the Northeast Power Council, the private carriers are all systems much larger than the individual and require—even though the business base is essentially individual consumption by the client—a total business climate that is socialistic rather than capitalistic in tone. As a result, an attitude within and about big business has developed that has endowed it with a kind of social and service image only distantly related to individualistic enterprise.

A corollary dilemma facing us as we have moved from the economy of individual consumption to that of broader services is the inadvertent effects of pollution and environmental degradation as business and industry carry out processes on a local or parochial basis. These are functions that must be socially measured. But in a society operating within the myth of individual property rights and business entrepreneurship, rational approaches are difficult to achieve.

Certain attitudes within and about American business directly affect the lives of all citizens. The first is the lack of historical perspective. There is a deep acceptance of the present as being almost unique, a desire to hold on to what has been gained and keep a foothold in reality by overrating the accomplishments of the present.

Rarely does a corporate executive have a sense of history or an understanding of where the corporate form originated, what its relationship is to other institutions, and what its antecedents for legitimacy might be. What view there is of the past is a romantic view. An ethos has developed built upon frontier images of a time that was sweet and innocent—a time in which individual risks might have been higher, yet when the gains of the simple life offset such risks.

But if the past is considered a separate and innocent time, the future has about it a terrible fascination. Many believe that the engines of business are taking us into a future over which we will have no control, and that the immediate effects of technology and the problems being engendered are almost too much to bear. Given the immense concern with the practical, and the complexity of problems already with us, it is natural for people to escape into considerations of the future.

An attitude that follows from the above is fear of change. In spite of great talk about change, no dramatic effort has been made to effect change by conscious and willful understanding of the present system and its major parameters, followed by a commitment to alter the system according to some determined goal. When the thrust of technology and science force rapid change, either the change is accommodated within the framework of the business system—that is, the technological development is converted to a consumable product or service—or the technology is instituted as a new system not directly related to the entrepreneurial business environment. The space program, the development of research in the universities, the poverty program are examples.

This inability to handle change is often manifested as a disregard for those who would seek change. The tensions of the so-called generation gap—the questioning of values by young people, their refusal to accept the authority of the establishment, and their desire to express themselves—run counter to the adult image of stability and goodness. Similarly, blacks, on the edges of the society demanding admission and equality, represent to business not so much a racial factor as a change factor—something that will break old patterns and demand new relationships. Only by conscious effort can the business community encourage admittance of these two groups.

Compounding the difficulty of dealing with those who are outsiders is the effect of automation and technology on job displacement. The business community is built upon the notion of the necessity for work. Yet the cult of efficiency has disciplined and rationalized work, has reduced most work to simple functions using only part of a man's capabilities. The aim of the analytic approach to work is to guarantee the interchangeability of people and to reduce to a minimum set of functions the skills required at each stage; the human reaction is frustration and boredom.

The changing nature of work has had its impact upon professionals as well. Lawyers, doctors, teachers, in order to have a freer materialistic individual life, have increasingly transferred much of their professional responsibility to a larger organization. Professional training has shifted the idea of competence in the service of human need from the shoulders of the individual and placed it within the context of bureaucracy, both business and nonprofit.

Another common attitude in the business community concerns fear of other types of political or economic systems. This failure to realize that democracy, socialism, and communism are all merely methods of dealing with social organization bespeaks fear of the outside, fear of possible change.

These attitudes within and about American business—lack of historical perspective, fear of change, inability to deal with the changing nature of work, absorption of the professional into the larger corporate organization, and a kind of isolationist ideology with respect to non-American enterprises—all affect the quality of life in this country.

How do these characteristics affect the quality of life—that is, the opportunity to have such things as a good and varied diet, adequate or better housing, sensible public and private transportation, adequate health services, an aesthetically pleasing environment, and the right to engage in artistic activities?

In its major assault on the quality of life, the business society brings to bear its enormous virtuosity in product marketing. The populace is conditioned to see life primarily in terms of materialistic gains, of possessions. An incredible richness of color, motion, shape, and form inundate the spirit, but all are directed toward the movement of goods and services rather than the development of human potential. Education becomes shaped primarily to materialistic ends and pays scant attention to art or aesthetics. Parochial and short-term thinking ignores the opportunity for the creation of a more beautiful environment. Art becomes a commercial venture since business society, through its communications media, is continuously ingesting the periphery of artistic endeavor, continuously reforming the new into the useful or commercially desired. In turn, the culture of the business society feeds upon itself, for its avant-garde springs principally from manipulating the very stuff of the business system —electronic media, concrete poetry, architectural sculpture, and so on. This is art that proceeds from the consideration of processes among men rather than the importance of the interior struggle of the human being.

In sum, ignoring some accomplishments, we might say the effect of business upon the quality of life is to present increasing material-istic glut; to guarantee that the future will simply be an extension of the present; to support the tensions between young and old which occur because of shifting attitudes on basic issues; to increase the pragmatic emphasis of education, with its paraphernalia of degrees and credentials; to lessen the aesthetic experience, converting it to a commercial enterprise; and to treat the land at best carelessly, and at worst to rape nature when local technological acts are consum-mated without regard to their social and ecological consequences.

If business attitudes and psychology have a direct effect upon the quality of life in America, it should be possible by certain policies and programs to raise the level of that quality.

Controls, restraints, and regulations upon those activities of busi-ness that contribute a negative effect to the general quality of life offer some small measure of help, but restraints and regulations rarely change policy or direction and tend to introduce counter-productive responses. As has been amply demonstrated by history, when regulation is imposed on an industry for the public good, after a period of time we are faced with the problem of keeping straight the identities of the regulated and the regulator.

Perhaps a more fruitful avenue would be the establishment of governmental subsidies to encourage business and industry to under-take programs for the general good. Tax incentives for plant and facilities beautification, rebates and flexible depreciation schedules for new equipment required to eliminate pollution, long-term finan-cial assistance for plant and process changes could all be available as tools for increasing the beauty of the environment and the quality of our life. Further, these incentives are easily adapted to the entre-preneurial and materialistic attitudes of the business society.

But of much greater importance are massive federal programs. Federal programs are urgently needed in housing, in public transportation, in health and educational services. Such programs would be a great source of strength, income, and profit to the private sector. Only the inability of business management to shake off the myth of the past prevents our movement into a new era. For example, instead of planning to invest great sums of money in rehabilitation of the large cities, it would probably be more in line with the psychology of the business manager and help those who are affected to have a program of rural and small-town rehabilitation, with dispersion of industry and resource. Because the condition of the small town is not an urgent and present problem requiring action, the present-minded business society cannot seem to acquire sufficient distance in its thinking to see that it is an important problem of the future. But if business management skills and resources are applied to the problem, particularly with the number of firms operating in national market and production setup, the effect could be electric.

Business society must look at the role of business with respect to the people who work. We must begin to tell the truth about the nature of work, about the ability or inability to use creativity in large organizations, and about the importance of establishing several careers. We should be encouraging young people not to make premature career decisions but rather to develop competencies of a general nature, and to invest much in their own personal development. We should stress the importance of liberal education, and the fact that late entrance into the work force and earlier retirement demand that an individual be stronger and more self-reliant than even the fathers and grandfathers who built this country. We must hammer home the idea that mobility and multiple careers during a lifetime should become the mode rather than the exception.

It is doubtful that the business community can take active singular leadership in any of the above. However, much could be done if the business community would look objectively at its past and its present. It must become free of its pragmatic, practical, and mythically bound notion of property rights and rugged individualism. In concert with humanists, concerned intellectuals, and ardent political thinkers, the business society could form the base for a new and truly great society.

WOLF VON ECKARDT

Business and Urban Order

Rhyme or Reason?

IT IS a cozy idea: Our cities are sick, bankrupt, inefficient, and wicked. Government, with some five hundred oversold and under-funded urban and antipoverty programs, has only made matters worse. Big business is healthy, prosperous, efficient, and virtuous and has mastered the management of a boundless technology. Ergo: Give business the right kind of profit incentives[1] and it will pull the cities out of their rut.

The trouble with this cozy idea is that it does not seem to work. The simplism seems, in fact, dangerous to both cities and business.

At best this naive approach to business involvement in "urban action" offers more of the same—the last thing we need. It spells the same fragmentation of the one thing that holds this or any other society together—its common habitat.

Like the government programs, the equally fragmented and frag-mentizing business projects now bandied about deny the urban ecology and the desperate need for a comprehensive approach, if you will, to the total man-made environment. Worse, with its mesmerized focus on the ghetto, it gives the wrong answer to the crucial life-and-death question the Kerner Commission has asked: Two societies or one?

The best remedy for urban disorder is not piecemeal urban pro-grams but the creation of urban order. Such order—as the National Committee on Urban Growth Policy, among others, has pointed out[2] and as I hope to explain further on—can be achieved. Business can and must play an important role in bringing it about. But this role does not call for speechmaking and piecemeal tinkering in the explosive inner city. That will not help the people who are cooped up in the ghetto. Nor will it do business much good.

Roger Lewis, chairman and president of General Dynamics Cor-poration, must have gotten a whiff of this at the second and most likely the last American Management Association conference on Mobilization for Urban Action in the spring of 1969. Lewis had made a fine, exhortative but innocuous speech on the Waldorf's Starlight Roof. "A leader in the Plans for Progress organization, he unquestionably came expecting a friendly audience," reports the biweekly *Business & Society*. "Instead he found rampant hostility grounded in the frustration of young activists who expected more from the business community. The response that probably produced the most anger was Mr. Lewis' admission that he did not know how many blacks General Dynamics had in its management ranks. He was therefore peremptorily informed that he had no right being chief executive officer of General Dynamics."[3]

Ah, well. We know all about frustrated black activists. But at Reston, Virginia, when the Gulf Oil Corporation took over and, in the interest of management efficiency, summarily fired Robert E. Simon, who had conceived and founded this New Town, white middle-class citizens threatened to burn their Gulf credit cards.

When business, or some segments of business, in the aftermath of the New Deal launched a wordy, star-spangled hurray-for-free-enterprise campaign, there was room for doubt, as William H. Whyte pointed out at the time, as to whether anybody was listening.[4] People are more irritable now. They do listen—and talk back.

Business could, perhaps, inject greater management efficiency into the business of building more low-cost housing and other urban hardware. And that, after all, is what we are talking about. Even public housing projects have obviously not been built by government clerks. They are built by contractors who are as much free-enterprise businessmen as Roger Lewis. Yet, as we shall see—with the exception of some turnkey housing—to date the trial performances in this area have not lived up to their advance billing. And efficient business management of such software urban services as health, education, and welfare is so far only talk—rather silly talk. Urban services suffer enough from the government's inane obsession with the cost-benefit syndrome. Their present inadequate delivery system is further jeopardized by noisy but justified demands for decentralization and local-citizen participation, which business management is even worse equipped to cope with than government management. Have you ever watched a hapless management consultant fidgeting with his charts in front of an angry neighborhood meeting?

But worse, where does the profit come in? Sure, it could be—

and that seems to be the idea—provided by a government magnanimous enough to admit its own failures and pay someone else to do its job. But such a government would not be long in office. America's taxpayers are not very likely to let much more of their money be used for more oily depletion allowances, for ransom to an establishment they are becoming increasingly disenchanted with.

What Has Business Done for Us Lately?

The disenchantment is not just with the military-industrial complex. The disenchanted are not just the young and the black. I am neither. And I am less than enthusiastic about being forced to make the journey to Penn Central's ticket office downtown to stand in line for thirty-five minutes for the privilege of purchasing a ticket from a surly agent for the fast new Metroliner between Washington and New York which my tax money largely paid for. This train might have been a fine example of what free enterprise, with the intelligent help of government, can do to make our urban environment more livable.

Surely fast trains with pleasant service between the cities of megalopolis could substantially ease dangerous congestion and pollution in the sky, around airports, and possible even on the freeways. That is why the government subsidized the Metroliner which, with all our glorious technology and management efficiency, took nearly three years longer to put into operation than the Penn Central had promised. At last it now runs—not as fast and as often as it might, but it runs—piping enervating Muzak into our ears all the way. Reservation, ticketing, food, and other services are, however, still far and, I suspect, deliberately behind those of the airlines which will sell you a ticket aboard or will at least make your reservation by telephone.

Although the Association of American Railroads professed our railroads to be "willing and anxious to do what they can—within their means—to help solve the transportation crisis," most of them, including the Metroliner, make passengers realize how unwelcome they are. There is no profit in moving people, not even with public subsidy, railroad executives told *The New York Times*.[5] But when the Canadian National Railroad decided a few years back to go all out to make its passengers happy with all kinds of delightful innovations, it soon found that passengers also paid their way.

Nor, as a resident of Washington, am I impressed with the

superior business management efficiency of O. Roy Chalk's D.C. Transit System. It is a sordid story which has angered even conservatives in Congress and which will end only when Congress turns the buses over to public ownership where they belong. Suffice it to say that in twelve years Chalk, according to the calculation of one angry Congressman, has made 878 per cent in earnings on a $500,000 investment. He has also made it just about impossible for thousands of Washington's blacks to go where the jobs are, despite one of the highest fares in the country. Chalk's "urban action" has, year after year, consisted of asking for and being granted another fare increase.

It can be argued, of course, that our railroad presidents are the visionless remnants, and the Chalks the shortsighted extremists, of an old-style capitalism that is becoming as obsolete as the steam engine and Adam Smith. And that the highway lobby, whose ruthless insensitivity to urban needs requires no specifics or elaboration, represents the old-fashioned robber-baron and slum-lord kind of business that is outside the consideration of this anthology. The promised new free-enterprise involvement in the city is to be one of the large corporations—the giant agglomerations with their ever-advancing technologies, systems analysis, and urban affairs departments.

Do They Mean What They Say?

Some spokesmen of the new technostructure, as Galbraith calls it, say they agree that the country must shift priorities. As soon as the government moves out of Saigon, they allow, the technostructure will move in on American cities with new know-how, new technological breakthroughs, and new massive investments. "We now have a military-industrial team with unique resources of experience, engineering talent, management, and problem-solving capacities," said Clark Clifford when he was Secretary of Defense in 1968, "a team that must be used to help find the answers to complex domestic problems as it has found the answers to complex weapons systems. These answers can be put to good use by our cities and our states, our schools, by large and small business alike."

But this is not as the leaders of this team in Dallas, Fort Worth, San Diego, and Los Angeles view a post-Vietnam world, if *Washington Post* writer Bernard D. Nossiter is any guide. Nossiter reported, in a story for which he won the Polk Award, that for the big defense contractors "the war's end means no uncomfortable conversion to alien civilian markets. Quite the contrary, and with no discoverable exception, they expect handsome increases in the complex planes and missiles, rich in electronics, that are the heart of their business." We meet General Dynamics again in Nossiter's story—not the boss mobilizing for urban action, but his vice-president in charge of the Washington office, Edward J. LeFevre. "Basically, we're a big systems builder for military weapons. Over 90 per cent of our business is military. We're in that business to stay," he told Nossiter. According to unofficial estimates, General Dynamics expects its military sales at the Fort Worth Division alone to rise from $800 million in 1968 to $1.4 billion in 1973.[6]

The *Report from the Iron Mountain on the Possibility and Desirability of Peace*, which concluded that lasting peace and bona fide world disarmament "would almost certainly not be in the best interests of a stable society," may have been a hoax. But I am afraid that its subsidiary conclusion is not too farfetched as an indication of the thinking in the power centers of the really big, big business world. This conclusion was that any serious attempt to improve our housing, urban development, health, education, welfare, and transportation would not be too expensive but rather "far too cheap" to keep our economic system going, and is "therefore inadequate as an economic substitute for war."[7] In the Calvinist tradition of American business there is very little room for creative imagination about the environment. Business cannot even conceive of what we might make of America if, in addition to social justice, beauty and the public happiness were our goals.

In any event, we cannot live by the sword alone. Not for long. As Jane Jacobs points out in her new book, *The Economy of Cities*,[8] business has always been involved in the city. It has, indeed, been the essence of the city ever since history began with the advent of cities. It will continue to be involved, with or without "urban action" rhetoric.

This involvement is largely responsible for what glory American cities have. What would they be without the skyscraping Promethean spirit of American enterprise? But short sighted and often greedy and socially and aesthetically callous urban action is lately just about all we see, hear, and smell. Business has more than its share of the responsibility for urban decay—for pollution of air, water, and land; for sprawl; for the catastrophic inundation of the city with combustion engines; the demise of public transportation; the misery of the slums; the ugliness of the billboards and speculative office buildings; and freak-out of the white, middle-class taxpayers.

These evils, Jane Jacobs notes, are conventionally blamed on progress. But they are, she says, evils of stagnation. The businessmen of the city have failed to come up, as they did in the past, with new technologies to solve the problems the older technologies have created. Air pollutants and other wastes, for instance, could and should be recycled into useful and profitable products. But where, among the hundreds of new and restyled products we are offered every year, are the desperately needed waste-conversion devices?

There are easier profits elsewhere, particularly in heavily subsidized defense and space paraphernalia. Thus, not free and enterprising progress but free-enterprise stagnation—combined with lopsided government spending—has led to the horrible happening that is our urban environment.

No, one does not need to be young, black, or, worse, a socialist to ask whether the free enterprise that got us into this mess can seriously be expected to have the capability, even if it has the intent, to pull us out. Has business ever on its own succeeded in overcoming its own stagnation?

Business, Bureaucrats, and Bulldozers

Let us not question motivation. The motives of the large business enterprises which joined the federal urban-renewal effort in the 1950's were mostly exemplary. And many of the gleaming new buildings which such corporations as Reynolds and Alcoa have built with federal land writedowns are assets to their cities. Without their participation, in fact, urban renewal could not have gotten underway. But business participation, eagerly solicited by the federal government, has so disastrously perverted the original aims of the program that prenatal death, in retrospect, may have been the lesser evil. In the absence of compensating measures, the program became largely counterproductive.

The original aim of the Urban Renewal Administration, as set forth in the 1949 Housing Act, was to prevent and eliminate blight in the cities. At first, private developers were not interested. Aided by the F.H.A. and expanding highways, they had their hands full building suburbia. Public housing had been getting nowhere.

The new legislation, however, empowered the cities to acquire and raze slum properties and then sell the cleared land at lower prices to private developers. The federal government meets two-thirds of the markdown, the local government the rest. The power of eminent domain, which previously could take private property only for public use, could now take it for a public *purpose*.

And what was that purpose? As long as it was low- and moderate-income housing construction for the people who lived in the slums, the private developers wanted no part of it. As a result, cleared slum sites in the heart of our cities grew weeds and remained vacant for far too many years.

Then, in 1954, the public purpose was shifted to downtown revitalization. That meant luxury apartments for bachelors, bunnies, and airlines stewardesses; motels; offices; department stores; theaters; and opera houses. Suddenly there was, as one entrepreneur put it at the time, "a lot of romance" in urban renewal. "There's no killing in it," he told me, "just a nice fair profit at little risk." There was and is an inordinate amount of red tape, of course. But the way the government, under pressure from the business interests it tried to woo into the program, set up the financing terms, there were very few foreclosures. Even the Chamber of Commerce suddenly came around to give its approval.

For a fleeting moment, as the Eisenhower years came to an end and the new downtown skyscrapers rose on the old slums, there was euphoria in the business community. Fine speeches drowned out the still muted charges of "Negro removal." Remember the brave words about business leadership, skill, and vision; of downtown progress, action, and ACTION (the American Council To Improve Our Neighborhoods)?

Neighborhood implies neighbors—people who live together. Congressman William B. Widnall of New Jersey, who is hardly a radical, kept score on that. In August 1966 he told the Ribicoff Committee[9] that in many cities only a fraction of urban-renewal funds were spent on residential and neighborhood renewal. In Atlanta, Widnall testified, 97 per cent of urban renewal funds were allocated to nonresidential development. In Baltimore, the figure was 77 per cent; in Boston, 60 per cent; in Chicago, 49 per cent; in New York City, 56 per cent; and in Philadelphia, 75 per cent.

"Every dollar spent for nonresidential renewal means that much less for our low-income citizen and our slum dwellers," the congressman explained. "I know all the reasons for commercial renewal by heart . . . business and employment opportunities . . . the increased tax base. [But] the reasons also include the fact that it is easier to get a developer for commercial projects, thus sparing the local officials the embarrassment of land lying idle and vacant."

The slum dweller, Mr. Widnall ventured, "might understand these arguments more readily, if he didn't know that private enterprise has little trouble building luxury apartments or office buildings in other cities or other parts of his own town. He might appreciate these arguments more if the business brought back into the city employed or trained the semiskilled slum dweller seeking employment, rather than for downtown office buildings housing professionals and white-collar workers. The slum dweller might understand more easily if he saw the increased taxes, when and if they occur, earmarked for the schools, playgrounds, and other public improvements his area needs but seldom obtains."

Although his tax money was being used for his alleged benefit, the slum dweller was worse off than before. The urban-renewal authorities kept reassuring us with their relocation statistics, but there was no question, as Mr. Widnall put it, that in most instances the displaced slum dwellers "were forced into circumstances and locations that are rather similar to the places they have vacated. In many instances . . . they are now in worse circumstances because more and more families are clubbed together in one lodging place." Most urban-renewal efforts only pushed the slums from one part of town to another.

And then came the reckoning. When the fires had been put out, the National Advisory Commission on Civil Disorders, headed by Illinois Governor Otto Kerner, found that in face of the fact that 20 million Americans live in substandard housing, government programs destroyed far more low-cost housing than they had built. For example:

In Detroit, a maximum of 758 low-income housing units have been assisted through [federal] programs since 1956. This amounts to 2 per cent of the substandard units and 1.7 per cent of the overcrowded units. Yet, since 1960, approximately 8,000 low-income units have been demolished for urban renewal.

Similarly, in Newark since 1959, a maximum of 3,700 low-income units have been assisted through the programs considered. This amounts to 16 per cent of the substandard units and 23 per cent of the overcrowded units. During the same period, more than 12,000 families, mostly low-income, have been displaced by such public uses as urban renewal, public housing and highways.

In New Haven since 1952, a maximum of 951 low-income housing units have been assisted through the programs considered. This amounts to 14 per cent of the substandard units and 20 per cent of the overcrowded units. Yet since 1956, approximately 6,500 housing units, mostly low-income, have been demolished for highway construction and urban renewal.[10]

Our Low-Cost Housing Failure

We cannot, of course, blame business for the government's failure to build or effectively stimulate the building of at least as many low-cost housing units as it bulldozes, let alone catch up with the backlog. But neither can we claim that American business has made much of an effort to produce decent housing at a price people of below-average income can afford.

The shocking fact is that less than half of American families—those who earn $8,000 a year or more—can afford ownership of a new house. And the cost of housing construction keeps going up at the rate of about 10 per cent a year, while productivity in the housing industry appears to be declining by perhaps as much as 4 per cent annually (in housing even the statistics are deficient).

The causes are complex. For one, the price of land keeps rising alarmingly, owing mainly to outrageous land speculation. Second, the cost of money keeps going up. Third, labor, business' partner in profit, is exploiting its monopoly. It is, of course, the workingman's perfect right to keep up with the general progressive standard of living. But the building trade unions also stubbornly hold on to the long-obsolete exclusivity of their specialized crafts with reactionary restrictions on use of materials, tools, methods, and the recruitment of apprentices. Building codes of which—in this land of standardized TV dinners and look-alike architecture—there are 5,000 different ones in as many communities, further impede building-component standardization, use of new materials, and building-construction productivity.

The building industry and its apologists like to blame it all on these three and other factors, accepting them, like inclement weather, as an act of God. The guts of the dilemma, however, is the building industry itself. It is, with few exceptions, a backward, stagnating, inefficient, and fragmented nonindustry that has been, in a fit of absent mindedness, overlooked by the Industrial Revolution. And the tragedy is not only that, with or without subsidies, it is presently unable to catch up with the nation's low-cost housing needs. It even fails, according to Theodore Larson, head of architectural research at the University of Michigan, to produce enough housing to keep up with the population increase.[11]

So far we have been getting by. The construction dust of gleaming skyscrapers downtown and fancy homes in suburbia has blinded us to the clear and present peril ahead. But other countries, notably France but also, for all its shoddy, look-alike highrises, the Soviet Union, are far ahead of us in industrialized housing production. If homes could be imported like Volkswagens, perhaps America's industry might be awakened to this sad failure of our free-enterprise system. The realization—if indeed it *is* realized—that, as George Romney, the Secretary of Housing and Urban Development has put it, "housing more than almost any other area of the economy, offers the greatest potential for job creation, business development, economic growth, environment improvement and human betterment," has not stirred much more than some luncheon-meeting oratory.

Now Romney says he wants to industrialize housing production. This is more than his predecessors with their paranoid fear of the building-trade unions and builders' associations could bring themselves to say. "But producing an economic and technological breakthrough of the magnitude our housing needs require will not be easy," Romney acknowledges. "It cannot be accomplished overnight. We will have to stop and then reverse some damaging, even crippling trends."[12]

The gist of these trends is that—as both the (Douglas) Commission on Urban Problems and the (Kaiser) Commission on Urban Housing have amply demonstrated—partly owing to government red tape and despite some brave talk about the potential of advanced technology and systems analysis, American business to date has made no serious attempt to provide, as Congress put it back in 1949, "a decent home in a suitable living environment for every American family."

There have been palliatives. After Watts, with more public hoopla than tangible success, some large firms such as U.S. Gypsum, Armstrong Cork, Reynolds, and U.S. Steel have experimented with the rehabilitation of slum housing. The so-called "instant rehabilitation" of New York "old-law" tenements has proved to be, as Charles Abrams pointed out, "the longest and most expensive instant on record." It is time, Abrams observed, "to identify current remedies as what they are—little programs with big promises, minuscule appropriations wrapped in high-sounding oratory, pilot programs that never sail into the wind and nostrums sold to the public as panaceas."[13]

The much-touted $1 billion ghetto-rehabilitation pledge of the insurance companies and the National Alliance of Businessmen's effort to provide jobs for hard-core ghetto youths also fall, I'm afraid, into the nostrum category. The insurance companies' gesture was not quite so noble as it may sound because the F.H.A. insures *them*. And it also has the usual drawback that it does not reach those in real need. They cannot pay the interest rates. And even if the entire billion were devoted to creating new dwelling units, which is very doubtful, it would, as Michael Harrington has pointed out, build only 80,000 units. This is less than 20 per cent of the annual need as defined by the federal government. As Harrington says, "justice is not a sound business investment. The poor *are* a bad financial risk."[14]

Eugene J. Conroy, senior vice-president and general counsel of the Prudential Insurance Company, agrees. He told a symposium on Business in the Ghetto in the summer of 1969 that the investments have been found to be "almost without exception, high risk and low yield." He added that "there is a limit to what private corporations, with duties to their stockholders, and particularly insurance companies with their fiduciary duties to their policyholders can do."

Quite so. The full-page advertisement that announced the program, however, contained no such caveat.

Business and Social Programs

As to job training, we have all seen the pretty magazine pictures of handsome, Afro-haired but clean-shaven youngsters in dashikis, turning lathes or welding wires. The captions inevitably cite impressive statistics of the number of dropouts business has generously taken to its bosom and trained for lucrative jobs.

Many corporate officials are critical of these statistics, however. They talk of "a phony numbers game."[15] It seems that many companies yield to pressure by the National Alliance of Businessmen and report as new "hard-core" recruits youngsters they would have hired anyway. A large percentage of those the N.A.B. claimed to have hired, furthermore, had been hired by one company in the normal course of events and received no special training.

But even if we accept a little puffery, the private-industry effort to help ghetto kids to jobs and upward mobility has so far not been overly impressive. Of the 2.8 million unemployed in 1968, 800,000 were teenagers. But less than 10,000 youngsters, according to industry figures, received special training that year.

Nor is successful job training assurance of a successful upward climb on the mobility ladder. In Washington, D.C., in the summer of 1968, twenty-three hard-core unemployed ghetto residents were trained in cooking and baking under the auspices of the Board of Trade Jobs Center. The cost was at least $4,000 a body, maybe more, according to Frank Lucente of Northern Gas Company, which held the training contract. The trainees were between seventeen and forty-four years old. Twelve of them were women. All of them were diligent. And all passed the course with flying colors and were placed on jobs. A few weeks later, however, only six of the twenty-three still held these jobs. Why?

Some of the women in the group had children and had difficulty finding baby-sitters. Most were dependent on buses, and traveling home late at night was therefore hazardous. A third of the group were given jobs in the suburbs, which meant paying double bus fares and spending as much as four hours a day commuting. The average wage for the graduates was $1.65 an hour and some restaurants balked at paying more than 90 cents for part-time help and $1.40 for fulltime kitchen employees. Once travel cost was subtracted, most of these people's simple arithmetic convinced them that welfare payments left them with more money.[16]

Such is the urban ecology. Job training alone—without swift, safe, and inexpensive public transportation, without day-care centers, without adequate wages, and a host of other things—is like staking a wilting plant in your garden without watering, fertilizing, and otherwise caring for it. It won't do.

Neither can you arbitrarily replant fruit trees into soil that has turned fallow and expect an instant harvest. Robert F. Kennedy was a foremost proponent of the notion that moral exhortation might move corporate employers back into the inner city, notably New York's downtrodden Bedford-Stuyvesant district. A roaring mountain of busy and illustrious magnanimity produced, in the end, one mouse—an IBM plant that makes computer components. It hired about 300 people. Most of them already had jobs. Some 2,200 hopeful applicants had to be turned away. In the view of some concerned Negro leaders, they were possibly more embittered than before. Another hope had been frustrated.

No, that IBM plant is not the only new enterprise Bobby Kennedy's concern has quickened in "Bed-Stuy." In 1968, according to a study by Sal Levitan of the Center for Manpower Policy Studies, twenty-two firms, all told, had been given financial and technical assistance to the tune of nearly $1 million. Their average potential is sixteen employees.[17]

Experience in several other places has shown that, with government assistance or without, free-enterprise transplants into the sick heart of the city promise to do little, if anything, to revive it. Nor has it proved easy to persuade many businesses to perform the operation. As one survey, by the Fantus Company, a Dun and Bradstreet subsidiary, has it, more than one hundred of seven hundred major corporations asked were willing to build new plants in or near the slums. But none of them said it would make such a move under current conditions. They all first wanted a reliable labor force, continuous job-training programs, lower land and construction costs for their plants, ample space with adequate roads and utilities, pleasant surroundings with good housing and without the vandalism and other hazards of ghetto blight.[18] In short, business is perfectly willing to take on the patient provided he is cured first. That hardly makes it the right doctor for this particular ill of our society.

But how could we ever expect that? As John A. Hamilton, a member of the editorial board of *The New York Times,* has stated it: "Business involvement in slum areas needs encouragement. . . . The limits of this involvement, however, need understanding. A business is not a social agency and cannot be expected to perform tasks that properly belong to government and society. A business is, in the end, a business."[19]

A National Policy

But neither can government and society cure the heart of our cities without treating the entire urban body. It is obvious, or should be, that we are not able to solve in isolation any one of whatever aspect of the urban problem one may choose to single out—poverty, housing, transportation, education, pollution, recreation, open space, downtown revitalization, and, most of all of course, racism. None can be solved within the context of the core city alone. We can permit the continued apartheid of two societies—one predominantly black and urban, the other predominantly white and suburban— only at deadly peril of both whites and blacks, city and suburb, law and order, at the deadly peril, in fact, of our whole economy and political and social tranquility. We need, as it has now come to be called, a National Urban Growth Policy.

Under such a strategy, coordinated physical and social reform of existing cities would become possible by building new communities, or New Towns, in our expanding metropolitan areas that are from their very inception racially and economically integrated—places with a sense of place where people of all income groups and backgrounds feel they belong because here they can stay put and can live, work, learn, enjoy, and advance themselves in dignity and comfort. New Towns have been called "essays in civilization."

The United States is the only major country in the world that has not yet adopted such a national settlement policy. But it is now clearly in the offing. Every major aspirant for the presidency, save George Wallace, advocated such a course in one form or another during the talkative summer and fall of 1968. A potent group of senators, congressmen, governors, and mayors (supported by the National Association of Counties, the National League of Cities, and the U.S. Conference of Mayors) has recently reasoned and charted a National Urban Growth Policy in some detail.[20] And leading members of the Nixon administration, notably George Romney, are strongly advocating it.

Let us not quibble here about whether we call the comprehensively planned settlements "New Communities," "New Towns," or "New Cities." The question of size, configuration, character, population density, and relation to the core city cannot be answered in generalities. It depends on location, need, purpose, and other specific circumstances. Since the British passed their New Towns Act of 1946, the term "New Towns" seems to me to be the most widely understood and best defined. It is a term, incidentally, which in Britain, as well as in this discussion, includes the creation of new communities by the planned, comprehensive, and instantaneous expansion of existing small towns.

Nor is this the place to elaborate on the New Town concept with its promise to arrest ecological and economic disaster of urban sprawl, open a way out of the ghetto, achieve the large-scale technological breakthrough in housing production George Romney is pushing for, and enhance the quality of urban life we are all talking about. There is no dearth of literature on the subject. The notion that we should build orderly new communities instead of taking pot luck on social justice, efficiency, beauty, and amenity in our place to live has been around since the London court stenographer, Ebenezer Howard, published his famous tract on Garden Cities some seventy years ago.

Let it here be noted only that Howard's historic and somewhat idyllic concept—new Garden Cities surrounded by permanent greenbelts—has now changed in one very important respect. As he saw it—or, rather, as his views have been interpreted—the virtuous Garden City, hugging the bosom of Mother Nature, was to replace the wicked Industrial City, or, at least, stunt its scabrous growth. Now New Towns—all kinds of New Towns, from verdant, spacious communities, like Tapiola in Finland, to bustling, high-density subcities, like Cumbernauld in Scotland—are conceived as instruments of metropolitan growth. The new satellites—and that, rather than science-fiction utopias hundreds of miles away from nowhere, is what we are talking about—will enable the city to live and prosper again.

It is rather silly, therefore, to charge, as Jane Jacobs did, that the New Town idea "viciously assumes that blacks are not going to solve their problems either for themselves or for the cities, that the cities can be rescued only by whites."[21] No one proposes to exclude blacks from running for municipal office and running the city if elected. Nor does anyone propose to ship people out of the ghetto in cattle cars and forcibly settle them in integrated communities.

As George Romney put it, the fact that our solutions cannot be centered merely on the slums does not mean that we should not also try to rehabilitate the ghetto. Many families, Romney said, "simply do not want to leave the homes of their fathers, and the neighborhood in which they were born. Rather than suffer the pains of dislocation, every effort should be made to make their homes and environment more attractive and livable." But to do that, and bring taxpayers, business, amenity, and viability back into the inner city, it must obviously be decongested in some areas. We cannot continue urban renewal without humane resettlement of the people living in the buildings we want to renew. The most humane way to resettle them is to offer them a new and better home in a new and better community close to new and better jobs. We would thus offer people additional choices of where, how, and next to whom they want to live.

Edward G. Sharp has therefore called New Towns "the black man's hope." Writing in the *Reston Times* he asserted "a new town, like Reston is fresh and innocent. Men can build a tenable, stable environment without first having to tear down pillars of old urban systems." And that is the point for whites, too.

Can private business build these New Towns? Of course not. Not alone. We are talking about complete communities, not real-estate ventures. And private business can no more provide all the facilities and operations of a complete community than it can provide for the common defense. Nor should it. Nor would it want to.[22]

It may be ephemeral fun for some business spokesmen to get high on the hubris that business can do anything better (including, as has been suggested in this book, running public education or trash disposal at a profit), but they tend to sober when they face up to the headaches.

It is true that the only two bona fide New Towns that have recently been launched in this country, Columbia and Reston, are private developments. But Columbia's idealistic developer, James Rouse, credits his success to a very unique set of circumstances not likely to be duplicated a second time. He would not venture it again. And the other, Reston, has already had one perilous shake-up and, although as a subsidiary of the Gulf Oil Corporation it may eventually become solvent, it is by no means certain that solvency can be achieved by the kind of complete, socially balanced, "fresh and innocent" town Edward Sharp hopes for and the country needs. We all know what happens to the freshness and innocence of girls when they get obsessed with the profit motive.

What is needed for New Towns, among many other things, are a large parcel of land in the right location with its own zoning and building codes and the authority to put in its own roads, sewers, and municipal services *and to run them.* The town will never be a real town if it remains at the mercy of often hostile or uncomprehending rural authorities. What it further needs is low-cost, that is, subsidized, housing and such public services as job training, family counseling, and fresh new education, transportation, and recreation, including inviolate open space. It needs state and national support under a regional growth policy to attract, lure, or cajole the right kinds and variety of employment centers. It needs protection from parasitic development around it that would destroy the integrity of the plan. Most of all, it needs the will and the money to go first class, to assure that new quality of life that the next generation has every right to expect of America.

Private business alone, the profit motive alone, the cost-benefit syndrome, cannot possibly provide this quality. Yet that is the issue today. The Affluent Society, as we should know by now, even without forceful reminders by the kids on the campus and the blacks in the ghetto, is no longer enough.

The Limits of Free Enterprise

An economic miracle was indeed wrought by Puerto Rico's Operation Bootstrap, as Eli Goldston suggests.[23] But the miracle, which, incidentally, required not only Puerto Rico's dispensation from federal taxes but also $4.8 billion of net federal expenditures in the years 1948-1967, is far from complete. In 1968, some 13 per cent of the island's total work force remained unemployed. Dire poverty still existed in the barrios—the squatters' colonies. Though a third of Puerto Rico's budget is devoted to education, it still does not meet needs. And so little has been invested in agriculture that a substantial part of the island's food must be shipped in at monopoly rates.[24]

It is also worth noting that an island that only started to build modern cities thirty years ago already finds it necessary to engage in some sixty projects to renew them. Much of the island is blighted. Behind the flashy facades of Miami-type beach hotels and bootstrap industrial buildings you will find all the schoolbook examples of the urban mess.

The chaotic jumble of mostly ugly buildings and uglier parking lots and utility poles is relentlessly sprawling along the traffic-choked roads that lead out of San Juan. Much of the lovely countryside is covered with a nebulous film of unlovely agglomerations of ticky-tacky housing and all kinds of jerry-built contraptions. Even the island's most enchanting mountain roads are blighted with the rusting corpses of junked cars.

This is progress American style. It has, to be sure, raised the standard of living in Puerto Rico. But not the standard of life, which is what the New Towns must pioneer. Unfortunately, however, there is no immediate financial gain of the kind that pleases the stockholders in a day-care center, or the beauty of a building, or the smell of a flower, or the splashing of a fountain, or even the happy laughter of a child who can walk to school without risk of colliding with a combustion engine.

General Electric, at any rate, did not find a prospect of profit in investing in a livable place to live. In August 1966, G.E. announced that it had set up a Community Development Division that would do research on and develop New Towns. The idea, the company proclaimed, was not only real-estate investment diversification. G.E.'s interest, it was said, encompassed such matters as the aesthetic quality of the new community, community services, the building process, innovations in construction techniques, new products, and new systems and subsystems.

In February 1969, G.E. called it quits. "After three years of intensive effort and exploration, the company has been unsuccessful in its efforts to locate the proper combination of circumstances that can make a large-scale, planned community venture possible and profitable," said George T. Bogard. "If you have gathered the impression by now that G.E. is discouraged about its prospects for developing new cities," he added, "you are right!"

The federal government alone, so help us, cannot be relied upon to do it either, though in Britain and other democratic countries it seems to manage. These countries also have their problems with government bureaucracies. But they do not have to contend with the penury and meddlesome distrust of a still largely uncomprehending Congress (overdiligently representing, to be sure, a still largely uncomprehending and antiurban electorate).

In America the most promising road would seem to be to organize public development corporations on which the state, local governments, and the public are represented. In New York, a State Development Corporation has assumed the task under the energetic leadership of Edward J. Logue. The details of organization, however, are less important than a substantial federal commitment and federal coordination. The cost, as the Committee on Urban Growth points out, "will be small compared to the cost incurred by the inefficiencies in the current approach to development and the lack of coordination among existing programs. . . . The building of new communities will produce efficiencies and returns to the national economy which dwarf the direct outlays involved."[25]

In part the money might come from a more realistic approach to the relocation of the victims of public works. Rather than pushing the slums around we should, before we destroy a home by public action, have a new home, which the displaced family can afford, ready and waiting for it to move into. When the Department of Transportation, for instance, finances the right-of-way for roads, it should, as Charles Abrams has suggested, at the same time finance the purchase of excess land for housing and new communities.[26] I would, under a National Replacement Housing Act, extend this concept to every public action—school, hospital, municipal or urban renewal, and model city—in which federal money is involved. It seems only fair and has long been a practice in Europe. Such legislation would accelerate both low-cost housing construction and necessary public works with the assurance, however, that urban rebuilding is not undertaken again at the expense of the poor who have no place to go. It would also make effective regional planning necessary and that, of course, is essential to a new urban order.

How Business Can Help Urban Order

What should business do to contribute to urban order? It can help in many simple ways that seem no less valid for their elementary simplicity.

In the first place, let business stop contributing to urban disorder. Let it assume a greater sense of responsibility—that is, let it cultivate an ability to respond far more readily than it now does to the desperate needs of our urban environment. It might be a good beginning if private industrialists would find it within their individual and collective hearts to stop throwing their garbage into our air and water instead of fighting every timid regulatory move by government. LIVES—a League of Industry Volunteering for Environmental Sanity—might be a welcome acronym to add to the roster of public-spirited business organizations. I could go on to other things that might so simply be stopped by one responsible decision up there in the executive office, such as the continued flight from the inner city or the use of land, not for private greed but for the public interest.

Second, as Charles Abrams has put it, "if private enterprise is to function in the cities, as I believe it should, we need a philosophy that acknowledges that central city and suburbs are an interdependent entity, a philosophy that puts maximum responsibility for the city's future on the federal government. When a constructive philosophy emerges, constructive legislation will follow."[27]

The above essays the parameter of such a philosophy. Let business get behind it and push and prod the Executive and Congress into accepting and refining it. There are untold profits to be made from urban order.

Third, let big business begin to think small. We cannot, to be sure, in this day and age of computer efficiency, set back the clock to the all-but-lost social and psychological benefits of the neighborhood Pa-and-Ma store, the friendly neighborhood service man who is smiles not just in the advertisements—the business, in short, that is not mysteriously inaccessible as in Kafka's anonymous Castle but, rather, that cares and serves people.

But is it really part of big computer management efficiency that all our chain stores from coast to shining coast look drearily alike? Are there not ways and indirect profits for Big Brother were he to assist rather than crush the small business of vending flour; of operating cafes and bars without Muzak and Formica where a man can linger and feel human; of running small restaurants where the food —just plain, simple fare for plain, simple fees—is cooked rather than defrozen and deprocessed; and of maintaining shops that cater to special tastes, needs, and eccentricities beyond the ken of the market analysts' statistical averages? This—not only corporate palaces and marble shopping malls with their ubiquitous and insipid stockbrokers' and airline offices—is the stuff that good cities are made of. This and, as Jane Jacobs says, the ingenious inventiveness of the small businessman in the big city, not the Research and Development Division removed from human life and needs way out there in suburbia or up there on the sixty-ninth floor. I, for one, don't care if the floor space and bank accounts of such vital, small, urban enterprises are all conglomerated by some super corporation as long as we find a way to save their souls and their humanity. Without them the soul and the humanity of the city is lost. And city is a word quite closely related to civilization.

Fourth, let business do what it does and must—only a little better and with somewhat greater social awareness. I can think of a great many business buildings, for instance, that might quite easily, and at only slightly greater expense, have been assets to our cityscape rather than eyesores. The businessmen in Rotterdam seem to gain more prestige from contributing beautiful statuary to the public parks and plazas than from erecting jarring billboards. But in the event that you hold, with some errant sociologists, that environment has no influence on human behavior, there are always, for every business, ways and means to extend special consideration and service to the underprivileged. The slums are slums largely because not only their public but also their private services tend to be less efficient, shoddier, and more expensive than in the respectable parts of town. If we are ever to catch up, we must shift into reverse.

These are, I admit, not dramatic, instant panaceas that will yield business quick-buck public-relations results. In fact, unlike the pleasant mirage of "urban-action programs," they will do little to change the business image. But they just might give this image that undefinable taint of forthright humility we admire in honest persons.

REFERENCES

1. Eli Goldston, "New Prospects for American Business," in this volume.

2. National Committee on Urban Growth, *The New City*, published for Urban America, Inc. (New York, 1969).

3. *Business & Society*, Vol. 1, No. 24 (June 10, 1969).

4. William H. Whyte, Jr., *Is Anybody Listening?*

5. *The New York Times*, June 15, 1969.

6. *The Washington Post*, December 8, 1968.

7. *Report From the Iron Mountain on the Possibility and Desirability of Peace*, with introductory material by Leonard C. Lewin (New York, 1967).

8. Jane Jacobs, *The Economy of Cities* (New York, 1969).

9. Hearings before the Subcommittee on Executive Reorganization of the Committee on Government Operations on the Federal Role in Urban Affairs, 88th Congress, August 15 and 16, 1696, p. 66*ff*.

10. *Report of the National Advisory Commission on Civil Disorders* (New York, 1968), p. 142.

11. Theodore Larson, "Contrary to the Sound of Battelle, "*Journal of the American Institute of Architects* (August, 1968), p. 47.

12. "New Directions at HUD," *Nation's Cities* (June, 1969), p. 18.

13. Princeton University Conference No. 88, "Cooperation of the Public and Private Sectors in Housing," April 18 and 19, 1968.

14. Michael Harrington, *Toward a Democratic Left* (New York, 1968), p. 102.

15. *The New York Times*, March 15, 1969.

16. *The Washington Post*, October 20, 1968.

17. Sal Levitan, "Developing Business and Entrepreneurs in the Ghetto," Record of the National Industrial Conference Board, July, 1969.

18. *The New York Times*, October 22, 1968.

19. *The New York Times,* February 10, 1969.

20. National Committee on Urban Growth, *op. cit.*

21. Leticia Kent, "Jane Jacobs: Against Urban Renewal, For Urban Life," *The New York Times Magazine,* May 25, 1969, p. 92.

22. The National Committee on Urban Growth professes itself impressed with growing interest by the private sector in New Towns, but "also finds that the development of new communities by solely private mechanisms will occur only in those rare circumstances where the dynamics of growth in particular areas will afford a timely and reasonable return on private investment" (*op. cit.,* p. 171).

23. Eli Goldston, "New Prospects for American Business," in this volume.

24. Reports on balance of payment by the Puerto Rico Planning Board.

25. National Committee on Urban Growth, *op. cit.,* p. 172.

26. Princeton University Conference, *op. cit.*

27. *Ibid.*

CHARLES S. SHOUP, JR.,
AND ROBERT A. CHARPIE

Business as an Agent of
Technological Change

ECONOMIC GROWTH resulting from technological innovation has been
the result of aggressive management of both large and small businesses. Early studies of the innovation process[1] showed technological innovation in small companies to have a disproportionately high
degree of success. As the result of a better understanding of the
innovation process itself, many of the sophisticated, technologically
oriented large corporations are today experimenting with altered
organizational structures in the hope of accelerating and enhancing
the impact of their internally generated developments on the economy. During the final third of this century, we can expect to see the
large corporation become a more important force for the generation
of technological innovations than has been historically true. If suitable motivation is provided by government, some of this innovative
effort can be channeled to attack the nation's most pressing social
problems.

Every systematic study of the innovation process points to the
role of the innovative individual as the pivotal factor in the process.
The innovator is typically a technically oriented, anti-establishment,
entrepreneurial individual totally committed to his own concept of
a new product or a new business. The innovator's characteristics
do not change just because he is employed by a big company instead
of a small enterprise. He is the type of individual who is not inhibited by his environment. He still demands the same freedom to
range over a wide field of business activities as his domain. Controls
that are imposed upon him by corporate management in an attempt
"to increase his effectiveness" are often a burden to the innovator
and have frequently resulted in disillusioning and handicapping
aspirant entrepreneurship. Once he feels shackled by constraints,

regardless of their purpose, his output as an entrepreneurial innovator may well diminish.

A second important factor at work in the classic picture of innovation is the business environment in which the entrepreneur is immersed. It is well known that consequential innovations have been made disproportionately often in small companies or by isolated individuals rather than within large well financed and technologically gifted organizations. The prime factor in this discrepancy has been the isolated entrepreneurial innovator who has had the ability to control his own destiny without being frustrated by the endless justification analyses and bureaucratic reports required in typical large organizations as a means of controlling the business to safeguard the interests of stockholders and corporate management.

An analysis of the needs of innovative enterprises indicates that their most important requirement for success is flexibility of action in their initial years—the opportunity to think and act imaginatively and the freedom to attempt to swim against the stream of competitive business "wisdom"—in short, the choice to be different in executing a fundamentally sound plan of action. In the period immediately following initial success, after the innovation has been clearly defined and successfully brought to market, the most important requirements for success change, and rationalization of the business becomes the prime objective. In this period, the greatest need of the business is the addition of highly qualified functional skills in marketing, manufacturing, financial control, and technology—to bring about the conversion of the embryonic enterprise from a highly individual one-product, few-customer activity to one that deals with many products or services and unseen customers throughout the world with equanimity, and to produce the organizational development that provides the structure required to evoke adequate confidence from potential investors and customers so that the enterprise may grow rapidly over a sustained period of time.

It is clear that *in principle* the large company has all the assets required for the rationalization of a successful nascent business. Large companies understand well, in terms of growth in profitability, the impact that an important innovation can have on their future. They are well organized and financially able to deal with major innovations. To that end they represent fertile ground for planting innovative seeds, provided certain other conditions are met. The oft-missing ingredient in the large company, however, has been an adequate understanding of the entire innovation phenomenon, a willingness to upset an established business routine and organization in order to be successful in the quest for change.

During the past few years, evidence has accumulated which indicates to us that large businesses are more concerned than ever before with their innovation record. The cult of performance and investor pressures in recent years for growth in earnings per share rather than consistently high dividends has led aggressive business managements to focus intense attention on new proprietary products or services as a means to rapid earnings growth. Many large companies are now attempting to create a more favorable climate for such innovations to proceed successfully within their organization, despite traditionally anathematic corporate attitudes toward the innovator. A widespread interest in the dynamics of innovation has resulted in a dramatic increase in the use of various forms of the "umbrella" concept which, we believe, makes it possible for the large company to accelerate rather than stifle the innovative forces in our society.

Aggressive business managements are quick to react to profit opportunities once the opportunities are pointed out to them. A significant example of such a reaction is the rather remarkable restructuring that has occurred among some of America's largest technological companies in recent years in order to focus management's attention on innovative opportunities generated and executed from within the company. Each of these reorganizations has had as one of its goals the launching and maintaining, under the umbrella of a big company, of many new ventures—each of which is, in effect, a small company operating by itself in the external business environment. Each such new venture, protected by the big company umbrella, has available to it for attacking problems the adequate financing and in-depth staff expertise so important to success and so difficult for the independent small company to acquire. Among companies that have experimented with some form of the umbrella concept are DuPont, Monsanto, 3M, and Ford—each of which has created a stable of small businesses or new ventures.

It is obvious that in order to cope with the problem of innovation in the large-company environment, it is desirable to have a detailed understanding of both the anatomy of the independent innovation process and those factors within the large company that tend to impinge on that process as it is practiced under the umbrella of the big company. In a certain sense, established business success is itself the greatest hindrance to future success based on technological innovation. This apparently contradictory statement can perhaps be better understood by considering the hypothetical case of a successful company with annual sales of $250,000,000, which has as one of its objectives sustained growth in both sales and earnings at an annual rate of 10 per cent.

Most such companies produce the bulk of their current earnings from their traditional businesses. These older businesses are typically ones that depend on product lines which are most subject to deterioration in profit margins either because of price or cost squeezes, or because of product obsolescence owing to innovations made by competition. The time comes in the life of every company when some of its profitable existing product lines or services begin to decay, initially in earnings performance and eventually in sales volume. Thus, it is not enough to look at the $250,000,000 company with a 10 per cent growth objective and conclude that it must grow by $25,000,000 a year in sales and appropriately in profits. Rather, it is necessary to consider the deterioration expected in the company's existing businesses as a part of the sales and earnings growth objectives established for new products and businesses. In the case of the hypothetical company, if its traditional businesses experience an annual 5 per cent deterioration in profitability, this must be offset by sales of new products or sales to new markets in addition to the improved performance required by the objective of a 10 per cent net growth rate. These replacement sales plus the fruits of the innovative process must generate total new sales of $37,500,000 or 15 per cent, instead of the $25,000,000 a 10 per cent growth rate seems to require.

This realization brings us sharply to the point that a successful established company, to remain successful, must accurately appraise and rank-order the opportunities within the company for innovation. This is one of the respects in which the large-company situation is remarkably different from the small-company entrepreneurial situation. Management's appraisal and rank-ordering of innovative opportunities within the large diversified corporation must necessarily include, as a factor, its own well-known returns on those investment opportunities available within the company's existing businesses. The company in the polymer business, for example, is able to predict reliably the return on additional investments in polyethylene plants. Thus an innovative project that has a higher risk must necessarily promise a significantly higher return than a new investment in an established business in order to compete successfully for funds within the large company.

The presence of experienced corporate management personnel, including financial, legal, and technical staffs, means the risk of a large company's failure in an uncertain new business area where the market is not yet understood (or does not even yet exist) may be much lower than the same risk taken by an individual or a small company. Nevertheless, it is much larger than the risk of enlarging businesses already well known to the company. In the large company, the management of investment risks is considered a part of the normal routine and, therefore, alternatives tend to be appraised, not only in terms of ultimate gains and potential rewards but in terms of the risks relative to the discounted values of those potential rewards and the limited resources available to the company for investing in new areas. The small innovative business, which has no option but to drive straight ahead with the idea to which the entrepreneur is committed, seldom has the opportunity to indulge itself in the luxury of considering sure things with small returns against the ultimate success of the larger gamble to which it is already committed. This may be the single most important reason why big companies have failed to originate many dramatic innovations within the field of their existing competence and activity—because they tend to invest in "for-sure" profits at lower gains rather than "might-be" long shots.

Another facet of the large company's consideration of alternatives is its ability to look outside. Here again, the large company, because of its resources and experience, has a sharper view (real or imagined) of who the established competitors and potential competitors are. These are often much better known to the big company than to the isolated individual in a small company who may not have had either the experience or the opportunity to learn the details of the competitive scene.

Finally, the potential antitrust problems, which are of no consequence to the individual entrepreneur, may loom very large to a major company when it appraises a business opportunity that involves either an acquisition or a new relationship to an established market in which it is already operating.

Notwithstanding the above, we believe the day is coming when more and more large companies in the process of managing risks will approach innovative new business opportunities in a variety of new ways—often on an integrated basis from the laboratory to the market place within an entrepreneurial framework, all the while under the protection of the corporate umbrella.

The initial step in the pursuit of an innovation opportunity is identification. For this purpose, many a large company will maintain a small but highly discerning specialist staff which is constantly on the lookout for new scientific concepts, new engineering developments, and, equally important, attractive technological entrepreneurs to form the cornerstones of new business opportunities. Once such an opportunity has been identified and tentatively appraised, either internally or externally, a venture analysis will be prepared to predict the near-term and ultimate performance of the opportunity as a business and to elucidate the resources required for that performance. Pricing policies, markets served and their approach, cost of sales, competitive advantages and disadvantages, and the means to achieve such advantages must all be considered in a candid and disciplined manner. The analysis will evaluate the possibilities of obtaining a useful proprietary position. Finally, the analysis must factor into the final appraisal the people who will be responsible for the venture. This analysis is hard to make and certain to be wrong in detail, but nevertheless is essential. It is the only available tool of which we are aware that can help us choose between alternatives when we are prepared to invest high-risk capital in order to create a new business.

If at this point the venture appears to be attractive, it is then necessary to determine systematically whether in fact it can be brought to success. This is accomplished in two major phases: (1) The establishment of a technical feasibility program in which intense laboratory and development work to create the product or service in question goes forward. In this phase, a major concern will be the establishment of proprietary control over the product and/or the market so that it cannot be easily copied or legally duplicated; and (2) the determination of the commercial feasibility of the business concept. The questions to be answered here include: How will the market accept the product or service, at what price can it be sold, and what will it cost to make and sell it?

One should realize that the technical and marketing feasibility programs may, in some cases, last many years. Therefore, it is important to discipline the "Go—No Go" decision in the venture analysis stage. In the initial planning stages, checkpoints must be carefully established for various critical points in the technical and marketing programs to require positive decisions to continue or withdraw, depending upon results compared to the plan at each point. The most experienced companies pursue only those few innovations that appear to offer extremely high profit opportunities. Our own rule of thumb has always been that a company should not normally undertake a major new business-innovation program unless, at the venture-analysis stage, it appears to offer as a minimum twice the profitability (according to that company's favorite yardstick) available to the company within its present well-established businesses.

After having finally established the technical and commercial feasibility, it is necessary to decide whether to introduce the new business to the market. At this stage, it is desirable to review completely the entire competitive environment in which the proposed new business or product would be established. Although this has been under continuing review during the entire lifetime of the development of the venture, experience teaches us it is prudent for corporate management to reexamine every possible facet of the new business at this point, in order to identify and evaluate existing and potential competitive products and services, and to estimate again the likelihood for technological obsolescence in light of knowledge gained during the development cycle. A negative result in either of these areas could well force the cancellation of a planned product introduction or the launching of a new business that had survived the difficult and often expensive technical and marketing-feasibility tests.

In many respects, the decision at this point is the most traumatic for corporate management, for this is the final pre-launch "Go—No Go" checkpoint. Very aggressive management in an unrelenting quest for growth sometimes fails to recognize fatal pitfalls that a detailed objective review at this stage may reveal, thereby committing the unnecessary error of "throwing good money after bad." On the other hand, a corporate management that has publicly touted its dedication to innovation but is privately conservative in nature is more likely to terminate a radically new business venture at this point, immediately prior to market exposure, because of fears of entering a competitive environment where risk is known to exist but is foreign to the experience of most of the company management.

When poised on the brink of public commitment, managements are usually understandably reluctant to render a decision which could modify the thrust of the corporation. If, however, this final review results in an unequivocal commitment to proceed, the large corporation has available far more of the resources necessary for an ultimate business success than does the isolated entrepreneur, and therefore has a much higher probability of successful innovation.

It should be remembered that hardly any of the new business embryos subjected to the venture analysis ever reach their planned market because the casualty rate is very high along the way. One of the most frequent questions we are asked is whether radical ideas are suppressed within business during this cycle simply because of major misjudgments of market receptivity. We have to answer that question: "Probably—but we don't know of any." There is considerably more highly visible evidence of what were considered to be major innovations that *were* introduced to market because of a misassessment of the market's readiness for such innovations. The most popular example of the latter is the Edsel, but each of us can think of many other significant examples. General Telephone & Electronics has even featured some of its past errors in a recent advertising campaign.

As part of our examination of the performance of business vis-à-vis technology, we should certainly consider how well the innovation process has been working for the nation as a whole. From the point of view of national economic growth, American industry has had a high degree of success in introducing and exploiting technological innovation by broadening its base of sales, thereby increasing the earnings both of individual companies and of American industry as a whole and improving the overall position of the economy. From the public point of view, however, some major weaknesses remain in our national innovative performance. Specifically, despite the general affluence of our society and the contribution of technological innovation to the overall strengthening of the economy, we have been unable to focus effectively the innovative capabilities of American business onto many of the nation's social problems.

Recent broadly based expressions of dissatisfaction with the social performance of business stem in part from the recognition that many of these social problems have technological components and that private industry could provide the management and technical strengths to attack and solve some of them. To draw the attention of business to such multifaceted social goals as humanization of the urban environment, assurance of equal opportunities for all, and elimination of environmental pollution, as much motivation must be supplied by the public sector as that supplied through profit opportunities in the private sector. We believe that such clear motivation by the public sector will require the creation of new profit opportunities, presumably under government auspices. For example, the wise employment of special tax credits, preferential interest rates, or relief from other restrictions on profit might be sufficient to catalyze the involvement of business in substantial social innovations outside the normal market economy on which shareholder wealth has traditionally been based. Such measures would hopefully be clearly defined as temporary, for the emergence of a new social conscience in American companies is already detectable. Enlightened corporate attitudes combined with appropriate positive motivating factors should entice industry to attack these recently acknowledged social ills with the sense of urgency which business is capable of generating when sufficiently motivated.

In terms of innovative performance, we expect the rest of this century to be dominated by a relatively small number of large companies that understand the innovation process implicitly. These companies will be organized for innovation on an integrated basis from the laboratory to the market place, applying their abilities in a wise and often generous manner toward solution of public problems that demand technological innovation as well as governmental or social restructuring. To hasten the day of substantial industrial involvement in complex sociotechnological problems, temporary encouragement must come in the form of opportunities for new, enhanced profits. We expect this nation to insist on long-term maintenance of a free market economy, however, in which companies will ultimately discover new and as yet unrecognized profit opportunities through an increase in their contribution to our national well-being.

REFERENCE

1. J. Jewkes, D. Sawers, and R. Stillerman, *The Sources of Invention* (New York, 1958), especially pp. 72-88, and Part II.

DONALD A. SCHON

Business as a Vehicle for the Diffusion of Innovation

DIFFUSION OF innovation is a dominant model or pattern for the transformation of societies. According to this pattern, novelty arises at one or more points and moves out from those points to permeate the society as a whole. Although there are several prevailing theories or models for the diffusion of innovations, no one of them is adequate. Social systems for diffusion change over time, but theories of diffusion tend to be based on old systems, and thus lag behind our own expanding competence. Moreover, the prevailing theories of diffusion rest on certain key assumptions that are inadequate even to the old social systems from which they are derived. They fail, therefore, as guides to directed diffusion, but, like the prevailing theories of central implementation of policy, they are remarkably stubborn and resilient.

The Center-Periphery Model

The concept of the center-periphery model has been at the heart of theories proposed by economists and anthropologists who have

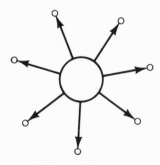

Figure I. The center-periphery model.

tried to account for social change via the diffusion of innovations. The language they have used reflects prevailing assumptions underlying the inquiry:

The innovation to be diffused exists, essentially fully realized, prior to its diffusion.

Diffusion is the movement of an innovation from a center or "source" out "to its ultimate users."

Directed diffusion is a centrally managed process of dissemination, training, and provision of resources and incentives.

In a center-periphery system, the scope of diffusion capability depends first upon the level of resources and energy at the center. These determine the number of points at the periphery and the length of the "radii" or "spokes" through which diffusion takes place. The diffusion capability of an agricultural extension agent, for example, depends upon his own energies and skills, the time available to him, and the location of the farmers he serves.

Scope also depends on infrastructure technology. Where the technology for the flow of men, materials, money, and information is more advanced, the scope of the center-periphery system can be more extensive; where the infrastructure technology is less advanced, the scope must be more limited. Public-health officials who try to spread new birth-control technology in India must reach thousands of small villages over roads difficult to pass at any time and impossible in certain seasons. The use of elephants as vehicles reflects not only an ingenious sense of public relations but a solution to the transportation problem. It is a reaction to the limits of diffusion set by poor infrastructure.

Finally, the scope of a center-periphery system depends on its capacity for generating and managing feedback. Because regulation of diffusion originates at the center, the effectiveness of the process depends upon the ways in which information moves from the periphery to the center. The center-periphery system fails when demands of the periphery exceed the resources or the energy at the center, when the capacity of the radii is overloaded, or when the system cannot incorporate feedback from the periphery. Failure takes the form of simple ineffectiveness in diffusion, distortion of the message, or disintegration of the system as a whole. Detail men working for a drug company communicate with doctors in their territory. When they have insufficient time to reach their quota of doctors, they may reduce their level of effort with each doctor to a point where they are unable to convey the company's message effectively, or they may lose contact with their own central office, garbling new messages. If, as a result, sales fall off and salesmen lose morale, the system as a whole may fall apart.

Normative Use of the Model. The center-periphery model is not only historically important but has also become the dominant normative model for diffusion. Agricultural-development programs in Africa and Latin America, for example, rest on a theory of the successful agricultural-extension program of the United States. The theory requires centers of technological competence—experiment stations, model farms, central laboratories, land-grant universities— and experts in technical assistance who communicate the new technologies of agriculture to the farmers.

When directed diffusion of innovation is at issue, the center-periphery model and its variants have inadequacies that go beyond the historical failings of actual center-periphery systems. In two crucial respects, the prevailing center-periphery theories fail to take historical phenomena into account.

Diffusion as Communication. Everett Rogers, who simply reflects current thinking on the subject, treats the act of diffusion as an act of communication. "The essence of the diffusion process is the human interaction in which one person communicates a new idea to another person."[1] The essential process is getting information out: "communication from A who knows about the innovation to B who does not." This concept does not take into account the dynamically conservative plenum into which information moves. The process is more nearly a battle than a communication.

Product or Technique as the Unit of Diffusion. Every social system has prevailing technologies and related theories around which it is organically built. Innovation in any aspect of the system threatens—to a greater or lesser extent—the system as a whole. The more significant innovations are those whose acceptance would require more radical transformation of the system. Hence, their threat to the system is greater.

Rogers and other exponents of center-periphery theory consider only the diffusion of new products or new techniques, any one of which presupposes a relatively stable technological system of which it is a part. A new weed-killer, for example, moves into a system of agricultural technology that includes mechanical plowing, harvesting, and spraying, the use of new genetic varieties, chemical fertilizer, crop rotation, mechanical packing equipment, and motorized transportation of crops. Within such a technological system, middle- to large-sized farms are dominant. The economic constraints on farming as well as the impact of previous technological innovations have already sharply reduced available farm labor. The acceptance of a new weed-killer depends on equipment that would permit its use over relatively large areas with relatively little labor. If the weed-killer could be shown to be effective and innocuous in its side effects, and if it permitted increase in land productivity or further reduction in farm labor, then managers of middle- to large-sized farms might accept it fairly readily.

The situation is quite different when the introduction of the innovation requires or produces significant disruption in the technological system as well as the social system. In such a case, diffusion of an innovation appears not as the dissemination of information, but as a sequence of related disruptions of complex systems, resulting in each case in a new systems configuration. The unit of diffusion is neither a product nor a technique, but a technological system.

The Bessemer converter, for example, was a significant innovation whose acceptance threatened to disrupt the technological and related social system of the established iron industry. After the first dissemination of information about the invention, its diffusion required a period of heroic entrepreneurship on the part of outsiders to the industry; the fortuitous pull of a vast new demand, the railroads; and the design and implementation of a whole new system of finance, protection, production, and control—all tailored to the new technology. This combination of fortuitous and deliberate processes gave the whole industrial-marketing system an entirely new configuration.[2]

Every complex that is in the broadest terms an industry represents just such a sociotechnical system. The "agricultural industry," the "food industry," the "primary metals industry," the "nuclear industry"—all are systems of technology, production, distribution, marketing, employment, and finance that have developed over time. Major nonindustrial institutions—institutions for health care, education, and social welfare, for example—represent socio-technical systems of a similar kind. Each has the same kind of dynamic conservatism. Taken function by function, and function-fulfilling institution by institution, our society represents a dynamically conservative plenum into which innovations must find their way if they are to be diffused. Within such a plenum, potential innovations can be ranked in a kind of target diagram depending on the magnitude of the disruption their acceptance would cause.

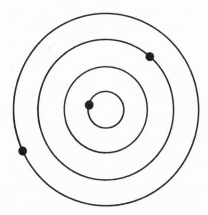

Figure 2. Target diagram for ranking potential innovations.

Innovations lying near the periphery are likely to undergo a diffusion process whose principal features have to do with the dissemination of information—the communication of information from A who knows about the invention to B who does not. Once the Bessemer process is in place, a more efficient recarbonization unit might be diffused in this manner. But for innovations located near the center of the diagram, like the Bessemer converter itself, the process of diffusion is a battle for broad and complex systems transformation. And within such a process, the assumptions underlying the classical diffusion model do not hold:

The innovation does not by any means entirely antedate the diffusion process; it evolves significantly within that process.

The process does not look like the fanning out of innovation from a single source. Many sources of related and reinforcing innovations are likely to be involved.

And the process does not consist primarily in centrally managed dissemination of information. This element is usually present, but is subordinate to the massive reorientation of existing sociotechnical systems.

Deliberate entrepreneurial intervention usually intermeshes with the emergence of new demands comparable in their force to the dynamic conservatism of the established system itself.

The whole matter is complicated somewhat because systems reaction to an innovation depends on the ways in which the innovation is perceived by those within the system. The threat inherent in a significant innovation may or may not be apparent at the outset. Where it is apparent, the system is likely to respond by ignoring or by actively resisting the innovation. Where the threat is not apparent, however, the system may accept the innovation fairly readily as a kind of Trojan horse, only to experience far-reaching and unanticipated disruption as a consequence. Such appears to have been the case in the well-known story of the adoption of the steel ax by Yir Yoront: Acceptance of the attractive and apparently innocuous implement led to a chain reaction of cultural disruption. Consumer acceptance of television in our own society may turn out to have been a similar phenomenon.

The system may also be structured in such a way that only a relatively powerless element experiences disruption as a consequence of acceptance. The acceptance of mechanical equipment, chemical fertilizer, and weed-killer by cotton planters in the Mississippi Delta transformed the Delta cotton system, and in the process dislocated thousands of black plantation workers who were unable to make their resistance felt.

Systems as Units of Diffusion

Diffusion of significant innovations turns out actually to require the generation of whole new sociotechnical systems. The unit of diffusion is more nearly a complete industrial system than a product or a technique. The process involved in the diffusion of a significant innovation, then, should be like the generation and diffusion of industries.

For purposes of comparison, let us examine the growth of the granite industry in New England in the late eighteenth and early nineteenth centuries. The industry depended, of course, on the geology of the New England region.[3] From earliest colonial times, surface granite in the form of boulders had been put to limited use, but until the late eighteenth century there had been no quarrying and no large-scale industry associated with granite.

Business as a Vehicle for the Diffusion of Innovation

The first impetus to the development of the granite industry came in the course of the Revolutionary War. Among the German mercenaries the British imported to fight the colonists were many stone cutters, and a group settled in Quincy (originally called Germantown).

This class of German artisans first introduced into this country the practice of preparing hewn or hammered stone, wrought to a plain surface, sufficiently straight and smooth to make a regular wall. The process as then practiced by them and those who were instructed by them was understood to be extremely laborious, and, of course, expensive, as the expense depended wholly on the amount of labor required for preparing it. . . . In this state of the trade, although stone might be gotten out and dressed and made suitable for building, yet few buildings were erected, probably on account of the great expense.[4]

The next phase in the development of the industry centered on a rather specialized demand.

Desirous of getting the stone for the prison [at Charlestown] on the best terms, and believing the prices high, though general, [Governor Robbins] thought much and conversed much on the subject. . . . In passing along a [Salem] street, he noticed a building apparently new, the basement story of which was stone. He stopped to look at it carefully. In doing so he perceived along the margin of each stone the marks of a tool at distances of six or seven inches apart. This was something new. He had never seen it on hewn stone. He immediately inquired for the owner and saw him and asked if he knew how and by what process these stones were got out and wrought. He said he did not, but referred him to the contractor who did most of that species of work in Salem, by the name of Galusha. . . . He then proceeded to find Mr. Galusha, and to ask him whether he got out these stones and by what process. He said he did not get them out himself; that they were obtained in Danvers, two or three miles distant, and were furnished by a man named Tarbox.[5]

Samuel Tarbox played a role in the emerging granite industry analogous to that of Bessemer or Kelley in the steel industry, but Tarbox was neither a scientist nor an entrepreneur.

Upon asking for directions to find Mr. Tarbox, Governor Robbins was told that he was a very poor man, being in an obscure situation in Danvers, near the place where the stone was quarried. Governor Robbins determined to pursue the inquiry, immediately proceeded to Danvers, and after considerable inquiry, he found Mr. Tarbox in a small house with a family, and with every appearance of poverty about him.[6]

311

Governor Robbins perceived the problem as one of directing the diffusion of an essential innovation.

Governor Robbins asked [Tarbox] if he would consent to go up to Quincy and work two or three months, and split stone in his mode, so that other workmen might practise it. . . . Governor Robbins . . . introduced Mr. Tarbox to several of the principal stone dealers, and . . . it was not three months before every stone cutter in Quincy could split stones with small wedges as well as Mr. Tarbox. . . . This improvement in the working of granite had in a very short time the effect to reduce the price to five-eighths of its former cost; that is, the cost of the dimension stone wanted for the prison, which had before been $4.00, was afterwards reduced to $2.50, and other granite work in similar proportion.[7]

As a consequence, Quincy emerged as a center of the new granite industry. It was a Quincy man, associated with South Shore quarrying operations, who first acted to exploit Cape Ann granite.

The quarry industry got its start on Cape Ann when Nehemiah Knowlton, in 1823, excavated some five hundred tons of stone at Pigeon Cove and advertised it for sale in a Boston newspaper. A Mr. Bates of Quincy, where quarries already were in operation, saw the advertisement and came to Pigeon Cove to investigate its resources. He deemed the prospects favorable and began operations there on a ledge which he leased. His venture was not successful, but a couple of years later William Torrey, who had been associated with Mr. Bates, opened a pit at another location in Pigeon Cove which became a large quarry. During the next fifteen years he supplied much of the granite used by the federal government in its construction work at Boston and Portsmouth, N.H.[8]

The early granite technology was simple.

When the first quarries were opened, all the work was done by hand-power or ox-power. The holes in which blasting powder was to be exploded were drilled by pounding a square drill with a hammer. Round drills with V-shaped points presently superseded the square drills, but it was not until 1883 that the first steam drill came into use. In the early years, furthermore, the rough slabs of granite were hoisted out of the pits either by manpower or by oxen, and the pumping of the water which flowed into the pits from the surface of the ledge or from springs underneath was done by hand. It was in 1853 that a steam engine was first used for hoisting and pumping. Late in the nineteenth century numerous mechanical devices were introduced for drilling, cutting, and polishing the granite.[9]

But it set in motion a chain of events which transformed not only the industry but the government, the population, and the infrastructure of Cape Ann.

From 1700 till after 1820 the settlements at Sandy Bay and Pigeon Cove increased only slowly in population. . . . In 1823, however, a new industry—granite quarrying—began to develop on a large scale at Pigeon Cove and in neighboring areas, and that led to such a growth of trade and such an increase of population that a movement eventually was started among the residents of Sandy Bay, Pigeon Cove, and adjoining neighborhoods to have that part of the Cape separated from Gloucester and set off as an independent town. As a result, in 1840, by action of the State Legislature, the Town of Rockport came into being.[10]

The new industry fed on the rapidly increasing demand for granite as a building material. And the requirements for increasing volume brought a chain of innovations in their wake.

For transporting stone from the quarries to the finishing sheds and the piers, several quarry companies built inclined railroad tracks down which the loaded cars traveled by gravity. When empty, they were towed back by oxen. As the ownership of the quarries became largely connected in the hands of a few companies, the railroad tracks were extended over a larger area and steam locomotives came into use. The Rockport Granite Company, for example, with quarries both in Pigeon Cove and in Lanesville, operated seven miles of railroad track and three locomotives.[11]

And waves of cheap, immigrant labor were imported to work the quarries.

When the first arrangements for employing Irish immigrants were broached in Pigeon Cove, strong opposition sprang up. "The house which was being prepared for them to occupy was two or three times blown up with powder; and other means were employed to keep out the unwelcome immigrants." That opposition undoubtedly was kindled by apprehension that the newcomers would accept employment at wages lower than the rates then being paid.

Immigrants of other nationalities followed the Irish, and in 1875, for example, French Canadian as well as Irish laborers were employed for unskilled work in the quarries at Bay View, and presumably also in Lanesville and Pigeon Cove. . . .

About 1880 the quarry companies' continued search for strong-bodied laborers who would work for relatively low wages led to the bringing in of Finnish immigrants. At first the Finns were housed in a couple of old barns which had been converted into dormitories, but they soon established their families in permanent residences. Thus the population of Lanesville came to include a large Finnish colony.[12]

By 1860 the Cape's granite industry had reached an impressive scale.

In 1860, John J. Babson reported that about 350 men were employed in quarrying the stone, in cutting it into the shapes and sizes called for in the market, in hauling the stone to the cutters and the shipping piers, and in manning the blacksmith shops which were always busy sharpening tools and repairing gear. Another 150 men then were employed on the sloops on which the stone was shipped.[13]

It took the beginning of World War I and the introduction of cement as a large-scale building material to initiate the sequence of events which led precipitously to the industry's decline.

World War I practically marked the end of the quarry industry on Cape Ann. For some years now only one quarry has been in operation on the Cape. The industry fell victim to technological changes. New and improved methods for the manufacture of cement were introduced just before the start of World War I, and the labor cost of putting up a building with reinforced concrete was so much less than the cost of erecting a building with granite blocks that granite construction, except for occasional trim, was largely discontinued. The rapid increase in the number of automobiles in use, which occurred at about the same time, called for smooth streets, and the market for paving stones vanished. Thus even an industry founded on bedrock could not withstand the force of technological change.[14]

The rise and fall of the granite industry contains in microcosm themes common to processes in the diffusion of new industrial systems.

The crucial role of war. The industry rose and fell in the interval between two major wars—the Revolutionary War and World War I. The first created the extraordinary conditions of mobility that brought the carriers of stone-cutting technology to the New World; the second set in motion a revolution in building that displaced stone.

The role of the inventor. Tarbox was a prototype of the independent inventor whose contribution triggered the new industry, although he himself was only dimly aware of his own importance and failed to gain any long-term profit from it.

Business as a Vehicle for the Diffusion of Innovation

The role of pulses of special demand. The new prison of Charlestown sparked Governor Robbins' search, which led to the takeoff of the Quincy operation. That operation, in turn, provided a new supply of relatively cheap granite cut to dimension, and reinforced a growing demand for new fireproof buildings that came with the development of Boston. Thenceforth, the demand and the industry reinforced one another in mutual growth.

The interaction of deliberate intervention and unforeseen occurrence. Governor Robbins took on himself the management of a segment of a process of diffusion when he brought Tarbox to Quincy to teach the local cutters his new method. Entrepreneurs from Quincy sought deliberately to create new, profitable centers of industry and, in so doing, triggered the industry's spread. But the industry's full development depended on waves of new demand that no one had anticipated or sought deliberately to create.

The clustering of innovations and the requirements for infrastructure. The growth of the industry in Cape Ann after 1823 depended not only on the new stone-cutting technology but on blasting methods, on wire rope and hoisting equipment, and later, on steam-powered drills and hoists, which permitted the exploitation of granite in quarries as deep as five hundred feet. Requirements for transport drew first on oxen and then on rail technology, and led to the creation of the wharf and sloop traffic to Boston. The growth of water and rail transport permitted Cape Ann products to travel as far as Washington, D.C., and fostered the development of a widespread market whose growth fed into the industry's.

The system of the granite industry grew in interaction with other related systems, and no one system caused the others to come into being. Each fed on and reinforced the others. There were precipitating events—the prison, the discovery of Tarbox—but no one of them can be said to have caused the development of the industry. Individuals and associations intervened at various times and tried, more or less consciously, to forward the industry's diffusion. No man or group, however, can be said to have directed or managed that diffusion. Each chapter in the diffusion of the granite industry represented a complex reconfiguration of related systems.

DONALD A. SCHON

The Business Firm as a Vehicle for the Diffusion of Innovations

Theories of directed diffusion lag behind the reality of emerging systems. Prevailing models of directed diffusion rest on the great social interventions of the late nineteenth and early twentieth centuries. They are center-periphery models, heightened by the addition of the concept of the proliferation of centers. Moreover, these models rest on assumptions that are inapplicable to the diffusion systems from which they are derived.

The diffusion of significant innovations or of whole industries reveals the demands placed on the process of diffusion by the dynamic conservatism of the plenum into which innovation moves. The process must be considered in terms of the diffusion of whole systems, although theories of diffusion have not yet taken these matters into account. The image of the county agent, the detail man, and the public-health officer still dominates historical accounts of diffusion as well as normative theories of diffusion.

The development of more adequate theories for the diffusion of innovation must begin by taking into account existing systems that are already in advance of theories in good currency. Some of these are to be found in the evolution of the business firm seen as a vehicle for the diffusion of innovations; they are variants on a new strain of diffusion systems that normative theory must learn to understand.

In modern industrial society, the business firm has been a major vehicle for the diffusion of innovations. Through production, distribution, and marketing, new products and techniques have permeated whole societies, bringing with them unanticipated waves of change. New facilities for production, distribution, and maintenance have proliferated by means of industrial expansion. Business firms have managed the diffusion of innovations, but because these functions are subsumed under names like marketing, distribution, and expansion, students of the diffusion process tend to ignore them. In Rogers' listing of the sources of inquiry into diffusion, no mention is made of the marketing and business literatures. Yet the business firm has been at least as important in this respect as departments of agriculture or public health.

A kind of functionalism in the definitions of "industry" and "business" has in the past hundred years led businesses to see themselves for the most part as managers of the diffusion of *products*, not of the larger technological systems of which the products are components.

Business as a Vehicle for the Diffusion of Innovation

Since the turn of the century, however, industries and business firms, seen as systems for diffusion and learning, have undergone a spectacular evolution.

The *Standard Industrial Classification Manual* reflects the definition and organization of industries as they existed in the early years of this century. Industries were defined around concepts like materials, energy, manufacture, and transportation. The "materials industry" broke down, in turn, into the industries associated with the production of specific materials—clay, paper, metals, and the like. "Manufacturing industries" clustered around specific classes of manufactured products—like shoes, textiles, shops, and toys. Within a manufacturing industry, a business firm defined itself by its "product line," a subset of its industrial product category. In the early years of the century, the definitions corresponded to the actual structure of the industry.

Within the classical business firm, divisions formed around functions like production, sales, and accounting. The firm was an organizational pyramid with functional units under the control of functional managers and functional managers under the control of top management. The firm existed as an intermediate link in a chain of supply that fed into it raw and intermediate materials and manufacturing equipment, and a chain of distribution and marketing that took its products to the ultimate consumer. The firm depended upon its interactions with other systems concerned with the provision of manpower and capital, and with the infrastructure functions governing the necessary flows of men, material, energy, and information.

The evolution of the business firm from this early stage has had several major turning points.

Growth: Horizontal and Vertical Integration. Although in the early decades of the twentieth century various corporate forms emerged that placed under central ownership firms representative of widely varying industries, these corporate forms did little to alter the structural and functional organization of the firms themselves. "Holding companies" were primarily vehicles for the consolidation of profits, the control of capital, the preempting of captive markets and captive sources of supply. Two forms of growth did, however, significantly change industrial and business organization. In horizontal integration, one firm acquired or established other firms engaged in similar processes of manufacture and marketing. It replicated the classical business firm, expanded it, gave it a more nearly secure position in its market, and permitted it economies of scale in purchasing, the use of manpower, expenditures for marketing, and the like. Vertical integration put more links in the manufacturing-marketing chain under single corporate control. Papermaking firms, for example, came to control their own woodlands and timber operations and their own end-product facilities for manufacture and marketing. Placing these vertical elements of the system under single corporate control made possible a more effective balancing of supply and demand for each intermediate operation, a reduction of costs through elimination of "middle-man" profits, and a tailoring of each intermediate operation to the changing requirements of operations further down the ladder.

Vertical and horizontal integration of firms received their impetus from the pressures and opportunities for business growth: the expansion of markets, the increasing availability of capital, the transition from family to public ownership and from family to professional management. The industrial giants of the 1930's and 1940's —the great steel, paper, automotive, and chemical companies, for example—assumed this form. They aggregated and compressed similar product-centered firms and the business links connecting them to sources of supply as well as to end-users. Throughout this process, however, the classical definition and organization of industries remained intact. A business firm of this type is compelled to set for itself the problem of diffusing whole industrial systems as comprehensive as the granite industry. Such a firm controls most of the elements of an industrial system. When a major steel or paper company sets up operations in a new region, it manages the entire process of replication and expansion.

The complexity of the process of diffusion as a chain of related systems transformations escapes notice only on the part of those who confine their attention to the movements of products and techniques within a broad systems context that remains (or is taken to be) relatively stable throughout the process. But the role of the diffusion of broad functional systems becomes more apparent as the rate of systems change increases. When the rise and fall of an industry takes a generation or more, attention goes to the faster-moving evolution and diffusion of specific products and techniques within the system. But today whole industries emerge, diffuse, and show signs of declining within ten or twenty years, as is true for the industries associated with aerospace equipment, solid-state electronics, numerically controlled machine tools, and synthetic textiles. Thus attention turns to the evolution and diffusion of the technological system of the industry as a whole, and concern with "directed diffusion" shifts from "product or technique" to "the industry"—where "industry" means the complex of technological and social systems involved in the filling of major functions.

The Emergence of the Constellation Firm. The next significant stages in the evolution of business firms date from World War II. They share certain broad transitional themes: from static product line to product innovation, from single product line to diversity, and from product- to process-based definition of the business firm. These transitions are multiply determined, occurring at different rates and in different ways in various industries. The transitions have revolutionized both what it is to be a business and what it is to be an industry.

Following World War II and into the late 1950's, it began to become commonplace in United States industry to think of invention as a necessary internal function of the firm. Previously firms had established themselves around inventions; but it began to be seen that regular and continuing invention was a necessary internal function of the firm. This phenomenon reflected, in part, the increasingly technological nature of industrial competition, the response to the twin ideologies of research and growth that had received much of their impetus from the development and use of technology in the war, and the increasing saturation of traditional markets that necessitated the creation of new markets through the development and marketing of new products.

Business firms began to take seriously not only the improvement of technological and marketing systems associated with their existing product lines but the internal generation of new businesses based on new product lines. The internalization of this development capability, initially seen as an instrument of corporate growth, required transformation of the nature of the firm itself.

Firms raised the level of generality at which they defined themselves. Shoe companies concerned themselves with "footwear," oil companies with "energy," business equipment firms with "information processing." Where the change in name was not merely nominal, it signaled a broadening of the industrial base away from traditional production and marketing functions. A "footwear" company has within its scope the manufacture and marketing of slippers, sneakers, rubbers, and boots. These are separate "businesses," depending on different materials, new sources of supply, different methods of production, new outlets, new channels of distribution.

319

No one could manage such a cluster of businesses and integrate them into an effective operating whole without giving up the old "shoe" and "leather" mentality. Such a business would have as its charter for innovation a scope far broader than newer and better varieties of shoes.

Science-based industries relatively advanced in their own research cycles invaded traditional industries, preempted markets, and served as carriers of new technological systems. New industrial complexes have made the *Standard Industrial Classification Manual* obsolete. Now we have not a textile industry, but a textile-chemical-paper complex; not a machine-tool industry, but a materials-forming industry. Individual firms have had to incorporate the elements of diverse technologies and businesses associated with these new industrial definitions: A major textile manufacturer has synthetic fiber, nonwoven, and information-processing divisions, while a large machine-tool builder has divisions for plastics, precision-forging, chemical-forming, and numerically controlled machine tools.

Research- and development-based companies have worked out the logical consequences of the concept of technological innovation as an inherent business function. 3M grew by spinning off semiautonomous companies, each centered on new technologies emerging from development. The result, in corporate form, is a constellation of semiautonomous firms surrounding a central bank and development facility. The result is a business that defines itself in terms of a certain kind of *process* for the exploitation of new technological and market potentials. 3M's products can be defined not as members of a class, all of which share common and unique characteristics, but as a family resemblance that reflects the process through which they grew.

All of these trends have combined to effect certain major shifts. In response to new technologies, industrial invasions, and diversification away from saturated markets, the firm has tended to evolve from a pyramid built on a single relatively static product line to a constellation of semiautonomous divisions. It has moved toward a definition of itself in terms of generalized product functions or of a process for technological and marketing exploitation.

Seen as a vehicle for the diffusion of inventions, the constellation firm offers both analogies and dis-analogies with the center-periphery model. The center-periphery structure remains, as does the differentiation of functions of primary and secondary centers.

Figure 3. The constellation firm.

The secondary center concerns itself with diffusion in the earlier sense—through marketing, decentralization, and expansion of facilities. The primary center takes on the functions of the creation and management of secondary centers and the maintenance of the network as a whole. The concept of "fixed message," however, has disappeared. Instead, there is a continuing proliferation of messages —each spun off from the center, each the basis of a distinct business. There *is* considerable stability in the definition of the message inherent in a given business once it has been established. There is stability also in the methodology for diffusion—that is, the methodology for the creation and spinning off of new businesses. But the content of the messages evolves over time on the basis of internal resources as well as constraints and opportunities provided by the external environment. As a diffusion system, the constellation firm is a vehicle for the diffusion of an ever-changing message through a relatively stable system of dissemination. According to the messages they embody, secondary centers vary in content and style.

From Products to Business Systems. In its evolution over the last half century, the business firm has acquired the capacity to diffuse whole industries and to sustain technological innovation within them. At the present time, they are shifting from the product as the unit of business organization toward integration around business systems.

The potency of the concept of business systems owes a great deal to the aerospace and weapons systems of the last thirty years. N.A.S.A., for example, cannot be said to be in any traditional sense an industry. It is an immense organization made up of government agencies, laboratories, and related contractors—all subordinated (until recently) to the aim of getting man to the moon. N.A.S.A.'s organization reflects this function.

DONALD A. SCHON

PROJECTS

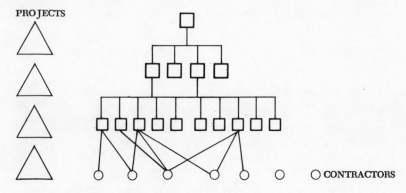

Figure 4. Administrative structure of N.A.S.A.

An administrator, together with associate administrators, oversees the central components of N.A.S.A.'s major functions: mission operations, management of laboratories, organization, and administration. A project organization cut across this basic administrative arrangement. Each project has its own subobjective and an array of organizational components responsible for functions associated with that subobjective—for example, propulsion systems, communications, guidance, life support. The project manager's task is to coordinate the complex of government agencies, laboratories, and contractors involved in performance of these functions. N.A.S.A.'s total budget for the performance of these functions has been on the order of $5 billion a year.

Contrast this with the manner in which the nation carries out another major function, which might be described as "keeping us in clean clothes." No person or agency is responsible for this function. It is carried out through the interaction of elements of what are usually considered separate industries:

The "textile chain" spins yarn from fiber or filament; makes cuts and converts cloth; and manufactures, distributes, and markets apparel.

The soap and chemical-complex manufactures, distributes, and markets soaps, solvents, detergents, and other cleaning materials.

The appliance-complex manufactures and distributes commercial and consumer equipment for laundering and cleaning garments.

Business as a Vehicle for the Diffusion of Innovation

The service industry consists of laundering and dry-cleaning establishments.

Consumers wear clothes, have them cleaned, and perform many of the maintenance and cleaning tasks themselves.

Although this description is oversimplified, the relations among its elements already appear to be extremely complex. Fiber and

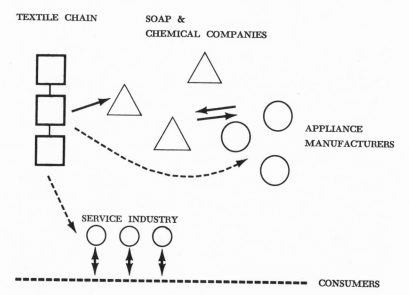

Figure 5. Industries involved in "keeping us in clean clothes."

apparel manufacturers produce the garments that are to be cleaned in the machines made by appliance makers, using materials produced by soap and chemical makers, in operations frequently carried out by consumers. When the process is found to be inadequate, responsibility is difficult to assign. With the proliferation of new fibers and finishes in the 1950's, there was considerable confusion as to what sorts of garments were to be cleaned, under what conditions, and with what sorts of cleaning materials. Appliance manufacturers blamed the textile industry for failing to adopt a clear and uniform labeling system; textile manufacturers blamed appliance and chemical companies for failing to adapt their products to the demands of the new fabrics; and all of them, at various times, blamed the consumer for lack of intelligence.

This complex of industries, organizations, and institutions—subsumed under the function of "keeping us in clean clothes"—we will call a business system. Any complex of firms related to one another in the performance of a major social function is a business system. On this particular business system the nation spends about $5 billion per year.

Within the system, "innovation" turns out frequently to be a response of one part of the system to what another part of the system has done.

In 1960, a group of consultants proposed to the Whirlpool Corporation that they produce a "solvent washer" which would be, in effect, a home dry-cleaning machine for all kinds of garments. Whirlpool, it turned out, already had a version of the idea. But its market studies had convinced it that women would resist any increase in their ironing load; home dry-cleaners would simply produce more clothes to be ironed.

In the early 1960's, however, "wash-and-wear" gained acceptance. And wash-and-wear fabrics could, in most cases be "finished" acceptably without ironing. The introduction of wash-and-wear released the idea of the coin-operated dry cleaner, which had been on Whirlpool's shelves. Norge had the same idea. And Whirlpool and Norge raced to be first to the market with the "coin-ops."

The introduction of the coin-ops confronted traditional private dry-cleaning establishments with a new form of competition. The result was to force such companies either to coin-op concessions, to more industrialized dry-cleaning establishments better able to meet the new competition, or to highly customized "craft" operations capable of outperforming the coin-ops in special areas.

In the meantime, people were cleaning their clothes in common equipment at room temperature. Bacterial problems arose which created the "need" for new bacteriostats capable of functioning effectively in coin-ops.

The business system as a whole was significantly transformed through a kind of systems interaction managed by no one. An innovation in one part of the system led to another, creating waves of new requirements to which others in the system had to respond in still different ways. To each element in the system, the wave brought requirements or opportunities for new products and services. The diffusion of product innovation contributed to an overall systems transformation whose emergent character became clear only after the fact.

It is a sign of the times, however, that in California new firms engage in "keeping customers in clean shirts." They are neither cleaning establishments, shirt manufacturers, retailers, nor manufacturers of cleaning equipment. They solicit and perform on contracts to keep their customers regularly supplied with clean shirts, meeting specifications of size, color, style, and cleanliness. They control, either by ownership or by contractual arrangement, sources of shirt manufacture as well as cleaning establishments. They retain the decision to supply the customer with a new shirt or to launder his old one. They retain control of the "make or buy" decision and of enough of the elements of the business system (at least as it applies to shirts) to be able to manage system-wide innovations—for example, to introduce new cleaning methods to accommodate new kinds of fabric. They are neither horizontally nor vertically integrated in the sense described earlier. They have taken a different cut at the business system involved in "keeping us in clean clothes."

It becomes possible, then, for firms to integrate around a mix of elements of a business system—elements that are neither horizontally nor vertically related to one another but that reinforce one another in allowing the firm to be effective in performing a major social function. Just as the vertically and horizontally integrated firm became capable of diffusing new industries, the firm integrated around business systems becomes capable of diffusing new business systems.

The management of a business-systems firm poses special problems. For such a firm, expansion *means* the diffusion of whole functional systems. It is as though a single firm were to take on the series of steps essential to the establishment of the whole granite industry, including the use of its products in construction. This would include the establishment of the quarries, the means of transport, the technologies for extraction and refinement, the supply of manpower, and the construction process itself.

"Management" now means the creation and maintenance of a network of components internal to the firm that would have been handled through a variety of transactions with institutions external to the firm. Changes of investment in one component produce chain reactions in the others; innovations in any one area penetrate all areas. The system must become capable of planning for all components in a balanced and comprehensive way, and its internal network of information and control must be able to detect and modulate events in one area that have significant implications for the system as a whole. As a diffusion system, the firm must take into account and generate in each wave of expansion all the elements required for performance of the system's function. It cannot make expansion decisions on the basis of assumed market for product alone, nor can it introduce a new product and let things take care of themselves. In order to make such decisions, it must assess the adequacy of a given functional system in a region, the problems associated with the introduction of a new system for performing that function, and the firm's own resources for carrying out that introduction—including the resulting dislocation of established firms and workers.

The firm has no stable base in particular product technologies and systems built around them. It is, therefore, an internal learning system in which the system's interactions must become a matter of directed systems transformation. These directed transformations are in part the justification for the business-systems firm, but they require internalization of processes of information flow and sequential innovation that have traditionally been left to the "market" and to the chain reactions within and across industry lines. The business firm, representing the entire functional system, must now learn to effect the transformation and diffusion of the system as a whole.

Public Systems. Within the last three presidential administrations, public concern about innovation and its diffusion has shifted from private to public systems, from the satisfaction of consumer needs to the satisfaction of public needs to which no single product or industry corresponds. The concern with innovation in public systems stemmed from a tradition of social progress traceable directly to the New Deal. In 1958, Galbraith uttered the war cry of that tradition's reawakening in *The Affluent Society:*

The family which takes its mauve and cerise, air-conditioned, power-steered and power-braked automobile out for a tour passes through cities that are badly paved, made hideous by litter, blighted buildings, billboards, and posts for wires that should long since have been put underground. They pass on into a countryside that has been rendered largely invisible by commercial art. . . . They picnic on exquisitely packaged food from a portable icebox by a polluted stream and go on to spend the night at a park which is a menace to public health and morals. Just before dozing off on an air mattress, beneath a nylon tent, amid the stench of decaying refuse, they may reflect vaguely on the curious unevenness of their blessings. Is this, indeed, the American genius? [15]

In the Kennedy administration, concern over what Galbraith called "social balance" became an idea in good currency. A laundry list of public systems emerged to which we had paid inadequate attention: water supply, waste disposal, pollution control, public health and health care, education, low-income housing, public transportation, welfare services, the care of the disabled, mental health, criminal justice. Often these problems were united under the heading of "urban problems."

Galbraith had posed the problems of public systems in terms of the reallocation of national priorities. His term "social balance" pointed toward a righting of the balance of national expenditure in the direction of public need. But expenditure to what ends and by what means? Why had American industry been unable to solve public-systems problems as it had "solved" the problems of product development? What was the proper division of labor between government and industry in work on public problems?

There had been, for some time, a disposition to treat the problem as technological. "Systems analysis," in particular, presented itself as a candidate technology for the solution of urban problems. Early discussions of the newly rediscovered public-systems problems tended to be elaborations of new public-systems technologies that, if adequately supported and implemented, could transform the public sector. New waste-disposal systems, low-cost housing systems, public transportation systems (combining individual and mass transit)—all were proposed and discussed.

The Commission on Automation, Technological Change and Economic Progress included in its report a volume on "unmet social needs" and the potentials for technological solution. Governor Brown of California sponsored a competition among California-based aerospace companies to devise new "systems solutions" to California's public-systems problems. But the Brown-sponsored proposals, as well as the federally-sponsored public-systems studies and prototypes, have in general come to nothing. It has become acceptable to notice that public-systems problems are also—or even primarily—problems of "social innovation."

This came as no surprise to the ten industrial firms that invested well over $1 million each in the design and development of "housing systems" during the decade of the 1950's. Monsanto, Koppers, Alcoa,

Johns Manville, and others had examined the growing housing market and its projected future growth as a percentage of the gross national product. They had observed that many of the elements of cost in a house—particularly the high cost of labor—seemed to derive from the fact that a house is assembled, largely by craft, out of a conglomeration of products. What if houses were designed, produced, and marketed as industrial systems?

Each company invested in the development of a housing system that would employ its own products. The Koppers house, for example, consisted of plywood-polystyrene "skin structure" sandwiches, fastened together with wooden splines. The components could be manufactured efficiently and cheaply in a factory and assembled on site with relatively little labor. But each company discovered independently that "public systems" are also a plenum. Prevailing public-systems technologies are linked to social systems that are dynamically conservative. The introduction of a new public-systems technology, like the introduction of the Bessemer converter, encounters the funded resistance of the established system that it threatens to disrupt.

Specifically, these industrial firms discovered that housing falls under the jurisdiction of approximately two thousand separate municipal building codes, each of which is supported by the complex of institutions (craft labor unions, code inspectors, building-material suppliers). It may be possible to persuade code inspectors in Duluth of the acceptability of the Koppers system, but the battle must be fought again in Cedar Rapids and again in Kansas City. Soon, the cost of marketing exceeds even the most optimistic estimate of profits. Thus public systems, like industrial systems, are dynamically conservative social and intellectual systems built around prevailing technology.

Between 1964 and 1966, a young architect, Ezra Ehrenkrantz of Building Systems Development, Inc., developed a new school construction system known as S.C.S.D. His purpose was to reduce the costs and improve the quality of school construction. He persuaded thirteen school districts to aggregate their purchases of schools in order to create a market of some $30 million—one large enough to attract industrial firms to invest in the development of new school-construction technology. He worked with school administrators, manufacturers, teachers, parent groups, building-code inspectors, and union officials to select the subsystems of the school most appropriate for innovation. He selected internal structures, roofing, light-

ing, environmental control, and partitioning; because of union resistance, he eliminated plumbing and exterior brickwork. He then
formulated user criteria for systems based on the interests and
behavior of various user groups—including teachers, students, and
laborers. He wanted to advance industrialized building through the
use of standard components, but he discovered that a major requirement of user groups had to do with flexibility—in lighting, environment, and use of space. As a result, a series of interlocking performance criteria gave rise to the development of interlocking flexible
systems based on standard components. It was possible, for example,
to redesign the interior of a school in twelve hours. Air conditioning
adaptable to varied uses of space could be installed with heating for
the previous cost of heating alone. Floors could be carpeted for the
cost of maintaining hardwood flooring.

Critical to all of this was the design of networks—structural,
electrical, means of connecting or disconnecting—that permit standard components to be realigned in a wide variety of relationships
cheaply and according to user need. Standardization of parts, allowing industrialized manufacture, became consistent with demands for
flexibility through the design of what might be called the infrastructure of the building.

At the present time, over two hundred buildings have been built
using the products developed for S.C.S.D. Even though it by no
means dealt with the most difficult or important of the public-
systems problems, S.C.S.D. is interesting for the light it throws on
the process of introducing and diffusing public-systems technology.
First, Ehrenkrantz was aware of the multiple actors who had a stake
in schools or school construction and tailored a strategy for transformation for each of them. The most important strategy for control
of elements of the social system, however, was the notion of the
aggregation of markets. By making the unit of innovation not one
school but $30 million worth of schools, Ehrenkrantz was able to
offer greater incentives to the purchasers for using inventions rather
than employing a stable product line. He recognized that the problem of redesign involved a dynamically conservative system of
powerful interests, and he developed and carried out a multiple
strategy to meet, overcome, or circumvent those interests. In this,
the aggregation of markets opened up new possibilities for leverage.

The S.C.S.D. buildings were metaphors for the process: They
consisted of interconnected systems, tailored to the interests of
participants and capable of great flexibility.

A number of the firms that have come to identify themselves with "business systems" rather than with products have chosen to identify themselves with public systems. In part, this is a matter of the projected growth of public-systems markets and a reflection of the growing recognition that the introduction of new public-systems technologies requires the capability to redesign and introduce whole systems. The established system will resist any significant technological innovation, and a significant technological innovation will fail in a situation favorable to the introduction of a *new* system unless the other complementary components of the system can be made available.

Firms like Raytheon, General Learning, and Xerox have organized divisions around "educational systems" and claim the capability for initiating and managing all of the functions associated with an educational objective—for example, planning the junior-college system of a community, developing curriculum and materials, training and recruiting teachers, and overseeing the construction of buildings.

General Electric and Westinghouse have entered the "city business," which means that they have defined whole communities as their units of development and, beginning with land speculation, are prepared to undertake land improvement, road-building, housing developments, construction of schools and community facilities, preparation of industrial sites, and attraction of industry.

Litton Industries and Corn Products Corporation have taken on programs of agricultural and industrial development in developing countries of a breadth usually associated only with big government. C.P.C., for example, is engaged in one Latin American country in performing a set of functions analogous to the work of the Department of Agriculture in the United States—introduction of new crop varieties and methods, construction of "packaged" food-processing plants, training of farmers, provision of technical assistance.

These firms have raised the level of aggregation at which they define their businesses. They have attempted to organize around the innovation and diffusion of new systems technologies in the public sector. So far, they have shown only indifferent success. It is one thing to develop the concept and capability of organization around

Business as a Vehicle for the Diffusion of Innovation

a business system and another to meet the conditions for its successful diffusion. Their future success depends on an understanding of the interests of the actors in the situations into which they move and their ability to develop multiple strategies of response. The behavior of the market will also be critical for their efforts. It is far more difficult to introduce broad new systems in a situation of limited market and intense competition for scarce resources than to do the same in an expanding market. These firms must be able to generate a scale of operation large enough to make it worthwhile to function as a business system and to provide leverage over resisting elements of their target systems. Even at their present stage of evaluation, however, they represent models of learning systems to which the traditional theories of diffusion are inadequate.

REFERENCES

1. Everett Rogers, *Diffusion of Innovations* (New York, 1962), pp. 13-14.

2. For a discussion of this diffusion, see Elting Morison, *Men, Machines, and Modern Times* (Cambridge, 1966).

3. Arthur W. Brayley, *History of the Granite Industry of New England* (Boston, 1913), Vol. I, p. 78.

4. *Ibid.*, pp. 15-16.

5. *Ibid.*, pp. 17-18.

6. *Ibid.*, pp. 18-19.

7. *Ibid.*

8. Melvin T. Copeland and Elliott C. Rogers, *The Saga of Cape Ann* (Freeport, Mass., 1960), p. 141.

9. *Ibid.*, p. 147.

10. *Ibid.*, pp. 124, 125.

11. *Ibid.*, p. 147.

12. *Ibid.*, pp. 147, 148.

13. *Ibid.*, p. 142.

14. *Ibid.*, pp. 150, 151.

15. J. K. Galbraith, *The Affluent Society* (New York, 1958), pp. 199-200.

JOHN W. HENNESSEY, JR.

Educating Managers for
Modern Society

WHITEHEAD WROTE of the university that its task is "the creation of
the future, so far as rational thought, and civilized modes of appreciation, can affect the issue." That the American university should
choose to create the future partly through the establishment and
nurture of professional schools of management would seem a logical
development. In a society as complex and dynamic as ours, what
kinds of people the managers and decision-makers are and how they
perform their tasks is clearly an important matter.

This article will briefly describe the standard business curriculum now being offered in most American graduate business schools.
Then, four unresolved issues in graduate business education will be
discussed. Finally, we will turn to the basic challenge of preparing
business students for a society where profit alone will not legitimatize
the role of the business enterprise. There is no need for an extended
historical introduction, for among professional schools, schools of
management or business administration are relatively new. The first
undergraduate program, at the Wharton School, was inaugurated in
1881. Dartmouth first sponsored graduate work in the field with the
founding in 1900 of the Amos Tuck School. In a short while, business
studies became an important part of the university curriculum.
Today, the most popular undergraduate major for men is business.
Graduate work in management is nearly as popular as the study of
law or medicine.

The Current Business Curriculum

Across the country, business school faculties appear to be generally satisfied with their master's programs, telling themselves,
"We must be doing something right." What are the causes for this
feeling?

Student demand for master's programs continues to rise with

a concomitant increase in the attitude that success in corporate life will require master's credentials.

Employers are quite eager to recruit graduates.

The beginning salary of master's graduates continues to rise, as does their immediate value to the organizations that hire them.

The discovery of the strong contributions to the study of management of quantitative methods and computers and of the behavioral sciences has added a luster—indeed, a mystique—to business schools, aided in no small measure by the parallel systemization of decision-making in industry and in the federal government.

Business-school faculties have attracted excellent professors from other disciplines to join their ranks.

International respect for management education is widespread, evident even in England and France.

At the same time, and perhaps understandably, there has not been much effective interest in most of our schools in basic experimentation or curriculum research or in deliberate planning for a changed future. Rather, in the last decade—following the Ford and Carnegie reports—we seem to be becoming more and more alike, keeping up with one another in curricular innovations, styles, and even fads. At its best, this is a rapid diffusion of solid innovation; at its worst, we are taking in one another's brainwashing.

Administrators have rarely asked explicitly that MBA program research and development be built into faculty assignments and (more important) budgets. A radical decentralization of curriculum research to each professor has been the implicit administrative decision, and not without good reason. The normal curriculum committee often appears to be a creaky instrument for study and change.

Attempts to solicit and use corporate testimony, or alumni counsel, or the advice of boards of advisers for program planning (short- and long-range) have been distinguished by their relative ineffectiveness in the area of curriculum development. The wise management of outside consultation is a process that we still have much to learn about. Maybe we are asking the wrong questions.

Business-school graduate students are working harder and enjoying it less. Although they may be the last on campus to revolt, there are signs that they may one day ask business schools to practice the modern management skills they teach, to apply some of the best analytical techniques to the educational enterprise and the teaching-learning process. The names of Bruner and Skinner may someday be as important in business school conversation as Forrester and Schlaifer.

These general observations have purposely been a bit hyperbolic because these are certainly not days for self-congratulation in higher education. Rather, these are days for questioning and for peering with a sharp eye into the foreseeable future. But amid this questioning stand some solid accomplishments in the specific courses presently taught. Within the curriculum, at both the undergraduate and graduate levels, we have seen and will continue to see that:

Marketing develops new models for understanding consumer behavior, for pricing, packaging, and promoting products, for using quantitative analysis, the computer, sociology, psychology (even anthropology) to plumb the secrets of marketing phenomena in all kinds of organizations.

Accounting asks new effective questions about the adequacy of usual forms of measurement, reporting, and control. Not only has the computer been a revolutionary force but the refreshing concepts of management-information systems have changed our understanding of decision-making strategy and operational control.

Production was one of the first areas of the neoclassical analytical approach to rationalizing operations. The automatic factory has become a reality. Work as we have known it since caveman days has been substantially redefined. Simulation and model building have come into their own. Technological literacy and an understanding of what research and development really mean have found a place in operations-management courses.

Finance and banking have blended with managerial economics and statistics and become both more quantitative and analytical. The computer has now really begun to work its revolutionary ways on financial decision.

Management, administration, and industrial relations have become less fields of intuitive empiricism and yielded slowly and cautiously to the systematic study of the social sciences. As the social sciences tune their educational ventures toward action (recent national meetings of political science, sociology, and psychology groups held discussions of such tuning), rapport with schools of management in common cause makes eminent sense. Parallel problems of policy and action will bring academics from these fields together almost as easily as the common need for computerized, quantified modeling and analytics. A recent report described the need of professional schools for a closer tie with the social sciences: "The social sciences can sensitize . . . professionals to the social consequences of their professional behavior, and alert them to the impact of their professional roles on the well-being of individuals and groups. More than this, of course, the social sciences provide resources both in knowledge and theory that, when joined with the professional's training and practical experience, help achieve the desired ends of a given profession."[1]

Business policy, as an integrating discipline, has been strengthened both by the behavioral sciences and their illumination of the job of the general manager and by systematic model building. Strategic planning has come into its own.

Business and society is the area in the curriculum which has opened a larger window to the environment and encouraged students to study all of the evolving relationships between business and other social, political, and economic institutions, including the international community and the urban ghetto.

More schools than ever before are analyzing the oral and written communication skills of their master's candidates and are planning to do something to meet the problems in this area.

Methodology has been an important concern in graduate business-school faculties. In addition to a flexible use of case studies and the development of an intercollegiate clearing house for cases, we have seen the rapid diffusion of business games and other kinds of simulation exercises, ways of bringing the computer into the classroom, small group experimentation, growing use of videotape and closed-circuit television, more systematic field trips, and independent-study projects sometimes extending into the summer and into internship experiences.

These developments have clearly enhanced the quality of graduate business education and made it more relevant not only for the

American businessman of the late 1960's but also for managers in other countries and in enterprises other than the commercial or industrial model.

And graduate business schools are beginning to encourage fluidity at the borders of traditional functional areas. This not only allows behavioral scientists and quantifier-analysts to enter and leave a territory freely but it also permits changes in the boundaries themselves, promising one of the most important evolutions in curriculum structure in the short history of business schools.

Some Unresolved Issues

In part because graduate study of business is a relatively new field and in part because of developments in the rest of the university and the outside world, business schools do not yet fit comfortably in some of their relationships. The four major issues seem to be:

1. *Business School or School of Management?* It is not too much to say that the world has come to see that the most significant modern American invention in the sphere of organized economic activity is not our vaunted skill in industrial production or mass marketing; rather, it is modern management. It is the refinement of the corporate form of organized and systematic activity—the development and use of human intellectual and social competence to define, analyze, and solve efficiently problems in the economic world.

Management-consulting firms now have as clients not just businesses but hospitals, universities, churches, scientific organizations, governments (including whole cities).

Countries in Eastern and Western Europe, Asia—indeed around the world—seek to understand (and improve) this American model of management. Jean Jacques Servan-Schreiber warns that U.S. managerial expertise is the new invasion, threatening to be its own force in world affairs.[2]

At the same time, American corporate management meets huge new challenges and must change to survive. New forms, new activities, new social values demand a wider and wiser introspection than U.S. industry has yet attempted. It will include going beyond the marketing mechanism to another way of establishing priorities, another way of relating the firm to its environment.

But the point is that the action in the modern business school is suddenly relevant to other forms of enterprise and this suggests an evolution to a wider educational scope.

Some graduates have always gone from MBA programs into public service or the management of museums, foundations, or schools. Now the burgeoning of rigorous analytical tools of wide applicability plus the blending of private and public goals in the interest of newer goals of quality in a postindustrial society—both lend a logic to the institutional reidentification of business schools. Models for such changes are developing in some of the strongest university settings, where the business school has built felicitous educational links with sister schools of government, education, and urban affairs.

Every school will feel the growth in its graduate curriculum of education with a wider relevance—courses as useful for a city manager as a plant manager. In this way, it is not a question of either-or —either all business school or none. Comparative analysis can be a useful educational tactic in many courses.

Especially at the graduate level there is much to be said for going all the way symbolically—by changing the institutional name. It is healthy that some schools have done it and more will follow. Still, there are good reasons for keeping and enhancing the school's fundamental relationship with the business community during a time of tense change for all. Some schools will fulfill the needs of this relationship better than others and will properly choose to keep their "business" name to enhance their function.

It is a mistake to respond to this as a matter of style or (worse) of fad. No school should change without deeply examining its competence to prepare students for nonbusiness careers, its understanding and attitude toward mixed student values, its relationship to the specific careers for which it presumes to prepare its students, and its optimal role in its particular university structure.

2. *Graduate School or Professional School at the Postbaccalaureate Level?* In response to the 1958 reports and other forces, some schools have sought to strengthen their master's work not only by emphasizing theory and research but by adopting these as strategic values guiding the whole program. For the professor who does this, master's candidates are junior versions of doctoral aspirants. The rationale is that nothing prepares a person for a world of rapid change better than an appreciation for the researcher and theorist whose models are much less tied to circumstance and time than those of the practitioner.

Other schools accept the study of research as a means but reject it as a guiding curriculum strategy. These programs see a difference in *professional* education, which blends with a body of knowledge skills of practice, habits of mind, and a responsibility for action.

The tension between these two attitudes can be a healthy one, if it is perceived by all and no doctrinaire battle results, and if it is subjected to research! But usually the tension is destructive, and we must face that. In many schools of business with both doctoral and master's work, a dysfunctional clash can be seen between the "doctoral faculty" and the "master's (and undergraduate) faculty." The result is invidious distinctions about which is better or more important, a split which all too often divides older and newer faculty people and leads to more heat than light in the academic grove.

One valuable way to bridge these two views is to recognize the common value of *a spirit of inquiry,* as C. W. Churchman has remarked. The social importance of such a spirit in a changing society is clear. An inquiring mind is essential to those qualities of mature flexibility we all talk about. And there is a responsibility on a professional school faculty to share with students the confusion, joy, and despair that go with the search for new and better ways of thought and action.

3. *What Relationship Between Undergraduate Business Programs and Master's Programs?* At the time of Abraham Flexner's famous report on medical education (1910), only a few medical programs required a bachelor's degree for entrance. The vast majority were undergraduate in character. Within several decades, undergraduate medical schools had become obsolescent.

In business schools, we have been asking ourselves—and the 1958 reports asked—whether we are also headed in the direction of education for business exclusively at the postbaccalaureate level, with undergraduate prerequisites in the social sciences, mathematics, and statistics. The answer would appear today to be negative. Special forces in the society and strong developments in undergraduate management education make the analogy with medicine imperfect.

We are concerned with finding a better guiding principle for the parallel existence of undergraduate and graduate work. We will surely have both for a very long time, despite the decision of some schools (like U.C.L.A., Northwestern, Pittsburgh, and others) to drop undergraduate business.

However, as in 1958, we still have students going from good two-year undergraduate business curricula into fixed two-year MBA courses that take none but the most superficial recognition of the undergraduate work, because they are designed primarily for the student with no past educational experience in business. There is a tension here which has yet to be adequately dealt with. The better the undergraduate programs are, the worse this problem is. Even insisting on restricting undergraduate business courses to those most liberal in quality does little to reduce the difficulty. It raises new questions.

4. *How To Handle Continuing Education?* Management-development programs have flourished more in this decade than in their great period of expansion in the 1948-1959 era. The new rhythm in this movement comes from the faster beat of change.

Alumni never used to say, "I've had my business degree for five years, but I want to come back to get some of the things your present students are getting." Today, one hears that request with increasing frequency. It is dramatized by the computer's presence but it goes beyond—into all areas of modern analytics. Simultaneously, corporations have vastly changed their ideas of management education, from the time of man's entry to later career education.

But there remains a desperate need for closer planning between business schools and companies. The tune cannot really be, "Anything you can do, I can do better"; rather, we want to save scarce resources and develop a system in which the functions of the undergraduate business school, the graduate school, and the corporation in industry are quite clear. Such a rationale will be one more step toward the professionalization of our field.

At the alumni or corporate level, every school must devise its own best contribution. For some, short conferences on special topics will be most suitable; for others, longer courses will be better. For many, this will be a good place to experiment with bringing together managers from different environments—business, health, education, government.

Internships, both during and post-school, seem a worthy adjunct to classroom learning. They will be really valuable only as people inside corporations can be made veritable partners in the teaching-learning process. Internships in public institutions can be a forceful way to expose business-school students to a different decision context and its values. This kind of extension of the campus has only begun to be used in a productive way. There is room for experimentation and innovation.

In addition, the school of management needs the company of fellows in law, medicine, and engineering on questions like: How can wisdom be taught? What is the route to self-fulfillment in a modern profession? How can self-renewal processes be effectively built into large-scale organizations? Where does professional responsibility begin and end? What is the ultimate goal of professional activity?

Business and the Great Issues of Modern Society

One of the great phenomena of recent years is the new kind of involvement of American businessmen in social problems, along with a new concern in society for the quality of life. In one sense, this is the era of postphilanthropy. The real interdependence of parts of society now comes clear. Profit is the measure of business and no more the end; serving society is the goal. It is certainly a proper role of business education to help students become aware of the power of the corporation to affect great issue areas.

Effective educational recognition of and response to such issues depend fundamentally on the skill, wisdom, and modernity of thinking of the entire business-school faculty. I would predict the development of new business-school programs that derive their guiding value or strategy from the link between the corporation and issues of modern society. Some of these issues are:

The growing gap between wealth and poverty, advantage and disadvantage. We are just beginning to understand this issue in America, where it is deeply complicated by racial antagonisms and the legacy of the urban ghettoes, and business has both a role and a stake in the effective management of the search for solutions.

The shrinking of the globe and a vastly increased internationalization of business. What form this will take makes a profound difference. Economic imperialism is one form, cultural invasion and its inevitable backlash is another. Surely business students must have the best possible exposure to ways of *thinking about* these issues—not specific country knowledge, but new frames of reference, new analytical tools.

Pollution, urban squalor, transportation, communication, population growth, conservation of resources, and other systems problems bring economics, management, technology, and politics together. Business has a key role to play in all of these national matters.

The relationship of business to other institutions such as government, the field of education, or the arts. To expand on the issue of new relationships between business and governments, there is a need at all levels to manage together what neither can manage better separately. This, of course, is not collusion, nor is it a new ideology. Rather, it is an emphasis on the priority goals of a society and how they can best be approached. In the field of education, business has a distinctive role to play, not only in the technology of education but in some aspects of its management and in the recognition that every manager in a corporation is fundamentally both a student and a teacher—on whose shoulders lays a responsibility for the enhancement of human potential.

Creativity, alienation, and the nature of work in formal organizations. Young people have persuasively rephrased the pain of being caught in the clash between the organization's increased demand for efficiency, large size, and controllability and the vital need of the individual for self-fulfillment. What has been popularly dubbed a disrespect for business is at root a revulsion at the authoritarianism, conservatism, and soullessness of all formal organizations, including those in law, medicine, and (certainly) education. In management studies, we have taken both a mechanistic and a behavioristic approach to this set of issues, and these have helped us understand. But now the matter goes deeper and wider. The crisis of the human spirit is more than a cliché, and the attitude of the new generation in their search for meaning demands more than our professional school research and practice can provide either on its own or through a tie with social science. I am convinced there must be a tapping of the reservoir of the humanities in one way or another—through new prerequisites or a changed business curriculum or other newer ways. Today, we cannot and dare not let liberal learning stop as the student begins his professional education in our schools of management. John Ciardi put the case to businessmen this way, in a speech some years ago:

The poem does not care and cannot care what happens to that rush order. The poem is of the humanity of the man. And despite the tendency . . . to admire only those men who "do things" and to scorn "dreamers," the fact is that no man can be wholly practical or wholly impractical, and that the humanity of any man's life requires some, at least, of both orders of the imagination.

There is no poetry for the practical man. There is poetry only for the mankind of the man who spends a certain amount of his life turning the mechanical wheel. But let him spend too much of his life at the mechanics of practicality and either he must become something less than a man, or his very mechanical efficiency will become impaired by the frustrations stored up in his irrational human personality.

An ulcer, gentlemen, is an unkissed imagination taking its revenge for having been jilted. It is an unwritten poem, a neglected music, an unpainted watercolor, an undanced dance. It is a declaration from the mankind of the man that a clear spring of joy has not been tapped, and that it must break through, muddily, on its own.

Poetry is one of the forms of joy, the most articulate, the most expanding, and, therefore, the most fulfilling form. It is no separation from the world; it is the mankind of the world, the most human language of man's uncertain romance with the universe.[3]

REFERENCES:

1. *The American Challenge* (New York, 1968).

2. *Knowledge Into Action: Improving the Nation's Use of the Social Sciences* (National Science Foundation, 1969), p. 21.

3. Reprinted in *Toward the Liberally Educated Executive,* Robert A. Goldwin and Charles A. Nelson, eds. (New York, 1960), pp. 68-69.

Notes on Contributors

ROBERT T. AVERITT, born in 1931, is professor of economics at Smith College. He is the author of *The Dual Economy* (New York, 1968) and has served as a consultant to the Small Business Administration. Currently he is applying general systems theory to the American economy.

NEIL W. CHAMBERLAIN, born in 1915, is the Armand G. Erpf Professor of the Modern Corporation at the Graduate School of Business at Columbia University. Mr. Chamberlain is the author of *The Labor Sector* (New York, 1965); *Private and Public Planning* (New York, 1965); *Enterprise and Environment* (New York, 1968); and *Beyond Malthus: Population and Power* (New York, 1970).

ALFRED D. CHANDLER, JR., born in 1918, is Straus Professor of Business History at the Harvard Business School. Mr. Chandler is the author of *Strategy and Structure: Chapters in the History of the Industrial Enterprise* (Cambridge, Mass., 1962); *Giant Enterprise: Ford, General Motors and the Automotive Industry* (New York, 1964); *The Railroads: The Nation's First Big Business* (New York, 1965); he is coauthor of *Pierre S. duPont and the Making of the Modern Corporation* (New York, 1971) and editor of *The Papers of Dwight David Eisenhower: The War Years* (Baltimore, 1970).

ROBERT A. CHARPIE, born in 1925, is president of Cabot Corporation, Boston. Mr. Charpie is a member of the National Science Board and a trustee of Mitre Corporation and the Draper Laboratory Division of the Massachusetts Institute of Technology. He was formerly president of Bell & Howell.

MAX B. E. CLARKSON, born in 1922, is chairman of Graphic Controls Corporation, Buffalo, New York, a company specializing in various aspects of recording and information processing. Mr. Clarkson is a former chairman of Printing Industries of America, Inc.

MICHEL CROZIER, born in 1922, is scientific director at the French National Center for Scientific Research and founder and director of the Centre de Sociologie des Organisations in Paris. He is a former fellow of the Center for Advanced Study at Stanford University and has taught at Harvard University and the University of Nanterre. Mr. Crozier is the author of *The Bureaucratic Phenomenon* (Chicago, 1964); *La Société Bloquée* (Paris, 1970); and *The World of the Office Worker* (Chicago, 1971).

CHARLES R. DECARLO, born in 1921, is president of Sarah Lawrence College.

NOTES ON CONTRIBUTORS

Mr. DeCarlo is coauthor of *Education in Business and Industry* (New York, 1966); research associate, the Program on Technology and Society, Harvard University; and associate, the Seminar on Technology and Social Change, Columbia University. He was formerly director of automation research, International Business Machines Corporation.

JOHN P. FISHWICK, born in 1916, is president and chief executive officer of the Norfolk and Western Railway. Mr. Fishwick was formerly chairman of the board and chief executive officer of the Erie-Lackawanna Railway and president of the Delaware and Hudson Railway.

ELI GOLDSTON, born in 1920, is president of Eastern Gas and Fuel Associates. Mr. Goldston is a director of the National Bureau of Economic Research, Inc., a member of the Visiting Committee of the Joint Center for Urban Studies of the Massachusetts Institute of Technology and Harvard University, and a member of the Advisory Committee of the Program on Technology and Society, Harvard University.

JOHN W. HENNESSEY, born in 1925, is dean of The Amos Tuck School of Business Administration, Dartmouth College. Mr. Hennessey is coauthor of *Organizational Behavior* (New York, 1960) and *Hospital Policy Decisions* (New York, 1966) and a director of the American Association of Collegiate Schools of Business.

RICHARD H. HOLTON, born in 1926, is dean of the Schools of Business Administration at the University of California, Berkeley. Mr. Holton is the coauthor of *The Canadian Economy: Prospect and Retrospect* (Cambridge, Mass., 1959) and was Assistant Secretary of Commerce for Economic Affairs during 1963–1965.

WILLIAM LETWIN, born in 1922, is Reader in political science at the London School of Economics and Political Science and visiting Senior Lecturer at the Sloan School of Management at the Massachusetts Institute of Technology. He is the author of *Documentary History of American Economic Policy* (New York, 1961); *The Origins of Scientific Economics* (New York, 1964); and *Law and Economic Policy in America: Evolution of the Sherman Act* (New York, 1965).

HERBERT C. MORTON, born in 1921, is associate commissioner of labor statistics in the United States Department of Labor and editor of the *Monthly Labor Review*. He was formerly director of publications for the Brookings Institution and an assistant professor at The Amos Tuck School of Business Administration, Dartmouth College. Mr. Morton is the author of *Public Contracts and Private Wages* (Washington, 1965) and coauthor of *An Introduction to Economic Reasoning*, 4th ed. (Washington, 1967).

G. NEAL RYLAND, born in 1941, is assistant to the president, Eastern Gas and Fuel Associates, a Boston-based industrial organization with operations principally in bituminous coal mining, barging, and natural-gas transmission and distribution. Mr. Ryland was formerly with the Bank of New York, New York City.

HOWARD J. SAMUELS, born in 1919, is a businessman-engineer and visiting lecturer in urban economics at the New School for Social Research, New York. He is currently chairman and president of the New York City Off-Track Betting Corporation and special counselor to Mayor John V. Lindsay. Mr. Samuels was administrator of the Small Business Administration, 1968–1969, and Under Secretary of Commerce, 1967–1968. He founded the Kordite Corporation, which merged with Mobil Oil.

DONALD A. SCHON, born in 1930, is president of the Organization for Social and Technical Innovation, Inc., Cambridge, Massachusetts. He is the author of *Technology and Change* (New York, 1967); *Invention and Evolution of Ideas* (London, 1963); and *Beyond the Stable State* (New York, 1971).

ANDREW SHONFIELD, born in 1917, has been chairman of the Social Science Research Council in London since 1969; he assumes the post of director of the Royal Institute of International Affairs from January 1972. He is the author of *British Economic Policy Since the War* (1958); *The Attack on World Poverty* (1960); and *Modern Capitalism: The Changing Balance of Public and Private Power* (1965). Mr. Shonfield was formerly economic editor of *The Observer* and foreign editor of *The Financial Times*.

CHARLES S. SHOUP, JR., born in 1935, is director of corporate research, Cabot Corporation, and vice president and general manager of National Research Corporation, a subsidiary of Cabot Corporation, Cambridge, Massachusetts. He is the author of papers on infrared spectroscopy and surface chemistry.

LEONARD S. SILK, born in 1918, is a member of the editorial board of the *New York Times*. Mr. Silk is the author of *Forecasting Business Trends* (New York, 1956); *The Research Revolution* (New York, 1960); *The Education of Businessmen* (Committee for Economic Development, 1962); *Veblen* (New York, 1966); and *Contemporary Economics: Principles and Issues* (1970).

RAYMOND VERNON, born in 1913, is Herbert F. Johnson Professor of International Business Management at the Harvard Business School. He is the author of *Metropolis 1985* (Cambridge, Mass., 1960); *Dilemma of Mexico's Development* (Cambridge, Mass., 1963); *Manager in the International Economy* (Cambridge, Mass., 1968); and *Sovereignty at Bay* (New York, 1971).

WOLF VON ECKARDT, born in 1918, is architecture critic for the *Washington Post*. He is the author of *Eric Mendelsohn* (New York, 1960) and *A Place to Live: The Crisis of the Cities* (New York, 1968).

Index